VAIṢṆAVISM

Vaiṣṇavism

Its Philosophy, Theology and Religious Discipline

S.M. SRINIVASA CHARI

MOTILAL BANARSIDASS PUBLISHERS
PRIVATE LIMITED • DELHI

4th Reprint: Delhi, ***2018***
First Edition: Delhi, 1994

ISBN: 978-81-208-1098-3 (Cloth)
ISBN: 978-81-208-4135-2 (Paper)

MOTILAL BANARSIDASS
41 U.A. Bungalow Road, Jawahar Nagar, Delhi 110 007
8 Mahalaxmi Chamber, 22 Bhulabhai Desai Road, Mumbai 400 026
236, 9th Main III Block, Jayanagar, Bangalore 560 011
120 Royapettah High Road, Mylapore, Chennai 600 004
Sanas Plaza, 1302 Baji Rao Road, Pune 411 002
8 Camac Street, Kolkata 700 017
Ashok Rajpath, Patna 800 004
Chowk, Varanasi 221 001

Printed in India
BY JAINENDRA PRAKASH JAIN AT SHRI JAINENDRA PRESS,
A-45 NARAINA, PHASE-I, NEW DELHI 110 028
AND PUBLISHED BY NARENDRA PRAKASH JAIN FOR
MOTILAL BANARSIDASS PUBLISHERS PRIVATE LIMITED,
BUNGALOW ROAD, DELHI 110 007

To
The Revered Memory of
My Acharya
Sri Gostipuram Sowmyanarayanacharya Swami
who was
An illustrious example of an ideal Śrī-vaiṣṇava
with profound Respect and Gratitude

FOREWORD

As early as 1943 the late Professor P.N. Srinivasachari, who was a pioneer in presenting a systematic and scholarly account of the essentials of Viśiṣṭādvaita, was of the view, when he wrote his *The Philosophy of Viśiṣṭādvaita* (The Adyar Library, Adyar), that "in contemporary Indian philosophy, Vedānta is overweighted on the side of Advaita" and that "the balance will be restored only when the other systems of Vedānta, notably, that of Rāmānuja, are widely known and appreciated in the west as well as in the east." He maintained that, for the purpose of a comparative study of Vedānta as a whole, Viśiṣṭādvaita must come "to its own in the world of modern Vedāntic thought as a *siddhānta* as well as a synthesis." (xlvi-vii). He claimed that his own work was "a humble attempt at presenting the central features of the philosophy of *Viśiṣṭādvaita* as an introduction to its detailed study." (xlviii) When he pleaded that Viśiṣṭādvaita must be given due importance for the purpose of maintaining a balance among the various systems of Vedānta, he was exhorting the scholars in general, and those belonging to the Vaiṣṇava tradition in particular, to expound and highlight, in a systematic way, the philosophical theism of Viśiṣṭādvaita not only for the purpose of maintaining a balance among the systems of Vedānta, but also for the "understanding of Indian culture and its synthetic genius." For nearly five decades his exhortation has remained unheeded. I am happy that closely following the recent publication of *Fundamentals of Viśiṣṭādvaita Vedānta*, a work which has been highly commended by scholars, Dr S.M. Srinivasa Chari has come forward with this scholarly work on the philosophical theology and religious discipline of Vaiṣṇavism as a supplement to it. Dr Chari is justified in his claim that for the first time "an attempt has been made to present in English and in a single volume a comprehensive account of philosophy, theology, and religious discipline of Vaiṣṇavism;" (p. xi) and he has, I am happy to say, succeeded in his attempt.

According to the Indian tradition, which insists on the unity of theory and practice, philosophy and religion are distinguishable, but not separable. Philosophy, which is *darśana*, is complementary to religion, which is *mata*. While philosophy, without being merely speculative, should lead to practice, religion, which calls for faith, should have a philosophical base. In other words, what we require is philosophy-based-religion and religion-biased-philosophy. Such a combination, as Dr Chari observes, is found in Vaiṣṇavism, which is Vedic in origion and "which has developed distinctive theological doctrines which are founded on sound philosophical theories enunciated in the *Upaniṣads*." (p. xxvi) With a view to distinguish the philosophical aspect from the religious in Vaiṣṇavism, the former is referred to as Viśiṣṭādvaita Vedānta, while the latter is called Vaiṣṇavism. But the two aspects, like the two sides of a coin, are inseparable.

Dr Chari substantiates the claim that Vaiṣṇavism is both philosophy and religion with reference to its Upaniṣadic base. The *Vedānta-sūtra* explains the teaching of the *Upaniṣads*, which, on a superficial reading, appear to be incoherent, by re-arranging them within the structural frame-work of reasoning (*tarka*). The main topics which constitute the subject matter of the *Upaniṣads* can be grouped in different ways. According to one method, they can be brought under three groups—*tattva*, *hita*, and *puruṣārtha*. Philosophy, which is mainly concerned with the nature of reality and the means of knowing it, deals with *tattva*. Ethics and religion, which deal with moral and spiritual practices required for attaining the goal, take care of *hita* and *puruṣārtha*. It means that *tattva*, *hita*, and *puruṣārtha* constitute the subject matter of both philosophy and religion. It is well known that, while the first two *adhyāyas* of the *Vedānta-sūtra* discuss exhaustively all issues connected with *tattva*, the remaining two *adhyāyas* elucidate the problems connected with *hita* and *puruṣārtha*. The expansion of the three categories into five called *artha-pañcaka*, for which there is textual support in the *Hārīta-saṁhitā*, has helped, so argues Dr Chari, to add "certain distinctive theological doctrines which are not stated explicitly in the *Vedānta-sūtra*". So, Dr Chari concludes: "Vaiṣṇavism has both a philosophy and religion. Its philosophy is the same as that of Vedānta and its religion is not basically different from that of Vedānta except that it has been further expanded to meet theological needs." (p. xxxiii)

Dr Chari's book is comprehensive covering the entire gamut of the philosophy and religion of Vaiṣṇavism. After setting forth very elaborately the historical development of Vaiṣṇavism in Part I, Dr Chari devotes as many as five chapters to the discussion of the philosophy of Vaiṣṇavism in Part II of his book. It is necessary to mention in this connection that he has dealt with *bhakti-yoga* and *mokṣa* against the philosophical back-ground of the *Upaniṣads* and the *Vedānta-sūtra* in this Part itself, after expounding the nature of Brahman *cit*, and *acit*. Part III of the book consisting of eight chapters deals with the theology of Vaiṣṇavism. The analysis and explanation of the concept of *śeṣatva* with all that it implies for the soul, which is seeking liberation from bondage, and of the doctrine of *prapatti* which brings in for consideration the role of God on the one hand and that of the *jīva* on the other in the context of divine grace and human effort are commendable. In Part IV of the book, Dr Chari explains the Vaiṣṇava way of life in which *ācāryas*, sacraments, practice of daily religious duties, and cultivation of ethical virtues find an integral place.

What preserves a religion is its universality. The philosophical base of Vaiṣṇavism, as Dr Chari points out, leads to the practice of *vaiṣṇava-dharma* which guarantees peace with others through peace with oneself. Viṣṇu, the all-pervading principle, which is no other than Brahman, includes every being and indwells in every being. One who is aware of this truth will realize that, since Viṣṇu is in all beings, all, being divine, are equal and that to love every being is to love Viṣṇu. One who orders one's life on the basis of this awareness will practise the ideals of love and equality; such a person is a *Vaiṣṇava*.

Dr Chari's book is not only comprehensive, but also analytical. The explanation of concepts and the formulation of arguments in support of the concepts are analytical. Also, they have been supported by textual authority wherever necessary. This is a book which every Hindu should read for appreciating the philosophical and religious heritage which she has inherited. This is a book which every scholar interested in Indian philosophy in general and Vaiṣṇavism in particular should read.

R. Balasubramanian
Chairman
Indian Council of Philosophical Research

PREFACE

This book is in response to a long-felt need for a comprehensive treatise on the fundamental philosophical and theological doctrines of Vaiṣṇavism which is one of the oldest living monotheistic religions of India. During the last few decades books have been published on Rāmānuja's Philosophy and Religion but these do not cover exhaustively all aspects of the Vaiṣṇava religion. Even the few books written in English on Vaiṣṇavism do not deal in detail with all the basic doctrines of Vaiṣṇava theology. Further, while presenting Rāmānuja's thoughts, a clear-cut distinction has also not been made between philosophy and religion and the two are often mixed up. The Viśiṣṭādvaita Vedānta expounded by Rāmānuja is essentially a philosophical system developed on the teachings contained in the Upaniṣads, the *Vedānta-sūtra* and the Bhagavadgītā. It also has a distinctive theology based on the Vedānta, as is the case also with Śaṁkara's Advaita. Though philosophy and religion are not separable in the Indian schools of thought, it should still be possible to make a distinction between what is a philosophical system (*darśana*) and what is a religious system (*mata*). In my opinion the Viśiṣṭādvaita Philosophy as presented by Rāmānuja is distinct from the Viśiṣṭādvaita Religion known more popularly as Vaiṣṇavism, although the two are complementary, representing two facets of the same system of thought. This fact has been ably established by Vedānta Deśika, an illustrious follower of Rāmānuja, in his *Tattva-muktā-kalāpa* and my other book *Fundamentals of Viśiṣṭādvaita Vedānta* published recently. I have, therefore, endeavoured in this volume to present the Religion of Viśiṣṭādvaita under the title of Vaiṣṇavism, as distinct from its Philosophy. The theological doctrines, each one of which constitutes a distinctive feature of this religion, have been delineated from the philosophical theories and discussed separately in detail. So far as I am aware, it is the first time that such an attempt has been made to present in English and in a single volume a comprehensive account of Philosophy, Theology and Religious Discipline of Vaiṣṇavism.

In writing this book I have taken material mostly from original sourcebooks. During the period extending from 10th to 15th century, eminent Vaiṣṇava *ācāryas* have contributed erudite works both in Sanskrit and Maṇipravāḷa language (Sanskritised Tamil prose) on Vaiṣṇavism on the authority of the Vedas, Upaniṣads, Āgamas, Epics, selected Purāṇas and the hymns of Āḻvārs (Vaiṣṇava saints). The material available in these treatises is very extensive. Without going into all the details contained therein, I have selected the essential teachings having philosophic and theological significance. My objective has been limited to presenting an authentic account of the philosophy and theology of Vaiṣṇavism in a coherent manner. For the same reason I have refrained from making a comparative study of this religion with other monotheistic religions. Wherever I was confronted with doctrinal differences among the Vaiṣṇava sects and other parallel cults, I have tried to maintain a non-partisan attitude and discussed the doctrines purely from a philosophical standpoint.

For reasons explained in the Introduction, I have preferred to adopt the term *Vaiṣṇavism* instead of *Śrī-vaiṣṇavism*, as is generally used by other scholars who have written on Rāmānuja's religion. In my opinion, it is not a regional cult confined to a limited area, though it was founded by Rāmānuja born in South India. Its relevance and sweep is far wider, and ethical values embedded in this system have universal appeal. In the post-Rāmānuja period several Vaiṣṇava movements represented by eminent religious reformers such as Madhva, Nimbārka, Rāmānanda, Vallabha, Caitanya and Jñāneśvara have come up in other parts of India. All these are the offshoots of the basic Vaiṣṇavism which was prevalent from Vedic time and systematised later by Rāmānuja. I have, therefore, restricted the scope of my book to the original Vaiṣṇavism as developed by him and his followers.

In a work of this type, the use of technical terms in Sanskrit is unavoidable. I have, however, tried to minimise their use. Wherever I have mentioned Sanskrit words and quotations in the body of the text, I have given their nearest English equivalent. Wherever English terms are used, their Sanskrit equivalent is also given to indicate their correct import. Except the commonly used words, all the Sanskrit words have been diacritically marked. The long compound Sanskrit words have been split up wherever necessary to facilitate easy reading. I have avoided as far as possible the use of the Tamil quotations from the hymns of Āḻvārs and the literature in Maṇipravāḷa language as these would be difficult to read and understand by a person not conversant with the language. I have taken special pains to express the highly technical concepts in as simple and lucid manner as possible to facilitate easy comprehension. I hope this publication will be found useful by students of comparative religion in general and in particular, by those who wish to make an in-depth study of this important religion.

In the preparation of this book, I am guided primarily by the knowledge of the essentials of Vaiṣṇavism imparted to me fifty years ago by my spiritual preceptor, the late Sri Gostipuram Sowmya Narayaṇācārya Swami (1878-1943), under whom I had the good fortune to study *Rahasyatrayasāra* of Vedānta Deśika, which is the basic sourcebook for Vaiṣṇavism. As a token of my gratitude, I respectfully dedicate this work to my Ācārya. He was an illustrious example of an ideal Śri-Vaiṣṇava in the present century. I am also indebted to another *ācārya*, the late Sri Madhurantakam Veeraraghavacharya Swami (1900-83) under whom I studied *Śrī-bhāṣya* and *Bhagavad-viṣaya* (commentary on Nammāḻvār Tiruvāymoḻi) which are also the important sourcebooks for Vaiṣṇavism. In the preparation of this book, I have consulted those few traditional Śrī-Vaiṣṇava scholars who are available today in South India. I take this opportunity to express my grateful thanks to all of them.

I have received considerable help from Dr. V. Varadachari who was good enough to go through the major part of the typescript of the book and make valuable suggestions. I express my sincere thanks to him. I should also thank Dr. N.S. Anantharangachar Prof. K.T. pandurangi and Dr. L.V. Rajagopal who have seen some of the draft chapters and offered useful comments. My special thanks are due to my esteemed friend, Sri S. Srinivasachar who patiently read the entire typescript and made useful corrections. My thanks are also due to all those who have helped me in one way or the other in completing this book. I should also express my grateful thanks to the esteemed professor R. Balasubramanian for evincing keen interest in my work and for graciously writing the Foreword.

Bangalore S.M. SRINIVASA CHARI
9th June, 1993.

CONTENTS

PART III

THEOLOGY OF VAIṢṆAVISM

SCHEME OF TRANSLITERATION

Vowels	a ā i ī u ū ṛ ṝ e ai o au
anusvara	ṁ
visarga	ḥ
Consonants	
gutturals	k kh g gh ṅ
palatals	c ch j jh ñ
cerebrals	ṭ ṭh ḍ ḍh ṇ
dentals	t th d dh n
labials	p ph b bh m
semi-vowels	y r l v
sibilants	s as in sun
	ś palatal sibilant pronounced like the soft s of Russian
	ṣ cerebral sibilant as in shun
aspirate	h
	ḷ for the Dravidian retroflex
	ḻ for the Tamil Guttural

LIST OF ABBREVIATIONS

Ahs	*Ahirbudhnya Saṁhitā* of the Pāñcarātrāgama, 2 vols. (Published by Adyar Library and Research Centre, Madras, Second Edition, 1986)
AiUp	*Aitareya Upaniṣad*
AV	*Advaita* and *Viśiṣṭādvaita*—A study based on *Śatadūṣaṇī*
BGD	*Bhagavadguṇa-darpaṇa* by Paraśara Bhattar (Published by Viśiṣṭādvaita Pracharini Sabha, Madras 1983)
BG	*Bhagavad-gītā*
BrUp	*Bṛhadāraṇyaka Upaniṣad* with Raṅgarāmānuja Bhāṣya (Ed. Uttampur T. Veeraraghavacharya, Madras and published by Tirumala-Tirupati Devasthanam, 1954)
ChUp	*Chāndogya Upaniṣad* with Raṅgarāmānuja Bhāṣya (Ed. Uttamur T. Veeraraghavacharya, Madras 1952)
FVV	*Fundamentals of Viśiṣṭādvaita Vedānta*
GB	*Gītābhāṣya* of Rāmānuja with *Tātparya-candrikā* (Ed. P.B. Annangaracharya, Conjeevaram, 1941)
GaBh	*Gadyatraya-bhāṣyam* by Vedānta Deśika (Ed. P.B. Annangaracharya, Conjeevaram, 1940)
GaVa	*Gadyavyākhyānas* by Periyavāccān Piḷḷai and Sudarśanasūri (Ed. S. Krishnaswamy Ayyangar, Trichy)
KaUp	*Kaṭha Upaniṣad*
LT	*Lakṣmī Tantra*—A Pāñcarātra Āgama (Published by The Adyar Library and Research Centre, 1959)
Mbh	*Mahābhārata* (Based on South Indian Texts, Ed. by T.R. Krishnamacharya, Kumbhakonam and printed by Nirnayasagara Press, 1910)
MUp	*Muṇḍaka Upaniṣad*
NP	*Nyāya-pariśuddhi* by Vedānta Deśika (Ed. P.B. Annangaracharya, Conjeevaram, 1940)
NS	*Nyāya-siddhāñjanam* by Vedānta Deśika (Ed. P.B. Annangaracharya, Conjeevaram, 1940)
NUp	*Nārāyaṇa Upaniṣad* (Ubhaya Vedānta Granthamālā Series, Madras, 1972)
PR	*Pāñcarātra-rakṣā* by Vedānta Deśika (Ed. P.B. Annangaracharya, Conjeevaram, 1941)

RB	*Rāmānuja Bhāṣya* on *Vedānta Sūtras* (2 Volumes) (Ed. Uttamur T. Veeraraghavacharya, Madras, 1968)
RRB	*Raṅgarāmānuja Bhāṣyam on Upaniṣads* (Ed. Uttamur T. Veeraraghavacharya, Madras).
RTS	*Rahasyatraya-sāra* by Vedānta Deśika (Ed. P.B. Annangaracharya, Conjeevaram, 1941 in Telugu script)
RV	*Ṛg-Veda Saṁhitā* (Published by Svadhyaya Mandal, Paradi, Gujarat State)
SB	*Śaṁkara Bhāṣya* on *Vedāntā Sūtras.*
SR	*Saccharitra-rakṣā* by Vedānta Deśika (Ed. P. B. Annangaracharya, Conjeevaram, 1941)
SD	*Śatadūṣaṇī* by Vedānta Deśika
SS	*Sarvārtha-siddhi on Tattva-muktā-kalāpa* by Vedānta Deśika (Ed. P.B. Annangaracharya, Conjeevaram, 1941)
SvUp	*Śvetāśvatara Upaniṣad*
SSB	*Śrīsūkta Bhāṣya* by Nañjīyar (Ed. A. Srinivasa Raghavan, Pudukotah, 1937)
SVB	*Śrīvacanabhūṣaṇam* of Piḷḷailokācārya with commentary of Maṇavāḷamāmuni. (Ed. P.B. Annangaracharya, Conjeevaram 1966)
TNUp	*Taittirīya Nārāyaṇa Upaniṣad* (Ed. Uttamur T. Veeraraghavacharya, Madras, 1951)
TUp	*Taittirīya Upaniṣad* (Ed. Uttamur T. Veeraraghavacharya, Madras, 1951)
TC	*Tātparya-candrikā* on *gītābhāṣya* by Vedānta Deśika (Ed. P.B. Annangaracharya, Conjeevaram, 1941)
TMK	*Tattva-muktā-kalāpa* with *Sarvārtha-siddhi* by Vedānta Deśika (Ed. P.B. Annangaracharya, Conjeevaram, 1941)
Up	*Upaniṣad*
VD	Vedānta Deśika
VDh	*Viṣṇu-darmottara*
Vp	*Viṣṇupurāṇa*
VS	Vedānta-sūtra
VSa	*Vedārtha-saṁgraha* by Rāmānuja (Ed. S.S. Raghavachar with English Translation and Published by Ramakrishna Ashram, 1956)

INTRODUCTION

Religion and Philosophy have been an indispensable part of Indian culture from remote past. The Ṛgveda which is the oldest religious literature of the world together with the principal Upaniṣads contains profound philosophical as well as religious thoughts which have provided the foundation for the later development of philosophical and religious systems of India. Though philosophy and religion in India are not totally separated from each other, they have grown together as complementary to each other.

The major philosophical schools which have accepted the authority of the Vedas, are the Sāṅkhya, Yoga, Nyāya, Vaiśeṣika, Pūrvamīmāṁsā and Vedānta categorised as *ṣaḍ-darśana* or the six systems of Indian Philosophy. Buddhism and Jainism which are also a part of Indian Philosophy fall outside this group as they do not acknowledge the authority of the Vedas. The Vedānta system comprises several schools which have arisen as a result of the different interpretations offered by exponents of the Upaniṣadic texts, the *Vedāntasūtra* and the *Bhagavadgītā*, the triple foundation of Vedānta. The principal ones among them are the Advaita of Śaṁkara, the Viśiṣṭādvaita of Rāmānuja and the Dvaita of Madhva.

There are also several religious cults of ancient origin. The sects which are referred to in the later religious literature are Vaiṣṇavism, Śaivism, Śāktaism, Saurya, Vaināyaka and Skanda. Of these the principal ones which are well developed with an extensive literature of their own and which have survived through centuries are Vaiṣṇavism, Śaivism and Śāktaism. The two other major living religions which have had their origin in India are Jainism and Buddhism, but these two do not owe any allegience to the *Vedas*. It is customary to call the religion of the vast majority of Indians as Hinduism or the religion of the Hindus as distinct from Buddhism, Jainism, Judaism, Christianity and Islam—the other major religions of the world. Hinduism itself does not stand for any specific creed. It includes several cults, each with a distinctive character, and devoted to the exclusive worship of a specific deity as the Supreme Being. Though the various religious cults do have certain commonly accepted doctrines and may be regarded as part of Hinduism in a broad sense, they are all identifiable as distinct. Each one is a well developed religious system with a long historical background and claims millions of followers. A comprehensive and separate study of each religion, therefore, would merit a closer study.

Vaiṣṇavism which is the main subject of this study is one of the oldest living religions of India. It is a monotheistic system based on the theory that Viṣṇu is the Ultimate Reality, the Supreme Deity (*paratattva*) and identical with Brahman of the Upaniṣads. It believes that the exclusive and devoted worship of Viṣṇu will lead to the attainment of the highest spiritual goal. It emphasises the observance of an ethical and religious way of life for the purpose of realization of Viṣṇu.

Vaiṣṇavism is not a mere cult. It is essentially a philosophy of religion. It has developed distinctive theological doctrines which are founded on sound philosophical theories enunciated in the Upaniṣads. There are religions which do not have a rational philosophical basis. The tribal religions, the older Pāśupata sects and some of the revealed theologies are of this type. On the other hand, we have metaphysical systems such as the Mādhyamika school of Buddhism and the Western schools of thought which do not include in them a theology. A philosophical system howsoever great and acceptable it might be, would lack practical value if it cannot regulate the religious life of human beings. In the same way, a good theological system without a philosophical foundation might influence the life of an individual through a religious discipline, but may lack a sound philosophy. A sound religious system must, therefore, be structured on a strong philosophical foundation. Vaiṣṇavism as a theological system pre-eminently fulfils this criteria. As a philosophy of religion it attempts to fuse religion and philosophy and reconcile the claims of revelation and reason.

The basis for the above claim is that Vaiṣṇavism is an outcome of the Vedānta as enshrined in the Upaniṣads, the *Vedānta-sūtra* and the *Bhagavad-gītā.* The Viśiṣṭādvaita Vedānta expounded by Rāmānuja which is essentially a philosophical system provides the philosophic foundation for it. Traditional scholars do not generally make a distinction between Viśiṣṭādvaita Philosophy and Vaiṣṇava Religion. According to them the Viśiṣṭādvaita *darśana* as it is rightly called like the Nyāya *darśana*, is not different from the Vaiṣṇava *mata*, as it is generally termed. Besides, in Indian philosophy, philosophy and religion are not treated as different from each other as is done in the West. The two are complementary and they often overlap. Nevertheless, we have to admit a distinction between what I would prefer to call Viśiṣṭādvaita Philosophy and Viśiṣṭādvaita Religion. The former represents the theoretical and systematic study of the nature of Reality, whereas the latter covers a practical way of life which will lead to the realization of the ultimate spiritual goal. The main theme of the Upaniṣadic teaching as summed up in the three significant words is: 'True knowledge of Brahman (*brahmavit*) should lead to the attainment of Brahman (*āpnoti param*).' It thus emphasises the ultimate value of philosophical pursuits as the attainment of Brahman.

Keeping this in mind, the sage Vyāsa, author of the *Vedānta-sūtra*, has divided his reputed treatise containing aphorisms into four parts (*adhyāyas*). The first part primarily deals with the nature of Ultimate Reality, termed as Brahman in the Upaniṣads. To maintain the rigour of the metaphysical character of the subject, the *Sūtras* do not identify the one Ultimate Reality with any of the deities accepted as God of the religion by various cults with different names. This is in the spirit of true philosophical investigation which does not bring in theological concepts. The second part is primarily concerned with the re-establishment of the same truth expounded in the first part by way of refuting the theories of the rival schools of thought. The third part is focused on the *sādhana* or the means of realizing the Ultimate Reality. The fourth part is devoted to a discussion of the spiritual goal or the *summum bonum* of human life (*puruṣārtha*). The two topics—*sādhana* and *puruṣārtha* are very important because they spell out the practical value of the philosophical study. *Sādhana* or discipline involves an ethical and religious way of life leading to the achievement of the spiritual goal. This, in my opinion, is the character of a true religion. Thus, both philosophy and religion are important as they are complementary. Mere philosophy as speculative thinking and intellectual exercise is of little practical value. Mere religion based on faith with a set of beliefs and ritualistic practices will not be rational. The two should be in harmony. The religious texts use the terms *jñāna* and *karma* in a broad sense to cover theoretical knowledge gained from a study of the Sacred texts and its practical application for achieving a spiritual goal. As an ancient verse states, mere *jñāna* without *karma* is useless and mere *karma* devoid of *jñāna* is equally futile.[1] Both are, therefore, important. Against this background, we have to understand the difference between the Philosophy of Viśiṣṭādvaita (*darśana*) and the Religion of Viśiṣṭādvaita (*Vaiṣṇava-mata*).

There is a view that Vaiṣṇavism as a religion has been developed primarily from the Vaiṣṇava Āgamas, the numerous Pāñcarātra treatises, more than the Vedānta texts. Some scholars believe that there existed in the ancient past a Bhāgavata religion or the religious practices of the Bhāgavatas who worshipped Bhagavān Vāsudeva and that Rāmānuja imposed this religion on Vedānta philosophy to fuse the two to make it a philosophy of religion.[2] This analysis may be true to some extent but it does not invalidate the view that Vaiṣṇavism is an outcome of the Vedānta philosophy. The Pāñcarātra Āgamas on which the Bhāgavata religion is founded have their origin in the *Vedas*. The *Āgama-prāmāṇya* of Yāmuna, the commentary of Rāmānuja on the relevant *Vedāntasūtras* referring to Pāñcarātra religion and the *Pāñcarātra-rakṣā* of Vedānta Deśika have established beyond any doubt that the Pāñcarātra Āgamas are of Vedic origin. This point becomes more evident if we compare Vaiṣṇavism with the older school of Śaivism, another important monotheistic religion. Śaivism is primarily developed on the basis of the teachings contained in the Śaiva Āgamas, which are as old as the Vaiṣṇava Āgamas. Nevertheless, it cannot be taken as a religion developed from the Vedānta, because the Śaiva Āgamas, unlike Vaiṣṇava Āgamas, are not claimed even by ancient Śaivites as of Vedic origin. They are regarded as treatises having independent divine origin and as different from the Vedānta.[3] This is obvious from the fact that the Advaita Vedānta of Śaṁkara, which is the oldest among the living Vedānta schools and whose followers also worship Śiva, does not have any place in it for Śaivism. Presumably, some later thinkers such as Śrīkaṇṭha (14th century) and Appayya Dīkṣita (16th century), after realizing the rift between the Vedānta and the religion of Śaivism, have attempted to accord a Vedāntic authority to Śaivism by interpreting the *Vedānta-sūtra* in terms of Śiva as the Supreme Being in the books entitled Śrikaṇṭha's *Brahmasūtra Bhāṣya* and Appayya Dīkṣita's

Śivārkamaṇidīpikā, a commentary on the *Bhāṣya*. These efforts made at a later period with sectarian bias at a time when open clashes had developed between the two rival religions, are not of much relevance to establish the basic fact whether or not a particular ancient religious cult is an outcome of the Vedānta. We do not face a similar problem in the case of the Viśiṣṭādvaita Vedānta and its complementary Vaiṣṇava religion. Historically the two have grown together as two facets of one and the same school of thought from the ancient past. We may, therefore, make a claim free from dogmatic assertion that Vaiṣṇavism is a religion which has developed out of the Vedānta and has thus, a strong philosophic foundation.

A few lines of explanation may be necessary to substantiate this conclusion. The main topics of Vedānta are *tattva* or Reality, *hita* or means of realization and *puruṣārtha* or ultimate goal. *Tattva* is divided into two categories—*para* or what is ultimate and *apara* or what is dependent on the one highest Reality. The *apara-tattva* is of two kinds; the sentient beings or the individual souls that have consciousness and the material entities which are non-sentient in character. As *Śvetāśvatara Upaniṣad* states, *tattvas* are broadly classified into three kinds—*bhoktā*, the one who experiences the universe, *bhogya* or the universe of experience and *preritāra* or the one who controls the former two. In the language of Vedānta, the three realities are called as Brahmān, the Supreme Being, *jīvātman*, the individual self and *jagat*, the material universe. In the Viśiṣṭādvaita terminology, they are named as *Īśvara*, *cit* and *acit* respectively. The three constitute the *tattva-traya*. All the schools of Vedānta have generally accepted the three *tattvas*. Differences arise when it comes to the question of determining the relationship between the *para-tattva* and *apara-tattvas*. The issues involved are whether all the three are absolutely real or whether the ultimate Reality alone is absolutely real, while the other two are either phenomenal in character or dependent realities. If all the three are real, the question also arises as to whether the dependent realities are organically related to the independent one or in some other manner. We get three different answers to these basic questions and thus we have three principal schools of Vedāntā—Advaita, Viśiṣṭādvaita and Dvaita.

From an epistemological standpoint, the schools of Vedānta

may be classified under three categories: *abheda-vāda*, based on the logical concept of non-difference, *bheda-vāda*, based on the concept of difference and *bhedābheda-vāda* or the theory of difference-cum-non-difference as a compromise of the other two views. The *abheda-vāda* can itself assume different forms. It may be taken as undifferentiated, absolute oneness (*tādātmya*) as in the case of the Advaita Vedānta. It may also be taken as non-difference or oneness in the sense of organic unity, as advocated by the Viśiṣṭādvaita Vedānta. It may also mean oneness in the sense that only the ultimate Reality is independent (*svatantra*), while the other two realities, though different from each other, are absolutely dependent (*paratantra*) on the one independent entity, as in the case of Madhva's Dvaita Vedānta. The concept of *bhedābheda* is also understood in different ways giving room to other schools of Vedānta such as those represented by Bhāskara and Yādava Prakāśa. This is hardly the place to go into the details of these theories but suffice it to say that all schools of Vedānta accept the three metaphysical entities of God, soul and the physical universe.

Regarding the second topic relating to *hita*, the main issue according to the Upaniṣadic texts is whether *jñāna*, the spiritual knowledge of Brahman or the *upāsanā*, the meditation on Brahman is the direct means to attain the supreme goal. The Advaita Vedānta lays emphasis on *jñāna*, whereas Viśiṣṭādvaita and Dvaita give greater importance to *upāsanā*, also known as the path of devotion (*bhakti-yoga*) aided by knowledge (*jñāna*) and *karma*. Some schools have attempted to adopt a combination of *jñāna* (*upāsanā*) and *karma*, as that of Yādava and Bhāskara.

Regarding the nature of the goal (*puruṣārtha*), the doctrines advanced by each school vary. But what is common to all is the acceptance of the concept of cessation of bondage leading to the realization of supreme end. According to the Viśiṣṭādvaita Vedānta, it is the complete and comprehensive experience of Brahman by the individual soul in a transcendental realm.

If we take into consideration these basic doctrines of Vedānta, we do not find that the religion of Vaiṣṇavism is in anyway different from the Viśiṣṭādvaita Vedānta. In fact, the former has adopted all the philosophical doctrines of the latter. The distinction, however, arises with regard to the manner in which these doctrines have been further expanded or developed without breaking away from the original sources in order to meet certain theological needs. The three main topics of Vedānta—*tattva, hita* and *puruṣārtha*—have been expanded to make it a fivefold scheme of categories known as *artha-pañcaka*. These are: (1) the nature of Brahman to be attained (*prāpya*); (2) the nature of the individual self who aspires to realize it (*prāptā*); (3) the method of achieving the goal (*prāptyupāya*); (4) the nature of the goal (*phala*) and (5) the obstacles in the way of realization of the goal (*prāpti-virodhi*). This scheme of classification is adopted on the basis of a verse found in *Hārīta Saṁhitā*, a Pāñcarātra treatise, which claims that these five topics encompass the essential teachings of the Vedas, the Itihāsas and Purāṇas.[4] The Vaiṣṇava treatises frequently quote it and have primarily focused their doctrines on these five categories.[5] Of these, the first two are covered by the first and second part of the *Vedānta-sūtra*; the third and fourth categories by the *sādhana* and *puruṣārtha* sections of *Vedānta sūtra*. The fifth is also covered indirectly in the *sādhana-pāda*. Nevertheless, it is considered important that an individual should be made aware of how he is caught up in bondage and the various kinds of obstacles standing in the way of attaining the final liberation so that he develops in him a sense of detachment towards worldly pleasures and a yearning for *mokṣa* before he embarks on the prescribed path of spiritual discipline. Vaiṣṇavism has, therefore, accorded importance to *prāpti-virodhi*.

The three *tattvas* referred to by the *Śvetāśvatara Upaniṣad* become part of the fivefold classification. However, these have been discussed by Vaiṣṇavism in a different manner and in greater detail with emphasis on the theological aspects of the doctrines.[6] This has led to the formulation of certain distinctive theological doctrines which are not stated explicitly in the *Vedānta-sūtra*.

By way of elucidation of the above point, we may briefly examine the doctrines of *Īśvara*, the *sādhana* and *mokṣa* in order to find out how these topics have been dealt with in the Vaiṣṇava treatises. Regarding *Īśvara*, the *Vedāntasūtra* is concerned primarily in determining the nature of the ultimate Reality. It focuses its attention on the criteria for determining a metaphysical entity as the ultimate Reality rather than going into the question whether that Reality is Viṣṇu or Śiva or some other deity. Even when it deals with the question of meditation on a specific deity for attaining liberation, the Upaniṣad merely states in general terms that which is the cause of the universe is to be meditated upon (*kāraṇaṁ tu dhyehaḥ*), without mentioning the name of the deity.[7] Though for metaphysics it is immaterial what name is given to this Reality, it becomes very important for theology to specify the particular deity which fulfills the criteria of Reality and which, therefore, serves as the appropriate object of worship and contemplation. This is what Vaiṣṇavism seeks to do as a theological system. It does not develop any new doctrine which has no basis in the Vedānta. On the other hand, it develops the same Vedānta theory by making it more specific by providing a practical guide for religious purpose. Thus, in Vaiṣṇavism the Brahman of Vedānta Philosophy is identified with a personal god in the name of Viṣṇu or Nārāyaṇa strictly on the authority of *Śruti* as well as Smṛti texts and well within the framework laid down by the Vedānta. As a logical corollary to the acceptance of a personal god, which is a necessity in any theistic system of religion, the Supreme Being is conceived in Vaiṣṇavism as one endowed with various attributes such as omniscience, omnipotence, Supreme Lordship, compassion, friendly disposition etc., including a divine bodily form in order to make the transcendental Reality a cognizable object of meditation and worship.

With regard to the *sādhana* or means of liberation, the *Vedāntasūtra*, following the general trend of the Upaniṣads, has laid greater stress on *upāsanā* and discusses in detail the several types of *vidyās* for Brahman-realization. Realizing the impracticability of this path of discipline for persons who are not qualified for *upāsanā*, the Vaiṣṇava theology advocate *nyāsa-vidyā* or the self-surrender to God which is one of the thirty-two *vidyās* laid down in the Upaniṣads and which is easier to observe being open to all irrespective of caste, creed and status of an individual. Here again it is not a novel doctrine brought into Vaiṣṇavism from elsewhere but it is a development of the basic theory implicit in the Vedānta.

On the subject of the *puruṣārtha*, the author of the *Vedānta-sūtra* takes a rationalistic stand. On the strength of the *Chāndogya Upaniṣad*,[8] he expresses the view that the individual self after becoming free from bondage, manifests itself in its true form. This means that after it attains Brahman, it becomes free from the shackles of *karma*. Once this state is reached, there is no return to mundane existence. This concept of *mokṣa*—a state in which the individual soul is freed from *karma* and attains Brahman—is further expanded in Vaiṣṇava theology to include, besides a positive state of existence for the *jīva* enjoying the bliss of Brahman, the divine service (*kaiṅkarya*) to God in a transcendental realm known as *paramapada*, the Supreme abode of God. This has led to the development of the doctrine of *nitya-vibhūti*, the transcendental spiritual realm with a picturesque description of *paramapada* and the concept of *kaiṅkarya* or divine service by the released souls. All these may appear as speculative doctrines conceived by Vaiṣṇava theology to create an interest in the devotees seeking liberation. But it is not so. These theories have come up as an outgrowth of the concept of *mokṣa* as outlined in the Vedānta.

Thus, Vaiṣṇavism as a monotheistic religion can be proved to have developed on the basis of sound philosophical theories, derived from the Upaniṣads and the *Vedāntasūtra*. Vaiṣṇavism has both a philosophy and religion. Its philosophy is the same as that of Vedānta and its religion is not basically different from that of Vedānta except that it has been further expanded to meet theological needs.

We shall present in this book the Philosophy of Vaiṣṇavism and Theology of Vaiṣṇavism separately. The philosophy will be dealt with under the following headings:

1. The Doctrine of Ultimate Reality.
2. The Doctrine of Individual Self.
3. The Doctrine of Cosmic Matter.
4. The Doctrine of Means (*bhakti-yoga*).
5. The Doctrine of Goal (*mokṣa*).

The theology of Vaiṣṇavism will be discussed under the following headings:

1. Viṣṇu as Supreme Being.
2. Viṣṇu and Goddess Śrī.
3. Viṣṇu and His Attributes.
4. Viṣṇu and His Incarnations.
5. Viṣṇu and the Nitya-vibhūti.

6. Viṣṇu and Jīva.
7. Prapatti as means of Attaining Viṣṇu.
8. Viṣṇu as Supreme Goal of Life.

As an orthodox religious system, Vaiṣṇavism advocates a way of life involving certain religious practices, sacraments and cultivation of ethical virtues. As these constitute an important feature of Vaiṣṇava religion, they have been dealt with separately under the following headings:

1. Role of Ācārya in Vaiṣṇavism.
2. The Sacraments of Vaiṣṇavism.
3. The Religious Duties of a Vaiṣṇava.
4. Kaiṅkarya for God and the Devotees of God.
5. The Vaiṣṇava Dharma.

The main objective of presenting the doctrines under separate headings is twofold. The first purpose is to establish that the Philosophy of Viśiṣṭādvaita is distinct from the Religion of Viśiṣṭādvaita, though the two are complementary representing two facets of the same one system. The second objective is to delineate the purely theological theories from the philosophical ones and present them with all the relevant details to enable the students of philosophy to understand them in the correct perspective. I have felt the necessity of such a presentation for the obvious reason that the extensive Vaiṣṇava treatises, particularly those written by the Vaiṣṇava *ācāryas* in the Maṇipravāḷa language (a mixture of Tamil and Sanskrit) which include the several elaborate commentaries on the hymns of the Ālvārs have mixed up philosophy and theology. In fact, they are more theological in character than philosophical, as compared with the classic *Śrī-bhāṣya* of Rāmānuja and the works of Vedānta Deśika in Sanskrit such as *Nyāya-siddhāñjana* and *Tattva-muktā-kalāpa*. This has created an impression in the minds of some scholars that Viśiṣṭādvaita is essentially a theology rather than philosophy. With a view to removing this wrong notion, I published a book recently under the title *Fundamentals of Viśiṣṭādvaita Vedānta* based on the study of Vedānta Deśika's *Tattva-muktā-kalāpa* which is mainly a philosophical treatise. That book seeks to establish that Viśiṣṭādvaita is essentially a philosophical system though it includes theology in it. In order to uphold the philosophical character of the system, theological doctrines were generally left out of the scope of that book, as Vedānta Deśika himself had done in his *Tattva-muktā-kalāpa*. As theology is important for a theistic system, I have attempted in the present book to expound the theological doctrines distinctive to Vaiṣṇavism along with its philosophy and religious discipline in order to bring out the distinction between the philosophy and theology.

The sourcebooks for the study of our subject are far too many.[9] Apart from the Vedas, the principal Upaniṣads, the Itihāsas (*Rāmāyaṇa* and *Mahābhārata*), the Vaiṣṇava Purāṇas, the Āgamas (both Vaikhānasa and Pāñcarātra), we have the erudite works in Sanskrit contributed by Yāmuna, Rāmānuja and his illustrious successor, Vedānta Deśika. We have also a large number of scholarly treatises written in Maṇipravāḷa language by Vaiṣṇava *ācāryas* between the 12th and 15th century. They fall into two categories: (*a*) those which primarily deal with the interpretation of the esoteric doctrines and hence are known as *Rahasya-granthas* or *Saṁpradāya granthas* and (*b*) those which are in the form of elaborate commentaries (*vyākhyāna*) on the hymns of the Āḻvārs (the Vaiṣṇava saints of South India). A large number of works written at a later period between 16th and 19th century are mostly in the form of commentaries on the works of earlier *ācāryas* and tracts dealing with certain doctrinal controversies between the two main sects of Vaiṣṇavas—Vaḍakalai and Tenkalai.[10] The literature that piled up in later years is indeed very extensive and it would run into volumes if one were to write on the subject expounding all the theories in detail as contained in these sourcebooks, both in Sanskrit and Maṇipravāḷa. It is not the objective of this book to write the History of Vaiṣṇavism. Its scope is confined, as already indicated, to present the essential philosophical and theological doctrines of Vaiṣṇavism comprehensively and in a lucid manner.

The school of Vaiṣṇavism which is covered in the present book is confined to the extant scholarly texts of Yāmuna, Rāmānuja and his immediate successors such as Kūreśa, Piḷḷān, Parāśara Bhattar, Nañjīyar, Periyavāccānpiḷḷai, Vātsya Varadācārya, Sudarśana Sūri, Piḷḷailokācārya, Vedānta Deśika and Maṇavāḷamāmuni. These Vaiṣṇava *ācāryas* who lived during the period extending from 10th to 15th century have developed the philosophical as well as the theological doctrines taking their stand on the authority of the Vedas, Upaniṣads, Itihāsas, Vaiṣṇava Purāṇas, Pāñcarātra Āgamas and the hymns of the Ālvārs. What is found in these authoritative sourcebooks truly represent the proper Vaiṣṇavism. The treatises which have appeared subsequent to the 15th century are generally in the form of commentaries, glossaries on the *Śrī-bhāṣya* of Rāmānuja, the hymns of the Āḻvārs and the works of Vedānta Deśika. They cannot be regarded as original works. I have, therefore, confined my study to the original sourcebooks written prior to the 15th century. With a view to presenting an objective exposition of the doctrines, I have avoided the mythological episodes from the epics and Purāṇas, generally used in the works of later Vaiṣṇava *ācāryas* to substantiate the theological concepts.

Many other schools of Vaiṣṇavism have come up in the post-Rāmānuja period such as those of Madhva, Nimbārka, Vallabha, Caitanya, Rāmānanda, Jayadeva and Jñāneśvara. These schools are generally the offshoots of original Vaiṣṇavism as expounded by Rāmānuja. They represent different forms of Vaiṣṇava movements which attained popularity in different parts of India and are a part of *bhakti* movement to meet the local social conditions and the religious aspirations of the people of the area. I have, therefore, left them out of the scope of my study except a brief account of them for comparative study. I have also refrained from the temptation of comparing Vaiṣṇavism with other Hindu monotheistic religions such as Śaivism and Śāktaism and the non-Hindu religions of Christianity and Islam.

Rāmānuja's Vaiṣṇavism is often designated as Śrī-vaiṣṇavism to distinguish it from that of Madhva and other religious reformers. It is also described by some scholars as Vaiṣṇavism of South India. These epithets, in my opinion, are misleading as it would give the impression that it is a religion confined to a small sect of a particular region. True Vaiṣṇavism, as will be explained in the next chapter, is the one which has been in existence from the time of Ṛgveda and which has been developed through successive stages over several centuries culminating in the reformulation as a systematized philosophy of religion at the hands of Rāmānuja. That Viṣṇu is the Supreme Deity as associated with Goddess Śrī or Lakṣmī as His consort is acceptable to all schools of Vaiṣṇavism, though there may be differences of opinion with regard to the ontological status of the Goddess. Hence it is not necessary to add the prefix 'Śrī', to Vaiṣṇavism except for the purpose of showing veneration to the religion.[11] Nor is it correct to call it the Vaiṣṇavism of Rāmānuja or of South India. Though Rāmānuja as its exponent was born in South India, he adopted the Vaiṣṇavism which was in vogue at that time all over India. The inscriptional evidence found in parts of North India and the fact that North India is the home of some of the important Pāñcarātra treatises which constitute one of the main sources for Vaiṣṇavism demonstrate the prevalence of the religion in other parts of India. It is not, therefore, a regional cult, though it may be widespread in the South since Rāmānuja's time due to historical reasons. It is in fact a cult having a universal appeal as it believes that Viṣṇu is the Supreme Deity who is immanent in all and that the worship offered to other deities will ultimately reach Him even as rain water fallen from the sky into the different streams eventually join the ocean.[12]

To my knowledge, this is the first time that an attempt has been made to present in English and in a single volume a comprehensive account of Vaiṣṇavism—its Philosophy, Theology and Religious Discipline based on original sourcebooks. It is my hope that this book may prove useful for students of comparative religion and in particular, for those who wish to make an in-depth study of Vaiṣṇavism.

Notes

1. *hataṁ jñānaṁ kriyāhīnaṁ hatā ca ajñāninām kriyā*
   (Quoted by Vedānta Deśika in SS II.33).
2. Dr. R.G. Bhandarkar; *Vaiṣṇavism, Śaivism etc.*, p. 6.
   See also M. Hiriyanna, *Outlines of Indian Philosophy*, p. 383.
3. See *Darśanodaya*, p. 246 and p. 496. *agamaikamūlamidaṁ darśanamiti prācyām abhiprāyaḥ.*
   See also the commentary of Aghoraśivācārya or Bhoja's *Tattvaprakāśa* (Quoted in *Darśanodaya* p. 496).
   śaivadarśanaṁ tu vedāntavāsanāvadbhiḥ vidvadbhiḥ vyākulikṛtam.
4. *Hārīta Saṁhitā*, *prāpyasya brahmaṇorūpaṁ prāptuśca pratyagātmanaḥ;*
   prāptyupāyaṁ phalaṁ caiva tathā prāpti-virodhi ca.
   vadanti sakalā vedāḥ setihāsa-purāṇakāḥ.
5. See RTS IV. *Arthapañacakādhikāra.*
   Also *Arthapañcakam* of Piḷḷailokācārya.

6. Piḷḷailokācārya has written a separate treatise in Maṇipravāḷa language under the title *Tattvatraya*. Vedānta Deśika has dealt with the subject in detail in a separate chapter in the *Rahasyatrayasāra* and also written an independent work under the title *Tattvatrayaculukaṁ*.
7. The mention of 'Śambhu' and 'Śiva' in this context as objects of meditation in the *Atharva-śiras* and *Śvetāśvatara* Upaniṣads does not mean a God of a particular cult. See Chapter VII pp. 145-46, 148.
8. ChUp VIII.12.2. See Chapter 6, p. 121.
9. See pp. 35-38.
10. See p. 29 for explanation of these terms.
11. It is customary among the Vaiṣṇavas since the time of Rāmānuja to use the prefix *Śri* or *Tiru* its Tamil equivalent to all the words that have some religious significance.
12. *ākāśāt patitaṁ toyaṁ yathā gacchati sāgaraṁ;*
sarvadeva namaskāraḥ keśavaṁ pratigacchati.

PART I

HISTORICAL DEVELOPMENT OF VAIṢṆAVISM

1

HISTORICAL DEVELOPMENT OF VAIṢṆAVISM

Vaiṣṇavism, one of the oldest living religions of India, is a monotheistic system which upholds Viṣṇu as the ultimate Reality (*paratattva*). It believes that the exclusive and devoted worship of Viṣṇu leads to the realization of the highest spiritual goal (*parama-puruṣārtha*) and for this purpose, it has laid down an ethical and religious discipline.

The origin of Vaiṣṇavism can be traced back to the Ṛgveda—the oldest religious literature of the world. Tradition, however, ascribes its origin to the oral teachings imparted by Viṣṇu himself to Goddess Lakṣmī and in turn to Viśvaksena, the divine angel. Judged on the basis of the extant recorded literature, we can find in the Ṛgveda adequate and unquestionable evidence for the basic tenets of Vaiṣṇavism. There is sufficient number of hymns in the Ṛgveda, some of which are also repeated in the Yajurveda and Sāmaveda, which speak of Viṣṇu as the highest personal God, who is the sole creator and controller of the universe and the saviour of humanity. The Western Indologists and some Indian scholars have, however, taken the view that Viṣṇu mentioned in the Ṛgveda is one among several deities such as Agni, Rudra, Prajāpati, Indra, Varuṇa, Soma etc., and that Viṣṇu is, therefore, not a Supreme Deity. A dispassionate study of the hymns related to Viṣṇu, on the basis of interpretations by ancient commentators such as Yāska and the exponents of Vedānta, bring out the true implications of the Vedic statements and reveal beyond doubt that the view of the Indologists is not correct.

Monotheism of Ṛgveda

Before we take up the import of the selected hymns of the Ṛgveda which support the above conclusion, we should examine whether the religion of Ṛgveda can be considered monotheistic upholding the theory of one Supreme Being. The common view of many Indologists is that the Vedic religion is polytheistic. The basis for this view is that the hymns of the Ṛgveda speak of numerous deities (*devatās*) with diverse characteristics. Each deity is described as having an individuality and a distinct status. According to one hymn the number of *devatās* is 3339.[1] In another place in the *Ṛk Saṁhitā* the deities are divided into three groups: (1) those who dwell in the heavens (*dyu-loka*); (2) those whose abode is the mid-region (*antarikṣa*); and (3) those who reside on earth (*pṛthivī*).[2] Their total number is counted as 33, eleven in each region. Therefore, on the face of it, it would appear that the religion of Ṛgveda cannot be considered monotheistic and that it would be difficult to accept the supremacy of Viṣṇu.

There is a significant statement in the *Taittirīya Upaniṣad* which provides an answer to the issue whether or not the Ṛgveda teaches monotheism. It states: '*Maha* is the Brahman, the Supreme Self and all other *devatās* (deities) constitute its limbs or aspects'.[3] This fact is reiterated in a more explicit way in the *Mahābhārata*. It points out that Nārāyaṇa, the highest personal God, is the Supreme Being; all deities are created by Him and all other deities are, therefore, parts (*aṅgas*) of that one great Being.[4] Another verse of the *Mahābhārata* offers the same explanation upholding the supremacy of Viṣṇu. Thus it states: "Viṣṇu is the unique and unparalleled Deity; He is the Supreme Being (*mahad-bhūtaṁ*); the other countless beings which are different from each other exist as His different aspects. He pervades all the three worlds and controls them but He Himself is untouched by their defects."[5]

From these statements it is obvious that the numerous deities referred to in the Ṛgveda are no more than 'functional appellations' of one fundamental Reality. Three or thirty-three or three thousand are numbers to which it would be wrong to attach a literal significance. They are to be understood as figures of speech adopted by the composers of the Vedic hymns to convey certain truth which the seers had realized.[6] This fact has been brought out by the *Bṛhadāraṇyaka Upaniṣad* in the dialogue between Sākalya and Yājñavalkya. In reply to a question addressed to the latter by the former regarding the number of gods, the number 3339 is reduced to 33, then to 3, later to 2, further to one and a half and finally to one. That one deity is described as *prāṇa* or Brahman. The same Upaniṣad further explains that this numerical description of gods signifies the divine glories of one ultimate Reality.[7] The ancient Vedic commentators, Yāska and Śaunaka, have adopted this explanation. According to Yāska only one Supreme Being is sung differently and all other deities are its different aspects.[8] Śaunaka, the author of *Bṛhaddevatā* states: 'There is but one deity. This deity has great powers and by its special powers it can assume many diverse forms. Hence the primary Reality which is single *Ātman* of the universe is described and praised under different names. Those who are described separately are part of this one *Paramātman*.'[9] Sāyaṇa, the well-known commentator on the Vedas, also maintains the view that one *Paramātman* is praised through the different deities.[10]

The view expressed by the Vedic commentators and the *Mahābhārata* is not a later innovation as some scholars contend, to support the monotheism of the Ṛgveda. There are hymns in the Ṛgveda itself, though these are fewer in number, which explicitly speak of the existence of one Supreme Being. Thus, an oft-quoted hymn states: There is one Being (*sat*) but wise men call it by different names (*ekaṁ sat viprā bahudhā vadanti*).[11] This is not the only stray statement but there are many others of this kind found in almost every *maṇḍala* (part) of the Ṛgveda. We may cite a few. In the very first *maṇḍala* we have another hymn stating that the *sūrya* (sun) is the soul of the universe and its support.[12] This emphasises the Upaniṣadic truth that the supreme Deity within the orbit of the sun is the controller of the entire universe as an indweller of the sentient and non-sentient entities. In the third *maṇḍala*, the hymn emphasises the oneness of the deity by stating that the worshipful divinity of gods is one.[13] In the fourth *maṇḍala*, the assertion of the Sage Vāmadeva that "I am Manu, I am Sūrya, I am indeed everything etc., refers to the unity of Reality".[14] A hymn in the fifth *maṇḍala* says that in whatever form He was seen in the same form He is described.[15] In the sixth *maṇḍala* we come across statements such as He is one to whom prayer is to be offered[16] corresponding to the *Taittirīya* Upaniṣadic text speaking of one ultimate Reality. Another text in the same *maṇḍala* explicitly points out that there is one monarch of the world.[17] The passage in eighth *maṇḍala* expresses in clear terms that the one verily has become all this.[18] A similar lucid statement can be found in the tenth *maṇḍala* which points out that wise people describe in many ways the one existent principle.[19] In another hymn it is stated that He who gives names to different deities is one Supreme Being.[20]

The *Ṛgveda Saṁhitā* not only acknowledges the existence of one ultimate Reality in general terms such as *sat*, *eka* etc., but it also refers to the essential characteristics of the one Reality in the same terms as the Upaniṣads speak of Brahman. The Supreme one Deity is regarded as primary cause of the universe (*sarva-kāraṇa*).[21] He is considered as the controller of all (*sarva-niyāmaka*)[22] and immanent in the hearts of men (*antaryāmī*).[23] He is described as the ruler of the entire universe[24] and the Lord of both the transcendental as well as the physical universe.[25] He is referred to as the saviour of mankind and giver of immortality.[26] We also come across other important attributes of the Supreme Being such as omniscient (*sarvajña*) omnipotent (*sarvaśakta*), endowed with unsurpassable glory (*sarvātiśāyi*) and the greatest of all.

Though the hymns of the Ṛgveda are addressed to different deities and are used to invoke them for sacrificial purposes they do contain philosophical thoughts. The Vedic seers who sang the glory of different deities were fully conscious of one Supreme Being who is the inner soul of these deities. As already pointed out this truth has been well brought out by Yāska and other Vedic commentators.[27] Further, according to the principle of interpretation adopted by the author of the *Vedānta-sūtra*, when a prayer is addressed to a specific deity such as Indra or Agni, it is not intended for that particular Being but on the contrary, it is meant for the *Paramātman*, the Supreme Being who is the indweller (*antarātmā*) of that Deity.[28] From the philosophical standpoint the various names such as Indra, Agni, Viśvadeva etc., denote ultimately *Paramātman*. The *Kaṭha Upaniṣad* also declares that the entire Vedas speak of the *svarūpa* of Brahman.[29] All the different deities referred to in the hymns are, therefore, regarded as the different aspects or appellations of one Supreme Being. Thus, the religion of Ṛgveda is basically monotheistic despite its reference to numercus deities. These monistic ideas of the *Ṛk Saṁhitā* have been well developed in the Upaniṣads which quote the hymns of the Ṛgveda.[30]

Viṣṇu in the Ṛgveda

We shall now consider whether or not Viṣṇu referred to in the Ṛgveda is that Supreme Deity, the one Reality (*sat*) as described by the hymns? Is not Viṣṇu also a general deity (*devatā-sāmānya*) like all other deities? There are greater number of hymns singing the glory of Agni, Indra and Rudra than that of Viṣṇu. In some places Viṣṇu is addressed along with Indra and Agni and is regarded as a solar deity (*āditya*). In view of this, some scholars are of the opinion that Viṣṇu of the Ṛgveda is one among the other deities and He was raised to the status of a Supreme Being at a later period by the Epics and Purāṇas.[31]

There is no doubt that Viṣṇu is accorded a higher place in the Ṛgveda even though fewer hymns are addressed to him.[32] The scriptural text itself states that Agni is the lowest of all the deities and Viṣṇu is the highest.[33] Whether or not Viṣṇu is the Supreme Deity is to be determined with reference to the essential characteristics which define the ultimate Reality. Vedānta Deśika has offered several definitions of *Īśvara* or Supreme Lord.[34] These serve as the criteria to determine the Supremacy of a deity. From the philosophical standpoint, the important criteria are that a deity which claims the status of the Supreme Being should be all-pervasive (*sarva-vyāpi*), that it should be immanent in all beings as inner controller (*antarātmā*), that it should be the ground (*ādhāra*) of all that exists in the universe and that it should be the sovereign of the entire universe (*sarveśvara*). If we examine the hymns of the Ṛgveda addressed to the different deities including Viṣṇu, taking into consideration the interpretations offered by ancient Vedic commentators and exponents of the Vedānta, we see that Viṣṇu of the Ṛgveda qualifies fully to be considered as the Supreme Being (*Īśvara*). Whether or not Viṣṇu of the Ṛgveda is the Brahman of the Upaniṣads will be discussed later. For the present we may examine the meaning and implications of a few selected hymns addressed to Viṣṇu.

In the first place, the all-pervasive character (*sarvavyāpakatva*) of Viṣṇu has been explicitly brought out in more than one hymn of the Ṛgveda. This characteristic feature, which is an important determining criterion of the Supreme Being, is not found in respect of any other deity. Even if it be found implicitly in respect of any other deity, that deity is to be regarded as Viṣṇu according to the principle adopted by the *Vedānta-sūtra.*[35] Eight hymns[36] appearing in the very first *maṇḍala* of the *Ṛgveda Saṁhitā* speak about the greatness of Viṣṇu by repeatedly referring to the three strides with which He measured the entire universe. The description of Viṣṇu with three strides signifies symbolically that the entire universe—the lower region (*pṛthivī*), the upper region (*antarikṣa*) and the higher region (*dyuloka*)—is pervaded by Viṣṇu. The incarnation of Viṣṇu as an *avatāra* as narrated in the later Purāṇas is not what is referred to here. On the other hand, it implies that Viṣṇu along with the creation of the entire universe, pervades all that is created. The created entities derive their existence (*sattā*) by the immanence of the creator as its inner self. The Upaniṣad expresses this truth in a different way. 'Brahman wills to become many; it creates and it enters into the same as its inner soul'.[37] According to the Vedic etymology (*nirukta*) of Yāska, the term *Viṣṇu* means the one who pervades everything (*yad viṣito bhavati tad viṣṇur-bhavati*).[38] It is also interpreted as the one who enters into all (*viṣṇuḥ viśatervā*).[39] The *Ahirbudhnya Saṁhitā*, an authoritative Pāñcarātra treatise, upholds both the meanings.[40] The philosophical significance of the three strides of Viṣṇu has been brought out more explicitly in the *Śatapatha Brāhmaṇa.*[41] The passage says: Viṣṇu is the very sacrifice (*yajña*). He measured the entire universe for the sake of divine beings (*devatās*); the strides are: the pervasion of the entire physical earth by the first step, the entire upper region (*antarikṣa*), by the second and the heavenly region (*divam*) by the third step.

Some ancient commentators on the Vedas and also a few Western scholars have taken the view that *Viṣṇu* is Sun-God (*sūrya*) and the three steps represent the rising sun in the early morning, the sun in the noon and the setting sun in the evening. The three steps are also interpreted as the manifestation of sun in three different forms, first as *agni* (fire) in the earthly region, the second one as *vidyut* (lightning) in the upper region (*antarikṣa*) and the third in the higher celestial region (*divi*) as *sūrya* (sun). Both the interpretations, though plausible stand opposed to the correct etymological meaning of the term *Viṣṇu* as explained earlier. It also conflicts with the Ṛgvedic hymn[42] which speaks of an eternal *Viṣṇupada* (either in the sense of abode of Viṣṇu or as *Viṣṇu-svarūpa*). The sun or the realm of sun (*sūryaloka*) is not eternal. The term *vicakrame* (strode) used repeatedly in the hymns along with the word *thredhā* (in threefold manner) has a special significance. The number three, as Madhva has interpreted, covers not merely the three worlds—*pṛthivī*, *antarikṣa* and *dyuloka*—but the three Vedas (*Ṛk*, *Yajus* and *Sāma*), the three time factors—past, present and future, the three kinds of *jīvas*—*devas*, *dānavas* and human beings, the three types of existents—sentient beings (*cetana*), non-sentient matter (*acetana*) and the mixed ones (*miśra*). The implication of it is that everything that exists in the spatio-temporal universe is pervaded by Viṣṇu. If this meaning is accepted it becomes obvious that Viṣṇu of the Ṛgveda is the Supreme Being by virtue of His all-pervasive character.

The purpose of Viṣṇu's pervasion is to provide protection to all beings in the universe. This is made evident in the words *Viṣṇuḥ gopāḥ*'[43] *Gopā* means one who is the protector of the universe and He carries out this function by upholding the *dharma* (*dharmāṇi dhārayan*).

The most important hymn which establishes beyond any doubt the supremacy of Viṣṇu is the one which speaks of the eternal abode (*paramapada*) of Viṣṇu. The hymn runs as follows: "The enlightened seers (*sūris*) always see that supreme abode of Viṣṇu, like the shining sun pervading the entire sky as if it were an eye fixed in the heaven".[44] The word *Viṣṇu* in this hymn refers to *Para-Brahma* because the supreme abode as existent eternally should belong to the eternal Supreme Being. The *sūris* (seers) as explained by Rāmānuja are the *nitya-sūris*, those individual souls who are eternally free (those who never had any bondage unlike the released souls). They are endowed with perfect knowledge implying that they are omniscient. Only such individuals can have the vision of Viṣṇu and His eternal abode.[45] The word *paramapada* also means the *svarūpa* or nature of Viṣṇu in the sense that he is to be attained. The bound souls and all other deities cannot have a direct vision of this abode.[46] The *Kaṭha Upaniṣad* also refers to *paramapada* of Viṣṇu.[47] The *Viṣṇupurāṇa* also reiterates this.[48] Human eye cannot grasp it because it is a transcendental spiritual entity. It is only through the spiritual knowledge acquired after release from the bondage that it is possible to have the vision of Viṣṇu's abode.

The description of Viṣṇu as *tridhātu* or one who mixes the three primary elements—*pṛthivī*, *ap* and *tejas* at the time of cosmic creation and offers support (*dādhāra*) to the entire universe brings out the supremacy of Viṣṇu as the sole cause of the universe and as one who after creating it sustains it.[49] This is the theory of cosmic creation advanced by the *Chāndogya Upaniṣad.*[50] One of the essential determining characteristics of *Īśvaratva* or Supreme Lordship is that He should be the ground or supporter of the entire universe (*sarvādhāratva*).

One other hymn[51] states explicitly that Viṣṇu is the protector of all (*sarvarakṣaka*) by using the term *trātā* and also that He is the Lord (*inasya*) which implies Lord of everything (*sarvasya swāmin*). The expansion of the three worlds by His three strides is described as an extraordinary feat of masculine character by using the expression *pauṁsyaṁ.* Such an epithet is not found in respect of any other *devatā* in the Ṛgveda.

The distinguishing characteristic of Vaiṣṇavism is the acceptance of the theory that Viṣṇu as associated with Goddess Śrī is the ultimate Reality (*Śriyaḥ-pati*). The root of this doctrine is found in one of the hymns.[52] The meaning of this passage is: An individual who surrenders himself to Viṣṇu who exists from time immemorial (*pūrvyāya*), who is the creator of the variegated universe (*vedhase*), who is at the same time looks as newly born (*navīyase*) and who possesses as His consort the one that delights the entire universe (*sumajjānaye*), such an individual not only lives an illustrious life in this world but also reaches the supreme spiritual goal. Though the name of Śrī or Lakṣmī is not explicitly mentioned in this hymn, the term *sumajjānaye* used here is interpreted by Sāyaṇa as the Goddess Śrī.[53] This hymn as well as the subsequent one refer to the concept of ultimate Reality (*tattva*), the theory of self-surrender to God as the means of salvation (*upāya*) and the idea of spiritual goal (*puruṣārtha*) as conceived by Vaiṣṇavism. The subsequent hymn emphasises in particular that the worship of such a Viṣṇu by way of reciting his name with sincere and deep devotion without any selfish purpose will promote the development of *jñāna* in the form of *bhakti* (*sumati*).[54]

According to the two hymns[55] in the seventh *maṇḍala* the greatness (*mahimā*) of Viṣṇu is immeasurable and inconceivable by any one, not even by other deities. The word *para* used in the hymn implies that Viṣṇu is the highest of all. This kind of description is not found in respect of any other deity of the Ṛgveda. He is regarded as the benevolent God who bestows not only material prosperity to his devotees but also the highest *puruṣārtha* in the form of attainment of *paramapada* (supreme abode) of which He is the Lord.[56]

A passage in the *Taittirīya Āraṇyaka* of Kṛṣṇa Yajurveda states more explicitly that Viṣṇu upholds both the universe and the higher region.[57] It further states that He holds them in their respective places through His power. He alone (*ekaḥ*) (implying that he is not dependent on any other power) sustains the entire universe, bringing out the fact that he is the *ādhāra* or supporter of the universe.[58] It also points out that this power of Viṣṇu is greater than that of air and fire. He is the controller of all other deities which are stated to be the cause of death and destruction such as Yama and Agni.[59]

Of all the hymns of the Ṛgveda, the *Puruṣa-sūkta* included in the tenth *maṇḍala*,[60] establishes decisively that *Puruṣa* who is equated with Viṣṇu, is the Supreme Being. It is extolled as the most important Vedic passage by the Pāñcarātra Saṁhitās and the Purāṇas because it expounds the doctrine of the ultimate Reality as enunciated in the Upaniṣads.[61] This *sūkta* is found in all the four Vedas and is, therefore, regarded as a scriptural text of greater authority.[62] This passage is recited during worship of God and is used for expiating sins and attainment of any desired object such as health, wealth, happiness and *mokṣa*. It is named as *Vaiṣṇavī Saṁhitā* and its recitation will secure the grace of Viṣṇu. Though there is no mention of *Viṣṇu* by name, the term *puruṣa* is interpreted by all the commentators as referring to Viṣṇu or Nārāyaṇa. According to the etymological meaning as provided by *Viṣṇu Smṛti* and *Padma Purāṇa*, the letter *puḥ* means the abode in the form of physical body and the letter *ṣa* means one who dwells in it. The *Praśna Upaniṣad* states that *Puruṣa* or the one who dwells in the body (*puriśayam puruṣa*) is the highest Being, Brahman.[63] The *Bṛhadāraṇyaka* uses the term *Puruṣa* in the sense of Brahman. The *Subāla Upaniṣad* identifies the term *Puruṣa* with Nārāyaṇa.[64] The *Śatapatha Brahmaṇa*[65] also uses the word *Puruṣa* as synonymous with Nārāyaṇa. It designates *Puruṣa-sūkta* as *Nārāyaṇa-sūkta*. In the *Taittirīya Nārāyaṇa Upaniṣad* which is a part of *Taittirīya Āraṇyaka*, *Puruṣa* referred to in *Puruṣa-sūkta* is identified with Nārāyaṇa.[66] It also explicitly mentions that Nārāyaṇa is *Para-Brahma*, to be meditated upon for *mokṣa*. The *Padma Purāṇa* identifies *Puruṣa* with Vāsudeva.[67] According to the *Taittirīya Āraṇyaka*, the passage following immediately after *Puruṣa-sūkta*, which is designated as *uttara-nārāyaṇa* by *Śatapatha Brāhmaṇa*, mentions that *Hṛī* (meaning *Bhū-devī*) and *Lakṣmī* are the consorts of the *Puruṣa*[68] referred to in the earlier part of *Puruṣa-sūkta*. The explicit mention of the Goddess Lakṣmī and Bhū as consorts rules out the possibility of taking *Puruṣa* of *Puruṣa-sūkta* as any other deity such as Caturmukha-Brahmā, Viśvakarma and Prajāpati and thereby establishing the fundamental tenet of Vaiṣṇavism that *Śriyaḥ-pati* or Viṣṇu as associated with Śrī is the Supreme Deity.[69] The *Puruṣa-sūkta* of the Ṛgveda covers briefly the fundamental concepts of Vaiṣṇavism that Viṣṇu or Nārāyaṇa is the Supreme Deity (*paratattva*), He is both immanent and transcendent, He is the creator of the universe and He is the sole object of meditation (*upāsanā*) for attaining *mokṣa*.

There is another important passage in the Ṛgveda known as *Śrī-sūkta* which comes at the end of fifth *maṇḍala* as an appendix. It is regarded as a *Khila-sūkta* or as one taken from some other *śākha* of Ṛgveda and appended to the extant Ṛgveda. This *sūkta* which comprises fifteen hymns speak of the greatness of Goddess Śrī or Lakṣmī, referred to in the later part of *Puruṣa-sūkta* as the consort of Viṣṇu. It is held in high esteem as a Vedic passage and there are several commentaries on it written by ancient Vedic scholars. The *Lakṣmī Tantra*, a Pāñcarātra treatise has offered detailed interpretation on every hymn. The important statement to be noted for our purpose is that it describes Śrī as Īśvarī or the Sovereign of all beings—divine as well as human (*īśvarīṁ sarva-bhūtānaṁ*).[70] This doctrine of Goddess, which constitutes an essential feature of Śrī-Vaiṣṇavism has its root in the Ṛgveda. That Goddess Lakṣmī is the consort of Viṣṇu (*viṣṇu-patnī*) is also stated explicitly in the *Taittirīya Saṁhitā* of *Kṛṣṇa Yajurveda*.[71]

Viṣṇu in the Upaniṣads

We have so far examined a few selected hymns of the Ṛgveda and passages of the Yajurveda to prove Viṣṇu as a Supreme Deity (*para-devatā*). The Upaniṣads present the philosophical and religious doctrines of Vaiṣṇavism in greater detail. In fact, the philosophical doctrines which constitute the foundation for Vaiṣṇavism are found in the Upaniṣads. The *tattva-trayas* or the three ontological entities, viz., *Īśvara* (God), *cit* (soul) and *acit* (matter), the nature of *Īśvara* as a personal God endowed with attributes, the *bhakti* or *upāsanā* as a *sādhana* or means of God-realization and the nature of *mokṣa* as conceived in Vaiṣṇavism are all taken from the Upaniṣadic teachings, as will be shown in the later chapters dealing with these topics. Brahman or *Ātman* (meaning *Paramātman*) is no doubt the ultimate Reality according to the Upaniṣads. Such a Reality is the material cause of the universe (*jagat-kāraṇa*). The term *Viṣṇu* is not frequently used in the Upaniṣads except in a few places. The *Kaṭha Upaniṣad* while speaking of the spiritual discipline, refers to Viṣṇu's *paramapada* as the goal of the aspirant.[72] The *Viṣṇupada* in this text is interpreted as the *svarūpa* of Supreme Being (*paramātma svarūpa*). It may also be taken as the abode of Viṣṇu referred to in the Ṛgveda.[73] The *Subāla Upaniṣad* uses the expression Nārāyaṇa as the sole reality existing prior to creation.[74] It also mentions the supreme abode of Viṣṇu as the goal to be achieved, reiterating what is said in the Ṛgvedic hymn. The *Mahopaniṣad* which is accepted as an authoritative Upaniṣad by Rāmānuja and also by Yādava Prakāśa, an earlier commentator on the *Vedānta-sūtra*, specifically states that in the beginning (prior to creation) only Nārāyaṇa existed. There was neither Brahmā, nor Rudra, nor Agni, nor earth nor heaven.[75] This passage which is identical to other Upaniṣadic passages relating to creation of the universe uses the term Nārāyaṇa in place of *Sat*, *Ātman* and Brahman. On the basis of the principle of interpretation provided by the Mīmāṁsaka, general terms bear the meaning of the specific term. Nārāyaṇa being a specific term as compared to the other three, Rāmānuja concludes that Nārāyaṇa is the same as *Para-Brahma* or *Paramātma* used in other Upaniṣads.[76] The *Nārāyaṇa Upaniṣad* at the very outset identifies the *Puruṣa* of *Puruṣa-sūkta* as Nārāyaṇa.[77] After stating that Nārāyaṇa is everything in the universe implying that He is the inner controller of all deities, it points out that the knower of this truth becomes Viṣṇu implying that he becomes equal to Viṣṇu.[78] Even if the authenticity of these Upaniṣads is questionable, as some critics maintain, the issue whether or not Viṣṇu or Nārāyaṇa is the *Para-Brahma* is settled by the *Taittirīya Nārāyaṇa Upaniṣad*, also known as *Mahānārāyaṇīya*, which is acknowledged as authoritative by all the Vedāntins.[79] This Upaniṣad clearly states that the *Puruṣa* referred to in the Ṛgveda is the Ruler of the universe and that He is Nārāyaṇa, the *Para-Brahma* and *Para-tattva*.[80] We can, therefore, take it that Viṣṇu of the Ṛgveda who is also identified with *Puruṣa* is the Supreme Deity. The *Aitareya Brāhmaṇa* also decisively states that among the deities, Agni is the lowest and Viṣṇu is the highest and that all other deities come in between.[81]

Vaiṣṇavism in the Āgamas

In the post-Vedic period, a fuller development of the important tenets of Vaiṣṇavism can be found in the Āgamas, a body of religious treatises devoted primarily to the modes of worship of God. The term *āgama* generally means sacred texts and refers in particular to the revealed scripture (*nigama*). But *āgama* as applied to the religious literature under our consideration means that which came later than the Vedas (the root *gam* with the preposition *ā* implies to move towards an object to be gained). The Āgama is also known as *tantra* or the system that elaborates the knowledge acquired from the Vedas (*tan* means to spread and *tra* means to save the aspirant from the fear of bondage). It is also designated as *saṁhitā* or the composition.

The dates of the Āgamas are disputed among the modern scholars varying from 3000 B.C. to A.D. 800.[82] But according to tradition the main source of the Vaiṣṇava doctrines contained in the Āgamas is the Vedas. The *Mahābhārata* in which we have the earliest and clear presentation of the essential teachings of the Pāñcarātra Āgamas states that Lord Nārāyaṇa is the promulgator of the Pāñcarātra system.[83] The *Vedānta-sūtra* whose author is the same Vyāsa as composed the *Mahābhārata*,[84] makes a reference to the Pāñcarātra system.[85] We should, therefore, accord to the Āgamas a period which is later than the Vedas and earlier than the *Mahābhārata*.

There are several types of Āgamas. Of these the *Vaiṣṇava*, *Śaiva* and *Śākta* Āgamas are considered important. The Vaiṣṇava Āgamas uphold the exclusive worship of Viṣṇu as the Supreme Deity. Śaiva Āgamas emphasise the worship of Śiva as the Supreme Deity. The Śākta Āgamas regard *Śakti* or a female energy known by the names of Goddess Devī, Durgā, Kālī etc., as the Supreme Deity. We are primarily concerned here with the Vaiṣṇava Āgamas which constitute the main source for the later development of Vaiṣṇavism.

The concept of Viṣṇu as the Supreme Deity as found in the Ṛgveda was developed into a cult in the Vaiṣṇava Āgamas emphasising the exclusive worship of Viṣṇu as a means to salvation. Realizing the need of offering worship to one deity in a concrete form these Āgamas have evolved the concept of worshipping it in an image form (*arcā*). As a follow up of this form of worship, the consecration of icons, the construction of temples for this purpose and the observance of certain prescribed daily rituals and other festivals in the temples have all been formulated in the Āgamas. All these have influenced the development of Vaiṣṇavism.

The Vaiṣṇava Āgamas fall under two categories—Vaikhānasa and Pāñcarātra. The former which is older in origin is based on the *Vaikhānasakalpa Sūtras* compiled by the Vedic Sage Vikhanas and claims that it has taken its teachings direct from the Vedas.[86] The Vaikhanasa system was expounded by four sages, Marīchi, Bhṛgu, Atri and Kaśyapa who are claimed to be the disciples of Vikhanas. On the authority of the hymn of the Ṛgveda[87] referring to the worship of Viṣṇu, it advocates that Brahmins should perform the *arcanā* of Viṣṇu daily.[88] Viṣṇu in this system is identified with Nārāyaṇa, the very Brahman, on the authority of the *Taittirīya Nārāyaṇa Upaniṣad.*[89] This sets aside the doubt whether Viṣṇu referred to in the Ṛgveda is Nārāyaṇa, the Brahman of the Upaniṣads.

The Pāñcarātra Āgamas are based on the Ekāyana recension of *Śukla Yajurveda* (which is not extant) and thus, these too are of Vedic origin. The term Pāñcarātra is explained in different ways but the one plausible interpretation as provided by Vedānta Deśika[90] is that it teaches the fivefold daily religious duty of a Vaiṣṇava, viz., *abhigamana*, *upādāna*, *ijyā*, *svādhyāya* and *yoga.*[91] As *Ahirbudhnya Saṁhitā* explains, the name is also derived from the concept of the fivefold manifestation of the Supreme Being as *para*, *vyūha*, *vibhava*, *arcā* and *antaryāmi*.[92] The names which are generally used for Viṣṇu in these Āgamas are Bhagavān and Vāsudeva. These names including that of Nārāyaṇa are identical. The *Ahirbudhnya Saṁhitā* has offered a detailed etymological interpretation for these terms[93] and if we take these into consideration, it is obvious that all the names represent the Supreme Being, the very *Brahman* of the Upaniṣads.

Some ancient as well as modern scholars have taken the view that Pāñcarātra is non-Vedic in origin and hence not authoritative. The validity of Pāñcarātra system has been vindicated by Yāmuna in his *Āgamaprāmāṇya*, by Rāmānuja in his commentary on the relevant *Vedānta-sūtras* and in a more emphatic way by Vedānta Désika in the *Pāñcarātrarakṣā*. The *Mahābhārata* extolls it as authoritative because it is taught by Lord Nārāyaṇa. The Pāñcarātra Saṁhitas claim their origin from the Vedas.[94] It is, therefore, definitely pro-Vedic. Śaṁkara in his commentary on the disputed *Vedānta-sūtra* regarding the validity of Pāñcarātra questions only some of its philosophic theories which apparently appear to contradict Vedic teachings such as the origin of the *jīva*, but he has not openly disputed the essential teachings of Pāñcarātra theology. In fact, Śaṁkara holds in high esteem the Bhāgavatas, the four Vyūhas, the concept of Vāsudeva as Supreme Deity and the fivefold religious practice of Bhāgavatas.[95]

The Pāñcarātra Saṁhitās or treatises are far too many. The Saṁhitās themselves enumerate them and the number varies from 108 to 154. Dr. Otto Schrader has listed about 210 and Pandit V. Krishnamacharya has mentioned 225.[96] They have been written at different periods. A few are most ancient, while many others are of later origin. The most ancient and authoritative Vaiṣṇava Āgamas are *Sāttvata*, *Pauṣkara* and *Jayākhya* claiming their source to the divine teachings (*divya*). Based on these, we have *Īśvara*, *Parameśvara* and *Pādma Saṁhitās* which have been contributed by the sages (*muni-bhāṣita*). Two other Āgamas from which material has been drawn extensively by the Vaiṣṇava *ācāryas* for expounding the doctrines of the *avatāra*, Goddess *Śrī* and *prapatti* are *Ahirbhudhnya Saṁhitā* and *Lakṣmī tantra*. The other important topics which have been adopted by Vaiṣṇavism from the Pāñcarātra texts are: the six principal attributes of God (*ṣaḍguṇa*), the mode of worship of God in the form of icon at temples as well as homes, the fivefold daily religious observances (*pañcakāla-prakriyā*), the theory of *nitya-vibhūti* and *paramapada* (divine abode) and the concept of *Bhāgavata.* In general, the theological aspect of Vaiṣṇavism has been greatly influenced by the Pāñcarātra system. On the philosophic side, the influence of the Āgamas has not been so great. The philosophical theories relating to the doctrines of *Īśvara*, *jīva*, *prakṛti*, their organic relationship, the means (*upāya*) and goal (*mokṣa*) are all taken direct from the Upaniṣadic teachings. We shall bring out the extent of influence of the Āgamas on Vaiṣṇavism when we discuss these doctrines in the respective chapters.

Vaiṣṇavism in the Rāmāyaṇa and Mahābhārata

After the Āgamas, the development of the essential tenets of Vaiṣṇava Philosophy and Religion has taken place in a comprehensive way in the two Itihāsas (epics), the *Rāmāyaṇa* and *Mahābhārata* which includes the *Bhagavadgītā*. The *Rāmāyaṇa* is the older epic since we have references to Rāma's *avatāra* in the *Mahābhārata*. It is regarded by the Vaiṣṇava *ācāryas* as a *Śaraṇāgati-śāstra*, a text expounding the doctrine of self-surrender. The episode of Vibhīṣaṇa who deserts his kingdom, family and all wealth and seeks the refuge of Śrī Rāma is a classic illustration of *śaraṇāgati*. It is also regarded as a text expounding the greatness of Goddess Lakṣmī through the character of Sītā. Vālmīki himself states that *Rāmāyaṇa* is essentially the portrayal of Sītā's character.[97] The *Rāmāyaṇa* depicts that the very Lord Viṣṇu incarnated Himself in the form of a human being as the son of the emperor Daśaratha, extolling the significance of *avatāra*. Lakṣmaṇa and Bharata are presented as the personification of the two important Vaiṣṇava concepts, viz., *dāsatva* or service to Bhagavān as the sole purpose of an individual soul and *Bhagavad-bhakti* or the worship of God with devotion. Śatrughna symbolises the *Bhāgavata-kaiṅkarya* or service to a God's devotee which is considered to be of greater spiritual value than *Bhagavat-kaiṅkarya* or service to God. The Vaiṣṇava *ācāryas* including Rāmānuja have freely drawn material from the Rāmāyaṇa in developing the theological doctrines of Vaiṣṇavism.

Next in importance comes the *Mahābhārata*, which is almost

the encyclopaedia of Vaiṣṇava Philosophy and Religion. Though it deals with many other topics relating to social and ethical values and also other religions such as Śaivism, it lays greater emphasis on the various doctrines of Vaiṣṇavism. It is regarded as the fifth Veda (*pañcama veda*).[98] The doctrines of Pāñcarātra are found recorded for the first time in the Nārāyaṇīya section of Śāntiparva of the *Mahābhārata*. The identity of Viṣṇu, with Vāsudeva, Nārāyaṇa and Bhagavān as well as with Kṛṣṇa is established in the *Mahābhārata*. The devoted worship of Viṣṇu or Vāsudeva as the sole means of *mokṣa* is brought out emphatically in this Itihāsa. The Mokṣa-dharma section of Śāntiparva is devoted to the presentation of the philosophy and religion of Vaiṣṇavism. The *Bhagavad-gītā* which forms part of *Mahābhārata* is the most important sourcebook and in fact it constitutes the foundation for the exposition of the *sādhana* for *mokṣa*. For the first time we find in this work a detailed account of *karma-yoga*, *jñāna-yoga*, *bhakti-yoga* and briefly *śaraṇāgati*. Rāmānuja in his introduction to the *Gītā* says that the Lord under the pretext of teaching to Arjuna imparted to us *bhakti-yoga* (*bhaktiyogam avatārayāmāsa*). Besides the exposition of Vāsudeva as the Supreme Deity, it offers a detailed account of Vaiṣṇavism. The *Sahasranāma* of Viṣṇu, the thousand names of Viṣṇu, narrated by Bhīṣma in the Anuśāsana-parva provides a deeper insight into the greatness of Viṣṇu and his numerous attributes. The supremacy of Viṣṇu as against all other deities including Śiva and Brahmā is upheld throughout the *Mahābhārata*. It is, therefore, no wonder that Rāmānuja and his followers have drawn material extensively from the *Mahābhārata* in not only expounding the Vaiṣṇava doctrines but also used it as an unquestionable evidence (*pramāṇa*) to support their teachings.

Vaiṣṇavism in the Purāṇas

The contribution of the Purāṇas in general and *Viṣṇupurāṇa* of Sage Parāśara in particular is significant in developing the Vaiṣṇava doctrines. The *Viṣṇupurāṇa* is acknowledged as the oldest and the most authoritative Purāṇa. Both Śaṁkara and Rāmānuja hold it in high esteem and have accepted it as an authentic sourcebook for determining the philosophical doctrines.[99] It presents all the basic doctrines, both philosophical and theological, of Vaiṣṇavism. This is the earliest text which treats

Godhead against the background of Pāñcarātra system.[100] Viṣṇu is held as the Supreme Deity (*para-tattva*) and is identified with the very Brahman of the Upaniṣad. At the very outset the Purāṇa asserts that Viṣṇu is the primary cause of creation, sustenance and dissolution of the universe, reiterating the definition offered by the *Taittirīya Upaniṣad* and *Vedāntasūtra* for Brahman.[101] The same Viṣṇu is also spoken of as Bhagavān and Vāsudeva.[102] He possesses six attributes (*ṣaḍguṇa*) and is also free from all defects. The concept of *ubhayaliṅgatva* as stated in the *Vedāntasūtra* is thus explicitly brought out in this Purāṇa.[103] The central doctrine of Vaiṣṇavism, viz., that Viṣṇu is inseparably associated with Goddess *Śrī*, that the latter is also all-pervasive (*vibhu*) like God and that She is also the giver of *mokṣa* finds a significant expression here.[104] The Vaiṣṇava concept of *paramapada*, (the eternal abode of Viṣṇu) is also referred to in this Purāṇa.[105]

The other Purāṇas are classified into three categories—*sāttvika*, *rājasa* and *tāmasa*. The *Sāttvika* Purāṇas are those which emphasise the greatness of *Viṣṇu*, *rājasa* speak about *Brahmā* and *tāmasa* refer to the greatness of *Śiva* and *Agni*. This classification is made in the *Matsya Purāṇa* for the purpose of determining the relative validity of the Purāṇas, whenever conflict arises between their teachings. The *Sāttvika* Purāṇas are, therefore, regarded as Vaiṣṇava Purāṇas. These are: *Viṣṇudharmottara*, *Padma*, *Garuḍa*, *Varāha*, *Nāradīya* and *Bhāgavata* besides *Viṣṇupurāṇa*. All these, therefore, contain material supporting the tenets of Vaiṣṇavism.

Vaiṣṇavism in the Tamil Hymns of Āḻvārs

The four thousand Tamil hymns composed by the twelve Vaiṣṇava saints known as Āḻvārs marks an important stage of development of Vaiṣṇavism. Ālvārs were born in different parts of South India long before Rāmānuja. The traditional date ascribed to the earliest Āḻvār is 4203 B.C. and the date of the latest Ālvār is 2706 B.C. But modern scholars assign it to the period between the A.D. 200 and A.D. 800.[106] They were great mystics deeply immersed in the divine experience. They have expressed their experience of God and His glory in the form of Tamil verses which are collectively entitled *Nālāyira Divyaprabandham* or four thousand Divine Hymns. These mystic outpourings contain rich philosophical and religious thoughts drawn from the Upaniṣads, Itihāsas and Purāṇas. They cover all the essential teachings of Vaiṣṇavism and have thus contributed to the further development of Vaiṣṇavism by Nāthamuni, Ālavandār and Rāmānuja, the three principal Vaiṣṇava apostles and by the later Vaiṣṇava *ācāryas*.

Of the four thousand hymns contributed by the different Āḻvār[107] varying in number, 1102 verses of Nammāḻvār which are called Tiruvāymoḻi are held in high esteem. They are regarded as *Dramiḍa Upaniṣad* or Tamil Veda (*Tamiḻ-marai*) because these contain the quintessence of the Upaniṣadic teachings. Its importance and popularity in the realm of Vaiṣṇavism may be judged by the number of commentaries and sub-commentaries written on these hymns. In fact, some of the Vaiṣṇava *ācāryas* after the 14th century have been so much attracted by the hymns of the Āḻvārs that they have devoted greater attention to the teachings contained in the hymns and the commentaries thereon in *Maṇipravāḷa* language in preference to the Vedānta texts in Sanskrit. Rāmānuja, though he did not write any commentary on the Tamil hymns, has definitely been influenced by their teachings. Under his direction, the very first commentary known as *Ārāyirappaḍi* was got written by his closest disciple named *Piḷḷān*. The main doctrines expounded in the Tamil hymns are: (*i*) that Viṣṇu or Nārāyaṇa associated with *Śrī* is the *paratattva*; (*ii*) *Bhakti* or *prapatti* is the means to attain *mokṣa*; (*iii*) *kaiṅkarya* or service to God and godly men is an important duty of a true Vaiṣṇava; (*iv*) *mokṣa* or release from bondage is the supreme goal. The three principal tenets of Viśiṣṭādvaita Vedānta, viz., *Tattva*, *Hita* and *Puruṣārtha* as presented in the *Vedānta-sūtra*, are developed by Nammāḻvār in the Tiruvāymoḻi. The Vaiṣṇavism expounded by Rāmānuja and his followers are based not only on the teachings of the Upaniṣads, *Vedānta-sūtra*, *Bhagavad-gītā* and the Pāñcarātra treatises but also on the teachings contained in the Tamil hymns of Āḻvārs. Hence it is designated as *ubhayavedānta* that is, Vedānta based on Sanskrit Vedānta texts and Tamil works of Āḻvārs.

From the brief outline of the historical development of Vaiṣṇavism presented so far, it may be observed that the religion and philosophy of Vaiṣṇavism has been prevalent since very ancient times up to the period of Nāthamuni, Yāmuna and

Rāmānuja, the three eminent Vaiṣṇava *ācāryas* who as its principal exponents, formulated it into a religious and philosophical system. There are four stages of development during this long period: (1) the Vedic period, (2) the post-Vedic period (when Āgamas developed), (3) the period of the Itihāsas and Purāṇas, (4) the period when the Āḻvārs survived. I would not like to venture the dates of these periods for two reasons: (1) the dates are under dispute between the traditional scholars and the modern scholars; (2) they are not relevant for the purpose of presenting the Philosophy and Religion of Vaiṣṇavism. If we go by tradition, Vaiṣṇavism has a divine origin, as in the first place it was taught by Lord Viṣṇu to Brahmā and in turn to Sanatkumāra etc. But taking the view of modern scholars, we may trace its origin to the Ṛgveda. The period of the Ṛgveda itself is disputable among scholars ranging from 5000 B.C. to 600 B.C. In the same way the period of the *Mahābhārata* according to some scholars is 300 B.C. and for some it is 3000 B.C. (beginning of the present age of *Kaliyuga*). Nammālvār was born, according to tradition in the beginning of *Kaliyuga.* If this is accepted, we have to place the age of the Āgamas which have had a direct influence on the Āḻvārs and to which references are found in the *Mahābhārata*, as far back as 5000 B.C. All that is important to note for our purpose is that Vaiṣṇavism has a long antiquity. Even going on the basis of the Ṛgveda, where we have noticed the hymns asserting the monotheistic religion of Viṣṇu, it is as old or older than the Ṛgveda.

Inscriptional Evidence for Antiquity of Vaiṣṇavism

On the basis of inscriptional and internal textual evidence, we can also safely attribute considerable antiquity to Vaiṣṇavism. An inscription found at Ghosundi in Rajasthan mentions the construction of a wall round the hall of worship of Saṁkarṣaṇa and Vāsudeva, the two important deities of Āgamas. On epigraphical evidence, it is believed to have been engraved about 200 B.C.[108] In another inscription discovered at Besnagar, Heliodara, a native of Taxsasila and an ambassador of the Yavana, King of Taxila, erected a column with the image of Garuḍa (the bird mount of Viṣṇu) at the top (*garuḍadhvaja*) in honour of *Vāsudeva*, the God of gods. He calls himself a Bhāgavata. This inscription is considered to belong to the earlier part of the 2nd century before Christian era. At that time Vāsudeva must have been worshipped as the God of gods or the Supreme Being and his worshippers were called Bhāgavatas. In another inscription found in the cave at Nanaghat (Maharashtra), the names of Saṁkarṣaṇa and Vāsudeva (as a compound word) occur along with those of other deities in the opening invocation. This inscription appears to belong to the 1st century B.C.[109] More important than this, *Pāṇini Sūtra*[110] makes mention of *Vāsudeva*. Pāṇini, the grammarian, belonged to a period long before Christian era. Patañjali, the commentator on the *Sūtras*, explains that *Vāsudeva* in the *Sūtra* refers only to God and it is not the name of a Kṣatriya. All these evidences indicate that long before these inscriptions were written, the Bhāgavata cult with the belief in Vāsudeva as the Supreme Being must have existed. The references to Vāsudeva and Saṁkarṣaṇa indicate the prevalence of Pāñcarātra system since these names are of the *Vyūha* forms of Viṣṇu or *Para-Vāsudeva*. The Bhāgavata religion is not distinct from Vaiṣṇava religion since the two deities, as has been explained earlier, refer to the same God. We will not be wrong in concluding that Vaiṣṇavism, both according to tradition as well as historical evidences, is a very ancient religion going back to pre-Christian era.

Development of Vaiṣṇavism by Nāthamuni, Yāmuna and Rāmānuja

The next stage of development of Vaiṣṇavism comes with the era of the advent of the three eminent *ācāryas*—Nāthamuni, Yāmuna and Rāmānuja, who are regarded as the three principal pontiffs of Vaiṣṇavism. Nāthamuni was born in A.D. 824; Yāmuna also known as Ālavandār was born in A.D. 916 and Rāmānuja in A.D. 1017. As already observed, Vaiṣṇava religion has been prevalent right from the Vedic period. Its teachings have been found scattered in the Vedas including the Upaniṣads, *Rāmāyaṇa* and *Mahābhārata*, the Purāṇas, the Āgamas and the hymns of the Āḻvārs. During this long period of its growth, several other rival schools of thought—both philosophical systems as well as religious cults have come up. We have had Buddhism, Jainism, Pāśupata and other forms of Śaivism and Śāktaism. On the philosophical side we have had Sāṅkhya, Yoga, Nyāya, Vaiśeṣika, Mīmāṁsā and Advaita as well as Bhedābheda schools of thought. The main opposition to Vaiṣṇavism as a religious cult, has come from Śaivism, Buhdhism and Jainism. In order to uphold the teachings of Vaiṣṇavism as against other rival religious creeds there was an urgent need to consolidate and systematise the thoughts found in different religious works and also for the propagation of the religion. This task was fulfilled to a large extent by Rāmānuja and his forerunners, Nāthamuni and Yāmuna. Though all the three *ācāryas* are the exponents of Vaiṣṇavism, major credit goes to Rāmānuja in terms of the contribution made by written works and propagation of the religion through a large number of well qualified apostles.[111] As will be shown presently, the monumental works such as *Śrī-bhāṣya* (commentary on the *Vedānta-sūtra*), *Gītābhāṣya*, *Vedārtha-saṁgraha* and the *Gadyas* (prose lyrics) bear evidence to the extant of his intellectual contribution to Viśiṣṭādvaita system and Vaiṣṇava theology. But Rāmānuja owes his knowledge to the works of both Nāthamuni and Yāmuna, as he himself acknowledges his debt of gratitude in the opening verse of the *Gītābhāṣya*.[112] In the same way, he states that he is following the views expressed by Bodhāyana and other *pūrvācāryas* in writing the commentary on the *Vedānta-sūtras*.[113]

Nāthamuni, the first pontiff of Śrīvaiṣṇavism, wrote two works: *Nyāyatattva* and *Yogarahasya*. Both the works are not extant and it is difficult to evaluate their contents. However, the *Nyāyatattva* must have been an important philosophical treatise since both Rāmānuja and Vedānta Deśika have referred to it. Nāthamuni made a significant contribution to Vaiṣṇavism by rediscovering the four thousand hymns of the Āḻvārs,[114] re-arranging them into four parts and introducing its recitation by the Vaiṣṇavas as part of the worship at temples. Following the teaching of Nammāḻvār, Nāthamuni seems to have advocated the adoption of *prapatti* or self-surrender as the means of salvation in place of the rigorous *bhakti-yoga*.

Yāmuna, the grandson of Nāthamuni has written a few important works: *Siddhitraya*, *Āgamaprāmāṇya*, *Mahāpuruṣanir-ṇaya*, *Gītārthasaṁgraha*, *Stotraratna* and *Catuḥślokī*. In the *Siddhitraya* comprising three parts each one dealing with God, soul and knowledge respectively Yāmuna has made a significant contribution to the Viśiṣṭādvaita Philosophy. The rest of his works have laid the foundation for the formulation of the important doctrines of Vaiṣṇavism—the supremacy of Viṣṇu as the ultimate Reality, the ontological status of Goddess *Śri* and the doctrine of *śaraṇāgati* or self-surrender. The *Āgamaprāmāṇya* vindicates the authoritativeness of the Pāñcarātra Āgamas on the basis of which the Theology of Vaiṣṇavism is developed. In fact, these are the first written extant works in Sanskrit contributed by a Vaiṣṇava *ācārya* for understanding the Vaiṣṇava theology. All these have helped Rāmānuja to systematise Viśiṣṭādvaita Religion and Philosophy.

The most significant contribution to the development and propagation of the Viśiṣṭādvaita Philosophy and the Vaiṣṇava Religion has been made by Rāmānuja. Rāmānuja was born at a time when the Advaita Vedānta propounded by Śaṁkara had taken a deep root in the minds of people. Though Śaṁkara himself was not an anti-vaiṣṇava,[115] the *māyā-vāda* advocated by him affected the ontological status of Viṣṇu or the personal God as *paratattva*. For Śaṁkara the ultimate Reality is *Nirguṇa Brahman*, whereas Viṣṇu or *Īśvara* is *Saguṇa Brahman* and from the transcendental point of view *Īśvara* is less real than the Absolute Brahman. The emphasis given to the one Absolute of the Upaniṣad as the sole Reality and the adoption of the doctrine of *Māyā* or *Avidyā* to account for the plurality of individual souls and the cosmic universe did not accord the absolute reality to the individual souls and cosmic matter. The emphasis given to *jñāna* or knowledge of Brahman derived from the study of sacred texts as the sole means of liberation did not acknowledge *upāsanā* or *bhakti* as the direct means to *mokṣa*. It was, therefore, necessary for Rāmānuja to criticise the teachings of Advaita Vedānta and re-establish on a sounder basis the tenets of Viśiṣṭādvaita Vedānta as adumbrated in the Upaniṣads, *Vedānta-sūtra* and *Bhagavad-gītā*. On the religious side the Supremacy of Viṣṇu as the ultimate Reality, the exclusive worship of Viṣṇu as the direct means for *mokṣa* and the restoration of individuality and reality of the souls and a positive state of blissful experience in a divine realm as the goal of human life had to be established in order to sustain the ancient teachings of Vaiṣṇavism as expounded in the Vedas, Āgamas and Purāṇas. This uphill task was undertaken by Rāmānuja and was executed perfectly by him through his works and through his missionary institutions. Thus, Rāmānuja stands as an important milestone in the history of Vaiṣṇavism.

Rāmānuja has written nine works: *Śrī-bhāṣya* (commentary on the *Vedānta-sūtra*), *Vedānta-dīpa* and *Vedānta-sāra* (both briefer commentaries on the *Vedānta-sūtra*), *Vedārtha-saṁgraha* (a consolidated presentation of his views on important Upaniṣadic texts), three *gadyas* (prose lyrics expounding the doctrine of *prapatti*), *Gītābhāṣya* (commentary on the *Gītā*) and *Nitya-grantha* (a treatise on the daily observance of Vaiṣṇavas). In the *Śrī-bhāṣya*, which is the most outstanding philosophical work, Rāmānuja presents the fundamental philosophical doctrines of Viśiṣṭādvaita Vedānta on the basis of the interpretation of the *Vedānta-sūtras* as provided by Bodhāyana and other earlier *ācāryas* along with detailed explanations of the relevant Upaniṣadic and Smṛti texts. The nature of the three *tattvas*, which form the fundamental philosophical tenets of Viśiṣṭādvaita, viz., *Īśvara* (God), *cit* (soul) and *acit* (cosmic matter) has been fully discussed and their organic relationship in the form of *śarīra-śarīri* (body-soul) is well established on the irrefutable authority of the *Antaryāmī Brāhmaṇa* of the *Bṛhadāraṇyaka Upaniṣad*. The doctrine of *bhakti* which is termed as *upāsanā* in the Upaniṣads as the direct means or *sādhana* for *mokṣa* is discussed in detail. The nature of *mokṣa*, the supreme goal of human life is also presented on the basis of the Upaniṣadic authority. The *Gītābhāṣya* is equally an important work in which, apart from establishing the Supremacy of Vāsudeva, the same as Viṣṇu or Nārāyaṇa as the *para-tattva*, the details of *bhakti-yoga*, aided by *karma-yoga* and *jñāna-yoga* as the *sādhana* for *mokṣa* is brought out. The theory of *avatāra* or incarnation of Viṣṇu is fully discussed on the basis of the *Gītā* verses.[116] In fact, a fuller presentation of *avatāra-rahasya* is found only in the *Gītābhāṣya*. The doctrine of *prapatti* is also mentioned briefly while commenting on the sixty-sixth verse of the last chapter of the *Gītā*. The *Vedārtha-saṁgraha* devoted to an exposition of the Philosophy of the Upaniṣads, contains Viśiṣṭādvaita views on *Tattva* (Reality), *Hita* (means) and *Puruṣārtha* (supreme goal of life), besides the Supremacy of Viṣṇu and the doctrine of *Nitya-vibhuti*. The three *gadyas—Śaraṇāgati-gadya*, *Śrīraṅga-gadya* and *Vaikuṇṭha-gadya*—expound in detail the theological doctrine of *śaranāgati* and the numerous attributes of God. The

Nityagrantha sets out the daily observance of Vaiṣṇavas as enjoined in the sacred texts along with the mode of worship of God. Thus, for the first time in the History of Vaiṣṇavism, we get a comprehensive and an authoritative account of its philosophy, theology and ethical discipline.

Development of Vaiṣṇavism in the Post-Rāmānuja Period

The post-Rāmānuja period witnessed further growth of Vaiṣṇavism through three successive stages. The first one extended for a period of two centuries up to the advent of Vedānta Deśika and Piḷḷailokācārya who were contemporaries. The second stage covers their life period and the third stage refers to the post-Vedānta Deśika period extending nearly six centuries. During the first stage a few immediate disciples of Rāmānuja and his later successors expounded the teachings of their spiritual leader faithfully through oral discourses and writings which were in the nature of glossaries on Rāmānuja's works. An interesting feature of the literature that grew up during this period is that it was written in a popular style known as *Maṇipravāḷa*[117] which is Tamil language interspersed with Sanskrit words or Sanskritised Tamil prose and therefore, easier to understand by persons not too well versed in Sanskrit. These works are mostly in the form of commentaries (*vyākhyāna*) on some of the Sanskrit works of Yāmuna and Rāmānuja and more importantly on the Tamil hymns of the Āḻvārs. It was for the first time that a commentary was written on the hymns of Nammāḻvār by Kurukeśa also known as Piḷḷān, the closest disciple of Rāmānuja under the latter's direction. This commentary is titled *Ārāyirappaḍi*, which literally means a work of six thousand units (*granthas*).[118] This marks the beginning of popularisation of the teachings of Āḻvārs. The Piḷḷān's commentary was followed up by many other more detailed commentaries. Nañjīyar (A.D. 1182) wrote a commentary called *Onpatināyirappaḍi* (9000 *granthas*) on Tiruvāymoḻi. He was followed by Periyavaccān Piḷḷai (A.D. 1228) who for the first time wrote commentaries on all the four thousand hymns of Āḻvārs. Another important contribution was made to the Maṇipravāḷa literature by Vaḍakkuttiruvīdi Piḷḷai (A.D. 1217) who wrote an elaborate, scholarly commentary on Tiruvāymoḻi entitled *Muppattiyārāyirappaḍi* (36000) popularly known as *Īḍu*.[119] All these works in Maṇipravāḷa style helped considerably to popularise the teachings of Vaiṣṇavism, thereby establishing the claim of *ubhaya-vedānta* for the Viśiṣṭādvaita. The *ubhaya-vedānta* signifies that the system of Rāmānuja is based on the Upaniṣads (the Vedānta as expounded in Sanskrit language) and the Tamil hymns of the Āḻvārs which are accorded the status of revealed Scripture (*veda*) in so far as it contains the teachings of the Upaniṣads. During this period a few important works in Sanskrit were also composed both as independent treatises and commentaries. These have thrown light on specific topics of Vaiṣṇava theology. The *Śrīstava* of Śrīvatsānka Miśra, the *Śrīguṇaratnakośa* of Parāśara Bhattar, the commentary of Nañjīyar on the *Śrī-Sūkta* of the Ṛgveda and the commentary of Periyavāccān Piḷḷai on the *Catuḥślokī* have expounded for the first time the doctrine of Goddess *Śrī* in Vaiṣṇavism. Similarly, the four other lyrics of Śrīvatsānka Miśra—*Atimanuṣāstava*, *Varadarājastava*, *Vaikuṇṭhastava* and *Sundarabāhustava*—the *Bhagavadguṇa darpaṇa* of Parāśara Bhattar, the commentaries of Periyavāccān Piḷḷai on Rāmānuja's *gadyas* and Yāmuna's *Stotraratna* provide a detailed exposition of the Supremacy of Viṣṇu and His attributes. The *Śrutaprakāśikā*, the learned commentary on Rāmānuja's *Śrī-bhāṣya*, written by Sudarśana Sūri in this period has provided a solid foundation for the Viśiṣṭādvaita Vedānta.

Development of Vaiṣṇavism during the Period of Vedānta Deśika and Piḷḷailokācārya

The second and more significant development of Vaiṣṇavism in the post-Rāmānuja period comes from Vedānta Deśika, also known as Venkaṭanātha (A.D. 1268-1369), an illustrious successor to Rāmānuja. In fact, his advent marks an outstanding milestone in the history of both the Viśiṣṭādvaita Vedānta and Vaiṣṇava theology. He was an intellectual giant and as a distinguished scholar of all branches of traditional learning (*sarvatantra-svatantra*),[120] he wrote more than 100 works covering practically all aspects of the Viśiṣṭādvaita Philosophy and Religion. He wrote both in Sanskrit and also in the Maṇipravāḷa language which had become popular in his time. The philosophical works written in Sanskrit are: *Tattva-muktā-kalāpa* with his own commentary known as *Sarvārthasiddhi*,

Adhikaraṇa-sārāvalī, *Nyāya-siddhāñjana*, *Nyāya-pariśuddhi*, *Śatadūṣaṇī*, *Tattvaṭīkā*, an incomplete commentary on *Śrī-bhāṣya*, *Tātparya-candrikā* (glossary on *Gītā-bhāṣya*), *Mīmāṁsā-pādukā*, *Seśvara-mīmāṁsā*, *Īśāvāsyopaniṣad-bhāṣya*, *Gadyatraya-bhāṣya* (commentary on three *gadyas* of Rāmānuja) *Stotraratna-bhāṣya*, *Catuḥślokī-bhāṣya* (commentary on two Yāmuna's lyrics) and Gītārtha-*saṁgraha-rakṣā* (commentary on Yāmuna's work on the *Gītā*). Through these works he strengthened the Viśiṣṭādvaita Philosophy on a solid ground. The *Rahasyatraya-sāra* and thirty three other *Rahasya granthas*[121] written in Maṇipravāḷa language strengthened the theological and esoteric doctrines of Śrīvaiṣṇavism. The *Pāñcarātrarakṣā* written in Sanskrit vindicated the unquestionable validity of the Pāñcarātra Āgamas. The *Saccaritrarakṣā* has given a meaningful significance to religious practices of Vaiṣṇavas. The *Nikṣeparakṣa* a treatise on *Śaraṇāgati*, has provided a strong defence for the practice of self-surrender to God as the *sādhana* for *mokṣa*. His commentary on Yāmuna's *Catuḥślokī* and *Stotraratna* has upheld the theological concepts of the Supremacy of Viṣṇu over other deities and that Goddess Lakṣmī is an integral part of the ultimate Reality. Through his *Dramiḍopaniṣad-tātpayaratnāvaḷī* and *Dramiḍopaniṣad-sāra*, the hymns of Nammāḻvār secured a respectful place in the philosophical realm. His allegorical drama known as *Saṅkalpsūryodaya*, the poetical works—*Yādavābhyudaya* and *Haṁsasandeśa* and several devotional lyrics[122] and *Pādukāsahasra* (1000 verses on the sandals of the Lord Raṅganātha), apart from exhibiting his poetic skill, are full of philosophical significance. Indeed in the hands of Vedānta Deśika Śrīvaiṣṇavism—both its philosophy, theology and religious discipline—as expounded by his spiritual master, Rāmānuja, got further strengthened and developed beyond anybody's imagination. In fact, the works which were contributed by his predecessors, who were immediate successors to Rāmānuja, were almost eclipsed. In the same way, the works which were written in later period, barring those of Piḷḷailokācārya along with the commentaries of his successor, Maṇavāḷamāmuni, could not stand comparison with the brilliance, originality and depth of scholarship of Vedānta Deśika. Most of them as will be shown presently, were mere elaboration or commentaries on the works of earlier *ācāryas* or tracts on individual topics which had already been covered by Vedānta Deśika.

This remarkable development of Vaiṣṇavism through the scholarly works of Vedānta Deśika was further supplemented by the contribution of Piḷḷailokācārya (A.D. 1264-1369). He wrote a total of eighteen works in Maṇipravāḷa language which are collectively called *Aṣṭādaśa-rahasya*. The major works which deal with the essentials of Vaiṣṇavism are *Tattvatrayam*, *Śrīvacanabhūṣaṇam*, *Arthapañcakam* and *Mumukṣuppadi*. His other works are relatively of minor character as they deal with the esoteric doctrines (*rahasyas*) of Vaiṣṇavism.[123]

Some of Piḷḷailokācārya's views differ from those of Vedānta Deśika on certain theological issues such as the ontological status of Goddess *Śrī*, the nature of *prapatti* as a means to *mokṣa*, the operation of God's grace vis-a-vis human endeavour, concept of *vātsalya* and the observance of *varṇāśramadharma* by persons engaged in divine service. Besides, there are few other minor doctrinal differences between the two *ācāryas* which seem to have erupted at an academic level, involving the interpretation of certain basic concepts. Piḷḷailokācārya was a senior contemporary of Vedānta Deśika and as two scholars, they were on friendly terms and bore no animosity to each other. At this stage there was no split in the Śrīvaiṣṇava community into two sects as Vaḍakalai and Tenkalai, although the seeds of rift might have been sown. It became pronounced at a later period long after the advent of Varavaramuni, popularly known as Maṇavāḷamāmuni. The split into two sects, each claiming an allegiance to a particular *ācārya* might have arisen much later, presumably in the eighteenth century on account of the rivalry caused by the temple administration at Śrīraṅgam which was at that time in the hands of the successors of Maṇavāḷamāmuni.[124] The terms Vaḍakalai and Tenkalai literally mean Northern culture and southern culture. But they bear a different implication. The Vaḍakalais are those who lay greater emphasis on the Vedānta texts in Sanskrit and the Tenkalais are those who give more prominence to the hymns of the Āḷvārs in Tamil. However, in actual practice the Veḍakalais are those Vaiṣṇavas who owe their allegiance to Vedānta Deśika, whereas Tenkalais are those who trace their allegiance to Maṇavālamāmuni. The distinction between the two is based on the doctrinal differences on a few theological issues. There are eighteen points of difference some of which are of major significance while many are of minor importance.[125] We shall discuss in the concerned chapters the important doctrinal differences and to what extent they are philosophically justifiable. For the present we may take note of the fact that at the religious level Vaiṣṇavism grew on two parallel lines in the later centuries as a result of the sectarian differences. But at the philosophical level, however, Viśiṣṭādvaita Vedānta as expounded by Rāmānuja has continued unaffected by these differences.

Development of Vaiṣṇavism in the Post-Deśika Period

In the post-Deśika period extending over six centuries, Śri-Vaiṣṇavism as it is popularly known, has developed on two parallel and schismatic lines, one sect owing its allegiance to Vedānta Deśika and the other to Maṇavāḷamāmuni. The Vaḍakalai sect has had a long line of succession of eminent *ācāryas*. Two important *maṭhams* or religious centres came into existence initially—one known as *Ahobila Maṭham* and the other as *Parakāla Maṭham*—both headed by eminent ascetics (*Sanyāsis*) for propagation of the Rāmānuja *Siddhānta* as interpreted by Vedānta Deśika. Subsequently in the 18th century, another centre known as *Āṇḍavan Āśramam* came into existence headed by ascetics. The important *ācāryas* who have contributed scholarly works are: Kumāra Vedāntācārya (1316-1401), son of Vedānta Deśika, Brahmatantra Parakāla Swāmi I (1286-1386), first pontiff of Parakāla Maṭham and some of his successors (who were the pontiffs of Parakāla Maṭham) Ādivaṇ Śaṭhakopayati (A.D. 1398), first pontiff of Ahobila Maṭham and some of his successors, Mahācārya (1509-91), Tātācārya (16th century), Raṅgarāmānujamuni (16th century), Śrinivāsācārya (17th century), Nṛsimharāja (17/18th century), Paravastu Vedāntācārya (18th century), Tātadeśika (18th century), Vedāntarāmānuja Swāmi (also known as Sākṣāt Swāmi), Gopāladeśika (18th century) and many others. The books written in Sanskrit are mostly in the form of commentaries/glossaries on the works of Rāmānuja and Vedānta Deśika. Some are devoted to a criticism of Advaita doctrines; some are intended to uphold the Supremacy of Viṣṇu as against the criticism of Śaivites; some are devoted to the explanation of the sacraments and certain daily rituals of

Srivaiṣṇavas. Some of these *ācāryas*, particularly Raṅgarāmānuja Muni, Vedāntarāmānuja and Periya Parakāla Swāmi (21st pontiff of Parakāla Maṭham) have written commentaries on the hymns of the Āḻvār.[126]

The other school of thought headed by Maṇavāḷamāmuni has carried on the propagation of Śrīvaiṣṇavism through a line of successive Tenkalai *ācāryas*. Maṇavāḷamāmuni also known as Varavaramuni was born in A.D. 1370 and lived up to A.D. 1443. He has commented extensively on the important Maṇipravāḷa works of Piḷḷailokācārya. He also wrote commentaries on the works of other *ācāryas*, one on the hymns of Periyaḻvār and three independent works in Tamil such as *Upadeśa rattinamālai*, *Tiruvāymoḻi-nūtrandādi* and *Ārtiprapandam*. His only work in Sanskrit is *Yatirāja-viṁśati*, laudatory twenty verses on Rāmānuja. He had a line of successors who spread his teachings all over the country. Their works are mostly in Maṇipravāḷa language and are devoted to an exposition of the esoteric doctrines of Śrīvaiṣṇavism and the hymns of Āḻvārs. The followers of Maṇavālamāmuni have generally given greater importance to the teachings of Āḻvārs.

As in the School of Vaḍakalai, the Tenkalai School of thought too had set up *maṭhams* or religious centres headed by on ascetic (*sanyāsi*) to propagate Vaiṣṇavism. The chief *maṭhams* of Tenkalai School are *Vānamāmalai Maṭham* at Nanguneri near Tirunalveli in South India (whose pontiff is called Vānamāmalai Jiyar), *Tirumalai Jiyar Maṭham* at Tirupati, one at Śrīraṅgam known as *Śrīraṅga-nārāyaṇa Jiyar Maṭham* and *Yatirāja Maṭham* at Melkote (Karnataka). All these *maṭhams* have served for centuries as important religious centres for the study of Vaiṣṇava philosophy and propagation of Vaiṣṇava religion.

Development of other Schools of Vaiṣṇavism

The historical account of Vaiṣṇavism would be incomplete if we do not take into consideration the spread of Vaiṣṇava movements in different ways in other parts of India. Though it is somewhat outside the scope of this book a brief mention of the later schools of Vaiṣṇavism is called for only to emphasize the vitality and universality of Vaiṣṇavism as a living religion of great antiquity. Rāmānuja was the original exponent of Vaiṣṇavism both as a school of philosophy and theological system. We have already noted how it developed under his guidance and was followed up by his devoted followers through centuries. In the post-Rāmānuja period, besides Śrīvaiṣṇavism as it is practised today by the followers of Vedānta Deśika and Maṇavāḷamāmuni, we had several other schools of thought developed in the western, northern and eastern parts of India by eminent *ācāryas* and religious reformers such as Madhva, Nimbārka, Rāmānanda, Vallabhācārya, Śrī-Kṛṣṇa Caitanya and Jñāneśvara.

Madhvācārya, born in A.D. 1238 nearly 200 years later than Rāmānuja, was the exponent of the Dvaita School of Vedānta. Though his dualistic system of Vedānta is different from that of Rāmānuja, he was a strong upholder of Vaiṣṇava theism. His teachings on Vaiṣṇavism marks an important epoch in the history of Vaiṣṇavism. Whether or not he was directly influenced by Rāmānuja, he has undoubtedly developed the *Bhakti* movement initiated by Rāmānuja and further strengthened Vaiṣṇavism by asserting that Viṣṇu is the very Brahman and *bhakti* or supreme devotion to God is the means to *mokṣa*. He travelled all over India and spread Vaiṣṇavism. His literary contribution to Vaiṣṇavism is significant. He wrote an independent work known as *Viṣṇu-tattva-nirṇaya* to establish the Supremacy of Viṣṇu. He has also written another work entitled *Tantrasāra-saṁgraha* which deals with practical aspects of Vaiṣṇavism. He accorded greater authority to *Bhāgavata Purāṇa* and wrote a commentary on it. Madhva holds in high esteem the Pāñcarātra Āgamas. The *Bhakti* movement initiated by Madhva was carried on further and spread all over the country through his able disciples, Jayatīrtha and Vyāsarāya. The latter promoted the devotional movement known as *Dāsa-kūṭa* comprising a band of saintly persons singing devotional songs. Notable among these are Purandara Dāsa and Kanaka Dāsa whose songs have greatly popularised the *Bhakti* cult. Basically, the Vaiṣṇavism of Madhva is not very different from that of Rāmānuja though there are some doctrinal differences in respect of certain theological details. However, Madhva's Vaiṣṇava theism had far-reaching influence on Caitanya and the Maharashtra saints.

Rāmānanda (1300-1411), another important religious reformer in Northern India, was deeply influenced by the teachings of Rāmānuja and spread the universal gospel of *bhakti*. He regarded Rāma, one of the incarnations of Viṣṇu, as Brahman.

Through his twelve devoted disciples he preached the religion in the mother tongue of the people. Since he did not believe in the caste system and accepted the concept of universal brotherhood, he was able to appeal to all classes of people and establish the faith in monotheism and *bhakti* cult. Kabir, born in 1338, was the greatest of his disciples. Tulasīdāsa (1532), another important follower of Rāmānanda spread Vaiṣṇavism through his classic epic in Hindi language known as Śrī *Rāmacaritamānasa.*

Nimbārka, a Telugu Brahmin who lived in the later part of 12th century A.D. after Rāmānuja, was the founder of Dvaitādvaita Vedānta. He developed a Vaiṣṇava cult under the name of Sanatkumāra Nārada Saṁpradāya which is similar in several respects to that of Rāmānuja. He maintains that Brahman is Rādhā-Kṛṣṇa, possessing the six principal attributes and many other auspicious qualities. He was also influenced by the Pāñcarātra although he did not advocate temple worship. He has accepted *prapatti* as a means of *mokṣa.* He had a large number of followers who have spread the Rādhā-Kṛṣṇa cult which is a type of Vaiṣṇavism.

Vallabhācārya, the founder of Suddhādvaita Vedānta, who was born in 1478 A.D. as a son of a Telugu Brahmin in Raipur (Madhya Pradesh), advocated yet another type of Vaiṣṇavism. According to this school, the Bhagavān of *Bhāgavata Purāṇa* or Lord Kṛṣṇa is the highest Brahman, Suprapersonal Puruṣottama with a divine body (*vigraha*), made of bliss (*ānanda*). He has also advanced the path of *bhakti* as the only way of attaining divine bliss.

Śrī Kṛṣṇa Caitanya, born in A.D. 1486 in Navadvipa (Bengal), founded the Bengal School of Vaiṣṇavism or popularly known as Caitanya Vaiṣṇavism. He was intoxicated with love for Kṛṣṇa (*Kṛṣṇa-prema*) and spread the gospel of devotion to Lord Kṛṣṇa throughout the country. Bhagavān as Kṛṣṇa is the Absolute Para Brahman (and not an *avatāra*). The concept of Rādhā-Kṛṣṇa incarnate in Caitanya brings out the full import of *Kṛṣṇa-lila.* He also believes that *bhakti* understood in the sense of loving service to God is the only means of attaining the bliss of Kṛṣṇa. There are gradations in the *bhakti* but the concept of erotic love between Rādhā-Kṛṣṇa (*prema-bhakti*) finds an important place. Jayadeva, one of his followers has immortalised this concept in his lyrical poem called *Gīta-govinda.* It captured the imagination of the people so greatly that *Bhakti* movement based on the Rādhā-Kṛṣṇa cult spread quickly in the eastern part of India.

One other important Vaiṣṇava movement which took its root in Assam was headed by Śaṁkaradeva (born in 1449). He was greatly influenced by the Philosophy of Rāmānuja. He travelled widely all over the country and spread Vaiṣṇavism, which may be called Assam Vaiṣṇavism or Neo-Vaiṣṇavism, throughout the country. Following the teaching of *Bhāgavata Purāṇa*, he emphasised the *Bhakti* movement and preached a religion and philosophy similar to that of Rāmānuja.

Jñāneśvara (1271-93) is the founder of the *Bhakti* school in Maharashtra. Lord Viṣṇu is worshipped as Viṭhoba or Viṭhala.[127] He advocated *bhakti* or devotion to God as the only means of realizing God. Following the teaching of Bhāgavata, he emphasised the nine forms of *bhakti* each having its own efficacy in securing salvation. His teachings caught the attention of a large number of devotees in Maharashtra. There appeared several mystics or *bhaktas* of God such as Nāmadeva, Ekanātha, Tukāram and Rāmadāsa. Nāmadeva (1270-1350), born in a tailor's family, became an ardent devotee of Lord Paṇḍarināth and his devotional outpourings to this Lord are embodied in his *abhaṅgas*, which have moved the hearts of devotees all over Maharashtra. Ekanātha (1533-98) dedicated himself to the service of God by singing *Saṅkīrtans* (devotional songs) in Marathi language. Tukāram (1607-49), the son of a farmer near Poona, advocated service to God as more important than salvation. Rāmadāsa (1608-81) was an ardent devotee of Rāma and emphasised the performance of duty with the heart set on God.

Among the recent Vaiṣṇava development, we may take note of the Kṛṣṇa-consciousness movement in the different parts of the world founded by Bhaktivedanta Swami Prabupāda who was a follower of the Caitanya School of Vaiṣṇavism. This modern movement has captured the attention of a large number of people in the United States of America and other parts of the world. They believe in the worship of Rādhā-Kṛṣṇa as the Supreme Being. The worship takes the form of *kīrtan* or chanting the name of Hare Kṛṣṇa. It has become so popular that one can witness large number of ardent devotees participating in it all over the world. The followers of this cult have adopted the *Bhagavad-gītā* and the *Bhāgavata Purāṇa* as the two important religious texts. They follow daily religious observances on the pattern of the Caitanya Vaiṣṇavites of Assam and Bengal. As devotees of Lord Kṛṣṇa, they are Vaiṣṇavas. Their missionary zeal has taken Vaiṣṇávism to many parts of the world.

Thus, it may be observed that Vaiṣṇavism as a living monotheistic religion is very ancient going back to Ṛgvedic times. It has developed itself and grown steadily through several centuries right through the present day. Though it has assumed different forms in different periods, it is basically the same religion as it believes in the exclusive worship of Viṣṇu or any one of his manifestations such as Rāma, Kṛṣṇa, Govinda and Pāṇḍuraṅga. *Bhakti* plays an important role as the means of salvation. There may be differences in the external forms and observance of certain daily rituals including mode of worship to suit the conditions in the different regions. But the basic tenets of Vaiṣṇavism have remained unchanged. The vitality of this religion lies in its universal appeal in terms of the reciprocal love of God and God's love to the *bhaktas* and thus promoting the universal brotherhood.

Sourcebooks for Vaiṣṇavism

Before we go into the discussion of the philosophical and theological doctrines of Vaiṣṇavism, we may note the sourcebooks for our study on this subject. A religion which has grown over a period of many centuries has to its credit a very extensive literature. We may, however, record the important source material for the benefit of research scholars and also to indicate the authoritative original sources from which the present book is written.

The following are the important source material:

1. Vedas

(i) *The Ṛg-veda Saṁhitās*—in particular the hymns referring to Viṣṇu (Viṣṇu-Sūktas); Puruṣa-Sūkta (X-90) and Śri-Sūkta along with their commentaries.

(ii) *Taittirīya Saṁhitā* (V-2).

(iii) *Śatapatha Brāhmaṇa* (I-1-2).

(iv) *Taittirīya Āraṇyaka* (I-VIII).

2. **The Upaniṣads**

Īśa, Kena, Kaṭha, Praśna, Muṇḍaka, Taittirīya, Bṛhadāraṇyaka, Chāndogya, Mahānārāyaṇīya, Śvetāśvatara, Atharvaśikha, Subāla, Nārāyaṇa, Narasimha-tāpanīya and Mahopaniṣad.

3. **Itihāsas**

(i) *Rāmāyaṇa* of Valmīki
(ii) *Mahābhārata* of Vyāsa—in particular Śāntiparva (Nārāyaṇīya section) and (Mokṣadharma section), Bhīṣmaparva (Bhagavadgītā section), Anuśāsanaparva (Viṣṇu-Sahasranāma section), Āśvamedhikaparva (Anugīta section).

4. **Vaiṣṇava Purāṇas**

(i) *Viṣṇu Purāṇa*
(ii) *Nārada Purāṇa*
(iii) *Viṣṇudharmottara*
(iv) *Padma Purāṇa*
(v) *Varāha Purāṇa*
(vi) *Garuḍa Purāṇa*
(vii) *Bhāgavata*

5. **Āgamas**

(a) *Vaikhānasa Saṁhitās*
(i) *Vimānaracana-kalpa* of Marīci (*Marīci Saṁhitā*)
(ii) *Samūrtarcanādhikaraṇa* of Atri (*Atri Saṁhitā*)
(iii) *Jñānakāṇḍa* of *Kaśyapa*
(iv) *Kriyādhikāra* of Bhṛgu

(b) *Pāñcarātra Saṁhitās*
(v) *Sāttvata Saṁhitā*
(vi) *Pauṣkara Saṁhitā*
(vii) *Jayākhya Saṁhitā*
(viii) *Pārameśvara Saṁhitā*
(ix) *Pādma Saṁhitā*
(x) *Īśvara Saṁhitā*
(xi) *Parama Saṁhitā*
(xii) *Lakṣmī Tantra*
(xiii) *Ahirbudhnya Saṁhitā*

(xiv) *Viśvaksena Saṁhitā*
(xv) *Nāradīya Saṁhitā*

6. **Nālāyira Divya-Prabandham** (Four thousand hymns in Tamil) of Āḻvārs and the commentaries on The Tiruvāymoḷi.
 (i) *Ārāyirappaḍi* of Piḷḷān
 (ii) *Oṅpatināyirappadi* of Nañjīyar
 (iii) Raṅgarāmānuja's *Oṅpatiṇāyirappaḍi* (in Sanskrit)
 (iv) Aḷahiya-maṇavāḻa Jīyar's *Pannirāyrappaḍi*
 (v) Periya Parakāla Swāmi's *Padinennayirappaḍi*
 (vi) Periavācchān Piḷḷai's *Irupattunālāyirappaḍi*
 (vii) Vadakkuttiruvīdi Pillai's *Īḍu Muppattiyārāyirappaḍi*
 (viii) Vedānta-rāmānuja's *Irupattu-nālāyirappaḍi*

7. **Yāmuna's works**
 (i) *Siddhitraya*
 (ii) *Āgamaprāmāṇya*
 (iii) *Strotraratna* and *Catuḥślokī*
 (iv) *Gitārtha-saṁgraha*

8. **Rāmānuja's works**
 (i) *Śrī-bhāṣya* with *Śrutaprakāśikā*
 (ii) *Vedānta-dīpa* and *Vedānta-sāra*
 (iii) *Bhagavdgītābhāṣya*
 (iv) *Vedārtha-Saṁgraha*
 (v) *Gadyatraya*
 (vi) *Nityagrantha*

9. **Śrivatsānka Miśra**: *Atimānuṣastava*, *Śrīstava*, *Varadarājastava*, *Vaikunṭhastava* and *Sundarabāhustava*
10. **Parāśara Bhattar**: *Bhagavadguṇa-darpaṇa*, *Aṣṭaśloki*, *Śrīguṇaratna-kośa*, *Śrīraṅgarājastava*
11. **Nāñjivar** : *Śrī-sūkta Bhāṣya*
12. **Vaṅgīvamśeśvara** : *Vaṅgīśvara-kārikā* (also known as *Āhnikakārikā*)
13. **Ātreya Rāmānuja** : *Nyāyakulīśa*
14. **Vāstya Vardācārya** : *Tattvasāra*, *Tattvanirṇaya*, *Prapannapārijāta*, *Prameyamāla*

15.	**Periyavaccāna-piḷḷai**	: Commentaries on *Jitante-strotra*, Rāmānuja's *Gadyatraya*, *Catuḥślokī*, *Paranda-rahasyam*, *Taniślokam*, *Māṇikkamālai*.
16.	**Piḷḷaiḷokācārya**	: *Śrivacanabhūṣaṇam*, *Tattvatrayam*, *Artha-pañcakam*, *Mumukṣuppaḍi* and other minor Rahasya granthas along with the commentaries of Maṇavāḷamāmuni thereon.
17.	**Vedānta Deśika's works**	: *Tattvā-muktā-kalāpa* with *Sarvārtha Siddhi* *Nyāya-paniśuddhi* *Nyāya-siddāñjana* *Adhikaraṇa-Sārāvaḷī* *Pāñcarātrarakṣā*, *Nikṣeparakṣā* and *Saccharitrarakṣā* *Tātparyacandrikā* (commentary on Rāmānuja's *Gītābhāṣya*) Commentaries on *Gadyatraya*, *Stotra-ratna* and *Catuḥślokī* *Īśāvāsyopaniṣad*; *Dramiḍopaniṣad-Sāra*, *Dramiḍopaniṣadtātparya Ratnāvaḷi*, *Rahasyatrayasāra* and other Rahasya granthas (in Maṇipravāḷa).

During the seven centuries following Vedānta Deśika and Piḷḷailokācārya, several works both in Sanskrit and Maṇipravāḷa language have been written by the Vaiṣṇava *ācāryas* and eminent Vaiṣṇava scholars belonging to both Vaḍakalai and Tenkalai sects. As observed earlier most of these books are in the form of further commentaries, glossaries on the hymns of the Āḷvārs and the works of Rāmānuja, Vedānta Deśika and other earlier *ācāryas*. The independent treatises which have come up in this period are generally in the form of tracts to elucidate the esoteric doctrines. Since these works cannot be strictly considered as original contributions they have not been mentioned here. Wherever they are used, references have been indicated in the footnotes and in the bibliography.

The literature on Vaiṣṇavism is very extensive and an exhaustive study of all this literature would run into volumes. It is not the purpose of this book to present the History of Vaiṣṇavism. Its scope as explained in the Introduction is confined to present the fundamental philosophical and theological doctrines of Vaiṣṇavism as propounded by Rāmānuja and his followers, on the basis of the authentic original sourcebooks.

References

1. RV III.9.9. *trīṇi śatā trī sahasrāṇyagniṁ triṁśacca devā nava cāsaparyan.*
   See also RV X.52.6.
2. RV I.139.11. See also RV I.34.11.
3. T. Up. I.1.5. *maha iti, tad-brahma, sa ātmā; aṅgānyanyā devatāḥ.*
4. Mbh. IV.3.16. *nārāyaṇastu puruṣo viśvarūpo mahādyutiḥ; nārāyaṇasya ca aṅgāni sarvā daivāni ca abhavan. anyāni sarvadaivāni tasyāṅgāni mahātmanaḥ.*
   See also *Stotraratna Bhāṣya*, p. 40.
5. Mbh. XIII.255.142. *eko viṣṇuḥ mahadbhūtaṁ pṛthagbhūtānyanekaśaḥ; trīn-lokān vyāpya bhūtātmā bhuṅkte viśvabhug-avyahaḥ.*
6. See G.N. Chakravarthy, *The Concept of Cosmic Harmony in the Ṛgveda*, p. 18.
7. See Br. Up. V.9.2. *sa ho-vāca mahimāna evaiṣāmete*. The word *mahimāna* is interpreted as glorious attributes.
   See RRB. p. 262. *mahimāna eva, guṇabhūto ityarthaḥ.*
8. See Yāska's Nirukta VII. 4.8. *eka ātmā bahudhā stūyate. ekasya ātmanaḥ anye devāḥ pratyaṅgāni bhavanti.*
9. See Bṛhaddevatā, I.70.71.
10. *Sāyaṇa Bhāṣya* (preface), *tasmāt sarvairapi parameśvara eva hūyate.*
11. RV I.164.46.
12. RV I.115.1. *sūrya ātmā jagatastasthuṣaśca.*
    See also *Sāyaṇa Bhāṣya*, Vol. I, p. 873. *āntarvartih sūryaḥ antaryāmitayā sarvasya prerakaḥ.*
    TUp *yaścāsau āditye sa ekaḥ.*
13. RV III.55.5. *mahddevānāmasuratvamekam.*
14. RV IV.26.1. See also Br. Up. III.4.10.
15. RV V.44.6. *yādṛgeva daḍṛśe tādṛgucyate.*
16. RV VI.45.16. *ya eka it-tamuṣṭuhi*
    T.Up. *sa ekaḥ sa ya evaṁ vit.*
17. RV VI.36.4. *eko viśvasya bhuvanasya rājā.*
18. RV VIII.58.2. *ekaṁ vā idaṁ vibabhūva sarvam.*
19. RV X.114.5. *ekaṁ santaṁ bahudhā kalpayanti.*
    See *Sāyaṇa Bhāṣya*, *ekaṁ santaṁ paramātmānaṁ vacobhiḥ stutilakṣaṇaiḥ vacanaiḥ bahuprakāraṁ kalpayanti kurvanti.*

20. RV X.82.3. *yo devānāṁ nāmadhā eka eva.*
See also *Sāyaṇa Bhāṣya*, Vol. VIII, p. 205.
21. RV VI.7.6. and X.5.7.
22. RV III.20.4. See also RV, IV.30.2.
23. RV VI.9.5. *dhruvaṁ jyotirnihitaṁ dṛśaye kaṁ mano javiṣṭhaṁ patayatsvantaḥ.*
Also VI.9.6. *idaṁ jyotirhṛdaya āhitaṁ yat.*
24. RV VI.36.4. *eko viśvasya bhuvanasya rājā.*
25. RV VI.19.10. *ikṣe hi vasva ubhayasya rājan.* See also RV, VI.22.9.
26. RV VI.7.7. *adabdho gopā amṛtasya rakṣitā.*
See also RV I.154.5. *sa hi bandhuritthā viṣṇoḥ pade parame.*
27. See fn. 8 and fn. 10.
28. See VS I.1.29.
In the *Kauśītakī Upaniṣad* (III.1), which is the basis for this *Vedānta Sūtra*, Pratardana is instructed by Indra to meditate on him, who is described as *prāṇa*, in order to attain the higher goal. The question is raised here whether the meditation on Indra as *prāṇa* means the individual self (the *jīva* of Indra) or the *Paramātman*. Both Rāmānuja and Śaṁkara explain that Indra as *prāṇa* here refers to Brahman who is the indweller of Indra.
29. Ka. Up. II.15. *sarve vedā yatpadam-āmananti.* The word *pada* is interpreted as *Brahma-svarūpa* by Rāmānuja and as goal by Śaṁkara. See also BG XV.15. *vedaiśca sarvaiḥ ahameva vedyaḥ.*
30. See Ch. Up. III.12.5. *tadetat ṛcā abhyuktam.*
See also Br. Up. VI.4.23. MUp III.2.10. Praśna Up I.7.
31. See R.G. Bhandarkar, *Vaiṣṇavism Śaivism and Minor Religious Systems*, pp. 47-48.
32. See AB. Keith, *The Religion and Philosophy of the Vedas*, p. 109. See also Aurobindo, *On the Vedas*, pp. 358-59.
33. *Aitareya Brāhmaṇa*, I.1.1. *agnirvai devānamavamo viṣṇuḥ paramaḥ.* See also *Taittirīya Saṁhitā*, V.5.1. *agniravamo devatānāṁ viṣṇuḥ paramaḥ.*
34. See NS III.1. *sarveśvaratvam, vyāpakatve sati cetanatvam, sarva-śeṣitvam, sarva-karma-samārādhyatvam, sarva-phala-pradatvam, sarvādhāratvam, sarva-kāryotpādakatvam, svajñāna-svetara-samasta-dravya śarīrakatvam, svataḥ satyasaṅkalpatvādikam ca īśvara lakṣaṇam.*
35. VS I.1.23. *ākāśastallingāt.* The issue raised in this *sūtra* is whether the term *ākāśa* used in the *Chāndogya Upaniṣad* refers to the physical ether or Brahman. The final view taken is that it applies to Brahman, because the descriptive characteristics such as being the cause of universe etc., apply only to Brahman.
36. RV I.22.16. *ato devā avantu no yato viṣṇurvicakrame; pṛthivyāḥsaptadhāmabhiḥ.*
RV I.22.17. *idaṁ viṣṇurvicakrame tredhā nidadhe padam.*
RV I.22.18. *trīṇi padā vicakrame viṣṇurgopā adābhyaḥ.*
RV I.154.1 *vicakramāṇastredhorugāyaḥ.*
RV I.154.2. *yasyoruṣu triṣuvikramaṇeṣvadhikṣiyanti bhuvanāni viśvā.*

RV I.154.3. *eko vimame tribhiritpadebhiḥ.*
See *Sāyaṇa Bhāṣya, eka eva advitīyassan.*
RV I.154.4. *yasya trīpūrṇa madhunā padāni.*
RV I.155.4. *yaḥ pārthivāni tribhirid-vigāmabhirurukramiṣṭa.*
RV VII.100.4. *vicakrame pṛthivīmeṣa etāṁ kṣetrāya viṣṇurmanuṣe daśasyan.*
For fuller explanation of these and other hymns, see *Sāyaṇa Bhāṣya* on the relevant hymns.

37. See TUp I.11. *so'kāmayata bahusyāṁ prajāyeyeti,...tat sṛṣṭva tadevānuprāviśat.*
38. See Yāska's *Nirukta* XII.18.
39. Ibid. Yāska also offers one more interpretation of the term on the basis of the views of some earlier commentators *Vyaśnoter-vā* which implies as one who pervades through the rays. Accordingly Viṣṇu means *Sūrya* (Sun).
40. See Ahs LII.39 and 42.
See also Chapter 7, p. 132-33.
41. *Śatapatha Brāhmaṇa* I.1.2. and I.4.2.
42. RV I.22.20. See fn. 44
43. RV I.22.18. *trīṇi padā vicakrame viṣṇurgopā adābhyaḥ ato dharmāṇi dhārayan.*
The word *gopā* is interpreted by Sāyaṇa as *sarvasya jagataḥ rakṣako viṣṇuḥ* (Viṣṇu as the protector of the entire universe).
See *Sāyaṇa Bhāṣya*, Vol. I, p. 198.
44. RV I.22.20. *tadviṣṇoḥ paramaṁ padaṁ sadā paśyanti sūrayaḥ; divīva cakṣurātatam. tadviprāso vipanyavo jagṛvāṁsassamindhate; viṣṇoryatparamaṁ padam.*
45. See VSa p. 161.
46. VP I.9.55.
47. KaUp III.9. *sodhvanaḥ pāramāpnoti tadviṣṇoḥ paramaṁ padam.*
48. VP I.6.39 and I.22.53 and 54.
49. RV I.154.4. *ya u tridhātu pṛthivīmutadyāmeko dādhāra bhuvanāni viśvā.*
See *Sāyaṇa Bhāṣya. pṛthivī ap tejorūpa dhātutraya viśiṣṭaṁ yathā bhavati tathā dādhāra dhṛtavān. . . .ityarthaḥ.*
50. ChUp VI.3.
51. RV I.155.4. *tattaditadidasya pauṁsyaṁ graṇimasīnasya trātuḥ*
See *Sāyaṇa Bhāṣya. inasya sarvasya svāminaḥ.*
52. RV I.156.2. *yaḥ pūrvyāya vedhase navīyase sumajjānaye viśṇave dadāśati.* This passage is also found in the *Kṛṣna Yajurveda Brāhmaṇa* II.4.
53. See *Sāyaṇa Bhāṣya, sutarāṁ mādayatīti sumat; tādṛśījāyā yasya sa tathoktaḥ; tasmai jaganmādanaśīla śrīpataya ityarthaḥ.*
54. RV I.156.3. *mahaste viṣṇo sumatiṁ bhajāmahe.*
55. RV VII.99.1 and 2. *paro mātrayā tanuvā vṛdhāna na te mahitvamanvaśnuvanti. na te viṣṇo jāyamāno na jāto, deva mahimnaḥ paramantamāpa.*
56. RV VII.99.3 and RV VII.100.5. *kṣayantamasya rajasaḥ parāke.*

57. *Taittirīya Āraṇyaka*, I.8. *viṣṇunā vidhṛte bhūmī iti vatsasya vedanā*
58. Ibid. *eko yaddhārayad-devaḥ.*
59. Ibid.
60. RV X.90.1.
61. Ahs LIX.2. *sūktaṁ tu pauruṣaṁ puṁsaḥ parasmāt utthitaṁ purā.* See also *Stotraratna Bhāṣya*, p. 41.
62. See Mbh XII.360.5. *idaṁ puruṣa-sūktaṁhi sarva-vedeṣu paṭhyate; ataḥ srutibhyaḥ sarvābhyo balavat samudīritam.*
63. *Praśna* Up V.5. *parātparaṁ puriśayaṁ puruṣam-īkṣate.*
64. *Subāla* Up VI.
65. *Śatapatha Brāhmaṇa*, XIII.6.1.1. *puruṣo ha nārāyaṇo akāmayata.*
66. TNUp 90 and 91. See fn. 80.
67. *Padma-purāṇa*, VI.254.66. *bhagavāniti śabdoyam tathā puruṣa ityapi; nirupādhi ca vartete vāsudeve sanātane.*
68. *Puruṣa-sūkta* (Yajurveda recension), II.6. *hṛīśca te lakṣmīśca patnyau.*
69. See TMK III.8.
70. *Śrī-sūkta*, hymn 9. See also SSB, p. 42.
71. *Taittirīya Saṁhitā*, IV.4.12. *asyeśānā jagato viṣṇupatnī.*
72. KaUp III.9. *sodhvanaḥ pāramāpnoti tadviṣṇoḥ paramaṁ padam.*
73. See RRB, p. 100.
74. *Subāla* Up VI.1. *naiveha kiñcana āsīt....divya deva eko nārāyaṇaḥ.*
75. *Mahopaniṣad. eko ha vai nārāyaṇa āsīt, na brahmā neśāno nāpo nāgniṣomau ne-me dyāvā pṛthivī....*
76. See Chapter 2, pp. 53-4.
77. NUp *atha puruṣo ha vai nārāyaṇo akāmayata prajāḥ sṛjeyeti.*
78. Ibid. *ya evam veda sa viṣṇureva bhavati.*
79. Though Śaṁkara has not written a commentary on the *Taittirīya Nārāyaṇa Upaniṣad*, it is accepted as an authoritative Upaniṣad by his followers. Ānandagiri who has written a glossary on the *vārtika* of Sureśvara (a disciple of Śaṁkara), which itself is a sub-commentary on *Śaṁkara Bhāsya* on the *Bṛhadāraṇyaka Upaniṣad*, quotes the *Taittirīya Nārāyaṇa Upaniṣad* to support the theory that *Puruṣa* of *Puruṣa-sūkta* is Nārāyaṇa.
80. TNUp 90.93. *sahasra-śīrṣaṁ devaṁ viśvākṣaṁ viśvaśambhuvam; viśvaṁ nārāyaṇaṁ devam-akṣaraṁ paramaṁ prabhum....nārāyaṇa paraṁbrahma tattvaṁ nārāyaṇaḥ paraḥ.*

    The mention of *deva* (deity) with thousand heads is reiteration of the *Puruṣa* of *Puruṣa-sūkta*. Such a *Puruṣa* is described as the ruler of the entire universe (*patiṁ viśvasya*). Later in the passage this Deity is identified with Nārāyaṇa who is described as *Para-Brahma* and *Para-tattva.*

    See also *Āpastamba Śrauta* (Quoted by VD in *Stotraratna Bhāṣya* p. 41). "*sahasra-śīrṣā puruṣaḥ*" *ity-upahitaṁ puruṣeṇa nārāyaṇena yajamāna upatiṣṭate.*

    A similar statement is also found in the *Kalpasūtra.*

81. *Aitareya Brāhmaṇa* I.1.1. *agnirvai devānāmavamo viṣṇuḥ paramaḥ. tadantareṇa sarvā anyā devatāḥ.*
82. See Otto Schrader, *Introduction to the Pāñcarātra* and *Ahirbudhnya Saṁhitā*, p. 22.
See also V. Varadachari, *Āgamas and South Indian Vaiṣṇavism*, p. 42.
83. Mbh XII.359.68. *pāñcarātrasya kṛtsnasya vaktā nārāyaṇaḥ svayam.*
84. According to tradition the two authors are identical.
See RTS, *Guruparaṁparā-Sāra*, p. 70.
85. VS II.2.39 and 40 (acc. to RB). II.2.42 and 43 (acc. to SB). Both Śaṁkara and Rāmānuja are agreed that these *Sūtras* refer to the theory of Pāñcarātra system.
86. *Vimānaracana Kalpa*, pp. 3-4. *ādikāle tu bhagavān brahmā tu vikhanā muniḥ; yajuḥ-śākhānu-sāreṇa cakre sūtraṁ mahattaram.*
87. RV I.155.1. *pravaḥ pāntamandhaso dhiyāyate mahe śūrāya viṣṇave cārcata.*
88. *Vimānaracana Kalpa*, p. 503. *tasmāt viṣṇu arcanameva dvijaiḥ aharahaḥ kartavyam-iti vijñāyate.*
Śaunaka, the author of *Kalpa-sūtra* also quotes the same Ṛk hymn in support of daily worship of Viṣṇu.
See VD's *Stotraratna Bhāṣya*, p. 41, See fn 2 on p. 377.
89. Ibid. p. 492. *tasya bhāvaḥ tattvamiti tasya para-brahmaṇaḥ nārāyaṇasya bhāvaḥ; tattvaṁ narayaṇaḥ para iti śrutiḥ.*
90. See PR I, p. 108. *pañcakāla vyavasthityai veṅkateśa vipaścitā; śrīpāñcarātra-siddhānta vyavastheyaṁ samarthitā.*
91. For explanation of these terms see Chapter 15.
92. See Ahs XI.63. *tatpara-vyūha-vibhava-svabhāvādi-nirūpaṇam; pañcarātrāhvyaṁ tantraṁ mokṣaika-phalalakṣaṇam.*
For explanation of these terms see Chapter 10.
93. See Ahs LII.34 to 70.
See also LT II.5 and 6.
sa vāsudevo bhagavān kṣetrajñaḥ paramo mataḥ;
viṣṇurnārāyaṇo viśvo viśvarūpa itiryate.
See also Chapter 7 pp. 132-34.
94. See *Mārkaṇḍeya Saṁhitā*, *śrutimūlamidam śāstraṁ pramāṇaṁ kalpasūtravat.*
See also *Viṣṇu-tantra*, I.36. *śrutimūlāni tānyeva pañcarātrāṇi paṅkaja.*
See also LT Introduction, pp. 4-5.
95. See SB II.2.42.
96. Otto Schrader, *Introduction to Pāñcarātra and AhS*, pp. 6–12.
LT Introduction by V. Krishnamacharya, pp. 10–13.
97. *Rāmāyaṇa* I.4.7. *kāvyam rāmāyaṇam kṛtsnaṁ sītāyāḥ caritam mahat.*
See *Śrī-guṇaratnakośa*, verse 14. *śrīmad-rāmāyaṇamapi paraṁ prāṇiti tvaccaritre.*
See also SVB sūtra 5.
98. TMK III.11. *ādyaṁ rāmāyaṇaṁ tat sa ca nigamagaṇe pañcamaḥ.*
See SS III.11, p. 123. *nigamagaṇe pañcamatvaṁ ca "vedān adhyāpayāṁāsa mahābhārata-pañcamān iti" pradarśitam.*
See Mbh XII.327.18.

99. See VSa p. 124. *sarvaśiṣṭaiḥ sarvadharma sarvatattva vyavasthāyāṁ idameva paryāptam....*
100. VP V.18.58.
101. VP I.1.31. See TUp III.1 and VS I.1.2.
102. VP VI.5.76, 78 and 80.
103. VP I.22.53, VI.5.79 and 85.
104. VP I.8.17, I.9.120 and I.9.126.
105. VP I.9.51 and 55, VP II.2.105.
106. See S.K. Aiyangar, *Early History of Vaiṣṇavism in South India*, pp. 4–13. See also S.N. Dasgupta, *History of Indian Philosophy*, Vol. III, pp. 64-65.
107. The names of twelve Āḻvārs in the chronological order as accepted by tradition are: 1. Poygai Āḻvār, 2. Pūtatt-Āḻvār, 3. Pey Āḻvār, 4. Tirumaḻaśai Āḻvār, 5. Nammāḻvār, 6. Madhurakavi Āḻvār, 7. Kulaśekhara Āḻvār, 8. Periyālvār, 9. Āṇḍāl, 10. Toṇḍaraḍippodi Ālvār, 11. Tiruppāṇālvār, 12. Tirumaṅgai Āḻvār. Tradition also maintains the view that they are all Divine incarnations for the purpose of propagating the spiritual knowledge through the popular language.
For details regarding their biographies and the hymns written by them, see *Guruparaṁparā Prabhāvam* (*ārāyirappaḍi*) in Maṇipravāḷa language by Pinpaḻakiya Perumāḷjiyar.
See also *Guruparaṁparā Prabhāvam* (*mūvayirappaḍi*) by Tṛtīya Brahmatantra Parakāla Swāmi.
See also *Divyasūrī Caritam* by Garuḍavāhana Paṇḍita.
108. See Bhandarkar, *Vaiṣṇavism* etc., p. 4.
109. Ibid., p. 5.
110. *Paṇini Sūtra* IV.3.98. *vāsudeva arjunābhyāṁ bun.*
111. According to the biography of Rāmānuja, he appointed 74 well qualified apostles for the purpose of propagation of Vaiṣṇavism. These are regarded as *Siṁhāsanādhipatis*, and also known as *Ācārya-puruṣas* or preceptors.
112. GB (opening verse), *vastutāṁ upayāto'ham yāmuneyaṁ namāmi tam.*
113. See RB (opening statement) *bhagavad-bodhāyanakṛtāṁ vistirṇāṁ brahmasūtra-vṛttiṁ pūrvācāryaḥ sañcikṣupuḥ; tanmatānusāreṇa sūtrākṣarāni vyākhyāsyante.*
114. The *Guruparaṁparā-prabhāvam* speaks of the recovery of the hymns which had almost been lost in Nāthamuni's time, by performing yogic meditation by Nāthamuni to whom these were revealed by Nammāḻvār.
115. See SB on VS II.2.43, where he acknowledges his acceptance of Bhāgavata Religion. In his *Bhāṣya* on the *Gītā* and the Upaniṣads, he repeatedly mentions with high respect Vāsudeva or Nārāyaṇa as Paramātman.
See Śaṁkara's *Gītā-bhāṣya*, VIII.5, VIII.15, XV.16.
See also Chapter 7, fn. 21 p. 152.
116. See Chapter 10, pp. 208–11.
117. Maṇipravāla literally means pearl (*mani*) and coral (*pravāla*). Just as the two are strung together alternatively to form a beautiful necklace,

Sanskrit words are intermixed with Tamil words to form a Sanskritised Tamil prose.

118. A *grantha* consists of thirty-two syllables. It was a common practice in those days to entitle the commentaries written on the hymns of Āḻvārs in terms of the number of units the work comprises.

119. The word *iḍu* means equal to or similar, since this work is considered similar to the *Śrutaprakāśikā*, the detailed commentary of Sudarśana Sūri on Ramanuja's *Śrī-bhāṣya*. It is also interpreted as *iḍu-paḍutal* which means to get attracted by the teachings of Āḻvār.

120. This is a title conferred on him in recognition of his mastery over all branches of learning.

121. See V.K.S.N. Raghavan, *History of Viśiṣṭādvaita Literature*, pp. 33–44 for details of these works.

122. Ibid., pp. 33–39.

123. See K.K.A. Venkatachari, *Śrīvaiṣṇava Maṇiprauāḷa*,, pp. 124–41 for details of these works.

124. See Ibid., pp. 165-66.

125. These have been outlined in a work of 19th century entitled *Aṣṭādaśa-bheda-vicāra* by Varavaraguru.

126. See V.K.S.N. Raghavan, *History of Viśiṣṭādvaita Literature*, pp. 52–68, for a fuller account of the literature that appeared in this period.

127. The word Viṣṇu became Bitti in Kannada and Viṭhala in Maharashtra. The Deity at Pandharpur temple is worshipped as Pāṇḍuraṅga Vithala.

PART II

PHILOSOPHY OF VAIṢṆAVISM

2

THE DOCTRINE OF ULTIMATE REALITY

In the previous chapter we have outlined the historical development of Vaiṣṇavism from the period of Ṛgveda to the present time. Apart from its being a monotheistic religion having Vedic origin, it contains distinctive theological doctrines based on philosophical theories as enunciated in the Upaniṣads and the *Vedānta-sūtra* which provide the rational basis for the Vaiṣṇava theology. We shall now present in this part of the book an exposition of the main philosophical doctrines of the Viśiṣṭādvaita Vedānta to show how the theological concepts of Vaiṣṇavism have their roots in the Vedānta theories.

The present chapter deals with the doctrine of Ultimate Reality which is the most important philosophical topic of Vedānta. The central theme of Vaiṣṇavism is that Viṣṇu is the Supreme Deity and the entire universe consisting of sentient souls and non-sentient matter is pervaded by Him. This theory is the direct outcome of the philosophy of the Ultimate Reality as enunciated in the Vedānta. The scope of our study will be confined to the discussion of the important aspects of the doctrine of Reality which have a direct bearing on the theory of Viṣṇu as Supreme Being.

Definition of Ultimate Reality

The first issue to be considered is: What is the Ultimate Reality? As true philosophers, the Upaniṣadic seers were more concerned with finding a solution to the metaphysical problem of Ultimate Reality than answering the theological question as to which of the deities is the Supreme Being. The Upaniṣads, therefore, describe the Reality in general terms such as *Sat*, *Ātman*, *Brahman*, *Para-tattva*, *Paraṁ-jyotis* etc. In the famous dialogue between Varuṇa and Bhṛgu in the *Taittirīya Upaniṣad*, the former in reply to a question of the latter regarding Brahman, says: 'That from which all these beings are born, that by which, when born they live, and that unto which, when departing, they enter; desire to know that; that is Brahman'.[1] On the basis of this text the author of the *Vedānta-sūtra* defines Brahman as that from which proceed the creation, sustenance and dissolution of the universe.[2] Accordingly Brahman, the Ultimate Reality of metaphysics, should be the primary cause of the creation, sustenance and dissolution of the universe. In other words, *jagat-kāraṇatva* or being the primary cause of the universe constitutes an important criterion for accepting an ontological entity as the Ultimate Reality. By applying this criterion, the *Vedānta-sūtra* eliminates all other ontological entities such as the individual self (*jīva*), the primordial cosmic matter (*pradhāna*) of the Sāṅkhya system, the physical *ākāśa*, the vital *prāṇa*, the light of the sun etc.; which *prima facie* appear to be the primary causal substance, from the purview of the concept of Ultimate Reality. *Jagat-kāraṇatva* is, therefore, the distinguishing characteristic of the Supreme Being. The first *two adhyāyas* (parts) of the *Vedānta-sūtra* are devoted to a discussion of this important aspect of Reality.

Proof for Existence of Reality

The first question that arises in this regard is: What is the proof of the existence of such a Reality? Is it possible to prove the existence of Brahman or God on the basis of logical arguments? According to the Naiyāyikas it is possible to establish it by means of logic. They have adopted among others, the cosmological argument based on the idea of causation to prove the existence of God. Every effect must have a cause and the universe being an effect must have been produced by an agent or creator called Īśvara. The argument is expressed in the following syllogistic form: 'The physical universe must have been caused by an agent, because it is an effect just as a pot.'[3] The Vedāntins reject the purely logical argument because it cannot conclusively establish the existence of the Supreme Being as conceived in the Upaniṣads. Besides it suffers from logical fallacies.[4] All that can be proved by means of syllogistic argument is that a super-individual possessing unlimited capacity and knowledge is the creator of the universe, such as Caturmukha-Brahmā, a Vedic deity of lower order entrusted with the specific act of creation and therefore, not an omniscient, omnipresent and omnipotent *Īśvara* as distinct from *jīva*. Hence the author of the *Vedānta-sūtra* asserts that Revealed Scripture (*śāstra*) alone is the supreme authority for our belief in the existence of God.[5] The justification for this claim is that neither perception nor logical argument can arrive at an unquestionable final conclusion in respect of matters which are super-normal. What is established by logic can also be disproved by adopting the same logical method as the Mādhyamikas have done on the question of the existence of God. The author of the *Vedānta-sūtra*, therefore, asserts that *tarka* (logic) is inconclusive.[6] This does not mean that the Vedāntins reject reasoning. They do accept it but it should not be the sole means of proof because in a matter which is super-normal such as God or Soul, it cannot establish it conclusively. *Śruti* or Scripture should be taken as the final authority and logical arguments should be adopted to support Scripture. The sage Manu also supports this view. Thus he says: 'A person who ascertains the teachings of the sages and those relating to *dharma* with the aid of the sound logical arguments which are not opposed to Scripture, he alone truly knows the philosophic truth.'[7] Though the philosophical doctrines of Vedānta are based on scriptural teachings, they are not irrational.

Ultimate Reality as a Sentient Being

The fact that the Ultimate Reality known as Brahman is the primary causal substance of the universe (*jagatkāraṇa*) implies that it should be a sentient Being (*cetana-vastu*) endowed with omniscience and omnipotence, as otherwise the creation of an orderly universe would be logically inconceivable. As in the case of a human being who needs physical aids besides knowledge and power to produce a product, God as a creator does not need them, because He can create the universe with His will (*saṅkalpa*). The Upaniṣadic statements relating to the creation of the universe known as *kāraṇa-vākyas* speak of the creation as caused by the *saṅkalpa* of Brahman. The *Chāndogya Upaniṣad* says: 'In the beginning, my dear, this was Being alone (*sadeva*), one only, without a second'.... 'The Being willed, "may I become many", "may I grow forth", it created fire (*tejas*) etc.'[8] Without going into the different interpretations offered by

Śaṁkara and Rāmānuja on this text in accordance with their ontological positions, we should take note of the fact that the *sat*, which is understood by all Vedāntins as Brahman, causes the universe by *will* (*saṅkalpa*). The attribution of 'will' (*īkṣaṇa*) to Brahman implies that the metaphysical Reality should be a sentient Being endowed with knowledge and power to create the universe. Rāmānuja, therefore, asserts that Brahman is *Puruṣottama*, the Supreme Personal Being qualified with numerous attributes.[9] This would mean that Reality is *saviśeṣa*, a differentiated Being and not *nirviśeṣa*, a transcendental undifferentiated Being as Śaṁkara maintains. The latter type of Reality cannot have any causal relation with the universe. Such a Reality can have no bearing on the universe. It is as good as a non-entity in the opinion of Rāmānuja. The Advaitin gets over these difficulties by postulating the theory of *saguṇa* Brahman or Brahman as endowed with the attributes of knowledge, power etc., similar to the Brahman accepted by Rāmānuja by adopting the doctrine of *māyā*, an inexplicable cosmic principle causing illusory manifestation, but this theory when subjected to logical scrutiny would become untenable.

Brahman as Supreme Person

What is this Brahman of the Upaniṣads? Taking the root verb *bṛh* 'to grow', the term etymologically means that which grows (*bṛhati*) and causes to grow (*bṛhmayati*). This meaning is upheld by the Scriptural text.[10] The same is also reiterated by the Smṛti text.[11] The two epithets—*bṛhatva* and *bṛhmaṇatva*—which convey the primary import of the term Brahman, signify that which possesses infinite greatness both in respect of its intrinsic nature (*svarūpa*) and also attributes (*guṇataḥ*) is Brahman. These two attributes are applicable only to the Supreme Personal Being (*Sarveśvara*) and not to an undifferentiated Being (*nirviśeṣa Brahma*).[12] In view of this, Rāmānuja states that the term brahman denotes *Puruṣottama* or Supreme Personal Being who by its very nature is free from all imperfections (*nirasta-nikhila-doṣaḥ*) and possesses infinite auspicious attributes of unsurpassable excellence (*ananta-kalyāṇa-guṇa-gaṇaḥ*).[13] The concept of *Puruṣottama* as qualified by the two specific attributes distinguishes Brahman from every other being such as Caturmukha-Brahmā and Rudra, the individual souls including those which are eternally free and even the *nirguṇa* and *saguṇa* Brahman of the Advaita Vedānta because none of these is totally free from defects and possesses unsurpassable infinite attributes.[14]

Brahman as God of Religion

How does the Brahman of the Upaniṣads stand equated with the Personal God of Religion, Viṣṇu or Nārāyaṇa? The identification of Brahman with Nārāyaṇa is established on the basis of the Upaniṣadic texts by adopting the principle of interpretation laid down by the Mīmāṁsakas. According to them, when several terms are used in the same context in a passage, the words bearing the general meaning should bear the meaning of the specific word. Thus, for instance, one Vedic text enjoins that the sacrifice is to be performed by using *paśu* which means, as a general term, any kind of animal. In another Vedic statement in the same context, it enjoins that the sacrifice is to be done by using a specific animal, viz., *chāga*, which means goat. *Paśu*, the general term is thus taken to mean *chāga* or goat. The same logic is adopted in the matter of determining the meaning of the terms such as *Sat*, *Brahman*, *Ātman* and *Nārāyaṇa*. All these four terms are used in the Upaniṣadic passages in the same context of explaining the causation of the universe by Brahman at the time of creation. Thus states the *Chāndogya Upaniṣad*: 'This was in the beginning *Sat* only'.[15] The *Aitareya Upaniṣad* says: 'All this was *Ātman* only in the beginning.'[16] The *Bṛhadāraṇyaka* points out: 'All this was *Brahman* only in the beginning.'[17] Three different terms—*Sat*, *Ātman* and *Brahman* are used. Since several entities cannot be the cause of the universe, it is obvious that only one particular entity can be the sole cause of the universe. Among these which one could be the cause? The word *Sat* is too general a term and may mean anything that exists. The term *Ātman* is a little more specific but it may mean both *jīvātman* and *Paramātman*. The word *Brahman* is relatively even more specific but it is applicable to more than one entity such as *jīva* and *prakṛti*. Another Upaniṣadic passage, speaking of the creation of the universe, mentions *Nārāyaṇa* as the cause of the universe. Thus, the *Mahopaniṣad* says: 'Only Nārāyaṇa existed (in the beginning).'[18] The word *Nārāyaṇa* is used in this passage in place of the terms *Sat*, *Ātman* and *Brahman* mentioned in the other passages as the cause of the universe. According to the grammatical rule formulated by Pāṇini, the term Nārāyaṇa is treated as a specific proper name (*saṁjñā-pada*),[19] and is applicable to one specific Being only but not to any other entity as other general terms do. Rāmānuja, therefore, concludes on the basis of the principle of interpretation explained above that Brahman, the cause of the universe, is the same as *Nārāyaṇa.*[20]

Further, the *Taittirīya Nārāyaṇa Upaniṣad* (which is part of *Taittirīya Āraṇyaka*) emphatically asserts that Nārāyaṇa is *Para-Brahma*, Nārāyaṇa is *Para-tattva* and Nārāyaṇa is *Paramātmā.*[21] The *Subāla Upaniṣad* describes Nārāyaṇa as *antarātmā*,[22] the inner controller of all beings in the universe. Only that which creates the universe becomes *Antaryāmī* as is evident from the Upaniṣadic statement which says that after creating it, the same Brahman entered into it. Nārāyaṇa is not a mere name of the God of a particular cult. It is a term which connotes all the essential characteristics of the concept of the ultimate Reality of philosophy. According to the etymological meaning of the word, Nārāyaṇa is one who is the ground of the entire universe of *cit* and *acit*. *Nārā* means the universe of sentient and non-sentient beings. *Ayana* means one who is the ground for it (*nārāṇām ayanaṁ*). It also means one who is immanent in all (*nārāḥ ayanaṁ yasya saḥ*).[23] That is, all that exists in the universe has for its ground Nārāyaṇa. As the terms Viṣṇu and Vāsudeva bear the same etymological meaning as that of Nārāyaṇa, Brahman is also equated with these two names. This matter will be discussed further in a later chapter.[24] The important point to be noted in this context is that the ultimate Reality of metaphysics will have to be conceived as a Supreme Personal Being (*Puruṣottama*). It is philosophically justified because any other concept of Reality as a transcendental undifferentiated Being cannot have any causal relation with the universe. The acceptance of such a theory bridges the gulf between religion and philosophy because the personal God of a religion is not, and cannot be basically distinct from the ultimate Reality of philosophy.

Nature of Brahman

We now come to the consideration of the nature of the ultimate Reality. The *Taittirīya Upaniṣad* defines the nature (*svarūpa*) of Brahman in terms of *satyam*, *jñānam* and *anantam*. That is, Brahman is *satyam* or reality, *jñānam* or knowledge and *anantam* or infinite. The term *satya* means, according to Rāmānuja, absolutely non-conditioned existence of Brahman.[26] In other words, it implies the eternal self-existent and self-contained substance without being subject to any kind of modification. Brahman is *satyam* in the sense that it exists forever without undergoing any kind of change (*vikāra*). This characteristic of Brahman distinguishes it from the non-sentient matter since the latter undergoes constant change. It also distinguishes Brahman from the individual souls which are associated with physical body because the latter undergoes continuous modification through the cycle of births and deaths. The term *jñāna* means, according to Rāmānuja, eternal knowledge which is not subject to contraction and expansion.[27] When Brahman is described as *jñānam* what is meant is that Brahman possesses as its essential attribute infinite, eternal knowledge. The term *jñānam* applied to Brahman also implies that the very *svarūpa* of Brahman is knowledge.[28] According to the Viśiṣṭādvaita Vedānta, Brahman is both *jñāna-svarūpa* and *jñāna-guṇaka*.[29] The latter is also infinite in character (*asañkucita*), that is, not subject to contraction and expansion unlike the finite knowledge of the bound individual souls. By virtue of this character, Brahman is distinguished from the released souls whose knowledge was subject to contraction and expansion during the state of bondage. The term *ananta* means that which is not conditioned by space, time and another entity.[30] Brahman is *anantam* or infinite because it is omnipresent, it exists all the time and it pervades all other objects in the universe. This characteristic of Brahman distinguishes it from the souls which are eternally free (*nityas*) because the latter are monadic in character (*aṇu*). Not only the *svarūpa* of Brahman but also its attributes (*guṇas*) are infinite in the sense that they are countless and unsurpassable in excellence. These three characteristics which are thus unique to Brahman reveal its true nature (*svarūpa-nirūpaka-dharma*). In reply to the question, viz., what is the *svarūpa* of Brahman, the answer of the Viśiṣṭādvaita Vedānta is that which is characterised by *satyatva*, *jñānatva* and *anantatva*.[31] In other words, Brahma *svarūpa* is *satyam*, *jñānam* and *anantam*, as the Upaniṣad declares. These three terms do not denote the mere *svarūpa* of Brahman, as maintained by the Advaita Vedānta. On the contrary, they denote Brahman as possessing the three distinct attributes. According to the grammatical principle of *samānādhikaraṇa-vākya* (a sentence in which the terms are found in apposition), the terms which connote different qualities denote one entity as qualified by the attributes.[32]

The Upaniṣads speak of Brahman as bliss (*ānanda*). Thus says *Taittirīya Upaniṣad*: 'Brahman is known as *ānanda*.'[33] That is, Brahman is blissful in nature (*ānanda-svarūpa*). The description of Brahman as *ānanda* is meant to emphasise its aesthetic character and make it a most desired object of meditation and attainment.

Besides the four positive essential attributes, the scriptural as well as Smṛti texts describe the nature of Brahman as free from any kind of imperfection (*samasta-heyapratyanīka*). Thus says the *Bṛhadāraṇyaka Upaniṣad*: 'Brahman' is neither gross nor minute, neither short nor long etc.[34] The *Muṇḍaka Upaniṣad* describes the imperishable higher Reality as unperceivable, ungraspable, without family lineage (*agotram*), without caste, without sight or hearing, without hands or feet etc.[35] The *Chāndogya Upaniṣad* states that Brahman is free from sin, free from old age, free from death, free from sorrow, free from hunger, free from thirst etc.[36] The *Viṣṇupurāṇa* explicitly mentions that the nature of Viṣṇu is free from all imperfections.[37] Taking into consideration these negative descriptions of Brahman, Rāmānuja takes the view that defectlessness or *heyapratyanīkatva* itself constitutes an essential attribute of Brahman because it serves to distinguish Brahman from the universe comprising the souls and non-sentient matter.[38] According to the Viśiṣṭādvaita Vedānta, Brahman has a twofold aspect—*ubhayaliṅgaṁ*, as declared in the *Vedānta-sūtra*.[39] It is absolutely free from all defects and it is also endowed numerous auspicious attributes.

Brahman and its Attributes

Besides the five essential characteristics, Brahman possesses numerous other attributes. According to the Viśiṣṭādvaita Vedānta, Brahman is *ananta-kalyāṇaguṇa-viśiṣṭa*, that is, one who is qualified by infinite number of auspicious attributes. As most of these *guṇas* have theological significance, we shall take up this subject in a separate chapter.[40] We may however take note of a few important ones that have philosophical implication. The Pāñcarātra Āgamas have mentioned six attributes as very important. These are: *jñāna* or knowledge, *bala* or strength, *aiśvarya* or lordship, *vīrya* or enegry, *tejas* or splendour and *śakti* or power. The fuller meaning and significance of each of these attributes will be discussed later.[41] According to the Pāñcarātra treatises, the possession of these six qualities makes the Supreme Being perfect in all respects. All these attributes have also been acknowledged by the Upaniṣads. The *Muṇḍaka Upaniṣad* states that Brahman is omniscient (*sarvajñaḥ*) and knows everything comprehensively.[42] *Sarvajña* means, as Nāthamuni has explained, the capacity to comprehend everything in the universe as it is at all times by direct intuition without the aid of the sense organs.[43] *Jñāna* here refers to the functional or attributive knowledge of *Īśvara* as distinct from the *svarūpa-jñāna* referred to in the *Taittirīya Upaniṣad* defining Brahman as *jñānam*. Philosophically, this is the most important attribute because the creation of the universe by the Supreme Being is done by *saṅkalpa*, which is a modification of knowledge. Theologically too, *jñāna* is essential for *Īśvara* because God, as the protector and redeemer of human beings, should know their sins and their needs. *Śakti* is the other important attribute of Brahman. The *Śvetāśvatara Upaniṣad* states: 'The super divine power of the Supreme Being is revealed in different ways; so also its action manifested by *jñāna* and *bala*.'[44] The implication of this statement is that with the help of *jñāna* and *bala*, Brahman carries out the functions of creation and dissolution of the universe.[45] From the philosophical standpoint Brahman, which is the primary cause of the universe, should be endowed with *jñāna* and *śakti*. God is, therefore, conceived in all the theological systems as omniscient and omnipotent. Realizing the importance of these two attributes, Vedānta Deśika is of the view that all His other *guṇas* are only modifications of these two. The numerous other personal qualities of God which are enumerated by Rāmānuja and the Vaiṣṇava treatises are the offshoots of these six principal attributes.[46]

The most important characteristic of the ultimate Reality which has ontological significance is that Brahman is the *Śarīrī* or the Universal Self. The concept of *Śarīrī* as fully explained by Rāmānuja implies three aspects of Reality: that Brahman is the ground or source (*ādhāra*) of the entire universe; that it is the controller (*niyantā*) of all things in the universe and that it is the Lord (*śeṣī*) of all. All these have far-reaching philosophical and theological implications and need detailed examination.

Brahman as the Ground of the Universe

Brahman as the primary cause of the universe establishes the fact that it is the ground or *ādhāra* of the universe of *cit* and *acit*. The *Chāndogya Upaniṣad* also affirms that all beings have their root in the *Sat* (Brahman), that they abide in the *Sat* and that they are grounded in the *Sat*.[47] The *Sat* brings forth the universe by its will. According to the Viśiṣṭādvaita theory of cosmic evolution, which will be explained later, creation is not production of something new from what does not exist but on the contrary, it is the unfolding of what already exists in an unmanifest form into a manifested form. The *Sadvidyā* of the *Chāndogya Upaniṣad* expounds the Vedāntic truth that Brahman is the cause of the universe and by knowing that Reality everything else is known. According to the theory of causality accepted by Viśiṣṭādvaita, the effect is the modified state of the cause and the two are non-distinct in the sense that causal substance is immanent in the effected products like the lump of clay in the pot, vase, etc. The *cit* and *acit* exist in Brahman in their subtle form and Brahman by His *saṅkalpa*, causes their evolution into the manifested form. Brahman is, therefore, the material cause of the universe (*upādāna-kāraṇa*) and all beings proceed from it. This theory will be discussed in detail in a later chapter.[48] At present we may note that the universe of *cit* and *acit* has its being in Brahman and sustained by it.

Brahman as the Inner Controller of the Universe

The concept of Brahman as *śarīrī* of *cit* and *acit* constitutes the central doctrine of Viśiṣṭādvaita. It emerges from the teachings of the Upaniṣad contained in the famous dialogue between Uddālaka and Yājñavalkya in the *Bṛhadāraṇyaka Upaniṣad*. Uddālaka poses an important question to Yājñavalkya: 'Do you know that inner controller (*antaryāmin*) who controls from within this world as well as the next and all things?'[49] In reply to this question Yājñavalkya states: 'He who dwells in the earth, yet is within the earth, whom the earth does not know, whose *body* (*śarīra*) the earth is, who controls the earth from within,

He is your self (*ātmā*), the *inner controller* (*antaryāmin*), the immortal (*amṛtaḥ*).'[50] He repeats the same kind of statement twenty times covering in each statement the following entities successively including the individual soul: water (*ap*), fire (*agni*), sky (*antarikṣa*), air (*vāyu*), heaven (*divi*), sun (*āditya*), space (*dik*), moon and the stars (*candra-tāraka*), ether (*ākāśa*), darkness (*tamas*), light (*tejas*), all beings (*sarva-bhūta*), life-breath (*prāṇa*), speech (*vāk*), eye (*cakṣus*), ear (*śrotra*), mind (*manas*), skin (*tvak*), the individual self (*vijñāna* or *Ātman*)[51] and semen (*retas*). The passage which is designated as *Antaryāmi Brāhmaṇa*, covers in an exhaustive way both the non-sentient entities as well as sentient beings starting from the five elements which constitute the physical world of space and time and concluding with the subjective world of *jīva*. It emphasises that Brahman is the *antaryāmin*, the indwelling self that abides in all beings, both sentient and non-sentient, as their controller and rules them from within. As *antrātmā*, indweller within all things, Brahman is able to control them. It is, therefore, regarded as *niyantā* or the Ruler. This brings out the immanent character of Brahman. That is, Brahman is immanent in the universe. It may be noted that Brahman is in the universe but it is not the universe as the Pantheists believe. This theory of immanence gives divineness to all things in the universe. Brahman is also described by the Upaniṣad as *amṛta* or immortal. The implication of it is that even though Brahman is immanent in the universe it is transcendent and remains pure and untouched by the defects of the universe. This truth is established by the fact that Brahman by virtue of its intrinsic nature is spiritual as *jñāna-svarūpa* and also free from all imperfections (*akhila-heyapratyanīka*). The Upaniṣads declare Brahman as *apahatapāpmā*, that is, untouched by evil. This is explained by two analogies of the sun and space (*ākāśa*).[52] In the first illustration, the sun is reflected in the waves of water but the defects found in the water waves do not affect the sun. The sun is not actually present in the waves, just as *Paramātman* resides in the physical entities but the analogy is intended to convey the fact that the movements etc., found in water waves do not apply to the sun. In the second example, the space (*ākāśa*) when conditioned by several pots of varying sizes becomes manifold; but the differences in the dimension of the receptacles do not apply to the space. In the same way,

Brahman though immanent in the objects of universe, is unaffected. This is the implication of the expression *amṛta.* As stated in the *Vedānta-sūtra,* both the characteristics—*niyantṛīva* and *amṛtatva* are unique to Brahman.[53]

Brahman as Śarīrī of the Universe

By virtue of its being the controller of all beings in the universe Brahman is regarded as *Śarīrī* or the Universal Self. The word *Ātman* always refers to a *śarīra* or body as its counterpart just as a physical body is always associated with a *jīva* or soul. In the case of the Paramātman as the *śarīrin,* the entire universe comprising both sentient souls and non-sentient material entities constitute His body (*śarīra*). This is what is implied in the *Antaryāmi Brāhmaṇa.* How can earth, water etc., be body of *Īśvara*? Rāmānuja furnishes the answer by explaining the proper and fuller implications of the term *śarīra* used in the passage repeatedly twenty-one times in respect of both the physical elements such as earth etc., and the sense organs such as mind, *prāṇa* and the spiritual entity such as *jīva* (soul). The word *śarīra* understood in the ordinary sense as the aggregate of physical components with a mind and the sense organs and also as the media of action as well as experience do not apply to any of the entities included in the Upaniṣadic passage. Even among living beings, there are great variations in respect of the pattern of the physical components such as in the case of a worm, reptile, tree etc., as compared to human body. In order to fit in with every kind of the entity in the universe both physical and spiritual, Rāmānuja offers a correct definition of *śarīra.* Any substance which a sentient self can completely control and support for its own purpose and which stands to that self in an entirely dependent relation is called its *śarīra.*[54] This definition has several important implications and brings out the metaphysical relation of Brahman to the universe. The concept of *śarīra* implies four factors. Firstly, only a substance (*dravya*) in relation to a spiritual entity (*cetana*), which may be either *jīvātman* or *Paramātman,* can be qualified to be a *śarīra.* Secondly, it is to be supported by the sentient being wholly and all the time (*sarvātmanā*). Thirdly, it is to be controlled by the latter at all times, unlike the relation of a dependent servant on his master. Fourthly the substance should subserve the purpose of the spiritual being. There are three concepts involved in this relationship: *ādhāra-ādheya* (the sustainer and sustained), *niyantā-niyāmya* (the controller and controlled) and *śeṣi-śeṣa* (the master and the subservient). In the light of this explanation, all the sentient and non-sentient beings are regarded as the *śarīra* of *Īśvara* in the *technical sense*, viz., the former are wholly dependent on the latter for their existence (*sattā*), they are completely controlled by *Īśvara*; and they also subserve the purpose of the Supreme Lord. *Īśvara* is called the *śarīrin* or *Ātman* because He, as has been explained earlier, is the main support (*ādhāra*) for the entire universe of *cit* and *acit*; He is the controller (*niyantā*) and He uses it for His own purposes (*śeṣī*). The *ādhāra-ādheya* concept brings out the ontological relation of Brahman to the universe. The *niyantā-niyāmya* idea explains the spiritual and moral aspect of the relation of Brahman to the individual souls. The theory of *śeṣī-śeṣa* brings out the teleological relation of the universe to Brahman. We shall discuss these theories in a later chapter.[55] For the present we should take note of the fact that Brahman is the universal Soul (*śarīrī*) which is its distinctive characteristic according to Viśiṣṭādvaita Vedānta.

Brahman as Viśiṣṭa Reality

The above theory of Brahman as *śarīrin* connected with the universe as its *śarīra* emphasises the organic relation that obtains between the two in the same way as the individual soul (*jīva*) is organically related to the physical body. The physical body is dependent upon the soul for its very existence. When the soul leaves the body, the latter ceases to exist as a living body (a dead body is not strictly considered as body). As long as the body lasts, it is not separable from the soul. The soul is the *ādhāra*, supporter of the body. The soul also controls the body in the waking state, that is, the voluntary movements of the body take place with the will of the soul (*saṅkalpa*). The purpose of the existence of body is for the use of the soul. On the basis of the threefold concept, relationship between the *jīva* and body is described as *śārīra-śarīri-bhāva* or body-soul relation. Such a relation is not a mere *saṁyoga* or conjunction as between two separable physical objects but on the contrary, it is an inherent relation as between substance and its essential attribute. The technical word used for inherent relation is *apṛthaksiddha* or inseparability. According to the Viśiṣṭādvaita epistemology, a substance is inseparable from the attribute. If we take the example of a blue lotus, the blueness which is the attribute of lotus cannot exist independently except as inherent in the lotus. In the same way, lotus as a substance cannot be conceived devoid of the blue colour. The two together always coexist (*apṛthak-sthiti*) and also seen as integrally related (*apṛthak-pratīti*). It is an inherent relation which is the very *svarūpa* of the relata (*svarūpa-sambandha*). It is not a separate category like *samavāya* over and above the relata linking the two inseparable entities, as the Naiyāyikas postulate. Such a relation is unacceptable to the Vedāntins. *Apṛthak-siddha* is a name given to two relata which are inherently and inseparably related. This is the type of relation that holds good between *jīva* and the physical body which is technically termed as *śarīra-śarīri-bhāva*. On the basis of this analogy of *Jīva* and body, the relationship that exists between Brahman and the universe of *cit* and *acit* is also described in the Viśiṣṭādvaita Vedānta as *śarīra-śarīribhāva-sambandha*. The metaphysical implication of it is that Brahman is always inseparably related to the universe of sentient souls and non-sentient entities. This means, that both in the state of dissolution and the state after creation of the universe, Brahman is associated with *cit* and *acit*. In the state prior to creation, the *cit* and *acit* abide with Brahman in a subtle form and Brahman in that state is associated with *cit* and *acit* in their subtle state (*sūkṣma-cid-acid-viśiṣṭa*). In the state after the creation of the universe, Brahman abides with the manifested *cit* and *acit* in their gross form (*sthūla-cid-acid-viśiṣṭa*). According to the Viśiṣṭādvaita Vedānta, Brahman is always (*sarvadā*) associated with *cit* and *acit*.[56] Brahman which is considered as the primary cause of the universe (*jagatkāraṇa*) means Brahman as associated with *cit* and *acit* and not a pure undifferentiated Being. Only the *Viśiṣṭa-Brahman* or Brahman as organically related to the universe of *cit* and *acit* by virtue of its being the ground, controller and Supreme Lord of the universe is the Ultimate Reality of the Viśiṣṭādvaita metaphysics. Though *cit*, *acit* and Brahman are distinct, Brahman, the Ultimate Reality as organically related to the two dependent realities is one (*viśiṣṭa-vivakṣayā ekatva*).[57] This is the central doctrine of Viśiṣṭādvaita.

On the basis of these Upaniṣadic teachings the Vaiṣṇava

theology has formulated other theories of Reality. These are: (1) Viṣṇu or Nārāyaṇa is the same as Brahman of the Upaniṣads and that He is the Supreme Being (*paratattva*) implying that other deities such as Caturmukha Brahmā, Rudra, Indra etc., do not enjoy that status; (2) Viṣṇu is *Śriyaḥpati* or Viṣṇu as inseparably associated with Goddess *Śrī* constitutes the Ultimate Reality; (3) Viṣṇu as the Supreme Being is endowed with numerous attributes including a divine body bedecked with ornaments and weapons; (4) that Viṣṇu as a benevolent deity manifests Himself in different forms (*avatāras*) for protecting His devotees and to carry out other divine functions; (5) Viṣṇu as the supreme goal (*parama-puruṣārtha*) to be attained by the aspirants for *mokṣa* is also the means (*upāya*) for *mokṣa*. As these topics have greater theological significance, we shall discuss them separately in the section on Theology.

NOTES

1. TUp III.1. *yato va imāni bhūtāni jāyante; yena jātāni jīvanti; yat prayanty-abhisaṁviśanti; tad vijijñāsasva; tad brahmeti.*
2. VS I.1.2. *janmādyasya yataḥ.*
3. *pṛthivyādikaṁ sakartṛkaṁ, kāryatvāt, ghaṭavat.*
4. See FVV pp. 220-23.
5. VS I.1.3. *śāstra-yonitvāt.*
6. VS II.1.11. *tarkāpratiṣṭhānādapi.*
7. *Manu Smṛti*, XII.106. *ārṣaṁ dharmopadeśaṁ ca vedaśāstrāvirodhinā; yastarkeṇanusandhatte sa dharmaṁ veda netaraḥ.*
8. See ChUp VI.2.1. *sadeva somyedam-agra āsīdekamevādvitiyam.... tadaikṣata bahusyāṁ prajāyeyeti; tattejo asṛjata.*
9. See fn. 13
10. See *Atharvaśiras* Up (quoted in *Śrutaprakāśikā*, p. 18) *bṛhati bṛhmayati tasmād-ucyate paraṁbrahma.*
11. See Vp III.3.23. *bṛhatvāt brahmaṇatvācca tad-brahmety-abhidhīyate.*
12. See SD Vāda 1.
13. RB I.1.1. *brahma-śabdena ca svabhāvato nirasta-nikhila-doṣaḥ anavadhikātiśyāsaṅkhyeya-kalyāṇa-guṇa-gaṇaḥ puruṣottamo abhidhīyate.*
14. See *Śrutaprakāśikā*, I.1.1, p. 17.
15. ChUp VI.2.1 *sadeva somyedam-agra āsīt.*
16. AiUp I.1. *ātmā vā idameka evāgra āsīt.*
17. BrUp III.4.10. *brhamā vā idamekamevāgra āsīt.*
18. *Mahopaniṣad*, I.1. *eko ha vai nārāyaṇa āsīt.*
19. *Pāṇini sūtra*, 8.4.3. *pūrva-padāt saṁjñyāyāṁ.*

20. VSa p. 108.
See also RB II.1.15. pp. 485-86 and TMK III.5.
21. TNUp 93.
22. *Sūbāla* Up *eṣasarvabhūtāntarātmā apahatapāpmā divyo deva eko nārāyaṇaḥ.*
23. See RTS XXVII, p. 203.
See also Chapter 7, pp. 133-34.
24. See Chapter 7.
25. TUp II.1. *satyaṁ jñanam anantaṁ brahma.*
26. RB I.1.2. *satyapadaṁ nirupādhika sattāyogi brahma.*
27. Ibid. *jñāna-padaṁ nitya asaṅkucita jñānaikākāram-āha.*
28. See *Śrutaprakāśikā*, I.1.1 p. 114.
jñāna-śabdasya svaprakāśatārūpaṁ jñānatvaṁ pravṛttinimittam.
29. Ibid. p. 115. *ataḥ paramātmanaḥ jñānaśabdena jñānadharmakatva-jñāṅa-svarūpatvābhidhānaṁ yuktam.*
30. RB I.1.2. *anantapadaṁ deśakālavastu-pariccheda-rahitaṁ svarūpam-āha.*
31. In Viśiṣṭādvaita epistemology, a distinction is made between *svarūpa* or the essential nature of an entity and its *dharma* or the essential characteristics. The former is the substrate which is characterised by the latter (*svāsādhāraṇa-dharma-nirūpita-dharmī*). The *dharmas* are those qualities which are unique to the entity without which it cannot be even conceived. For details see Chapter 9 pp. 185-86.
32. See FVV pp. 131-37 for details regarding the logical import of *samānādhikaraṇa-vākya.*
33. TUp III. *ānando brahmeti vyajānāt.*
See also RB I.1.13. *ānandamayah paramātmā.*
34. BrUp V.8.8. *tadakṣaram. . .asthūlam, anaṇu, ahṛasvam, adīrgham, alohitam. . .*
35. MUp I.1.6. *yattad adṛeśyam agrāhyam, agotram, avarṇam, acakṣuḥ-śrotram tad-apāṇi-pādaṁ.*
36. ChUp VIII.1.5. *esa ātmā apahatapāpmā vijaro vimṛtyurviśoko vijighutso apipāsaḥ. . .*
37. VP I.22.53. *samastaheyarahitaṁ viṣṇvākhyaṁ paramaṁ padam.*
See also VP VI.5.85.
38. RB III.3.33. *heyapratyanīkohy-ānandādi brahmaṇaḥ asādhāraṇaṁ rūpam.*
39. VS III.2.11. *na sthānato'pi parasyo-bhayaliṅgaṁ sarvatra hi.*
40. See Chapter 9.
41. Ibid.
42. MUp I.1.10. *yasarvajñaḥ sarvavit yasya jñānamayaṁ tapaḥ.*
43. *Nyāyatattva* (quoted by Vedānta Deśika in GaBh p. 111).
yo vetti yugapat sarvaṁ pratyakṣeṇa sadā svataḥ.
44. SvUp VI.8. *parāsya śaktir-vividhaiva śrūyate svābhāvikī jñānabala-kriyā ca.*
45. See RRB p. 432.
46. See TMK V.97. *ṣāḍguṇyasyaiva kukṣau guṇagaṇa itaraḥ śrīsakhasyeva viśvam.*

47. See ChUp VI.8.4. *sanmūlāḥ saumyemāḥ sarvāḥ prajāḥ sadāyatanāḥ sat-pratiṣṭāḥ.*
48. See Chapter 4.
49. BrUp V.7.2.
50. Ibid. V.7.7. *yaḥ pṛthivyāṁ tiṣṭhan pṛthivyā antaro yaṁ pṛthivī na veda, yasya pṛthivī śarīram, yaḥ pṛthivīm-antaro yamayati, yeṣa ta ātmā antaryāmy-amṛtaḥ.*
51. There are two recensions—Kāṇva and Mādhyandina—of this text. In the latter, the word *ātman* is used in place of *vijñāna* mentioned in the former. On the basis of it Rāmānuja interprets *vijñāna* as the very individual self (*ātman*).
52. See VS III.2.18 and 20.
53. See VS III.2.11 and 20.
54. See RB II.1.9. *yasya cetanasya yaddravyaṁ sarvātmanā svārthe niyantuṁ dhārayituṁ ca śakyam, taccheṣataikasvarūpam ca, tat tasya śarīram-iti śarīralakṣaṇam.*
55. See Chapter 4.
56. See RB II.3.18. *ataḥ sarvadā cid-acid-vastu-śarīratayā tat-prakaraṁ brahma.*
57. See NS p. 1. *prakāra-prakāriṇoḥ prakārāṇāṁ ca mitho atyanta-bhede'pi viśiṣṭaikyādi-vivakṣayā ekatva vyapadeśaḥ.*

3

THE DOCTRINE OF INDIVIDUAL SELF

In this chapter we shall examine the philosophic doctrine of *jīva* or the individual self as enunciated in the Vedānta. The Upaniṣads speak of the existence of *jīva* as a real spiritual entity and also as distinct from *Īśvara*. The classic illustration offered by the *Muṇḍaka Upaniṣad*[1] of the two birds of the same character sitting on the same tree, one eating the sweet fruit and the other looking on without eating, brings out clearly the distinction between the *jīva* and *Īśvara*. Both are sentient beings (*cetanas*) but the former caught up in bondage is subject to the experience of the fruits of *karma*, whereas the latter is untouched by it. There are numerous other passages bringing out the difference between *Īśvara* and the *jīva* in terms of the ruler and the ruled, the all-knowing and the ignorant and the independent and the dependent.[2] Though both are spiritual in character, Brahman is infinite (*vibhu*), whereas the *jīva* is monadic in substance (*aṇu*). In view of this, the Viśiṣṭādvaita Vedānta has admitted *jīva* as a separate reality (*tattva*) and therefore, a detailed study of this doctrine is called for.

The word *jīva* means that which lives or sustains life (*jīvati iti jīvah*). It is also known as *ātman*, a term which is more often used in the Upaniṣads. The word *ātman* means that which pervades the body (*āpnoti iti*). It is applicable to both Brahman and the individual soul and in order to distinguish between the two, the terms *Paramātman* and *jīvātman* are used respectively. The other terms used for *jīva* are *cit* or *cetana*, that which has consciousness, *kṣetrajña* or the knower of the field of knowledge and *ahaṁ-padārtha* or the entity denoted by 'I'. All these terms are synonymous in Viśiṣṭādvaita.

Jīva as Eternal

Jīva is an eternal spiritual entity. It is eternal (*nitya*) in the sense that it is neither born nor does it die, as stated in the *Kaṭha Upaniṣad* and the *Bhagavad-gītā*.[3] The birth and death of an individual is the association and dissociation respectively of a physical body with the soul. Due to the bondage caused by the beginningless *avidyā* or ignorance of the true nature of the self, *jīva* passes through the cycle of births and deaths until it attains final liberation from *karma* by means of prescribed spiritual discipline. We shall discuss this in greater detail in a later chapter.

Jīva as the Subject of Knowledge

Jīva is essentially of the nature of knowledge (*jñāna-svarūpa*). The *Bṛhadāraṇyaka Upaniṣad* describes the self as a mass of intelligence only (*prajñānaghana eva*).[4] The implication of it is that it is not material but spiritual in character (*ajaḍa*). As a non-material entity it is different from the physical body, sense organs, vital breath (*prāṇa*), mind (*manas*) and intellect (*buddhi*).[5]

According to the Viśiṣṭādvaita Vedānta, the individual self is not merely of the nature of knowledge but it possesses knowledge as its essential attribute. In other words, it is the subject of knowledge (*jñātā*). The knowledge which is an attribute (*dharma*) of *jīva* is technically called as *dharmabhūta-jñāna* or attributive knowledge to distinguish it from the *svarūpa-jñāna* or knowledge that constitutes the very *svarūpa* of *jīva*. The basis for admission of *dharmabhūta-jñāna* is the Upaniṣadic text which states explicitly that *jīva* is the knower (*boddhā*). Thus says the *Praśna Upaniṣad*: 'This self (*puruṣa*) which is of the nature of consciousness (*vijñānātmā*) is verily the seer, the toucher, the hearer, the smeller, the taster, the knower (*boddhā*), the doer.'[6] The two terms—*vijñānātmā* and *boddhā*—used in this statement signify that the individual self is not merely of the nature of consciousness but it is also the knower or subject of knowledge. There is also a logical justification for admitting knowledge as a quality of the self. The self is immutable and if the functions such as knowing, feeling and willing pertain directly to the self, it would be subject to modification. In order to uphold the unchanging character of *ātman*, the *dharmabhūta-jñāna* is to be necessarily admitted. The modifications take place only in respect of the attributive knowledge, while its substrate remains unaffected by them. According to the theory of substance and attribute advanced by Viśiṣṭādvaita, the changes taking place in the attribute do not affect the substance, in the same way as the bodily changes such as boyhood, youth and old age do not apply to the self within. Based on the teachings of the Upaniṣads, the *Vedānta-sūtra* also states that *ātman* is a knower.[7] Commenting on this *Sūtra*, Rāmānuja explains that *jīvātman* is essentially a knower and not either mere knowledge, as the Advaitin contends or non-sentient in character (*jaḍa-svarūpa*), as Naiyāyikas believe.[8]

It may be asked whether it would be appropriate to regard the self which is of the nature of *jñāna* as a substrate for another knowledge as its attribute. As the substance and attribute are of the same nature, how can the former serve as a substrate for the latter? Such a possibility is admitted by the Viśiṣṭādvaitin. Knowledge in this system means that which reveals something (*artha-prakāśaḥ*). The self reveals itself and the attributive knowledge reveals the objects. As both reveal something, the term *jñāna* is applicable to both. Nevertheless, it is possible to conceive two entities of the same nature as substance and attribute. The flame of a lamp (*dīpa*) for instance, is of the same character as its luminosity (*prabhā*) in so far as brightness (*tejas*) is common to both, but the two are nevertheless distinct as substance and attribute. They are also different functionally; the flame illumines itself, whereas its luminosity (*prabhā*) illumines itself as well as other objects. In the same way, *jīva* and its attributive knowledge, though they may have a common characteristic feature, are distinct as substance and attribute.[9] They are also different in respect of their functions. *Jīva* constituted of knowledge which is known as *dharmi-jñāna* or substantive-knowledge reveals itself and not the external objects; it knows what is revealed to it. On the other hand, knowledge as the essential attribute of the self known as *dharmabhūta-jñāna* or attributive knowledge reveals itself as well as the external objects to the self and does not *know* them. In other words, the self (*ātman*) *knows* what is revealed to it by knowledge, whereas knowledge only *shows* but cannot *know*. The functional knowledge is comparable to a light which reveals the presence of an object but it does not know it. What is capable of knowing the object thus revealed is the self. Though the self is regarded as constituted of *jñāna* (*jñāna-svarūpa*) in order to emphasise its spiritual character, it cannot reveal the objects outside it. This revelation of external objects is the function of *dharmabhūta-jñāna* and not that of *dharmi-jñāna*. To make this distinction very clear the Viśiṣṭādvaita epistemology uses the two technical terms *pratyak* and *parāk* for self and its knowledge respectively. *Pratyak* means that which only *knows* but does not reveal the objects outside it except itself. It is also known as *svasmai-bhāsamānatva* or what reveals for itself. Both *jīva* and *Īśvara* come under this category. *Parāk* means that which only reveals to the *ātman* but does not know what it reveals. This is also described as *parasmā-eva-bhāsamānatva* or that which reveals the objects always for a knowing subject. The *dharmabhūta-jñāna* and another metaphysical category known as *śuddha-sattva*[10] or transcendental spiritual substance admitted in Viśiṣṭādvaita come under this category. The terms *cetana* and *acetana* are also used to describe these two categories of entities. *Cetana* means that which possesses consciousness (*caitanyaviśiṣṭa*). Both *Īśvara* and *jīva* are *cetanas*. *Acetana* means that which is devoid of consciousness. Both *dharmabhūta-jñāna* and *śuddha-sattva* are of this type. The term *acetana* is not to be confused with the term *jaḍa*. The latter is absolutely non-intelligent like a piece of stone and does not, therefore, possess the capacity to reveal anything, whereas, the former has such a power. This kind of categorisation of spiritual and material objects is unique to Viśiṣṭādvaita.

Jīva as Self-luminous

Jīva by virtue of its being of the nature of knowledge is self-luminous (*svayaṁprakāśa*). The term self-luminosity means in Viśiṣṭādvaita that which reveals itself without the aid of knowledge. It is applicable to the spiritual entities such as *Īśvara*, *jīva*, *jñāna* and *śuddha-sattva*. All these entities are self-revealed unlike the physical objects which need to be manifested by another knowledge. Knowledge, for instance, while revealing an object to the subject (self) does not require another knowledge to reveal it. The closest analogy to explain this point is the light (*dīpa*). Light reveals the object around it but does not require another light for it to be revealed. When cognition of an object arises, it simultaneously reveals both itself and the object.[11] This is possible because self-luminosity is the intrinsic capacity of knowledge even as heat is the intrinsic capacity of fire. In the same way *ātman* which is of the nature of knowledge is regarded as self-luminous, because it does not require another knowledge for its manifestation. It is known by itself and is not in need of another knowledge to know it. It manifests always as 'I' (*ahaṁ ātmā iti svenaiya siddhyati*).[12] According to the Viśiṣṭādvaitin, the entity denoted by 'I' (*ahamartha*) is the true self.[13] It is not the same as *ahaṁkāra* or the psychological ego which is caused by the delusion that the physical body itself is the soul. That the self is self-luminous is also upheld by the scriptural text. Thus says the *Bṛhadāraṇayaka Upaniṣad*: 'The self in that state (in the state of dreamless sleep) becomes self-luminous.'[14]

Jīva as Aṇu

Another distinctive character of the *jīva*, according to the Viśiṣṭādvaita Vedānta, is that it is *aṇu* or monadic in substance. The main justification for accepting this view is that the Upaniṣads describe *jīva* as infinitesimal. Thus says the *Muṇḍaka Upaniṣad*: 'This ātman is *aṇu* and to be known by mind.'[15] The *Śvetāśvatara Upaniṣad* describes the self as infinitely smaller than the hundredth part of the point of a hair divided a hundred times and yet it is infinite in range.[16] The *Bṛhadāraṇyaka Upaniṣad* speaks of the exit of *jīva* from the body after death.[17] The *Kauśītakī Upaniṣad* refers to its movement to the realm of moon.[18] The *Bṛhadāraṇyaka Upaniṣad* also speaks of its return to the earth to experience the effect of *karma*.[19] If the *jīva* were *vibhu* or all-pervasive as Naiyāyikas believe, such a movement is inconceivable. What is *vibhu* cannot have any movement. If it were of the size of the body of the individual which it occupies, as the Jainas believe, it would be subject to mutation corresponding to the sizes of the bodies it occupies. To overcome all these difficulties, the Viśiṣṭādvaita Vedānta upholds the theory of *jīva* as *aṇu* on the strength of the Upaniṣadic authority.[20] Even though *jīva* is infinitesimal, its attributive knowledge (*jñāna*) possesses the intrinsic capacity of becoming infinite (*vibhu*) in the state of *mokṣa* after it becomes totally free from *karma*, as stated in the *Chāndogya Upaniṣad*.[21] In Viśiṣṭādvaita *jīvas* are classified into three types: *baddhas* or those in bondage, *muktas* or those which are free from bondage and *nityas* or those which are eternally free. The *baddha-jīvas* are not omniscient as their knowledge is subject to contraction and expansion due to the influence of *karma*, whereas the other two types of *jīvas* are omniscient being totally free from obstructive factors.

Jīva as Kartā and Bhoktā

We have observed that *jīva* is the knower (*jñātā*) or the subject of knowledge. *Jīva* which is the knower is also the agent of action (*kartā*) and the enjoyer of pleasure and pain (*bhoktā*). This truth is evidenced not only by our perceptual experience but also by the scriptural text. The same Upaniṣadic text which speaks of *jīva* as *boddhā* or knower, asserts that it is also *kartā*.[22] It stands to reason that the same *jīvātman* which performs a particular deed (*karma*) should also enjoy the fruit of the deed. This apart, the scriptural texts which enjoin the performance of Vedic rites by an individual would become meaningless if the *jīvātman* were not admitted as both the agent of action and the enjoyer of the result. Hence the author of the *Vedānta-sūtra* says: '*Jīva* is an agent on account of Scripture (thus) having a purport.'[23] Commenting on this sūtra, Rāmānuja explains that when sacred texts (*śāstra*) enjoin the performance of *upāsanā* for attaining *mokṣa* or the performance of a Vedic ritual for the achievement of heaven, they are addressed only to the intelligent agents of action who can enjoy the fruit. *Śāstra* means to command (*śāsanācca śāstram*). A command is intended to induce one to do a particular act and it is meaningful only in respect of an intelligent agent and not for one who is non-sentient (*acetana*). In view of this an individual who is intelligent to understand a command, is actually the agent of action and he alone is the enjoyer of the fruit of action.

The admission of knowership, doership etc., in respect of *ātman* does not affect the immutable character of *jīvātman*. Cognisership, according to the Advaita Vedānta, involves change and in order to overcome this problem, all the psychological functions such as knowing, feeling and willing are attributed to the empirical ego, which is the consciousness conditioned by internal organ (*antaḥkaraṇāvacchinna-caitanya*). According to the Advaitin, cognisership actually belongs to the internal organ and the self appears to be the knower because of the superimposition of the internal organ on it. But this theory has serious limitations. According to Rāmānuja, superimposition of cognisership on the self is an impossibility. He, therefore, rejects this theory. Cognisership, it is pointed out, does not affect the immutable character of *jīvātman*, because a transformation in the form of change (*vikāra*) from one state to another as in the case of the lump of clay into jug does not take place in the self by its being an agent of knowledge. Whatever modifications take place in the process of knowing apply directly to the attributive knowledge which is distinct from the self which is the substrate for knowledge. Since a change in the attribute does not affect its substrate, the immutable character of the self is not affected by virtue of its becoming a knower (*jñātā*).

If we understand clearly in what sense *jīva* is *jñātā, kartā* and *bhoktā*, the above objection does not arise. As already explained, *jīva* is regarded as *jñātā* in the sense that it is the *āśraya* or substrate for the functional knowledge through which all experiences take place. By merely being an *āśraya* for *jñāna* which is actually subject to modification, *jīva* remains unchanged. In the same way, *jīva* is *kartā* or doer in the sense that it is the *āśraya* or substrate for *kṛti* (effort).[24] Effort is caused by a desire to do an act. The desire is a mental modification, an *avasthā* of *jñāna*. It is not to be confused with the actual physical activity which follows subsequent to the desire to do an act. In so far as *jīva* is an *āśraya* for *kṛti* or *prayatna* prompted by desire which is actually a particular state of the knowledge, *jīva* becomes the *kartā*. The change involved in the physical activity pertains directly to the body and sense organs and it does not affect the soul which is only a substrate for knowledge.

The same explanation holds good for *jīva* being the *bhoktā* or one who is the enjoyer of pleasure and pain. *Bhoga* is an experience in the form of pleasure or pain. Pleasure and pain are different states of *jñāna*. Pleasure, according to Viśiṣṭādvaita, is an agreeable disposition of the knowledge (*anukūla-jñāna*) and pain is its disagreeable disposition (*pratikūla-jñāna*). As *jīva* is *āśraya* for such states of experience, it is regarded as *bhoktā* or enjoyer of pleasure and pain. The changes involved in such mental disposition apply to the attributive knowledge and not to *jīva*. It is logically possible to maintain this position since according to Viśiṣṭādvaita, a substance is distinct from its attribute and what pertains to the latter does not directly apply to the former.

Though *jīvātman* is a *kartā*, its action (*kartṛtva*) is caused by *Paramātman* as stated by the *Vedānta-sūtra* which is based on the Śruti and Smṛti texts.[25] The *Bṛhadāraṇyaka Upaniṣad* to which we have referred earlier, points out that *Paramātman* as the indweller of all beings controls them.[26] Another scriptural text explicitly says: '*Īśvara* controls all individuals by residing within their bodies.'[27] The *Bhagavad-gītā* also reiterates that *Īśvara* resides in the hearts of all beings and thereby controls their activities by his divine power.[28] On the authority of these scriptural statements the Viśiṣṭādvaita Vedānta maintains the view that the activities of *jīvātman* are controlled by *Paramātman*.

Freedom of the Individual

This raises an important question related to the freedom of an individual. If the action of *jīva* is controlled by *Paramātman*, does the individual have any freedom at all to act? If he had no freedom to act, it would follow that scriptural injunctions enjoining certain moral duties would have no significance. Rāmānuja provides an answer to this question on the basis of the *Vedānta-sūtra*. A distinction is drawn between the initial action of an individual and the activities that follow subsequently. In all human effort, the individual initially *wills* to do a thing by exercising the mental faculty provided to all human beings by God as the creator of the universe. To this extent, he is free to do what he so desires. This desire arises as a result of the influence of the latent tendencies (*vāsanā*) acquired by the individual from his *karma* or deeds of the past. In the matter of initial action, God's will has no part to play. *Īśvara* remains a passive spectator (*upekṣaka*) allowing the law of *karma* to take its own course. It is entirely the choice of an individual and to this extent he is free to think and initiate any activity. Based on this initial action, the activity which subsequently follows is approved by *Īśvara* (*anumantā*). By according such an approval, *Īśvara* as *antaryāmin* prompts the individual to proceed further.[29] Were it not so, the Vedic injunctions in this regard would lose their value. By merely giving an approval to the activity initiated by an individual, *Īśvara* does not become a *kartā* or the doer. The actual *kartā* is the individual himself. The initial action, for which the individual has the responsibility, determines the moral responsibility of that individual. The mere according of an approval to an initial act does not put any blame on *Īśvara*. If God only accords mere approval to the subsequent act and remains a passive spectator of the subsequent act without preventing a sinful action, it is because the individual who primarily acts under the influence of his past *karma* is allowed to reap the consequences of his *karma*. There are two kinds of causal factors in the moral world: a general cause (*sādhāraṇa-kāraṇa*) and specific cause (*viśeṣa-kāraṇa*). For instance, the rainwater, which falls on a particular piece of land, is a common cause for the growth of plants. The special effort made by an individual to cultivate the land with the help of the rainwater is the special cause for getting a better yield on that land. In the same way, God acts as a general cause because he has granted to everyone the faculty to think and the physical ability to function. The individual is the special cause since he exercises his innate mental faculty and physical power granted to him by a compassionate God. The special effort is responsible for the final result. In this regard, God has no role to play. Any failure on the part of the individual to exercise his other abilities is not and cannot be the fault of *Īśvara*. Thus, the freedom given by God to an individual does not in any way affect the freedom of *Īśvara*. The issue relating to the absolute dependence of the *jīva* on *Īśvara* versus the freedom of the soul from ethical and religious point of view is discussed in a later chapter.[30]

Plurality of Jīvas

Before we go to the next important topic of the relation of *jīva* to *Īśvara*, we may take note of another theory regarding the plurality of *jīvas*. According to the Viśiṣṭādvaita Vedānta, *jīvas* are infinite in number and are also different from one another. Both the *Kaṭhopaniṣad* and *Śvetāśvatara Upaniṣad* say that ***cetanas*** (the individual selves) are eternal and many (***nityānāṁ bahūnāṁ cetanānām***).[31] Apart from this scriptural authority, the plurality of selves is evident from our own experience. The fact that knowledge, memory, desire, happiness and suffering, birth and death pertaining to each individual differ from each other proves that *jīvas* are different from one another. Otherwise, everybody would be conscious of the feelings and thought of everyone else. Except on the ground of each *jīva* being different from another it is not possible to explain satisfactorily the variation in experiences of different individuals.

Other theories are put forward by the Advaita Vedānta which do not admit the plurality of individual souls. According to the Advaitin true self which is the very Brahman is the only one Ultimate Reality but the same appears as many due to the cosmic ignorance known as *māyā* or *avidyā*. The plurality of *jīvas* which is apparent to our ordinary experience is explained on the basis of limiting adjuncts (*upādhi*). The one true self or *ātman* when conditioned by different internal organs (*antaḥkaraṇa*) are regarded as *jīvas*, in the same way as one *ākāśa* or space becomes many when conditioned by different pots. The plurality is also explained in a different way on the analogy of the single moon appearing as many when it is reflected in the waves. The self which is claimed to be one, appears as many when reflected in the different internal organs. Both these theories are rejected by the Viśiṣṭādvaitin as unsound. The major defect is that with the removal of the adjuncts causing the appearance of one as many, the *jīvas* cease to exist. Apart from the fact that the unreality of *jīvas* goes against scriptural teaching, it does not explain satisfactorily the concept of bondage and release of different souls from the bondage. It does not also account for the individual's endeavour to attain *mokṣa* by pursuing the prescribed spiritual discipline. If *jīvas* were illusory in character, there would be no point in any of their endeavours to attain a positive spiritual goal. The very doctrine of *māyā*, on the basis of which the 'one' appearing as 'many' is sought to be explained, stands refuted since it is riddled with contradictions.[32] Hence the Viśiṣṭādvaitin asserts, on the authority of both the scripture and experience, that *jīvas* are eternal and infinite in number.

Jīva as an Integral Part of Brahman

The *jīvas* as eternal spiritual entities are not only different from each other but are also distinct from Brahman. As we have observed earlier, the Upaniṣads teach that they are distinct realities. The *Śvetāśvatara Upaniṣad* says: 'There are two, the one omniscient and the other ignorant, both unborn, the one a ruler and the other not a ruler.'[33] The *Muṇḍaka Upaniṣad* describes *jīva* as one caught up in bondage, whereas *Īśvara* is free from it.[34] The famous statement of the *Antaryāmi Brāhmaṇa* referring to *Paramātman* as the indweller of *jivātman* is a clear proof of the distinction between two real entities. The ontological position of Brahman as the primary source of all sentient beings and non-sentient material entities in the universe brings out the distinction between the two as the independent and dependent.

The scriptural texts also speak of non-difference between Brahman and *jīva*. Thus says the *Chāndogya Upaniṣad*: 'Thou art that' (*tattvamasi*).[35] The *Bṛhadāraṇyaka* equally asserts the identity: 'This self is Brahman' (*Ayam-ātmā-Brahma*).[36] The non-dualists give greater importance and validity to these statements and thus uphold the identity of *jīva* and Brahman. They contend that this is the true purport of the Upaniṣadic teaching. On the contrary, the dualists accord greater significance and validity to the statements pointing out the difference between the *jīva* and Brahman and reject the theory of identity. As a compromise between the two extreme views, a school of thought represented by Bhāskara and Yādava subscribes to the view that there is difference as well as non-difference between *jīva* and Brahman. All these theories are unacceptable to the Viśiṣṭādvaita Vedānta. This is not a place to discuss the details of the criticism which are largely based on the interpretation of the concerned scriptural texts, and in particular the famous *Chāndogya* maxim *Tattvamasi*. It would suffice to note that the views of the non-dualists and dualists do not afford equal validity to all the Upaniṣadic texts which speak both difference as well as non-difference between the *jīva* and Brahman. Rāmānuja upholds the validity of all the texts by reconciling the apparent contradictions in the texts. He adopts for this purpose an ontological principle enunciated in the *Bṛhadāraṇyaka Upaniṣad*.

The *Antaryāmi Brāhmaṇa* of the *Bṛhadāraṇyaka* states repeatedly that Brahman abides as the inner controller in all the sentient and non-sentient entities in the universe. The latter are described as *śarīra* or body for *Paramātman*, whereas the former is the universal Self (*śarīrī*) controlling them from within. The implications of this ontological relation of Brahman and the universe as *śarīra* and *śarīrī* have been explained in an earlier chapter. This relation which is organic in nature is analogous to the relation of the soul to the physical body. It is also comparable to the logical relation of substance and attribute. According to the Viśiṣṭādvaita epistemology, an attribute is distinct by its very nature from the substance. But at the same time, the attribute cannot exist independently except as inherent in the substance. Similarly, the substance, though not dependent in the same manner on the attribute, cannot be conceived except in terms of the essential attributes. The two are inseparable (*apṛthaksiddha*) because the two exist together and also are apprehended together. Because of this inseparable character of the two relata, the substance as qualified with the attribute is taken as one entity. In other words, as substance and quality, they are distinct but as substance qualified by the attribute, it constitutes a single entity. Thus, wherever two entities are found inseparable it is possible to speak of difference as well as non-difference. Where two entities are separable, as between a pot and a vase, we can speak of only absolute difference and not non-difference too. The same logical principle is involved in the ontological relation of Brahman to the universe as *śarīrī* and *śarīra* enunciated in the *Antaryāmi Brāhmaṇa*. On the basis of this sound principle of relation, Rāmānuja reconciles the apparent conflict between the *bheda-śrutis*, (the texts speaking of difference between ontological realities) and *abheda-śrutis*, (the texts speaking of non-difference between such entities). The statements of *Antaryāmi Brāhmaṇa* provide the clue to resolve this conflict and hence these are regarded as *ghaṭaka—śrutis* or texts that provide the reconciliation.

In this context, we have to understand the relation of *jīva* to *Paramātman* or Brahman. The *Vedānta-sūtra*[37] uses the term *aṁśa* or part, to describe the relationship between the two. The author of the aphorism in using this expression seems to acknowledge both the views regarding the jīva-Brahman relation as is evident from the two phrases used in the *sūtra* viz., *nānā vyapadeśāt* which means because of the declaration of difference and also *anyathā ca* which means otherwise (as non-difference). In order to maintain the truth of both these views, Rāmānuja states that we should admit that jīva is an *aṁśa* or an integral part of Brahman.[38]

What is meant by *aṁśa* and how does this concept support both the views? *Aṁśa* or part does not mean a spatial part of the whole, because the soul as a spiritual entity does not admit of any spatial division. Nor is Brahman a quantitative infinite of which soul is a part. The term *aṁśa* is, therefore, defined by Rāmānuja as that which constitutes an integral part of an entity (*eka-vastu eka-deśatvaṁ hy-aṁśatvam*). What is meant by part of a whole is that it is an essential attribute of a complex whole (*viśiṣṭasya ekasya vastunaḥ viśeṣaṇam aṁśa eva*).[39] Thus, for instance, the luminosity radiating from a luminous body such as fire or sun is part of that body; the generic characteristic of a cow (*gotva*) as its essential attribute is part of the cow in which it inheres. In the same way, *jīva* is regarded as an integral part of Brahman. As we have already explained, there is a relationship between Brahman and *jīva* as *śarīrī* and *śarīra* and it is, therefore, justified to treat *jīva* as an integral part of Brahman in the ontological sense of 'supporter' and 'supported' and the 'ruler' and the 'ruled'. The terms *aṁśī* and *aṁśa* in the present context are synonymous with the terms of *śarīrī* and *śarīra*.[40] On the basis of the logical concept of substance and attribute, it is justifiable to speak of the difference between *Paramātman* and *jīvātman* by virtue of their different intrinsic character and also of non-difference as a *viśiṣṭa* entity or Brahman as integrally related to the *jīvātman*. From the religious point of view, *jīva* is regarded as *śeṣa*, as one who subserves God and God as *Śeṣin*, the Lord of all. We have already discussed the fuller ontological implications of *śarīri-śarīra-bhāva* in an earlier chapter. Accordingly, *jīva* is *ādheya* or the one who is controlled by *Paramātman*. We shall discuss the fuller theological implications of *jīva* as *śeṣa* or dependent on *Īśvara* in a later chapter.[41] From the philosophical point of view, *jīva* is an integral part of Brahman, and it is distinct but inseparable from it.

Notes

1. MUp III.1.1. *dvā suparṇā sayujā sakhāyā samānaṁ vṛkṣaṁ pariṣasvajāte; tayoranyaḥ pippalaṁ svādvatti anaśnan anyo abhicākaśīti.*
   See also VS II.1.22. *adhikaṁ tu bhedanirdeśāt.*
2. SvUp I.9. *jñā-jñau dvau ajau īśanīśau.*
   See also BrUp V.7.22.
3. KaUp 2.18. *na jāyate mriyate vā vipaścit...ajo nityaḥ śāśvato'yam purāṇo na hanyate hanyamāne śarīre.*
   See also BG II.20.
4. BrUp VI.5.13. *ayamātmā anantaroabāhyaḥ kṛtsnaḥ prajñānaghana eva.*

5. See *Ātmasiddhi*, p. 8. *dehendriya-manaḥ-prāṇa-dhībhyo anyaḥ.* For details see FVV pp. 188-90.
6. *Praśna* Up IV.9. *eṣa hi draṣṭā spraṣṭā śrotrā ghrātā rasayitā mantā boddhā kartā vijñānātmā puruṣaḥ.*
7. VS II.3.19. *jño' ta eva.*
8. RB II.3.19. *ayamātmā jñātṛsvarūpa eva, na jñānamātram, nāpi jaḍasvarūpaḥ.*
9. See RB 1.1.1 p. 69. See also NP p. 213. *svasyaiva bhāsako dīpaḥ svātmano anyasya ca prabhā; evaṁ bhedo' sti sāmye' pi jñānayoḥ dharma-dharmiṇoḥ.*
10. See Chapter 11.
11. See FVV pp. 142-44 for details.
12. TMK II.6.
13. See RB I.1.1 pp. 68-69 for details. Also AV pp. 62-65.
14. BrUp VI.3.9. *atra' yam puruṣah svayaṁjyotirbhavati.*
15. MUp 3.1.9. *eṣo aṇurātmā cetasā veditavyaḥ.* According to the interpretation of Rāmānuja, *ātman* in this text refers to jīvātman. See RB II.3.23.
16. SvUp V.9. *vālāgraśatabhāgasya śatadhā kalpitasya ca; bhāgo jīvassa vijñeyaḥ.*
17. BrUp VI.4.2.
18. *Kauṣitakī* Up I.9.
19. BrUp VI.4.6.
20. RB II.3.20 and II.3.23.
21. ChUp VII.26.2. *sarvaṁ ha paśyaḥ paśyati sarvam-āpnoti sarvaśaḥ.*
22. *Praśna* Up IV.9. See fn 6.
23. VS II.3.33. *kartā śāstrārthavattvāt.*
24. See GB XIII.20. *Śarīrādhiṣṭhāna-prayatna-hetutvameva hi puruṣasya kartṛtvam.*
25. VS II.3.40. *parāttu tat śruteḥ.* See RB *paramātmana eva hetoḥ bhavati.*
26. BrUp. V.7.22.
27. *Taittirīya Āraṇyaka*, III.11.10. *antaḥ praviṣṭaḥ śāstā janānāṁ sarvātmā.*
28. BG XVIII.61. *īśvaras-sarvabhūtānāṁ hṛddeśe arjuna tiṣṭati; bhrāmayan sarvabhūtāni yantrārūḍhāni māyayā.*
29. RB II.3.41. *sarvāsu kriyāsu puruṣeṇa kṛtaṁ prayatnam-udyogam-apekṣya antaryāmī paramātmā tadanumatidānena pravartayati.* See *Śrutaprakāśikā*, vol. II pp. 377-79 for detailed explanation. See also TC XVIII.15.
30. See Chapter 11.
31. KaUp II.2.13. and SvUp VI.13. *nityo nityānāṁ cetanaścetanānām-eko bahūnāṁ yo vidadhāti kāmān.* According to the interpretation of Rāmānuja the text is taken to read

as *nityānāṁ bahūnāṁ cetanānāṁ* (the several eternal souls). Śaṁkara's commentary reads the *kaṭha* text as *nityaḥ anityānāṁ cetanānāṁ* (the many non-eternal souls). Even if we take the reading of Śaṁkara, (*anityānāṁ cetanānāṁ*) it does not militate against the theory of plurality of selves. The eternal souls may be regarded as *anitya* with reference to the changing character of its attributive knowledge. See RRB p. 433.

32. See SD Vāda 36 for details reg. the criticism of Advaita theory of jīvas. See also FVV pp. 203-07.
33. SvUp I.9. *jñā-jñau dvau ajau iśanīśau.*
34. MUp III.1.1. see fn 1
35. ChUp VI.8.7. *aitadātmyamidaṁ sarvam; tat satyam; sa ātmā; tat tvamasi śvetaketo iti.*
36. BrUp VI.4.5.
37. VS II.3.42. *aṁśo nānāvyapadeśād-anyathā-cāpi daśakitavāditvam-adhīyata eke.*
38. RB II.3.42. *ata ubhayavyapadeśopapattaye jivo'yam brahmaṇo'ṁśa ityabhyupetyam.*
39. Ibid. II.3.45.
40. The *śarīra-śarīri* relation in Viśiṣṭādvaita system is not different from the logical relation of *aṁśa-aṁśi* or *viśeṣya-viśeṣaṇa* (substance and attribute). If an integral relation exists between a sentient soul and a substance (*dravya*) which may be either a spiritual one or a material one, such a relation is known by the terms of *śarīri* and *śarīra*. If, on the other hand, such a relation is found between a substance and its attribute such as a flower and its fragrance, it is termed as *aṁśi-aṁśa* or *viśeṣya-viśeṣaṇa* or *prakāri-prakāra*. In the present case, since both *Iśvara* and *jīva* are *cetana dravyas* (sentient entities), the description of their relation as *aṁśi-aṁśa* means same as *śarīri-śarīra-bhāva*.
41. See Chapter 12.

4

THE DOCTRINE OF COSMIC MATTER

On the basis of the Upaniṣadic teaching the Viśiṣṭādvaita Vedānta has admitted three real and distinct ontological entities—*Īśvara* (god), *cit* (soul) and *acit* (cosmic matter). We have considered the first two in the earlier chapters and shown how these philosophical theories have provided the basis for the theological doctrines of Vaiṣṇavism. With the same objective, we shall now examine the philosophical doctrine of the cosmic matter.

The word *acit* means that which does not have consciousness as contrasted to *cit*, which possesses knowledge. All material objects are *acit* or non-sentient, while all spiritual entities are *cit* or sentient in character. The terms *cetana* and *acetana* are also used to cover the sentient and non-sentient entities. The three kinds of individual souls come under the category of *cetana* entities. The *acetana* entities, according to the Viśiṣṭādvaita Vedānta are three. These are: (*a*) *Prakṛti* or the primordial cosmic matter along with all its evolutes including the material universe; (*b*) *Nitya-vibhūti* or the transcendental spiritual universe constituted of pure unalloyed *sāttvika* substance (*śuddha-sattva*); and (*c*) *Kāla* or time with all its modifications in terms of moments, minutes, hours, days, months, years etc. *Nitya-vibhūti* is a spiritual concept formulated on the basis of the scriptural authority, to account for certain theological doctrines. We shall, therefore, deal with it in a separate chapter under Theology and examine here the other two topics.

The Concept of Prakṛti

The word *prakṛti* means that which gives rise to various modifications (*vikārān prakaroti iti*).[1] It refers to the primordial cosmic matter from which the various evolutes such as *mahat*, *ahaṁkāra* etc., originate. The existence of such a primordial substance is accepted by the Sāṅkhya system and the Vedānta in order to explain a causal beginning for the physical universe of five elements. While the Sāṅkhya school adopts a logical argument based on the principle of cause and effect to prove the existence of primordial cosmic matter, the Viśiṣṭādvaita Vedānta resorts to the scriptural authority.[2] *Prakṛti* is also known as *māyā*, as stated in the *Śvetāśvatara Upaniṣad*.[3] It is called *māyā* in the sense that it serves as an instrument for the creation of variegated objects in the universe.[4] Another word which is commonly used in Vaiṣṇava treatises for *prakṛti* is *avidyā*. *Avidyā* with reference to *prakṛti* does not mean the cosmic ignorance which is the cause of illusory manifestation as understood in the Advaita Vedānta. On the contrary, it is taken to mean that which stands as an obstruction for true knowledge of Reality (*vidyāvirodhi*). The physical body and the sense organs are products of *prakṛti* and these prevent the soul from having the true knowledge of God due to the attachment of an individual to the physical body and the sensual pleasures. This aspect of *prakṛti* receives greater emphasis in the Vaiṣṇava theology because the attachment to *prakṛti* from a beginningless time constitutes the major obstacle for the attainment of God.[5] We shall explain later how the association of soul with *prakṛti* causes bondage.

Prakṛti and the Three Guṇas

As regards its nature, *prakṛti* is a non-sentient substance (*jaḍadravya*) characterised by three fundamental attributes known as *sattva*, *rajas* and *tamas*. *Sattva* stands for whatever is fine or light (*prakāśa*) and causes happiness (*sukha*) and knowledge. *Rajas* represents whatever is active and is the cause of suffering, attachment and passion. *Tamas* is whatever is heavy and is responsible for lethargy and ignorance. These are supernormal qualities and are present in all the evolutes of *prakṛti* including the gross physical objects of the universe. They are found in varying proportion, depending upon the nature of the objects. If an individual has pleasant and friendly disposition, the quality of *sattva* is considered to predominate his mind. If one is too passionate or angry, it is due to the predominance of *rajas*. If a person is lethargic, dull and ignorant, it is taken that the *tāmasic* quality is predominant in him. Thus, the presence of the three qualities and their influence are inferred from the type of activities and the nature of the object. In a piece of stone which is absolutely inert, *tamas* is the most predominant quality. The three *guṇas* remain in equilibrium in the causal state of *prakṛti*. That is, the primordial matter in the state of dissolution remains with all the three *guṇas* in equal proportion. In the state of evolution variation takes place in the *guṇas* by way of one of them being dominant, while others remaining subdued. In fact, evolution is the disturbed state of the *guṇas*, while dissolution is the state of their equilibrium.

Evolution of Prakṛti

When the equilibrium of the *guṇas* is disturbed, evolution of *prakṛti* starts. The question as to who causes the actual evolution and dissolution of *prakṛti* will be discussed later. For the present we may note down that according to the Vedānta the process of evolution of *prakṛti* into various modifications is initiated by the *will* of *Īśvara* or God who is immanent as controller in all the entities of the universe including *prakṛti* and its evolutes. This theory is advanced on the authority of the Upaniṣadic teachings. The view of the Sāṅkhyas that *prakṛti* evolves itself without the aid of *Īśvara* is rejected on the ground that what is non-sentient cannot undergo modifications in an orderly way and also at any particular point of time on its own accord. The presence of *puruṣa*, the eternal self, which is the only other reality accepted by the Sāṅkhyas is not considered sufficient to cause evolution because *puruṣa* in that system is present eternally. The Naiyāyikas, as true logicians try to trace the origin of the universe to the *paramāṇus*, the atoms which are eternal, partless, infinitesimal and suprasensible reals. Even this theory is rejected by the Vedānta as untenable because of the impossibility of the combination of the absolutely partless atoms to form an aggregate for purposes of evolution into a physical entity. Hence, the Vedānta accepts *prakṛti* as the primordial cosmic source for the physical universe as the Sāṅkhyas believe with one modification, viz. that the process of evolution is initiated by God's will.

The very first evolute is known as *mahat* and from the latter arises the evolute called *ahaṁkāra*. These two do not refer to the psychic entities, intellect (*buddhi*) and ego of an individual but on the other hand, they are technical terms used for the two ontological *tattvas* or evolutes of *prakṛti*—representing two important stages of evolution. Both *mahat* and *ahaṁkāra*, being products of *prakṛti*, consist of the three *guṇas*—*sattva*, *rajas* and *tamas*. The *ahaṁkāra-tattva* assumes three forms on the basis of the three *guṇas*: *sāttvika ahaṁkāra, rājasa ahaṁkāra* and *tāmasa ahaṁkāra*. From this stage the process of further evolution takes place on two different lines. From the *sāttvika ahaṁkāra* in which *sattva* element is predominant, the eleven sense organs including *manas* or mind evolve. From the *tāmasa ahaṁkāra* evolve the five *tanmātras* or the subtle elements—*śabda* or sound, *sparśa* or touch, *rūpa* or colour, *rasa* or taste and *gandha* or odour, in a successive order. From each of these subtle elements come the gross elements—*ākāśa* or space, *vāyu* or air, *tejas* or fire, *jala* or water and *pṛthivī* or earth. There is some difference of opinion between the Sāṅkhya and the Viśiṣṭādvaita regarding the order of evolution from *ahaṁkāra-tattva*.[6] The Purāṇas also present them in a slightly different manner. But these details are not of philosophic significance. What we should take note of is that the total number of evolutes including *prakṛti* is generally accepted to be twenty-four and that the five gross elements which are undeniable facts have their origin in the *prakṛti*. How the physical universe is formed out of the five elements is an important point for consideration.

Creation of the Universe

The Viśiṣṭādvaita Vedānta postulates two types of creation known as *samaṣṭi-sṛṣṭi* or creation of the aggregate universe and *vyaṣṭi-sṛṣṭi* or creation of the universe of space and time with all its diversity. In the first stage, Brahman or *Īśvara* as the creator of the universe causes the evolution of *prakṛti* through various stages as outlined above up to the five gross elements. After this stage is reached, the second kind of creation starts by admixing the five physical elements in certain proportion. This is technically called *pañcīkaraṇa* or quintuplication of the five elements. This is done as follows: first the aggregate of each of the five elements is divided into equal parts; then each half is subdivided into four parts; in the next stage, taking this one-eighth portion of each of the five elements it is mixed with the half part of each of the *bhūtas*. This means that each element such as *ākāśa* comprises half of that element and one-eighth portion of other four elements. The rest of the creation of the physical universe with all its diversity is made out of *pañca-bhūtas* or the five elements thus mixed up. The admixture of the elements is supported by the Upaniṣads. It is also justified by the fact that all objects in the universe including the human body are constituted of all the five elements in varying proportion.

The Purāṇas present a vivid description of creation (*sṛṣṭi* or *sarga*). In this connection they introduce the concept of *aṇḍa*, the cosmic egg in the vast stretch of water out of which the four-faced Brahmā originates for carrying out the rest of the actual creation of the universe.[7] Similarly, for carrying out the process of dissolution of the universe in a reverse order, the concept of Rudra as a deity entrusted with the physical task of dissolution is brought in. What is created needs to be well preserved and protected until the stage of dissolution. For this purpose, a third deity, Viṣṇu is admitted. The Pāñcarātra treatises which also deal with the cosmology, advance the theory of emanation and bring in the three *Vyūha* manifestations of Supreme Being—*Saṁkarṣaṇa*, *Pradyumna* and *Aniruddha*—for explaining the three major cosmic functions of creation, sustenance and dissolution. In order to accommodate the three other deities—Brahmā, Viṣṇu and Rudra—introduced by the Purāṇas, the Pāñcarātra system speaks of two stages of creation, viz., primary and secondary. The three *vyūha* deities are put in charge of the three cosmic functions at the first stage and the Purāṇic deities are entrusted with the three cosmic functions at the second stage. These are all matters of detail for the Vaiṣṇava theology and will be dealt with at the appropriate place.[8] From the philosophical point of view, Brahman is the primary cause of the universe (*jagat-kāraṇa*) as emphasised in the *Taittirīya Upaniṣad* and the second aphorism of Vedānta. Brahman, as the metaphysical ground of the universe, is responsible for creation, sustenance and dissolution. Even if other deities actually perform these three functions, it is Brahman as their *antarātmā* or in-dweller controlling them from within that causes the different cosmic functions. If we understand this central truth of Vedānta, there is no contradiction between the teachings of the Upaniṣads and the theological account of the Purāṇas.

Material Cause of the Universe

The Vedānta as a philosophical system is confronted with a different problem in accounting for the causation of the universe. There are three types of causes which are needed for the production of an effect, one is known as *upādāna-kāraṇa* or the material out of which a product is brought out; the second is *nimitta-kāraṇa* or the intelligent agent to bring forth the product and third is *sahakāri-kāraṇa* or the accessories needed to produce an object. Taking the example of a pot, which as a finished product is an effect, the clay is its material cause, the potter is the instrumental cause and the wheel, stick etc., the accessory cause. If Brahman is regarded as the primary cause of the universe as the Upaniṣads declare, the question arises: is it the material cause (*upādāna-kāraṇa*) or is it merely an instrumental cause (*nimitta-kāraṇa*) or is it both? This is a crucial issue in the Vedānta and different theories have been advanced on this. If the physical universe is an outcome of the evolution of the primordial substance known as *prakṛti*, we should accept, as the older school of Sāṅkhyas has done, that *prakṛti* is the material cause and attribute to it the capacity to evolve itself spontaneously of its own accord as modern scientists believe in the emergence of the universe from the original energy. This is known as *svabhāva-vāda* in Indian philosophic thought accepted by the Cārvākas. If an intelligent agent is needed to set the process of orderly evolution at a particular point of time, the concept of Brahman or God as the creator is to be admitted, as otherwise an orderly evolution is untenable. In that case, Brahman or *Īśvara* becomes an instrumental cause (*nimitta-kāraṇa*) in so far as His *saṅkalpa* or will is responsible for the evolution of the universe. This is the position which is accepted by later Sāṅkhya school, the Yoga system, the Pāśupata religion and among the Vedāntins, Madhva. The philosophical advantage of this theory is that Brahman or God will not be subject to change (*vikāra*) as a result of His becoming the material cause. But this theory is rejected by the author of the *Vedānta-sūtra* as it goes counter to the teaching of the Upaniṣads. The aphorisms related to the critical examination of Sāṅkhya, Yoga, Pāśupata and the specific *sūtra* which explicitly states that Brahman is the material cause (*prakṛtiśca*)[9] evidently indicate the view of Bādarāyaṇa.

Except Madhva, all the Vedāntins subscribe to the view that Brahman is the material cause as taught in the Upaniṣads.

The Upaniṣads speak of Brahman as the material cause of the universe on the analogy of the lump of clay being the material cause of the pot. If this illustration is taken into account, it would follow that Brahman itself transforms into the universe. The scriptural texts also categorily assert that Brahman is immutable (*nirvikāra*). The material causality of Brahman thus needs to be explained in such a way as it would not affect the immutable character of Brahman. Each school of Vedānta that accepts Brahman as material cause attempts to offer an explanation in this regard.

There are three important theories of material causality of Brahman. According to the first one, which is held by Yādava Prakāśa, Brahman itself through the threefold power (*śakti*) it possesses undergoes as God, individual souls and matter just as water of sea turns itself into waves, foam and bubbles. Brahman which is *sat* manifests itself in the triadic form. In this way the *svarūpa* of Brahman is not affected because the change takes place in respect of the *śakti*. Bhāskara, another Vedāntin belonging to the same school of thought, advances a slightly different theory. In place of *śakti*, he introduces a limiting adjunct (*upādhi*) as the media of change. Brahman itself emanates successively into the manifold of sentient souls and non-sentient matter on account of the *upādhi* or limiting adjunct. This *upādhi* is called *avidyā* but unlike in the Advaita system it is real, beginningless and non-sentient in character. It is different as well as non-different from Brahman. The illustration provided to explain this theory is the one all-pervasive space (*ākāśa*) becoming many when it is conditioned by different pots. Just as the spider weaves its web by its internal power, Brahman transforms into the relative by its evolving power (*periṇāma-śakti*). Both these theories are regarded as *Brahma-pariṇāmavāda*.[10]

The second important theory is put across bv the Advaita Vedānta of Śaṁkara, which is known as *vivarta-vāda*. According to this, Brahman which is pure Being devoid of any differentiation does not actually undergo any transformation into the universe. But at the same time, in order to account for the material causality of Brahman as taught by the Upaniṣads, the Advaita Vedānta postulates the doctrine of *māyā* or *avidyā*, the cosmic principle which causes world illusion. Brahman which is eternally unchanging and pure consciousness illusorily appears as the universe owing to *māyā*. The common illustration given to explain this view is the piece of rope which is mistaken for a snake due to the ignorance of the true nature of the rope. In the same way, owing to the influence of cosmic ignorance known as *māyā*, Brahman illusorily appears as the universe. In so far as Brahman is the substrate (*adhiṣṭhātā*) for *māyā*, Brahman is regarded as *upādāna-kāraṇa*, while the change in the form of manifestation as universe applies to *māyā*.

Both these theories are considered to be defective and are not therefore, accepted by the Viśiṣṭādvaita Vedānta. As the scope of the present chapter is confined to the presentation of the Viśiṣṭādvaita theory of cosmology, we need not go into the details of the criticisms of the other two theories. The criticism of the view of Advaita involves an elaborate discussion of the doctrine of *avidyā* on the basis of which the *vivarta-vāda* is developed. According to Rāmānuja, the doctrine, when it is subjected to logical scrutiny, is riddled with contradictions and as such it is untenable. Consequently, *vivarta-vāda* or the theory that the universe is a phenomenal appearance of Brahman also falls to the ground. The theories of Bhāskara and Yādava too are rejected as unsatisfactory. For both these Vedāntins, either the *śakti* or the *upādhi* postulated by them to account for the transformation of Brahman into universe is different as well as non-different from Brahman. If the *śakti* or *upādhi* to which change is attributed is absolutely different from Brahman, then the material causality is applicable only to the *śakti* or *upādhi* and not to Brahman. If, on the other hand, *upādhi* or *śakti* is non-different from Brahman, the change also applies to Brahman. Besides, the *jīvas* being non-different from Brahman, the suffering experienced by them would touch Brahman too.

Viśiṣṭādvaita Theory of Material Causality

We now come to the third theory advanced by the Viśiṣṭādvaita Vedānta to get over the defects pointed out in respect of the other two theories. According to this the mere *svarūpa* of Brahman cannot become the material cause of the universe since that would affect the immutable character of Brahman. Nor can the non-sentient *prakṛti* by itself serve as the material cause of the universe for the reason already explained. It is Brahman as organically related to the *cit* (individual souls) and *acit* (the cosmic matter) in their subtle state (*sūkṣma-cid-acid-viśiṣṭa-brahma*) that constitutes the material cause of the universe. In the chapter on the Doctrine of Ultimate Reality we have observed how Brahman is always, both in the state of dissolution and the state after creation, is associated with *cit* and *acit*. In the state of dissolution, the cosmic matter as well as the individual selves exist in Brahman in an unmanifest form as devoid of name and form. When creation takes place, they are unfolded and given name and form. That is, when Brahman which exists prior to creation with *cit* and *acit* in a state of non-differentiation *wills* to be 'many' as the *Chāndogya Upaniṣad* says, the same becomes Brahman with *cit* and *acit* in a state of differentiation with an infinity of distinctions in name and form. What actually evolves or undergoes modification is the *cit* and *acit* but not Brahman directly. In the case of the *acit* the transformation is complete from one state to another, as the lump of clay changes to a pot. In the case of *jīva*, there is no change in respect of its *svarūpa* which is immutable; but the change is only to the extent of its attributive knowledge which so far was dormant. As far as *Brahman* is concerned there is also no change in respect of its *svarūpa*. The only change that can be spoken of for Brahman is that it was *niyantā* or controller of the subtle *cit* and *acit* prior to the creation and it now becomes a *niyantā* of *cit* and *acit* in manifested form.[11] A change in the attribute does not affect the substance, which is its *āśraya* or substrate. Brahman as the *ādhāra* or ground of the *cit* and *acit*, remains unaffected by the change in the *acit*. Brahman is, therefore, regarded as the material cause by virtue of its being the *ādhāra* of *cit* and *acit*.

This theory is justified both on the strength of the scriptural texts and also on the logical ground. According to the theory of causality adopted by Viśiṣṭādvaita, cause and effect are different states of the same substance. The effect is not a new product which comes into existence from what does not already exist, as the Naiyāyikas believe (*asat-kārya-vāda*). It exists in the causal state in an unmanifest form and the same assumes a different state after causation. If we take the example of clay and pot, the lump of clay which is the cause becomes an effect when it is changed into a pot. Thus, the cause and effect are two different states (*avasthās*) of the same one substance. *Upādānatva* or material causality consists in the association of an entity with a different state (*avasthāntara-yogitvam*). That which serves as the ground for the changed states is regarded as the material cause. The clay is the *upādāna-kāraṇa* for pot, vase etc., since these are made of the same substance. A piece of gold is the material cause of ear-ring, necklace, bangles etc., made of gold. Thus the cause and effect are not distinct (*ananya*) because the two are different states of one common substance. The same one substance assumes different names as cause and effect due to the two changed states. It is in this sense that Brahman as cause and the universe as effect are spoken of as *ananya* or non-distinct in the *Vedānta-sūtra*[12] which is based on the *Chāndogya* text. We shall explain it when we come to the consideration of the causal relation of Brahman and the universe. For the present, we may note that Brahman as associated with *cit* and *acit* in their subtle states serves as the *upādāna-kāraṇa* for the universe.

The Upaniṣads also support the existence of Brahman in the state of dissolution with subtle *cit* and *acit*. The *Bṛhadāraṇyaka Upaniṣad* says: 'Now all this was undifferentiated; it became differentiated by name and form.'[13] The word 'this' in this statement, taking the context into consideration, refers to the universe of *cit* and *acit*. Existence in an undifferentiated form implies existence without name and form. This interpretation is further supported by the *Subāla Upaniṣad*, describing the process of dissolution in the reverse order, when it says that *tamas* (*prakṛti*) becomes united with *Paramātman.*[14] The *Chāndogya* passage dealing with the creation of the universe states that the word 'this' (*idaṁ*) meaning the physical universe was in the beginning only *sat*. The implication of this statement, as interpreted by Rāmānuja, is that the universe of *cit* and *acit* existed with *sat* or Brahman in an undifferentiated form. If this meaning were not accepted, it would not be possibi to explain how Brahman could become 'many' (*bahusyāṁ*) after it wills to create for the obvious reason that which does not already exist cannot be produced according to the principle of *satkārya-vāda* accepted by Viśiṣṭādvaita. We should also bear in mind in this connection that the universe of *cit* and *acit* constitutes the body (*śarīra*) of Brahman as stated in the *Antaryāmi Brāhmaṇa*. As *śarīra* and *śarīri* are organically related and are eternally inseparable, Brahman as *saririn* remains always associated with *cit* and *acit*. The changes taking place in the body do not affect the *svarūpa* of the soul within. This is explained on the analogy of the bodily changes taking place in a personality. A boy grows into youth, a youth attains manhood and from this state he becomes an old man. But these different states which actually belong to the physical body do not affect the *svarūpa* of the *jivātman* within. In the same way, Brahman as the *ādhāra* of the universe is not affected by the evolution of the universe which is its body. In the light of these explanations Brahman is admitted as the material cause of the universe.

The Causal Relation of Universe to Brahman

The causal relationship between Brahman and the universe as explained by Viśiṣṭādvaita offers a satisfactory solution to the metaphysical problem of 'one' and 'many'. The main issue that Monism is confronted with is how the one Absolute Reality becomes many as the universe of diversity. The same issue is raised in a classical manner in the *Chāndogya Upaniṣad*: 'What is that by knowing which everything else is known?' The illustrations offered by the Upaniṣad in this regard such as clay and its products, gold and the ornaments made of it, the piece of iron (*lohā*) and the products made out of it, only substantiate the theory that cause and its effect are non-distinct. Unless the cause is immanent in the effect and the two are non-distinct in respect of the material substance it is not possible to explain the Upaniṣadic thesis, viz., 'by knowing the cause the effects too become known'. Keeping this truth in mind the author of the *Vedānta-sūtra* uses the expression *ananya* or non-distinct.[15]

There are two ways of explaining the concept of *ananyatva* or non-distinct relation of Brahman to the universe. One way which appears to be an easier solution is to deny the reality of the manifold universe and hold that Brahman is the only Reality. If there are two absolutely real entities and if they are different by virtue of their nature, then we cannot speak of non-distinctness. If one is real and the other is illusory in character, which by logical implication means a non-existent, it becomes possible to assert the non-distinctness of Brahman and the universe.

Rāmānuja does not accept this explanation. If the universe were illusory (*mithyā*) as the Advaitin contends, it may be possible to support the theory of the Advaita. The various arguments advanced by the Advaitins to prove the *mithyātva* or the illusory character of the universe have been subjected to detailed critical examination and have been rejected as untenable.[16] There are stronger *pramāṇas*, both perceptual experience as well as scriptural evidence, to support the reality of the universe. Rāmānuja, therefore, offers a different explanation, by accepting the reality of the universe, to answer the metaphysical issue raised by the Vedānta. The concept of causality, to which we have already referred, provides the solution. If cause and effect are two different states (*avasthās*) of the same one substance, there is no problem in knowing the effects by the knowledge of the cause. By applying the same logic to the Brahman and manifold universe, it is pointed out that by the knowledge of Brahman as the primary cause, the universe which is its effect, also becomes known. As already pointed out, Brahman associated with *sūkṣma-cit* and *sūkṣma-acit* is the material cause and the effect is also the same Brahman as associated with *sthūla-cit* and *sthūla-acit*. It is in this sense that Brahman and universe are non-distinct and on the basis of this fact, both the declaration of the Upaniṣad (*pratijñā*), viz., by knowing that (Brahman) everything else becomes known and also the illustrations (*dṛṣṭānta*) offered by the Upaniṣad in support of it stand established.[17]

Universe and Brahman

We have explained the causal relationship between Brahman and universe. We may now consider the ontological relation between the two. In connection with the study of the doctrines of *Īśvara* and *jīva*, we have referred to the concept of *śarīra-śarīri-bhāva* or body-soul relationship that obtains between *Īśvara* and the individual souls. The same ontological relation with all its implications holds good between Brahman and the physical universe. That is, Brahman is the *śarīrin* or the Universal Self by virtue of its being the ground (*ādhāra*), inner controller (*niyantā*) and the Lord (*śeṣī*), while the universe is its body (*śarīra*) in the technical sense that it entirely depends for its very existence on Brahman (*ādheya*), it is wholly controlled by Brahman (*niyāmya*) and it exists to serve the purpose of *Īśvara* (*śeṣa*). As Brahman is the primary cause of the universe, the latter derives its *sattā* or existence from the former. Its continuance is dependent on the *saṅkalpa* or will of *Īśvara*. Thus, it is stated in the *Mahābhārata*:[18] 'The heavens, the sky with the moon, the sun and the stars, the different quarters, the earth, the great ocean—all these are supported by the might of the Supreme Being, Vāsudeva.' The *prakṛti* by its very nature is *parārtha*, that is, intended for the pleasure of someone else just as a fruit or any other material object is meant for the use of others. The universe, which is evolved from the cosmic matter in its manifold form is intended for the pleasure of *Īśvara* and to provide the field of experience for the individual selves. The very purpose of creation of the universe by God is to provide an opportunity for the souls which have been submerged in the ocean of bondage from the beginningless time to escape from it through the spiritual pursuits. Without a body, mind and sense organs a soul cannot function. Physical body and the sense organs are the products of *prakṛti*. The creation and dissolution of the universe is a sport (*līlā*) for *Īśvara*, as stated by the *Vedānta-sūtra*.[19] Thus, *Īśvara* who creates the universe as an object of sport for His pleasure becomes the *śeṣin* or the Supreme Lord to enjoy it and the universe is His *śeṣa*, an object meant to serve His purpose. This concept of *śeṣi-śeṣa* is important for theological purposes, because it provides the intimate relation of the individual to the Supreme Lord. On the basis of this concept, Vaiṣṇava theology has developed the theory of divine service (*kaiṅkarya*) as an obligatory sacred duty of an individual, who is a subservient being (*dāsa*) to the Supreme Lord, who is his master (*swāmin*). We shall discuss this theory in detail in a later chapter.

The doctrine of universe comprising the *cit* and *acit* as the *śarīra* or body of *Īśvara* gives a divine character to all the living beings in the universe. All things are sacred because God is immanent in all that exists in the universe. In view of this, the *Chāndogya Upaniṣad* states: 'All this is Brahman'.[20] The *Puruṣa-sūkta* of Ṛgveda says: 'All this is *puruṣa*'.[21] The *Viṣṇupurāṇa* reiterates the same truth: 'All that exists—the illuminaries, the worlds, the forests, the mountains, the quarters (*dik*), the rivers, the oceans—are Viṣṇu'.[22] The Vaiṣṇava theology describes that the entire *jagat* (universe) is pervaded by Viṣṇu (*sarvaṁ viṣṇu-mayaṁ jagat*). The equation of Brahman and universe in such statements which are regarded as *samānādhikaraṇa-vākyas* (sentences in which the terms are found in apposition), is to be understood in the sense of the ontological relation that exists between Brahman and the universe.[23] An identity of two such entities is inconceivable, because the two are absolutely different in nature. Nor is it possible to explain such equations, as the Advaitins have done, by negating the reality of the universe and upholding the absolute reality of Brahman. The universe is as real as Brahman and the only plausible explanation of the equation is that the universe is the *śarīra* (body) of the *Paramātman*. In this sense Vaiṣṇavism speaks of the whole universe as *viṣṇumaya* which signifies that it is the body of Viṣṇu by virtue of the former pervading the entire universe. This is the true relation of universe to Brahman or Viṣṇu.

The Theory of Time (*kāla*)

Kāla is one of the three *acetana tattvas* or non-sentient entities admitted in Viśiṣṭādvaita. It is an independent and real substance, enjoying the same status as *prakṛti*. It is, however, not part of *prakṛti* but it exists along with *prakṛti*. It is also distinct from *Īśvara* but co-exists with Him since both are *vibhu* (infinite). However, like other ontological entities, it is the *śarīra* of *Īśvara* in the technical sense. It is also eternal. This means that it has neither a beginning nor an end.[24] As a substance (*dravya*) it undergoes modifications as minutes, hours, day, weeks, months, years etc.

Though time is one and infinite, it is conditioned and divisible into many units in the form of minutes, hours etc., due to the conditioning objects such as the movement of the sun. *Ākāśa* is one and all-pervasive but it is regarded as many when it is conditioned by objects such as pots. Similarly, on account of *upādhi* or limiting adjuncts, *kāla* though it is one infinite entity, is regarded as many. What we regard as time in terms of hours, days, weeks, etc., are modifications or different states of one infinite *kāla* (*akhaṇḍa-kāla*).

Notes

1. NS p. 190.
   See also *Tattvatraya*, 86.
2. TMK I.1. *svacchandenāgamena prakṛti. . .siddheḥ.*
3. SvUp IV.10. *māyāṁtu prakṛtiṁ vidyāt māyinaṁ tu maheśvaram.*
4. NS p. 190. *vicitra-sṛṣṭy-upakaraṇatvāt māyā.*

5. See *Śaraṇāgati-gadya*, p. 124. *madīya anādikarma-pravāha-pravaṛttāṁ bhagavat-svarūpa-tirodhānakarīm....guṇamayīṁ māyāṁ.*
6. See FVV pp. 318-19.
7. See *Manusmṛti*, I.8. *so abhidhyāya śarīrāt svāt sisṛkṣuḥ vividhāḥ prajāḥ; apa eva sasrajādau tāsu vīryam apāsṛjat...tadaṇḍaṁ abhavat haimaṁ sahasrāṁśu-samaprabham.*

   See also *Tattvatraya*, 110.
8. See Chapter 10, pp. 214-15.
9. VS I.4.23. *prakṛtiśca pratijñādṛṣṭāntānuparodhāt.*

   The term *prakṛti* is interpreted both by Śaṁkara and Rāmānuja as *upādāna-kāraṇaṁ Brahma.*
10. There is an ancient school of thought represented by Bhartṛprapañca according to which Brahman itself transforms into the souls and universe. This theory is rejected by all the other schools of Vedānta.
11. See RB II.3.18. *ubhaya-prakāra-viśiṣṭe niyantṛāṁśe tadavastha-tadubhaya-viśiṣṭatārūpa-vikāro bhavati.*
12. VS II.1.15. *tad-ananyatvam-ārambhaṇa-śabdādibhyaḥ.*
13. BrUp III.4.7. *taddhedaṁ tarhy-avyākṛtam-āsīt; tannāmarūpābhyām-eva vyākriyate.*
14. *Subāla Up* II. *tamaḥ pare deva ekī-bhavati.*
15. VS II.1.15. *tadananyatvam-ārambhaṇa-śabdādibhyaḥ.*

    See also RB II.1.15. p. 484. *tadevam-ārambhaṇa-śabdādibhyo jagataḥ paramakāraṇāt parasmāt brahmaṇo ananyatvam-upapādyate.*
16. See AV pp. 100–07. Also FVV pp. 260-71.
17. VS I.4.23. *prakṛtiśca pratijñā-dṛṣṭāntānuparodhāt.*
18. Mbh XIII,254.136.

    dyauḥ sacandrāka-nakṣatrā khaṁ diśo bhūr-mahodadhiḥ; vāsudevasya vīryeṇa vidhṛtāni mahātmanaḥ.
19. VS II.1.33. *lokavattu līlākaivalyam.*
20. ChUp III.14.1. *sarvaṁ khalvidaṁ brahma.*
21. *Puruṣa-sūkta, puruṣa evedaṁ sarvaṁ.*
22. VP II.12.38. *jyotīṁṣi viṣṇur-bhuvanāni viṣṇur-vanāni viṣṇur-girayo diśaśca; nadyaḥ samudrāśca sa eva sarvaṁ.*
23. See RB I.1.1. p. 142. *samānādhikaraṇyasya...śarīrātmabhāva eva nibandhanam.*
24. See VP I.2.26. *anādirbhagavān kālo nānto'sya dvijavidyate.*

5

THE DOCTRINE OF BHAKTI-YOGA

Vedānta based on the Upaniṣadic teachings is primarily devoted to the study of the three fundamental topics—*Tattva* or the nature of Reality, *Hita* or the ways and means of realizing it and *Puruṣārtha* or the ultimate spiritual goal to be attained. Thus, the four chapters (*adhyāyas*) of the *Vedānta-sūtra* deal with them in succession. The sole purpose of Brahman-knowledge is to attain Brahman, as the *Taittirīya Upaniṣad* says. Philosophic knowledge should culminate in the attainment of the highest spiritual goal. This important teaching of the Upaniṣad presupposes a practical discipline or means (*upāya*) to be undertaken in order to attain the goal. What is that *upāya*? According to the Viśiṣṭādvaita Vedānta, it is either *bhakti-yoga* or *prapatti-yoga* that serves as the direct means to achieve the supreme human goal (*parama-puruṣārtha*).[1] Both are important means for *mokṣa* and have been advocated as alternative methods intended for two different categories of individuals having different capacities and conditions of eligibility. The Upaniṣads and the *Vedānta-sūtra* have given greater emphasis to *bhakti-yoga*, also known as *upāsanā*, whereas the Vaiṣṇava treatises have accorded prominence to *prapatti*. We shall take up the doctrine of *prapatti* separately and examine in this chapter the doctrine of *bhakti-yoga* along with *karma-yoga* and *jñāna-yoga* which are regarded as the aids to *bhakti-yoga*.

Meaning of the term Bhakti

The term *bhakti* is derived from the root word *bhaj* which means *sevā* or meditation (*bhaj sevāyām*).[2] In common usage it is understood in the sense of love towards the respected or elderly person (*mahanīyaviṣaye prītiḥ*). *Prīti* or love is a state of knowledge, a mental disposition. *Bhakti* with reference to God, therefore, means unceasing meditation with intense love for the Supreme Being (*snehapūrvam-anudhyānam*).[3]

The general concept of *bhakti* in the sense of devotion or reverence to a deity is accepted by all religions. This kind of *bhakti* of a general character is not regarded as the direct means to *mokṣa* by the Viśiṣṭādvaita Vedānta. As will be explained presently, *bhakti* as a *sādhana* for *mokṣa* refers to the rigorous religio-spiritual discipline to be undertaken by a qualified aspirant for *mokṣa* and it is to be pursued continuously for the life-time until the total liberation from bondage is secured. A more appropriate term used for *bhakti* as *upāya* is *bhakti-yoga* as outlined in the *Bhagavad-gītā*. In the Upaniṣadic parlance it is termed as *upāsanā*. The *bhakti-yoga* or *upāsanā* of Brahman involves not merely the *bhakti* in a general sense but the entire *aṣṭāṅga-yoga* or the eightfold ethico-religious discipline as explained in the Yoga system. It should also be preceded by the acquisition of philosophic knowledge of *jīvātman* and *Paramātman*, the strict performance of prescribed rituals (*karma*) without any selfish motive purely as divine service and also the practice of meditation on the *jīvātman*, as enunciated in the *Bhagavad-gītā*. Thus, there is a wide difference between *bhakti* as understood in common parlance and *bhakti* as a yogic discipline leading to the attainment of *mokṣa*.

The Concept of Bhakti in the Upaniṣads

Before we take up a detailed study of the doctrine of *bhakti-yoga*, we should consider an important issue, viz., whether or not *bhakti-yoga* is advocated in the Upaniṣads as a direct means to *mokṣa*. This question arises because of two reasons. In the first place, the term *bhakti* is not mentioned in the Upaniṣads. The texts which speak of the *upāya* for *mokṣa* use other terms such as *jñāna*, *vedana*, *darśana*, *dhyāna*, *dhruvā-smṛti*, *nididhyāsana* and *upāsanā*. Secondly, the Upaniṣads also state explicitly that *jñāna* or knowledge of Brahman is the only means to *mokṣa*. Thus says the *Śvetāśavatara Upaniṣad*: 'Having *known* Him, he (the individual) transgresses death (bondage) and there is no other means to attain Him.'[4] The *Taittirīya Upaniṣad* also asserts: 'He who *knows* Brahman attains the highest.'[5] In fact, the Advaita Vedānta maintains, on the authority of such scriptural texts, that *jñāna* alone is the sole means to *mokṣa*. The practice of *upāsanā* or *nididhyāsana* (meditation) referred to in other texts is considered by the Advaitin as a subsidiary means to *jñāna*.

Regarding the first point, we have already pointed out that the term *upāsanā* bears the same meaning as *bhakti*. Though the term *bhakti* is not used in the Upaniṣadic texts, the concept of *bhakti* is implied in them. This fact is evident from the verses of the *Bhagavad-gītā* which explicitly mention the term *bhakti*, while elucidating the Upaniṣadic text in which *bhakti* is implied. Thus the *Muṇḍaka Upaniṣad* says: 'This Self (Brahman) cannot be attained by the study of Vedas, nor by meditation nor through much hearing. He is to be attained only by one whom the Self chooses. To such a person, the Self reveals Its true nature.'[6] The implication of this statement, as explained by Rāmānuja, is that mere *śravaṇa* (hearing), *manana* (reflection) and *nididhyāsana* (meditation) undertaken without intense love for God (*bhakti*) cannot serve as means to attain God. Only that individual on whom God showers His grace can achieve Him. The question then arises: whom does God choose to receive His grace? The answer, according to Rāmānuja, is that one who is dearest to God is chosen by Him (*priyatama eva hi varaṇīyo bhavati*).[7] The *Bhagavad-gītā* provides the answer to the question as to who is the person most dear to God and why he is regarded so. Thus says the *Gītā*: 'To those who crave for eternal union (with Me) and meditate (on Me), I bestow with love that clear divine vision (*buddhiyoga*) by which they attain Me.'[8] It also says: 'One who is most devoted to God is the one dearest to Me.'[9] By way of elucidating the statement of *Muṇḍaka Upaniṣad*, it further points out that there is no other way of attaining God except by *bhakti* or intense loving meditation on God.[10]

Further, according to Rāmānuja the different terms used in the Upaniṣads such as *upāsanā*, *dhyāna*, *smṛti-santati*, *vedana* and *darśana* are to be taken to mean the same as *bhakti* referred to in the *Gītā*. If these terms are understood differently, it would amount to the admission of several means to *mokṣa*. Since the goal to be achieved is the same, the means cannot be different. It should, therefore, be admitted that all these terms bear the same import. According to the principle of interpretation laid down by the Mīmāṁsaka, when different terms are used in the same context, the general term should be taken to bear the meaning of the specific term.[11] Accordingly, in the present context, *jñāna, vedana, darśana, dhyāna, upāsanā* etc., are treated as general terms indicative of *bhakti* and *bhaktī* as a specific term meaning unswerving devotion to God.[12] Besides, *vedana* (knowledge) and *upāsanā* (meditation), which are the two key words indicating *prima facie* two different paths to *mokṣa*, are used in the Upaniṣadic passages as interchangeable words.[13] Rāmānuja, therefore, comes to the conclusion that *bhakti* or *upāsanā* as a spiritual discipline is the *upāya* to *mokṣa*.

As regards the statement of the Upaniṣad that *jñāna* is the sole means to *mokṣa*, Rāmānuja does not question this basic view. The issue which he raises is: what is the kind of knowledge that serves as the means to *mokṣa*? Is it the knowledge about Brahman as generated by the Upaniṣadic texts? Or is it *jñāna* in some other form? The first kind of knowledge is known as *vākyārtha-jñāna* or the knowledge which arises from the study of the sacred texts teaching the identity of Brahman with the individual self. This is the view advanced by some Advaitins. But such a knowledge, it is contended by Rāmānuja, is not found to remove the bondage. A more modified view is presented by the Advaitin that it is not mere verbal knowledge derived by the study of the sacred texts but a kind of intensive knowledge of immediate character (*aparokṣa-jñāna*) generated by constant meditation on the purport of the Upaniṣadic texts which can serve as the means to liberation. Even this theory is rejected as untenable by the Viśiṣṭādvaitin. This conclusion is reached after an elaborate critical examination of Advaitin's theory from several points of view. We need not go into these details.[14] What is important for our purpose is that while Rāmānuja accepts the basic fact that knowledge (*jñāna*) is the sole means to *mokṣa*, he qualifies it with the statement that true *jñāna* should develop into steadfast meditation or *bhakti*. That alone would constitute the direct means to *mokṣa* (*bhaktirūpāpanna-jñāna*).

The view that knowledge derived by the study of sacred texts leads to *upāsanā* is established by Rāmānuja on the basis of the Upaniṣadic teachings. The *Bṛhadāraṇyaka Upaniṣad* points out that only after knowing Brahman (by means of study of Scripture and reflection thereon) the *upāsanā* is to be performed.[15] The same Upaniṣad enjoins more specifically: 'Verily, the self (Brahman) is to be seen, to be heard, to be reflected on, to be meditated upon.'[16] The *Chāndogya Upaniṣad* also states: 'He who understands the *self* seeks it.'[17] The implication of all these statements, according to Rāmānuja, is that *upāsanā* or meditation presupposes the knowledge of Brahman. That is, only after acquiring the knowledge of Brahman by means of the study of the sacred texts (*śravaṇa*) with the guidance of a preceptor and after repeatedly reflecting over the teachings (*manana*) to gain conviction in the theoretical knowledge, one should undertake meditation on Brahman. The knowledge of Brahman generated by the study of the Upaniṣads thus serves as an aid to *nididhyāsana* or meditation and it is not the other way, as the Advaitin would contend. What is enjoined by the Upaniṣadic texts in question is *nididhyāsana* proper. The *darśana*, *vedana* etc., as already explained, only refer to *upāsanā*. The constant and unceasing meditation on Brahman practised over a long period reaches a stage of perfection resulting in the vivid experience of Brahman almost similar to a visual perception of an object (*darśana-samānākārata*). This kind of perfected meditation is implied by the word *darśana* in the *Bṛhadāraṇyaka Upaniṣad* and not the goal, viz., the actual intuition of Brahman itself which is possible according to Rāmānuja, only after the soul is disembodied by totally shedding off *karma*. *Darśana* is, therefore, a specific term used for *nididhyāsana*, whereas the latter is taken as a general term. As will be explained later, there are various stages of development in the long process of *upāsanā* or *bhakti-yoga* and also gradations of *bhakti* corresponding to the degrees of its intensity. The starting point is a proper philosophic knowledge of Reality without which even ordinary *bhakti* or devotion to God does not arise. The point to be noted is that mere knowledge of Brahman cannot serve as the direct means to *mokṣa* but on the other hand, it is *jñāna* culminating in the practice of *upāsanā* or *bhakti-yoga* that constitutes the direct means to the spiritual goal.

The Concept of Bhakti-yoga in the Bhagavad-gītā

What is the nature of *bhakti-yoga* which is advocated by the Viśiṣṭādvaita Vedānta as a direct *upāya* to *mokṣa*? The principal Upaniṣads which generally speak of *Brahma-vidyās* or *upāsanās* of different types do not throw much light on the method of practising it except certain general characteristics of *upāsanā*. Nor does the *Vedānta-sūtra*, which accords such an important place to it (the major part of third *adhyāya* is devoted to a discussion of the issues relating to the *vidyās*) present a comprehensive and consolidated account of its practice step by step, as the *Yoga-sūtras* describe the eight limbs of yoga discipline. Though the later religious literature such as the Itihāsas and Purāṇas with the exception of the *Bhagavad-gītā*, commend the practice of *bhakti-yoga* and other forms of yogas, they do not provide us a practical guide to the practice of *bhakti-yoga*. The only important Vedānta treatise, which deals in detail about *bhakti-yoga* is the *Bhagavad-gītā*. The first six chapters deal with *karma-yoga* and *jñāna-yoga* which are considered by Rāmānuja as subsidiary means to *bhakti-yoga* and the later chapters (7 to 12) are devoted to *bhakti-yoga*. In fact, Rāmānuja in his introduction to the *Gītābhāṣya* openly states that the *Gītā* is primarily intended to teach *bhakti-yoga*. In his own words, 'The Supreme Being out of compassion towards humanity incarnated Himself as Lord Kṛṣṇa and under the pretext of inducing Arjuna to fight the war, he introduced *bhakti-yoga* aided by *jñāna* and *karma* which is enjoined in the Upaniṣads as the direct means to *mokṣa*, the highest goal of human endeavour.'[18] Though the *Bhagavad-gītā* gives sufficient details about *bhakti-yoga*, yet it does not throw much light on the method of its practice. However, both the *Vedānta-sūtra* as well as the *Gītā* refer to certain aspects of *Pātañjala yoga* but nevertheless they do not mention specifically that the very *aṣṭāṅga-yoga* itself is *bhakti-yoga* discipline. The commentators on the *Vedānta-sūtra* also acknowledge the need of yogic practice. However, *bhakti-yoga* seems to include much more than *aṣṭāṅga-yoga*. The obvious reason for this difference in the nature of two disciplines is that the final goal of *Pātañjala yoga* is *kaivalya* or the realization of the true nature of one's own self,[19] whereas it is the God-realization (*paramātma-sākṣātkāra*) for *bhakti-yoga*. The self-realization referred to in the Sāṅkhya-yoga system is considered subsidiary to God-realization in Viśiṣṭādvaita. This point has been manifestly brought out in the *Bhagavad-gītā*. We shall present a brief outline of the same in the following pages to bring out the essential features of *bhakti-yoga*.

The Theory of Karma-yoga

The main goal of *bhakti-yoga* is God-realization. This needs to be preceded by the self-realization or the vision of one's own self (*ātmāvalokana*). For this purpose both the *karma-yoga* and *jñāna-yoga* have been laid down as direct means (*upāya*). According to the *Bhagavad-gītā*, *karma-yoga* can serve as an aid to *jñāna-yoga* which secures the realization of the self. It can also serve as a direct means to self-realization since the practice of *karma-yoga* in the prescribed manner includes in it the *jñāna-yoga*. *Jñāna-yoga*, by itself, without the aid of *karma-yoga* is a difficult path for self-realization and the *Gītā*, therefore, recommends the observance of *karma-yoga* as an aid to *jñāna-yoga*.

Karma-yoga is the first step in the spiritual discipline (*sādhana*) to be adopted for *mokṣa*. The term *karma* bears different meanings. In a general sense it means action or any activity. It also refers to the merit and demerit (*puṇya* and *pāpa*) acquired as a result of the performance of good and bad deeds respectively. It is also understood as the observance of the prescribed religious acts and in this sense the term is used in the present context. Yoga means *upāya* or method to be adopted to achieve a goal. So the compound word *karma-yoga* means a specific religious act adopted as a means or *upāya* for self-realization.

There are several religious duties laid down by the sacred texts. The *Gītā* has enumerated the following as illustrative:[20] (1) worship of God (*devārcanā*); (2) performance of the sacrifice (*yāga*) in the consecrated fire; (3) control of the sense organs (*indriya-saṁyama*) by arresting their outward movement towards external objects; (4) control of the mind (*manas-saṁyama*); (5) giving away the money earned in a righteous way in charity (*dāna*) either for the worship of God or for performance of *homa* or to deserving persons etc.; (6) observance of austerities (*tapas*) in the form of performance of prescribed rites such as fasting; (7) visiting holy religious centres and bathing in sacred waters (*puṇyatīrtha-puṇyasthāna-prāpti*); (8) recitation of the Vedas and study of the teachings of the sacred texts (*svādhyāya tadartha-jñānābhyāṣa*); and (9) practice of breath control (*prāṇāyāma*). It is not necessary that all of these religious duties have to be observed for the purpose of *karma-yoga*. Any one of them, depending upon the capacity and choice of an individual, adopted as a *sādhana* or religious discipline can become *karma-yoga* for self-realization. Each one of these acts is called *yajña* in the *Gītā* thereby implying that it is to be performed with the spirit of a sacrifice (*yāga*) for the sole purpose of self-realization.

There are several important requirements to be fulfilled for a successful performance of *karma-yoga* by an aspirant. In the first instance, he should acquire adequate philosophic knowledge about the true nature of *jīvātman* and *Paramātman* through the study of the sacred texts under the guidance of a qualified preceptor (*guru*). The need of such knowledge is obvious because without knowing the true nature of the self, one cannot endeavour for its realization. For this reason Arjuna was imparted at the very outset with a detailed knowledge of the self. The second important requirement is that a person performing *karma-yoga* is required to observe without fail all the other religious duties which have been laid down by the sacred texts, in accordance with one's *varṇa* (caste) and *āśrama* (stages of life). These duties are generally called *karmas*. These *karmas* are of three types: (*a*) *nitya* or those prescribed religious duties which are mandatory and to be performed unconditionally; (*b*) *naimittika* or those prescribed rituals which have to be observed necessarily but only on certain occasions or for certain specific purposes; and (*c*) *kāmya* or those which may be performed only when one desires to attain some specific result such as heaven or wealth. The first two are obligatory duties because the non-performance of them will result in sin. The third one is purely optional. These duties vary in accordance with one's caste and the stages of life. Anyone who embarks on *karma-yoga* should necessarily observe the performance of *nitya* and *naimittika karmas* as auxiliaries to the spiritual discipline.

The third requirement, which is the most important one, is that the religious act which is adopted as a *sādhana* for the purpose of self-realization should be performed without any attachment either to oneself, or to the *karma* itself or even to the result arising from it. There are three factors involved in the performance of *karma-yoga* emphasising a spirit of renunciation. The first one is the renunciation of egoism in the form that 'I am the doer of the act' (*kartṛtva-tyāga*); the second is the renunciation of selfish attachment to the act, viz., that 'it is my act' (*mamatā-tyāga*); and third one is the renunciation of the desire in the fruit accruing from the deed, viz., that 'I am reaping the benefit for my purpose' (*phala-tyāga*). Thus says the *Gītā*: 'You have a right only to (do) the *karma* and never to its fruit; you are not to think that you are the cause of it.'[21] It teaches the disinterested performance of *karma* as a duty for duty's sake. This is the highest ethical ideal upheld in the *Bhagavad-gītā*. When an individual seeking *mokṣa* undertakes the performance of the prescribed *karma* as a *sādhana* for liberation from bondage, it is imperative on his part to develop this sense of renunciation.

It is not an easy task to follow this ideal. It is natural for an individual, being influenced by an attachment to the physical body, to have the egoism, the feeling that he himself is the agent of the action. It is also natural to be influenced by a desire for the result when an activity is undertaken by him. Constant and sincere effort is, therefore, needed to get over these factors. Two practical suggestions have been made in the *Gītā* in this regard. The first one is to ascribe the doership to the three qualities or *guṇas—sattva, rajas* and *tamas*—which are inherent in the mind. As we have explained elsewhere, all things in the universe—both physical as well as psychical—are the products of *prakṛti*, which is constituted of the three *guṇas*. These *guṇas* influence all our thoughts and physical activities. So what is responsible for a particular act is the influence of the *guṇas* more than the individual self. The second suggestion is to put the responsibility of the action on *Īśvara* or God who is the inner controller of all human beings. According to the Viśiṣṭādvaita Vedānta, God is the indweller of all sentient beings and as *antarātmā*, He controls all the activities of human beings from within. The *Gītā* also reiterates the same truth.[22] The individual self (*jīva*) is absolutely dependent on God and the very capacity to act (*kartṛtva*) is also endowed by God. By realizing this truth, it will become easy to develop the spirit of renunciation in the performance of a religious act as a part of *karma-yoga*.

The disinterested performance of *karma*, which is known as *niṣkāma-karma* as a divine service for the pleasure of God, has the advantage of securing the grace of God. It also gives mental tranquillity and inner purity of mind which are essential requirements for performing the meditation on the self. This helps the aspirant to realize the goal of self-realization in an easier way than pursuing the rigorous path of *jñāna-yoga*. In view of it, *karma-yoga* is considered better than *jñāna-yoga* and it can serve as a direct aid to *ātmāvalokana*, the vision of the *jīvātman*, which is the goal of *jñāna-yoga.* In a sense *karma-yoga* includes in it an element of *jñāna-yoga* since true knowledge of self (*ātma-jñāna*) is involved in the practice of *karma-yoga.* Even *jñāna-yoga,* as will be explained presently, will need *karma-yoga* as an aid to it. The two are interrelated. But it is easier to practise *karma-yoga* as it takes less effort and time to realize the goal because of the divine grace showered on the individual in response to the disinterested performance of *karma.*

The practice of *karma-yoga* leads the aspirant to a state of steadfastness in self-knowledge. The *Gītā* describes him as a *sthitaprajña* and extolls him as the ideal person. He has conquered the senses and mind, which cause attachment to worldly pleasures and thereby further bondage. He enjoys such a state of mental tranquillity that neither joy nor sorrow affect him. He neither develops hatred towards others nor any attachment to any because he has conquered the two unethical mental qualities of *kāma* or desire and *krodha* or anger. Being immersed in the delight of the self-knowledge, he enjoys perfect peace of mind (*śānti*). He thus becomes the fittest person for the practice of *jñāna-yoga* to attain the direct vision of the self or even the practice of *bhakti-yoga* to attain God-realization.

The Theory of Jñāna-yoga

Jñāna-yoga is the next important stage of the *sādhana* for *mokṣa.* Its goal is *ātma-sākṣātkāra* or the direct vision of the true nature of *jīvātman.*[23] It serves as an important means to *bhakti-yoga.* After an aspirant for *mokṣa* has successfully completed the practice of *karma-yoga* he can undertake *jñāna-yoga.* A *karma-yogī* can achieve *ātma-sākṣātkāra* without observing *jñāna-yoga,* whereas a *jñāna-yogī* cannot avoid altogether the practice of *karma-yoga. Jñāna-yoga* requires the concentration of mind and the latter cannot be obtained without the observance of the prescribed religious duties. *Karma-yoga* is thus an essential prerequisite for *jñāna-yoga.*

Before discussing the nature of *jñāna-yoga* we should understand what exactly it means in the Viśiṣṭādvaita Vedānta. There is a wide difference in the theories advanced by the Advaita Vedānta and Viśiṣṭādvaita regarding *jñāna-yoga* due to the different ontological positions held by the two schools of thought. According to the Advaita, the individual self (*jīvātman*) is not a distinct real entity other than Brahman and the two are identical. Owing to *avidyā*, the cosmic ignorance, *jīvas* appear to be many and as different from Brahman. The ignorance of the true nature of Brahman is the cause of bondage and its removal is possible only by knowledge of the true nature of Brahman. In Advaita, self-realization is actually the same as Brahman-realization. It is this realization of the identity of the *jīva* and Brahman as taught in the Upaniṣadic text 'Thou art that' (*tat-tvam-asi*) that removes bondage. The removal of *avidyā* or cosmic ignorance by Brahman-knowledge is *mokṣa* or the liberation from bondage. Self-realization which is the same as Brahman-realization is thus the goal of the spiritual discipline (*sādhana*). The *nididhyāsana* or meditation according to the Advaitin serves as an aid to *jñāna-yoga*.

The Viśiṣṭādvaitin holds diametrically an opposite view. *Jīvātman* is a real entity distinct from Brahman. Both are absolutely real and are different from each other. Bondage is caused by *karma* in the form of merit and sin arising from the performance of good and bad deeds. Its removal is possible only through the grace of God for which purpose *bhakti-yoga* or *upāsanā* in the form of unceasing meditation on God with devotion is to be performed. *Bhakti-yoga* needs the aid of both *karma-yoga* and *jñāna-yoga*. *Ātma-sākṣātkāra* which is the aim of both helps to achieve *Brahma-sākṣātkāra* or attainment of Brahman.

In the light of this explanation, *jñāna-yoga* in Viśiṣṭādvaita refers to the unceasing meditation on the true nature of the *ātman* of an individual after he has achieved control over his mind and senses.[24] Vedānta Deśika describes it as *nirantara ātma-cintanam* which means constant meditation on the true nature of the self (*ātman*).[25] The purpose of the meditation on the self is to obtain the direct vision of the self (*ātmāvalokana*) which in turn helps to achieve the direct *sākṣātkāra* or realization of God by means of *bhakti-yoga*.

The practice of *jñāna-yoga* for the purpose of *ātmāvalokana* requires the strict observance of the yoga practice (*yogābhyāṣa*) as described in the *Bhagavad-gītā*.[26] In a broad sense, it comprises the eightfold moral and spiritual discipline (*aṣṭāṅga-yoga*) of the Yoga system. In the first place, the aspirant needs the concentration of mind. In order to secure the steadiness of the mind, the impurities of the mind in the form of *rajas* and *tamas* and other unethical qualities such as *kāma* (passion), *krodha* (anger) have to be eradicated by the observance of prescribed religious acts. This means the scrupulous observance of all the mandatory religious duties. In other words, the observance of *karma-yoga* is imperative for the success of *jñāna-yoga*. The control of sense organs and development of the spirit of detachment (*vairāgya*) are also needed for the practice of *jñāna-yoga*. The mind and sense organs have a natural tendency to flow outwardly and attract the individual towards worldly pleasures. These are the obstacles coming in the way of practice of yoga and have, therefore, to be totally overcome. There are a few other requirements which are common to all kinds of meditation such as the selection of a quiet and suitable place, need to sit in a steady posture, control of breath, restriction on diet etc. Obstacles are bound to arise in the way of yogic practice and in order to overcome them, the *Gītā* advocates that one should seek the grace of God by meditation upon Him.[27] With the fulfilment of all these requirements an aspirant should practise the meditation upon the *jīvātman* over a long period. This will ultimately lead to the direct vision of the self (*ātmāvalokana*), which is the goal of *jñāna-yoga*.

The *ātma-sākṣātkāra* or self-realization comes gradually in stages. In the initial stage, the constant and unceasing meditation upon the self gives him the philosophic insight about the true nature of the self, viz., that the self is essentially of the nature of *jñāna* and *ānanda* and that all selves are of the same character. This helps to develop an attitude of looking upon all living beings as equal in so far as their intrinsic nature is concerned. Thus says the *Gītā*: 'The wise men regard as equal a person blessed with knowledge and humility, an ordinary Brahman, a cow, an elephant, a dog and an outcaste.'[28] The difference between one living being and another is all due to the physical bodies they assume on account of *karma*. In the next stage, he realizes that *Īśvara* or God is immanent in the soul and that the individual selves are supported, controlled and are intended for the service of *Paramātman*. At the next stage, when he gets the direct vision of the self, he enjoys the blissful character of the self and becomes absorbed in the joy of this spiritual experience, which is the culmination of *jñāna-yoga*. This state of the experience of the unique spiritual bliss is regarded in the Sāṅkhya-yoga system as *kaivalya* or the state of self in its own true nature (*kevalāvasthā*), devoid of all external experience. This state itself is liberation (*mokṣa*) for the *Sāṅkhya* and Yoga. But according to the Viśiṣṭādvaita Vedānta, this is not an end in itself but only a means to God-realization. It is not a goal because in the state of *kaivalya* the individual self, though it becomes free from bondage,[29] does not experience the bliss of *Paramātman*. It, therefore, advocates the practice of *bhakti-yoga* or the meditation on God as the next step from the stage of *jñāna-yoga*. The *ānanda* or bliss derived from the *paramātma-sākṣātkāra* is far superior to the bliss obtained from *ātmāvalokana*. Thus, *jñāna-yoga* is a subsidiary means to *bhakti-yoga*, which alone is the direct means to *mokṣa*.

The Theory of Bhakti-yoga

We have already explained the meaning and implication of the term *bhakti-yoga* and also its prerequisites. We shall now consider its main features as a spiritual discipline for *mokṣa*. The *Bhagavad-gītā* which sums up the essential features of *bhakti-yoga* in one significant verse,[30] refers to three points. First, the aspirant is required to fix his mind on the *Paramātman* (*manmanā bhava*) with deep devotion to Him (*madbhakta*). Secondly, he should engage himself in the worship of the Supreme Being (*madyājī*). Thirdly, he should do other acts such as offering salutations (*namaskāra*) to Him. The first one is *dhyāna* or contemplation. The second is *yajana* which in its broadest sense means the different modes of worship of God. The third is *namaskāra* which means dedicating oneself to God. Each one of these is full of significance and a proper understanding of it will give an idea of what *bhakti-yoga* is.

Dhyāna does not mean mere meditation on an object as it is ordinarily understood. In the initial stage, the mind is to be focused on the object of contemplation, which in the Yoga system is called *dhāraṇa* or concentration. *Dhyāna* follows *dhāraṇa*. It signifies a constant and continuous reflection on the divine form with all its glory.[31] To be more specific, it means, as Rāmānuja explains, reflection on the *svarūpa* or the essential nature, *rūpa* or the divine personality, *guṇa* or the auspicious attributes of Brahman.[32] It amounts to a conscious effort to think of all the glory of God not for a short period but continuously and repeatedly until such time as the goal is achieved. The flow of thought towards God should be like an unbroken stream of oil poured from a vessel.[33] This is what is intended in the expression *dhruvāsmṛtiḥ* used in the *Chāndogya Upaniṣad* for *dhyāna* or *upāsanā*.[34] The same truth is reiterated by the *Vedānta-sūtra* when it states that meditation is to be repeated often.[35] This is to be done with deep devotion towards God. Anything done devoid of love to God is not pleasing to Him and will not lead to the desired goal.

Dhyāna implies the entire eightfold yogic discipline known as *aṣṭāṅga-yoga* of Yoga system. Though the word *aṣṭāṅga-yoga* is not explicitly mentioned either in the *Gītā* or the *Vedānta-sūtra* it is implicit because without going through the prescribed yogic discipline, *dhyāna* for achieving God-realization is not possible. Rāmānuja acknowledges the need of *yogāṅgas* for *dhyāna* as he quotes a verse from *Viṣṇupurāṇa* which explicitly states that *dhyāna* on *Paramātman* is to be accomplished with the aid of the first six *yogāṅgas* (*prathamaiḥ ṣaḍbhiḥ aṅgaiḥ niṣpādyate*).[36] Before embarking on *dhyāna*, *dhāraṇa* or concentration on the object of contemplation is needed. This is the sixth limb of yoga discipline. Concentration of mind presupposes invariably the mental purity by way of cultivation of ethical virtues (*yama*), observance of religious duties (*niyama*), a steady posture (*āsana*), control of breath (*prāṇāyāma*) and control of sense organs (*pratyāhāra*). Then follows *dhāraṇa*, concentration and *dhyāna*, meditation. The same when perfected over a long period of practice culminates in the actual realization or the vision of the object of contemplation. This final stage of yoga practice is known as *samādhi* in Yoga system leading to the state of *kaivalya*. In Viśiṣṭādvaita, the final stage of *bhakti-yoga* culminates in *paramātma-sākṣātkāra* leading to *mokṣa*.

Though *bhakti-yoga* covers *aṣṭāṅga-yoga* of Patañjali, its scope is far wider and covers much more than *aṣṭāṅga-yoga*. The *Vedānta-sūtra* refers to the need of a steadyposture,[37] concentration of mind (*acalatva*) and proper congenial atmosphere for contemplation.[38] While discussing the practice of *jñāna-yoga*, the *Gītā* also refers to the need of sitting in a proper place for doing meditation with concentration.[39] There is no specific mention of *yamas* and *niyamas* of Yoga system in the *Vedānta-sūtra*. But it emphasises the need of development of calmness (*śama*), control of senses (*dama*) etc., as an aid to *upāsanā*.[40] Further, the sevenfold ethical discipline known as *sādhana-saptaka* which is prescribed by Rāmānuja as an essential requirement for *upāsanā* or *bhakti-yoga* on the authority of the ancient commentator, referred to as Vākyakāra[41] covers some of the features of *yama* and *niyamas*. These are: (1) *viveka* or the purification of body by consumption of *sāttvik* food which leads to purity of mind, (2) *vimoka* or getting rid of sensual attachment and anger for securing mental tranquillity, (3) *abhyāsa* or repeated reflection of God who is immanent in human souls, (4) *kriyā* or the performance of fivefold religious duty which will provide inner mental strength, (5) *kalyāṇa* or development of ethical virtues such as honesty, integrity, compassion, benevolence, non-violence etc., which will give inner purity, (6) *anavasāda* or freedom from despair due to disappointments and unexpected calamities, and lastly (7) *anuddharṣa* or not to be over-powered by excessive joy so that tranquillity of mind is not disturbed. The sevenfold ethical discipline helps the individual practising *bhakti-yoga* to achieve good progress in the meditation on Brahman.

In addition to the ethical discipline the *upāsaka* embarking on *bhakti-yoga* is required to perform without fail all the *nitya* and *naimittika karmas* or the religious duties laid down as obligatory by the sacred texts purely for the pleasure of God. The ethical principle of *niṣkāma-karma* advocated in respect of the observance of *karma-yoga* is also to be followed by the *upāsaka* seeking *mokṣa*. On the strength of the teachings of the Upaniṣads, the *Vedānta-Sūtra* and the *Bhagavad-gītā*,[42] Rāmānuja emphasises repeatedly that under no circumstances the *upāsaka* should give up the performance of the prescribed religious duties and that these have to be observed for the lifetime until the *upāsanā* is successfully completed culminating in the God-realization.[43] According to the Viśiṣṭādvaita Vedānta, *karma* or the performance of religious duties is an *aṅga* or subsidiary to *upāsanā*. Thus, it may be observed that *dhyāna* which is the first essential feature of *bhakti-yoga*, as stated in the *Gītā*, covers not only the entire eightfold yoga discipline but much more than that.

Dhyāna, which may be appropriately termed as *dhyāna-yoga*, is primarily a mental act (*mānasa*) in the form of unceasing, loving meditation on God. The other two features of *bhakti-yoga*, viz., *yajana* and *namaskāra* represent the physical (*kāyika*) and oral (*vācika*) acts. *Yajana* in its broad sense includes physical as well as oral acts such as *arcana* or worship, in the form of recitation of the names of God, offering flowers, fruits and food, litting lights, offering incense and sandal paste. In other words, the entire mode of worship prescribed by the Pāñcarātra Āgamas is covered by *yajana*.[44]

The *Bhāgavata Purāṇa* mentions nine modes of worship of God.[45] These are: *śravaṇa*, listening the glory of God, *kīrtana*, singing His glory, *smaraṇa*, contemplating of His greatness, *pādasevana*, offering worship to His feet, *arcana*, offering flowers with recitation of His names, *vandana*, prostrating before God, *dāsya*, feeling the utter dependence on God, *sakhyam*, loving disposition towards God and *ātma-nivedanam*, surrendering one-self to God. The last one is referred to by *namaskāra* mentioned in the *Gītā* and the rest of it are different forms of *yajana*. All these mental, physical and oral religious activities are to be carried on as part of *bhakti-yoga*. Thus, *bhakti-yoga* is not a simple meditation upon God but it is a multi-form ethical, religious and spiritual discipline to be undertaken and continued over a long time for the purpose of attaining God.

Stages of Bhakti-yoga

A psycho-religious discipline to be pursued over a long period has its stages of development. Rāmānuja, who is the foremost exponent of *bhakti-yoga* as a direct means to *mokṣa*, has conceived of three important stages. These are termed as *para-bhakti*, *para-jñāna* and *parama-bhakti*. In the Vaiṣṇava treatises Rāmānuja was the first to use these terms.[46] These concepts seem to have been taken from the hymns of Nammāḻvār and the *Bhagavad-gītā*. Though these phrases are not found explicitly either in the verses of the *Gītā* or the Tamil hymns, they are implicit in them. The *Gītā* verse says: 'To those who seek permanent union with me, and meditate on me, I (the Lord) bestow to them with love, *buddhiyoga* by means of which they attain me.'[47] The term *buddhiyoga* in this verse does not mean as it is generally understood, the wisdom or knowledge, because such a knowledge does not help to attain God. What is, therefore, intended here is *bhakti* which has been perfected to the extent of becoming something similar to a vision of God (*darśana-samānākāra*). Rāmānuja uses in his *Gītabhāṣya* the phrase '*vipāka-daśāpanna*' which means *bhakti* which has reached a stage of perfection. In the *Śrī-bhāṣya*, he repeatedly uses the expression *darśana-samānākāra*, something similar to an actual vision. The implication of it is that the actual direct and comprehensive vision of God with all His full splendour is not possible at the stage of the practice of *bhakti-yoga*. It comes after the soul is disembodied only in the state of *mokṣa*. When the unceasing meditation on God is perfected to the extent of its becoming similar to a clear vision, it is regarded as *para-bhakti*, or higher form of *bhakti*, to distinguish it from the ordinary *bhakti*, which is just devotion to God needed in the initial stages of *upāsanā*. The *para-bhakti* itself, in the opinion of Rāmānuja, is *dhruvānusmṛti*[48] or *nididhyāsana* which is enjoined by the Upaniṣads as a direct means to *mokṣa*. The word *darśana* also means the same as *nididhyāsana* except that the former is taken as a specific form of the latter signifying contemplation as characterised by vividness (*darśana-samānākāra*). The term *para-bhakti* is not a state of *jivan-mukti* of the Advaita Vedānta or God-vision or a state of *bhakti* to be developed after release as opined by some scholars. It is just the *bhakti-yoga* which is enjoined as the means for *mokṣa*.[49]

The other two terms—*para-jñāna* and *parama-bhakti* represent the next two stages of *bhakti-yoga* signifying the *intensity* of *bhakti* of the *upāsaka* as evidenced in the mystic experience of God by Nammāḻvār. Vedānta Deśika has explained clearly the differences between the three stages of *bhakti-yoga*. *Bhakti* which is the general term refers to the development of love towards God which arises from the contact with pious religious men, or by listening to the religious discourses etc. Consequently this produces a desire to know more about the nature of God and His glory. Such a desire leads to the practice of *bhakti-yoga* proper with all its prerequisites. When this practice reaches a stage of perfection resulting in the experience similar to a vision of God, it assumes the name of *para-bhakti*. The *para-bhakti* in turn produces an intense desire and determination to see the Lord and makes the *upāsaka* implore as in the words of Arjuna: 'O Lord, be pleased to show thy whole Self, if I can see you'[50] or as expressed in the fervent prayers of the Nammāḻvār: 'Vouchsafe Thy grace so that I may see Thee', 'May I see Thee some day'.[51] In response to these ardent appeals, the Supreme Being blesses him with an occasional glimpse of God for a very short duration. This type of temporary *sākṣātkāra* of God granted to the devotee out of the grace of the Lord is known as *para-jñāna* or vision of God. The several glimpses of God obtained by Nammāḷvār for short duration, as is evident from his hymns, are examples of *para-jñāna*. Such temporary glimpses of God do not satisfy the devotee and it produces in him further intense craving to have a fuller and permanent vision. Being restless, the *upāsaka* makes pathetic appeals to God to grant him an everlasting perfect vision of God.[52] This type of *bhakti* culminating in the deep craving for a permanent vision of God is regarded as *parama-bhakti*, the highest form of *bhakti*. Only when this final stage is reached, the aspirant, with the Grace of God, becomes disembodied and the individual soul reaches the supra-mundane realm where he enjoys perfect bliss of the Supreme Being (*paripūrṇa-brahmānubhava*). This is the state of *mokṣa*, the final goal of *bhakti-yoga* according to Viśiṣṭādvaita. Thus, *bhakti* leads through yoga practice to *para-bhakti*, which leads to *para-jñāna*, which in its turn to *parama-bhakti* resulting in the attainment of *mokṣa*. These are all gradations (*avasthās*) of *bhakti*. Such gradations are also admitted in the state of *mokṣa* during the unceasing experience of the released soul. In the *Śaraṇāgati-gadya*, when Rāmānuja prays to God while observing *śaraṇāgati*, to grant him *para-bhakti*, *para-jñāna* and *parama-bhakti*, he refers to the *bhakti* not as a means (*upāya*) for *mokṣa* but for doing divine service in the state of *mokṣa*.[53] There is a difference between the *bhakti* in the state of *mokṣa* and that during the stage of practice of *bhakti-yoga*. In the latter case, it is the *sādhana* or means of God-realization (*sādhana-bhakti*), whereas in the former case it is *bhakti* in the form of God's experience achieved by the observance of the prescribed *sādhana*. It is, therefore, called *phala-bhakti*.

Bhakti-yoga can also serve as a means for attainment of other goals such as *aiśvarya* or wealth, *kaivalya* or state of blissful existence of the self and wordly prosperity. Accordingly, the *Gītā* classifies the *bhaktas* or devotees into four groups:[54] *ārta* or the one who aspires for recovery of the lost wealth, *jijñāsu* or one who desires to attain the blissful state of one's self, *arthā-*

rthī or one who wishes to acquire material wealth and *jñānī* or one who craves to attain God. Of all these, *jñānī* is held in high esteem because he is the one who does meditation without any selfish purpose exclusively for attaining God. He is regarded by God as His dearest (*atyartha-priyaḥ*). The *bhakti-yoga* adopted as a direct means for *mokṣa* is, therefore, the best one. All the thirty-two *upāsanās* enjoined in the Upaniṣads are intended for the realization of Brahman. As the goal of these *upāsanās* is the same, viz., the attainment of *mokṣa*, they are regarded as alternative means. They are named differently because of the difference in the description of the object of contemplation, viz., Brahman in terms of its attributes. Thus, for instance, the *upāsanā* on Brahman as *sat* or the ground of the entire universe is named *sadvidyā*. The *upāsanā* of Brahman as an indweller in the inner recess of the heart (*dahara*) is known as *dahara-vidyā*. In all these cases, the mode of meditation along with the various ethical and religious requirements explained earlier in connection with *bhakti-yoga* remains the same.

This is indeed an arduous pathway to *mokṣa*. It is beset with innumerable difficulties and hardships. The most competent person like Arjuna even after he was fully instructed by no less a preceptor than the very God-incarnate, expressed grief towards the end indicating his incapability for the observance of *bhakti-yoga*. At this stage, the benevolent Lord Kṛṣṇa out of compassion and friendly disposition towards Arjuna comes out with the advice to adopt the method of absolute self-surrender as an easier pathway to *mokṣa*.[55] This is the doctrine of *śaraṇāgati* or *prapatti* as it is popularly known. This has been accepted by Vaiṣṇava *Ācāryas* as an easier alternative means to *mokṣa* and it constitutes the most important doctrine of Vaiṣṇava theology. We shall discuss it in a separate chapter.

Notes

1. See RTS XXIX p. 234. (quoted by Vedānta Désika from some pāñcarātra treatise).

   bhaktyā paramayā vāpi prapattyā vā mahāmate;
   prāpyo'ham nānyathā prāpyo mama kaiṅkaryalipsubhiḥ.

2. According to the *Nighantu* (glossary of Vedic terms), the terms *sevā*, *bhakti* and *upāsti* convey the same meaning. The word *sevā* is, therefore, understood as *bhakti*.

See *Śrutaprakāśikā*, I.1.1. p. 61.

3. Ibid. *snehapūrvam-anudhyānaṁ bhaktirityabhidhīyate.*
4. SvUp III.8. *tameva viditvā atimṛtyumeti nānyaḥ panthā vidyate ayanāya.*
   See also *Puruṣa-sūkta*, 17. *tamevaṁ vidvān amṛta iha bhavati nānyaḥ panthā ayanāya vidyate.*
5. TUp II.1. *brahmavid-āpnoti param.*
6. MUp III.2.3. *nāyamātmā pravacanena labhyo na medhayā na bahunā śrutena; yamevaiṣa vṛṇute tena labhyaḥ tasyaiṣa ātmā vivṛṇute tanūṁ svām.*
   See also KaUp I.2.23.
7. RB I.1.1. p. 19.
8. BG X.10. *teṣāṁ satatayuktānāṁ bhajatāṁ prītipūrvakam; dadāmi buddhiyogaṁ taṁ yena mām-upayānti te.*
9. BG VII.17. *priyo hi jñānino'tyartham-ahaṁ sa ca mama priyaḥ.*
10. BG XI.53.54. *nāhaṁ Vedair-na tapasā na dānena na cejyayā; śakya evaṁ-vidho draṣṭuṁ. . .bhaktyā tvananyayā śakya aham-evam-vidho'-rjuna.*
11. See Chapter 2, p. 53.
12. In a technical sense, these terms represent different stages of *bhakti*, one leading to the other.
    See TMK II.30. See also *Darśanodaya*, p. 235.
    Vedanaṁ dhyāna-viśrāntaṁ dhyānaṁ śrāntaṁ dhruvāsmṛtau;
    sā ca dṛṣṭitvam-abhyeti, dṛṣṭiḥ bhaktitvamṛ-cchati.
13. ChUp III.18 and IV.1.4 and IV.2.2.
    See also RB I.1.1. p. 17. *vidyupāsyoḥ vyatikareṇa upakrama upasaṁhāra darśanāt.*
14. See FVV pp. 289-95 for details regarding criticisms of Advaitin's theory.
15. BrUp VI.4.21. *tameva dhiro vijñāya prajñāṁ kurvīta.*
16. Ibid. VI.5.6. *ātmā vā are draṣṭavyaḥ śrotavyo mantavyo nididhyāsitavyaḥ.*
17. ChUp VIII.12.6. *yas-tam-ātmānam-anuvidya vijānāti.*
18. GB (Introduction). *pāṇḍutanaya-yuddhaprotsāhanavyājena paramapuruṣārtha-lakṣaṇa-mokṣasādhanatayā vedāntoditaṁ svaviṣayaṁ jñānakarmānugṛhītaṁ bhakti-yogam-avatārayāmāsa.*
19. See *Yoga-sūtra*, I.3. *tadā draṣṭuḥ svarūpe avasthānam.*
20. See BG IV.25.29.
    See also GB IV.25.29.
21. BG II.47. *karmaṇyevādhikāraste mā phaleṣu kadācana; mā karmaphalaheturbhūḥ mā te saṅgo'stvakarmaṇi.*
22. See BG XVIII.61. *īśvara ssarvabhūtānāṁ hṛddeśe arjuna tiṣṭati; bhrāmayansarvabhūtāni yantrārūḍhāni māyayā.*
23. See GB VII.1. *pratyagātmanaḥ yāthārthya-darśanam.*
24. *Gītārtha-saṁgraha*, 23. *jñānayogo jitasvāntaiḥ pariśuddhātmani sthitiḥ.*
25. RTS Ch. IX, p. 106.
26. GB VI.1. *jñānayogasādhya ātmāvalokanarūpa-yogābhāysa-vidhirucyate.*
27. GB VI.15.

See also *Yoga-sūtra, Īśvara praṇidhānādvā.*

28. BG V.18. *vidyāvinayasaṁpanne brāhmaṇe gavi hastini;*
śuni caiva śvapāke ca paṇḍitāḥ samadarśinaḥ.

29. According to the *Gītā* (VIII.21), an individual who has attained the state of *kaivalya*, does not return to the state of bondage. Nevertheless Rāmānuja does not regard it as equal to the final state of *mokṣa* enjoying the bliss of Brahman. There are two views on the theory of *kaivalya* among the Vaiṣṇavas. According to Vaḍakalai sect, *kaivalya* is half way to *mukti* and eventually the *kevala* (the *jīva* in this state) reaches the Divine Abode by practising *bhakti-yoga.* According to the Tenkalai sect, it is not half way to *mukti* but it is *mukti* itself in which the *mukta* enjoys the bliss of the self for ever remaining in the outskirts of *paramapada* or the Divine Abode without any hope of intuiting God.

30. BG IX.34. *manmanā bhava madbhakto madyājī māṁ namaskuru;*
māmevaiṣyasi yuktvaivam-ātmānaṁ matparāyaṇaḥ.

31. See RB IV.1.1. *dhyānaṁ ca cintanam; cintanaṁ ca smṛtisantatirūpam.*

32. The various types of *upāsanās* known as *Brahma-vidyās* enjoined by the Vedānta specify certain special aspects or attributes of Brahman besides the basic essential attributes for purposes of different *upāsanās.*

33. See RB I.1.1. p. 17. *tailadhārāvad-avicchinna-smṛtisantānarūpam.*

34. ChUp VII.26.2. *Sattvaśuddhau dhrūvāsmṛtiḥ;*
smṛtilambhe sarvagranthīnāṁ vipramokṣaḥ.

35. VS IV.1.1. *āvṛttiḥ asakṛdupadeśāt.*

36. See VP VI.7.91. *tadrūpa-pratyayācaikā santatiśca anyanispṛhā;*
tad-dhyānaṁ prathamairaṅgaiḥ ṣaḍbhirniṣpādyate nṛpa.

37. VS IV.1.7.

38. Ibid. IV.1.11. *yatra ekāgratā tatra aviśeṣāt.*

39. BG VI.11 and 12.

40. VS III.4.27. *śama-damādyupetassyāt tathāpi tu tadvidhestadangatayā.*
teṣāmapy-avaśyānuṣṭe yatvāt. See also BrUp VI.4.23.

41. See RB p. 19. *Tallabdhir-viveka-vimokābhyāsa-kriyā-kalyāṇa-anavasādaanuddharṣebhyaḥ saṁbhavān-nirvacanācca.*
Statement of Vākyakāra quoted by Rāmānuja.

42. BrUp VI.4.22; VS III.4.26 and BG XVIII.5.

43. GB XVIII.5. *yājñadānatapaḥ-prabhṛti vaidikaṁ karma mumukṣuṇā na kadācidapi tyājyam; apitu āprayāṇād-aharahaḥ kāryameva.*

44. TC IX-34, p. 276.
bhagavat śāstrādi-prapañcita viṣayo'yam yajiriti.
See also Chapter XV, pp. 313-14.

45. *Bhāgavata,* VII.5.23.

46. See *Śaraṇāgati-gadya,* 2, 15 and 16.

47. See BG X.10. *teṣāṁ satatayuktānāṁ bhajatāṁ prītipūrvakam;*
dadāmi boddhiyogaṁ taṁ yena mām-upayānti te.

48. See RB I.1.1. p. 19. *evam-rupā dhruvāṇusmṛtireva bhakti-śabdena abhidhīyate upāsanā paryāyatvāt bhakti-śabdasya.*

49. VSa p. 191. *parabhaktirūpāpannameva vedanaṁ tattvato bhagavat-prāpti-sādhanam.*
 See also RTS IX. *parabhakti mokṣopāya-vihita-bhaktiyogaṁ* (translated from Tamil to Sanskrit).
50. See BG XI.4. *yogeśvara tato me tvaṁ darśayātmānamavyayam.*
51. *Tiruvāymoḻi*, V.8.9; VIII.1.1, VIII.5.1.
52. See *Tiruvāymoḻi*, X.10.1.9.
53. *Śaraṇāgati-gadya*, 15. *parabhakti parajñāna paramabhaktyaika-sva-bhāvaṁ māṁ kuruṣva.*
 See GaBh. *muktidaśābhāvināṁ parabhaktyādīnāṁ idam-apekṣaṇam.*
 See also GaVa and commentary of Sudarśana Sūri.
 atha bandha-nivṛtteranantarabhāvinīḥ parabhakti-parajñāna-parama-bhaktīḥ prārthayate.
 In a strict sense, the *bhakti* towards God in the state of *mokṣa* is of one type viz. *parama-bhakti*, because the question of *para-bhakti* as a means for God-realization and *para-jñāna* or momentary glimses of God-experience do not arise in that state. However, Rāmānuja in his prayer desires for all the three types of *bhakti* in the sense of gradations in the *phala-bhakti*.
54. BG VII.16.
55. BG XVIII.66. *sarvadharmān parityajya māmekaṁ śaraṇaṁ vrja;*
 ahaṁ tvā sarvapāpebhyo mokṣayiṣyāmi ma śucaḥ.
 Rāmānuja, while commenting on this verse has taken the view in the context of the Gītā's teachings that *śaraṇāgati* is to be adopted as a subsidiary means (*aṅga*) to *bhakti-yoga*. However, in his *Śaraṇāgati-gadya*, *prapatti* is advocated as a direct means to *mokṣa*. All the Vaiṣṇava Ācāryas have accordingly interpreted this *Gītā* verse in the sense of *śaraṇāgati* as a direct, alternative path to *mokṣa*.
 See RTS XXIV, p. 173.

6

THE DOCTRINE OF MOKṢA

We have considered in the previous chapters the nature of *Tattva,* the ultimate Reality and *Hita,* means, the two major topics of Vedānta Philosophy. We shall now take up the third important topic, *Puruṣārtha* or the supreme spiritual goal. As in the case of the other topics, we shall present the philosophic view of *mokṣa* as enunciated in the Upaniṣads and the *Vedānta-sūtra* with a view to demonstrating how this has provided the basis for the theological concept of *mokṣa* as leading to *kaiṅkarya* or divine service by the individual self (*jīva*) in a supramundane realm known as *paramapada.*

The Concept of Mokṣa in the Upaniṣads

The concept of *mokṣa* in the sense of freedom or liberation of the soul from bondage is generally accepted by all the schools of Indian Philosophy. Its origin can be traced to the Vedic times. There are several hymns in the Ṛgveda pleading the Vedic deities to grant immortality (*amṛtatva*).[1] The main teaching of the Upaniṣads is centred on the realization of Brahman as the ideal *Puruṣārtha* or the ultimate human goal. The *Taittirīya Upaniṣad* says: 'The knower of Brahman attains the highest.'[2] While the basic concept of attainment of the spiritual highest is acceptable to all Vedāntins, divergent theories have been advanced by the different schools of Vedānta regarding the nature of the supreme goal. We are concerned here with the presentation of the view of Viśiṣṭādvaita Vedānta.

The *Chāndogya Upaniṣad* dealing with the subject of *mokṣa* states: 'Even so the *jīvātman,* when it raises up from this body and reaches the Supreme Light (Brahman), manifests in its true form.'[3] The same Upaniṣad in its concluding passage, adds: 'He who reaches *Brahma-loka* does not return to this world.'[4] The *Taittirīya Upaniṣad* specifically points out that the individual self enjoys Brahman together with all its auspicious attributes.[5]

The *Muṇḍaka Upaniṣad* mentions that when the Brahman-knower sees the Lord, he attains supreme equality with Him.[6] Based on these authoritative Upaniṣadic teachings, the Viśiṣṭādvaita Vedānta maintains the view that *mokṣa* is not merely the negative concept of freedom of the individual soul from bondage but a positive state of existence of *jīva* in a supra-mundane realm (*Brahma-loka*) where it regains its true form and enjoys the full glory of Brahman. In the words of Vedānta Deśika, it is *paripūrṇa-brahmānubhava*, a complete and comprehensive experience of Brahman. The fuller implications of this view will bring out the nature of *mokṣa* in Viśiṣṭādvaita.

•

The Nature of Jīva in the State of Mokṣa

That the individual self is eternal and different from the physical body and that at the time of death it leaves the body is an accepted fact of orthodox Indian philosophical systems. In the case of an individual who has successfully completed the *upāsanā* on Brahman or *bhakti-yoga*, the soul is believed to depart from the body through the crown of the head with the help of *Paramātman* and pass through the path of the gods (*arcirādi*) until it reaches the realm of Brahman. Descriptive accounts of the exit of the soul (*utkrānti*) and the divine path through which it passes are furnished by the Upaniṣads.[7] We shall consider these details in a separate chapter.[8] The points we should take note of for the present are: that the soul in the state of *mokṣa* manifests itself in its true form, that it enjoys in full measure Brahman and its glory, that it attains a status of equality with Brahman and that the soul does not become merged with Brahman but on the contrary, retains its individuality even in the state of *mokṣa*.

An important implication of these views is that the true nature of the soul which is omniscient in character, becomes fully revealed only after reaching the state of *mokṣa*. As we have observed in the chapter on *jīva*, its knowledge is constrained in the state of bondage due to *karma*. With the total eradication of *karma* by the observance of *upāsanā*, the knowledge of *jīva* becomes fully manifest. Thus says the *Chāndogya Upaniṣad*: 'He who sees (Brahman), sees everything.'[9] The omniscience of *jīva* is not a quality which is newly acquired by the *jīva* in the state of *mokṣa*. It was already there as its inherent character.

What was unmanifest in the state of bondage due to *karma* becomes now manifest in the state of *mokṣa* with the removal of the veil in the form of *karma*. The *Viṣṇudharmottara* makes this point more explicit with the analogy of gem and its lustre. The lustre of a gem when it is enveloped by dirt does not show itself but the same becomes manifest after the dirt is removed.[10] Even as the lustre is not newly created when the gem is cleaned, *jīva's* omniscience is not newly brought into existence. What was already inherent in *jīva* becomes manifest in the state of *mokṣa*. This is the implication of the, expression *'svena rūpeṇa abhiniṣpadyate'* (manifests itself in its own true form), used in the Chāndogya text. Based on this Upaniṣadic statement the *Vedānta-sūtra*[11] uses the term *āvirbhāva*, which according to Rāmānuja, means not a quality newly produced in *jīva* but a mere manifestation of its true nature that was already inherent in it.[12] The removal of the veil in the form of *karma* is accomplished by the observance of *upāsanā* and the former can, therefore, be regarded as the goal to be attained (*sādhya*) by a *sādhana* or the spiritual discipline. In other words, the removal of bondage is the goal of spiritual discipline and the restoration of the true character of *jīva* in the state of *mokṣa* is a mere consequence of it. Thus philosophically, the nature of *mokṣa* in Viśiṣṭādvaita is two-fold: removal of the bondage which is undesirable (*aniṣṭa nivṛttiḥ*) and the regainment of the true character of the soul which is desirable (*iṣṭa-prāptiḥ*). The former is important since the latter is consequential to it.

Eternal Freedom of Jīva from Bondage

Another important implication of this doctrine of liberation of the soul is that it is total and permanent. As the *Chāndogya Upaniṣad*[13] says, once the soul reaches the state of *mokṣa*, there is no return of it to mundane existence. The concluding aphorism of Vedānta asserts the same truth.[14] The same fact is reiterated in the *Gītā*.[15] Philosophically, the concept of *mokṣa* would be meaningless if the soul were to be caught up again in bondage. Theoretically, there are two possibilities of return of the soul to the world of bondage. An individual out of ignorance may of his own choice desire to come back. Alternatively, God who possesses unchecked freedom and to whom *jīva* is absolutely subordinate may command it to go back. Rāmānuja, while commenting on the significance of this *Vedānta-sūtra*, rules out both the possibilities. The individual who has totally become free from *karma* after realizing that other than the enjoyment of Supreme Being nothing else is of value and who has also become omniscient after attaining *mokṣa*, is most unlikely to desire anything other than the bliss of Brahman. *Paramātman* who has abundant love and compassion for the individual self and whom He considers as His dearest (*atyartha-priyaḥ*) will never think of sending him back. Thus, under no circumstances the *jīva* which has reached the state of *mokṣa* will ever return to the bondage.

Equal Status of Jīva with Brahman

The next important implication of the nature of *mokṣa* is that *jīva* enjoys a status of equality with Brahman (*sāmya*), as stated by the *Muṇḍaka Upaniṣad*. This is a significant point for Viśiṣṭādvaita as it upholds the ontological difference between *jīva* and Brahman. According to the Upaniṣadic teaching, *jīva* continues to retain its distinct spiritual entity even in the state of *mokṣa*. In other words, it rules out the view of the Advaitin that *jīva* becomes one with Brahman in the sense of the identity of the two (*tādātmya*). If the soul is an eternal, spiritual entity as distinct from Brahman by virtue of the two possessing distinctive characteristics, the two entities becoming one is logically untenable. If, on the other hand, the soul is illusory in character, which by logical implication amounts to its non-existence, its becoming one with Brahman does not constitute a goal for the obvious reason that the soul ever exists as Brahman. Nothing is newly accomplished to constitute an object of attainment except the removal of the ignorance of the identity. The Viśiṣṭādvaitin, therefore, upholds the view that the individual self attains the status of Brahman (*sādharmya*) rather than believe in the identity (*tādātmya*) of the two.

The concept of *sāmya* or equality does not mean, according to Viśiṣṭādvaita, equality in all respects. Ontologically, there is a fundamental distinction between Brahman and *jīva*. According to the Vedānta, the most distinguishing characteristic of Brahman is that it is the primary cause of the universe (*jagat-kāraṇa*). Brahman is that which is the cause of creation, sustenance and dissolution. This unique characteristic of Brahman is not applicable to any other entity, either the individual soul (*jīva*) or the cosmic matter (*prakṛti*). This is an established truth of Vedānta and it cannot change. Hence, the soul when it attains equality with Brahman, the function of creation which exclusively belongs to Brahman is denied to the soul. The *Vedānta-sūtra*, therefore, asserts that with the exception of the cosmic function (*jagatvyāpāra*), the released soul enjoys equal status with Brahman.[16] The equality is only in respect of the enjoyment of the bliss of Brahman (*bhogamātra-sāmya*).[17] The *Taittirīya Upaniṣad* points out that *jīva* experiences along with Brahman all its glory. The implication of this statement is that the object of experience is common to both *jīva* and Brahman. In what sense, then is the experience common? Brahman is essentially of the nature of *ānanda* or bliss. If the *svarūpa* of Brahman is blissful, it is taken that all that belongs to Brahman, its attributes as well as the *vibhūtis*—are also blissful in the sense that it is joyful (*sukha-rūpa*) for Brahman. In view of it Brahman is described in the Vedānta as *bhūmā* which is interpreted as infinite joy.[18] *Paramātman* experiences Himself as well as His glory as blissful. *Jīva* too in the state of *mokṣa* experiences Brahman as well as its glory as blissful. This is the implication of the term *bhoga* which is common to both *Paramātman* and *jīvātman*. In view of this, the Viśiṣṭādvaita Vedānta describes *mokṣa* as *sāyujya*. *Sāyujya* means the state of experiencing the same object of enjoyment by two individuals together (*sayujo-bhāvaḥ*), like two persons, father and son, eating together the same delicious food. *Jīva* is regarded as having an equal status (*sāmya*) with Brahman only so far as the experience of bliss is concerned and not with regard to the cosmic functions of Brahman.

The state of *sāyujya* or the attainment of equal status with Brahman by *jīva* along with the enjoyment of the bliss of Brahman constitutes the *mokṣa* proper in Viśiṣṭādvaita. The religious literature speaks of other concepts of *mokṣa* such as *sālokya* or living in *Viṣṇu-loka*, *sāmīpya* or staying close to Viṣṇu and *sārūpya* or assuming the bodily form similar to that of Viṣṇu. But none of these is regarded as equal to the *mokṣa* in the sense of *sāyujya*.[19] *Sāyujya* alone is *mokṣa*. Such a theory of *sāyujya* provides a meaningful significance to the concept of *mokṣa* as it ensures not merely the continuity of the soul free from all bondage but also a positive state of existence enjoying the bliss of Brahman.

Divine Service in Mokṣa

The *Chāndogya Upaniṣad* mentions that the individual self becomes free in the state of *mokṣa* and that it is capable of moving in all worlds according to its wishes. It also refers to such physical activities as eating, playing, moving from place to place.[20] This would, therefore, imply that the *jīva* should be possessed of body to perform such acts. If the *jīva* were associated with a body, the question arises whether it would not again be subject to bondage?

In reply to this, Viśiṣṭādvaita explains that *jīva* can assume a body out of its own free will (*saṅkalpa*) to perform some divine service or for the purpose of movement. Such a body taken on by *jīva* is constituted of spiritual substance (*śuddha-sattva*) and not made of the five elements as in the case of human beings. What brings bondage to the soul is the body caused by *karma* out of physical elements. The body constituted of spiritual substance out of its *saṅkalpa* does not cause any bondage to the soul. On the basis of the Upaniṣadic teaching, the author of the *Vedānta-sūtra* admits the possibility of a body for the released souls out of free-will.[21]

The assumption of a body by *jīva* in the state of *mokṣa* is purely optional. The soul can remain without a body enjoying the bliss of Brahman through its attributive knowledge without any need of the body and sense organs. It can also take on a body, if it so chooses, out of its *saṅkalpa* (will), for doing divine service or carrying out the divine commands of rendering some service to humanity. The soul becomes free (*svarāḍ*) as *Chāndogya Upaniṣad* says, only in the sense that it is not again subject to *karma* (*akarmavaśyaḥ*).[22] But as a dependent entity the soul functions even in the state of *mokṣa* in accordance with the wishes of *Paramātman*. Such a subordination to the will of the God does not cause any suffering to it since *kaiṅkarya* or doing service for the pleasure of God is the intrinsic nature of *jīva*.

The theory of the possibility of a spiritual body to *jīva* in the state of *mokṣa*, warranted by the Upaniṣads and the *Vedānta-sūtra* has led to the formulation of the theological concept of *kaiṅkarya* or divine service in the realm of God known as *paramapada*. Philoṣophically, *mokṣa* according to the Viśiṣṭādvaita Vedānta, is *paripūrṇa-brahmānubhava*, a complete and comprehensive enjoyment of Brahman. But the Vaiṣṇava theology has, however, conceived *kaiṅkarya* or divine service as an important spiritual goal. The *kaiṅkarya* itself is not the *mokṣa* in the technical sense. As Vedānta Deśika has explained, *kaiṅkarya* is an outflow of the experience of *Paramātman*. We shall discuss this matter in detail in the section on Theology of Vaiṣṇavism.

Notes

1. RV IX.113.11. *yatrānandāśca modāśca mudaḥ pramudaāsate; kāmasya yatrāptāḥ kāmāstatra māmamṛtam kṛdhī.*
2. TUp II.1. *brahmavidāpnoti param.*
   See also MUp III.2.9. *brahma veda brahmaiva bhavati.*
3. ChUp VIII.12.2. *evamevaiṣa saṁprasādoasmāt śarīrāt samutthāya paraṁ-jyotir-upasaṁpadya svena rūpeṇa abhiniṣpadyate.*
4. Ibid. VIII.15.1. *sa khalvevaṁ vartayan-yāvadāyuṣaṁ brahmalokam-abhisaṁpadyate na ca punarāvartate....*
5. TUp I.ii. *so aśnute sarvān kamān saha; brahmaṇā vipaściteti.*
6. MUp III.1.3. *yadā paśyaḥ paśyate rukmavarṇaṁ kartāram-īśaṁ puruṣaṁ brahmayonim; tadā vidvān puṇya-pāpe vidhūya nirañjanaḥ paramaṁ sāmyam-upaiti.*
7. See KaUp VI.16; ChUp VIII.6, IV.15.5, VIII.6.5; BrUp VIII.2.15, VII.10.1; *Kauṣītaki*, Up I.21.
8. See Chapter 14.
9. ChUp VII.26.2. *sarvaṁ ha paśyaḥ paśyati.*
10. VDh 104.55. *yathā na kriyate jyotsnā malaprakṣālanāt maṇeḥ; doṣaprahāṇāt na jñānaṁ ātmanaḥ kriyate tathā.*
11. VS IV.4.1. *sampadyāvirbhāvaḥ svena-śabdāt.*
12. RB IV.4.1. *sa svarūpāvirbhāvarūpaḥ nāpūrvākārotpattirūpaḥ.*
13. ChUp VIII.15.1. See fn. 4
14. VS IV.4.22. *anāvṛttiḥ śabdāt....*
15. BG VIII.15. *māmupetya punarjanma duḥkhālayamaśāśvatam; nāpnuvanti mahātmānaḥ saṁsiddhiṁ paramāṁ gatāḥ.*
16. VS IV.4.17. *jagadvyāpāravarjam prakaraṇād-asannihitatvācca.*
17. VS IV.4.21. *bhogamātrā-sāmya-liṅgācca.*
18. ChUp VII.24.1.
    See RB I.3.7.
19. See RTS XXII, p. 148. See also TMK II.67.
20. ChUp VIII.12.3. *sa tatra paryeti jakṣat-krīdan-ramamānaḥ....*
21. See VS IV.4.8. *saṅkalpādeva tatśruteḥ.*
22. See RRB on ChUp VII.25.2.

PART III

THEOLOGY OF VAIṢṆAVISM

7

VIṢṆU AS SUPREME BEING

In the earlier part of the book we have presented the philosophical theories of Vaiṣṇavism as expounded in the Viśiṣṭādvaita Vedānta. Based on the teachings contained in the Upaniṣads, the Āgamas, the Itihāsas, the Vaiṣṇava Purāṇas and the hymns of the Āḻvārs, Vaiṣṇava religion has formulated a few important and distinctive theological doctrines. As we have explained in the introduction, these doctrines are not at variance from the philosophical ones but on the other hand, they are further developments of the basic philosophic concepts in order to meet the needs of the religion as a way of life and as such they have assumed an added theological significance. Though it is often difficult to draw a line of distinction between philosophy and religion in the Indian philosophical systems as the two get closely intermixed, it should still be possible to distinguish between the philosophical and theological doctrines. An attempt is, therefore, made to separate those which are theological in character and discuss them separately in this part of the book to enable modern students to understand them in all their aspects.

Viṣṇu as the Ultimate Reality

We shall first take up the doctrine of Viṣṇu as the Supreme Being (*paratattva*) which constitutes the central theme of Vaiṣṇavism. In an earlier chapter we have discussed the nature of the ultimate Reality as enunciated in the Vedānta which represents the philosophic view of *Īśvara* or God. Brahman, the term commonly used to designate the ultimate Reality, is the primary cause of the universe (*jagat-kāraṇa*). It is defined by the Upaniṣad as *satyam* or Reality, *jñānam* or knowledge and *anantam* or infinite. It is also blissful in character and free from all defects. It is endowed with numerous attributes of unsurpassable excellence. The *Vedānta-sūtra* which is primarily concerned with the discussion of the criteria of Reality does not identify it with any particular deity of religion. This identification of the ultimate Reality of Vedānta with a deity is very essential for Vaiṣṇava religion for the purpose of worship and meditation. This is the task which has been accomplished by Vaiṣṇava theology by equating Brahman with *Viṣṇu.*

Identity of Viṣṇu with Nārāyaṇa Vāsudeva and Brahman

According to Vaiṣṇavism, Viṣṇu is the Supreme Deity (*paradevatā*) as revealed in the hymns of the Ṛgveda, the Upaniṣads, the Āgamas and the *Viṣṇupurāṇa.* The same is known by the name of Nārāyaṇa in the Upaniṣads, as Vāsudeva in the Pāñcarātra Āgamas and as Viṣṇu in the Itihāsas and Purāṇas. As we have explained earlier, the terms *sat*, *ātman* and Brahman used in the Upaniṣads to denote the ultimate Reality mean the same as Nārāyaṇa in accordance with the Mīmāṁsā principle of general terms bearing the meaning of specific term.[1] Viṣṇu, Vāsudeva and Nārāyaṇa are the three names which are generally used in the Vaiṣṇava literature to designate *Īśvara* or God.[2] The different names do not imply different deities conceived at different periods of the history of Vaiṣṇavism as some scholars believe. They are synonymous terms denoting the one and only ultimate Reality of the Vedānta metaphysics. This identity of the three names was established in the Vedic time itself. Thus, the famous hymn known as *Viṣṇu-gāyatrī* appearing in the *Taittirīya Nārāyaṇa Upaniṣad* (which is part of *Taittirīya Āraṇyaka*) states: 'We endeavour to know Nārāyaṇa, we meditate on Vāsudeva and let Viṣṇu bestow wisdom on us.'[3] This Vedic statement evidently reveals the identity of all the three deities. In the post-Vedic period the Āgamas, the Rāmāyaṇa and Mahābhārata and the Vaiṣṇava Purāṇas have used these names repeatedly to denote the same one ultimate Reality of the Upaniṣads.

Etymologically all the names bear the same meaning. Taking the root verb *viṣḷ* which means pervasiveness (*viṣḷ vyāptau*), the term Viṣṇu is defined as one who is all-pervasive. Among the scriptural texts, the *Nṛsimhatāpanīya Upaniṣad* offers this interpretation of the term more explicitly. This Upaniṣad says that the highest Reality is called *Viṣṇu* because He pervades all the worlds, all the celestial deities, all the living beings, all the entities in the universe.[4] Yāska, the author of the *Nirukta* (Vedic etymology) defines Viṣṇu as one who pervades everything (*viṣṇuḥ yadviṣitobhavati*). He also interprets it as one who enters into all (*viṣṇuḥ viśatervā*).[5] The *Ahirbudhnya Saṁhitā*, one of the older and authoritative Pāñcarātra treatises, offers four meanings for this term. Taking the root verb *viṣḷṛ* (pervasion), it first defines Viṣṇu as one who pervades space, time and all entities.[6] Secondly, on the basis of the root verb *viś* meaning to enter (*viś praveśane*), it explains that Viṣṇu is regarded as Supreme Being because He enters into all sentient as well as non-sentient entities, the greatest as well as the smallest, emphasising the immanent character of the Reality.[7] Thirdly, Viṣṇu is so-called because He possesses all the great attributes such as knowledge, power etc., (*vaś kāntau*). Fourthly, He is Supreme Being because He is always desired by all the souls (*iṣ iccāyām*).[8] The *Viṣṇupurāṇa*, the oldest and most authoritative Purāṇa for determining the nature of *tattvas*, points out at the very outset that the entire universe is originated, sustained and dissolved by Viṣṇu, reiterating the definition offered for Brahman by the *Taittirīya Upaniṣad* and the *Vedānta-sūtra*.[9]

The term *Vāsudeva* (derived from the root verb *vas* meaning to reside) is interpreted by the *Viṣṇupurāṇa* as one who abides everywhere and who is also the source of everything,[10] emphasising the all-pervasive character of the Reality, as stated in the *Taittirīya Nārāyaṇa Upaniṣad*.[11] The suffix '*deva*' added to *vasu* implies that He shines forth (*dīvyati*) untouched by any defects, though He abides in everything. It also signifies that He enjoys himself with the creation of the universe which is a sport to Him and that the celestial beings (*devas*) sing His glory.[12] The *Ahirbhudhynya Saṁhitā* also upholds the same etymological meaning for Vāsudeva. Besides, it offers a significant meaning to every letter of the term bringing out the essential characteristics of the ultimate Reality.[13]

The word Nārāyaṇa which is a far more comprehensive term implying all the characteristics of the ultimate Reality, bears the same etymological meaning as that of Viṣṇu and Vāsudeva. This compound word is interpreted in two ways on the basis of etymology. *Nārās* stand for sentient and non-sentient beings (*narasambandhino nārāḥ*) and *nara* means the Supreme Being (*puruṣottama*). *Ayana* means abode or ground. So Nārāyaṇa means one who is the ground of all sentient and non-sentient entities in the universe (*nārāṇām-ayanam*). It can also mean one who is immanent in all (*nārāḥ ayanaṁ yasya saḥ*).[14] The term thus signifies all the important characteristics of Brahman of the Upaniṣad, viz., that Nārāyaṇa is the ground and primary cause of the universe, that He is all-pervasive and immanent in all. This term has several other implications, both philosophical and theological, as fully explained in the Vaiṣṇava treatises.[15]

The term *Brahman* also means etymologically (taking the root verb *bṛh*) as the one which grows and causes to grow.[16] It implies that which is infinite (*ananta*) in respect of its *svarūpa* and also its attributes (*guṇtaḥ*) is Brahman.

Bhagavān is another term which is used more often in the Pāñcarātra treatises to denote Brahman. The *Ahirbhudhynya Saṁhitā* interprets every letter of the word and explains how the term *Bhagavān* implies the essential characteristics of the Supreme Reality.[17] The *Viṣṇupurāṇa* states explicitly that the term refers to Vāsudeva who is the *Para-Brahma*.[18] It also points out that Bhagavān means the Supreme Being who is endowed with the six attributes, viz., knowledge, power, strength, lordship, virility and splendour and who is also free from all defects.[19]

Thus all these terms—Viṣṇu, Nārāyaṇa, Vāsudeva, Bhagavān, Brahman—bear the same import and denote the same one ultimate Reality referred to in the Upaniṣads. Keeping this truth in mind, Rāmānuja states that the term *Brahman* denotes *Puruṣottama*, the Supreme Personal Being who is identified with the name of Nārāyaṇa, on the authority of the Upaniṣads.[20] The same Nārāyaṇa is known by the name of Viṣṇu in the *Viṣṇupurāṇa*, as Hari in the *Harivaṁśa*, as Rāma in *Rāmāyaṇa*, as Vāsudeva in the *Bhagavad-gītā*, as Kṛṣṇa in the *Bhāgavata Purāṇa*, as Narasimha in the *Nṛsimha-tāpanīya Upaniṣad* etc., indicating the different manifestations of Viṣṇu.

The nature of Brahman as the ultimate Reality of Vedānta has been fully discussed in an earlier chapter. Since Brahman is identical with the personal God of Vaiṣṇava religion, all that has been stated about Brahman will equally apply to Viṣṇu. Vaiṣṇavism has formulated a few additional theologicai theories related to the doctrine of God. These are: (1) Viṣṇu is the Supreme Deity over and above Rudra and Brahmā; (2) Viṣṇu is *Śriyaḥpati*, that is, He is inseparably associated with Goddess *Śrī*;

(3) Viṣṇu is endowed with infinite attributes and a spiritual body (*vigraha*); (4) Viṣṇu manifests Himself in different forms (*avatāra*); and (5) Viṣṇu is the means (*upāya*) and goal to be attained (*upeya*). As each theory has far-reaching theological implications, it needs to be discussed separately. The first one is taken up in this chapter and the rest will follow in the subsequent chapters.

Viṣṇu as Para-devatā

That Viṣṇu is the Supreme Deity constitutes an important subject of discussion of all Vaiṣṇava treatises. It has assumed special significance because of the inclusion of Viṣṇu on par with Brahmā and Rudra in the popular concept of trinity (*trimūrti*). Historically speaking, right from the Vedic period it is an established fact that Viṣṇu is the highest deity. We have already shown how the hymns of Ṛgveda speak of the supremacy of Viṣṇu. Though the Ṛgveda refers to numerous different deities including Rudra and Brahmā, it acknowledges the existence of one sole Reality in the name of *Sat*, *Ekam* etc. We have explained on the authority of *Puruṣa-sūkta* that the one Reality described as *Puruṣa* in this passage denotes *Viṣṇu* or Nārāyaṇa, as is evident in the Upaniṣads and the *Śathapatha Brāhmaṇa*. This truth is reiterated more explicitly in the Āgamas and the *Viṣṇu-purāṇa* as well as the *Rāmāyaṇa* and *Mahābhārata* including the *Bhagavad-gītā*. In the minds of the ancient sages, there was absolutely no doubt regarding the supremacy of Viṣṇu. All the Vedic commentators have acknowledged this fact. Even in the post-Vedic period right up to A.D. 800 this fact was not questioned seriously by anyone. This is evident from the fact that Śaṁkara born in A.D. 788 who was an outstanding Vedāntin and who is also claimed by the Advaitins to have accepted the worship of *Śiva*, has upheld the supremacy of Viṣṇu in all his writings. In his commentaries on the Upaniṣads, the *Vedānta-sūtra* and the *Bhagavad-gītā*, he has frequently referred to Viṣṇu, Nārāyaṇa and Vāsudeva as the Supreme Personal God.[21] The *saguṇa* Brahman in the Advaita Vedānta is Viṣṇu or Nārāyaṇa. Thus, right from the ancient time up to A.D. 800 there does not seem to have been any serious dispute regarding the supremacy of Viṣṇu. Śaivism, which is also one of the oldest religions and which upholds Śiva as the Supreme Being, existed along with Vaiṣṇavism.

But there was no rivalry between the two religions, probably due to the fact that the worshippers of *Śiva* in the earlier centuries did not question that *Viṣṇu* is the highest God. It was at a later period, some time after 8th century, that rivalry appears to have started between the two religions.[22] With the royal patronage, this was aggravated by building big temples for either Śiva or Viṣṇu and by writing works to prove the relative superiority of each cult. It reached a climax in the 16th century when Appayya Deekṣita (1552-1624), a follower of Śaṁkara school of Vedānta, wrote a book under the name of *Śivārkamaṇidīpikā* as a commentary on *Śrīkanṭha's Bhāṣya* which itself is a commentary on the *Vedānta-sūtras* in favour of Śiva as the ultimate Reality.[23] Books have been written in the last few centuries disputing, the claims of Vaiṣṇavas and Śaivites. Against this historical background, it became necessary for the Vaiṣṇava *ācāryas*, such as Ālavandār, Rāmānuja and particularly those who came in the post-Rāmānuja period to defend the supremacy of Viṣṇu with elaborate arguments supported with scriptural and Smṛti texts.

Without going into the details of arguments and counter-arguments which have assumed a sectarian bias, we shall examine this subject from a philosophical standpoint. The Upaniṣad enjoins that meditation is to be done on the entity which is the primary cause of the universe[24] for achieving *mokṣa*. In other words, the Ultimate Reality which is accepted as the material cause of the universe is to be meditated upon for attaining the spiritual goal. According to the teaching of Vedānta, *Īśvara* or God, who is the saviour of mankind and who is the bestower of *mokṣa*, is to be meditated upon for salvation. One should have a clear conception of who is that *Īśvara* before one embarks on meditation. Meditation is not possible on an impersonal Being or an absolutely undifferentiated Being. The object of meditation should be such as the mind is able to concentrate on it (*dhāraṇa*). The question arises: what is that *kāraṇavastu*, in terms of the Vedānta? Or theologically, who is that specific Deity (*devatā-viśeṣaḥ*) on whom meditation is to be done? Since the religious texts including the Vedas speak of several deities the question has assumed greater significance.

Regarding the first question, the Upaniṣads state that Brahman is the *kāraṇa-vastu*, the primary cause of the universe and it is to be meditated upon. The *Bṛhadāraṇyaka Upaniṣad* which refers to the creation of the universe, says that in the beginning there was only Brahman.[25] In *Chāndogya Upaniṣad*, it is stated that in the beginning '*sat*' alone existed.[26] In the same context, the *Aitareya Upaniṣad* says that this was in the beginning only *ātman*.[27] All the three terms, *sat*, *ātman* and Brahman bear the same meaning. Those terms are not equated with any specific deity as the object of meditation. The *Mahopaniṣad*[28] in a similar context, states at the outset that only Nārāyaṇa existed (*eko ha vai nārāyaṇa āsīt*) and there was neither Brahmā nor Īśāna (Rudra) nor other entities such as *agni*, *soma*, *ap* (water), heaven, *pṛthivī* (earth), stars, sun and moon.[29] The word Nārāyaṇa is used in place of the terms *sat*, *ātman* and Brahman mentioned in other passages as the cause of the universe. As we have explained in an earlier chapter, when terms are used in the same context, the term having the general meaning should bear the meaning of the specific term. Further, according to the grammatical rule laid down by Pāṇini, the term Nārāyaṇa must be treated as a specific proper name (*saṁjñā-pada*) and it is applicable to one specific Being but not to any other entity as in the case of the general terms such as Brahman, *sat* and *ātman*. On the strength of these authorities Rāmānuja concludes that Brahman referred to in the Upaniṣads as the cause of the universe is the same as Nārāyaṇa, which is the name of the Supreme Being (*puruṣottama*), or the *para-tattva* of Vaiṣṇava religion. The *Taittirīya Nārāyaṇa Upaniṣad* (which is also part of the *Taittirīya Āraṇyaka*) emphatically asserts that Nārāyaṇa is *para-brahma*, Nārāyaṇa is *para-tattva* and Nārāyaṇa is *paramātmā*.

The *Mahopaniṣad*, while stating that in the beginning only Nārāyaṇa existed, categorically denies the existence of Brahmā and Rudra. Another Upaniṣad named as *Nārāyaṇa Upaniṣad* mentions that *Puruṣa Nārāyaṇa* (equating Puruṣa of *Puruṣa-sūkta* with Nārāyaṇa) willed to create the beings.[30] It clearly states that from Nārāyaṇa was born Rudra, Indra etc. It further asserts that the only one Reality is Nārāyaṇa (*śuddho deva eko nārāyaṇaḥ*) and that there is no second as equal to Him and that the whole universe is pervaded by Nārāyaṇa (*nārāyaṇa evedaṁ sarvaṁ*).

As we have already observed, Nārāyaṇa is the same as Viṣṇu. These two terms denote the same Supreme Deity and they are used frequently as synonymous terms in the Āgamas (both

Pāñcarātra and Vaikhānasa) and the *Mahābhārata* and *Rāmāyaṇa*. The hymns of Ṛgveda relating to Viṣṇu extoll Him as the Supreme Deity. As pointed out in the chapter on 'Historical Development', the religion of Ṛgveda is monotheistic and the one *devatā* which fulfills the criteria of *Īśvara* or Supreme Lord is Viṣṇu. The hymn speaking of the eternal abode of Viṣṇu which is perceived all the time by the *sūris* (*nitya-muktas*) establishes beyond any doubt the supremacy of Viṣṇu. The *Puruṣa-sūkta* too extolls the supremacy of *Puruṣa*, who, as explained earlier is equated with Nārāyaṇa or *Viṣṇu*. The statement found in the *uttarānuvāka* of *Puruṣa-sūkta* that *Hṛī* and *Lakṣmī* are the consorts of *Puruṣa* dispels all doubts regarding *Puruṣa* being any other Vedic deity such as Rudra or Brahmā.

The Pūrva-Mīmāṁsā, which deals with the subject-matter of the *pūrvakāṇḍa* of the Vedas or the ritualistic portions, comprises sixteen sections or *adhyāyas*. Jaimini is the author of the first twelve sections of the *Mīmāṁsā-sūtras*; Saṁkarṣaṇa is the author of the later four sections which is known as *Saṁkarṣaṇa-kāṇḍa* or *Devatā-kāṇḍa*. This part of Pūrva-Mīmāṁsā is not extant. However, references are made to it by Rāmānuja on the authority of Bodhāyana who is the earliest commentator on the *Vedāntasūtra* and also by Vedānta Deśika.[31] The concluding *sūtras* as quoted by Vedānta Deśika, state: "The ultimate Deity to be worshipped is Hari who is called Viṣṇu and the same is described as Brahman"[32] The implication of these aphorisms is that of the several deities referred to in the Vedas, the one who is important and the highest and who is to be worshipped is Viṣṇu because He is *antarātmā* or the indwelling self of all deities by virtue of His all-pervasive character and that very deity is no other than Brahman referred to in the Vedānta. This view, Vedānta Deśika states truly represents the traditional theory of those who have true philosophic insight (*tattvavidāṁ sampradāya*).[33] The Vedic seers and the ancient commentators on the Vedas did not have any element of doubt regarding the Supremacy of Viṣṇu as *para-tattva*. The great sages such as Vālmiki, the author of the *Rāmāyaṇa*, Vyāsa, the author of the *Mahābhārata*, Manu and Yājñavalkya, the authors of the *Dharmaśāstras*, Parāśara, the author of the *Viṣṇu-purāṇa* and Śaunaka, the author of the *Viṣṇu-dharmottara*, have all upheld the same opinion. The Pāñcarātra Āgamas, which is based on the *ekāyana*-

śākha of the Śukla Yajurveda and the Sāttvika Purāṇas also speak of the Supremacy of Viṣṇu.

Place of Viṣṇu Among the Trinity of Gods

Now we come to the theological question, viz., whether Viṣṇu is on par with Brahmā and Rudra or is He greater than the other deities? This issue arises because the Purāṇas refer to the concept of the trinity of Gods—Brahmā, Viṣṇu and Rudra. According to the *Vedānta-sūtra* based on the *Taittirīya Upaniṣad*, Brahman is that which is the cause of origination (*janma*), sustenance (*sthiti*) and dissolution (*pralaya*) of the universe. In other words, what is accepted as *para-tattva* or Supreme Being should have the threefold functions of creation, sustenance and dissolution of the universe. The Purāṇas speak of three deities—Brahmā, Viṣṇu and Rudra—as in charge of each of the functions of creation, sustenance and destruction respectively.[34] This would mean that *Viṣṇu* is one of the three deities in charge of protection, whereas Brahmā performs the act of actual creation of the universe and Rudra is its destroyer. The questions, therefore, arise: (*a*) whether all the three deities together constitute the ultimate Reality; (*b*) whether Viṣṇu included in the trinity is the same as the Supreme Being; (*c*) whether either of the other two, viz., Brahmā or Rudra is Supreme; (*d*) finally, whether there is a Supreme Being over and above these. Unless these issues are clarified, it is not possible to assert that Viṣṇu is *para-tattva*.

These questions have engaged the attention of all the Vaiṣṇava Saints (Āḻvārs) and the Vaiṣṇava *acāryas* right from Nāthamuni. Each one has discussed this theory in detail and provided an answer. Taking their stand on the authority of the scriptural texts, the *Viṣṇupurāṇa* and the Pāñcarātra Āgamas, they have established conclusively the supremacy of Viṣṇu and the subordinate status of the other two deities.

The most important argument advanced in support of the above conclusion is that Brahmā and Rudra were created by Viṣṇu, whereas the latter has no such origin. Philosophically, what is created, cannot be eternal and cannot, therefore, become the Ultimate Reality. The scriptural texts as well as the numerous statements found in the Purāṇas support this view. The *Mahopaniṣad* to which we have already referred denies the existence of Īśāna (Rudra) and Brahmā prior to creation.[35] The *Muṇḍaka*

Upaniṣad speaks of Brahmā as the first deity to have been created.[36] The *Nārāyaṇa Upaniṣad* explicitly says: 'From Nārāyaṇa is born Brahmā; from Nārāyaṇa is born Rudra.'[37] The same Upaniṣad at the very outset points out that Nārāyaṇa, on the contrary, is the one who wills to create the universe. He is, therefore, taken as the primary cause of all. This view is supported by the *Mahābhārata* when it says: 'When the entire universe is dissolved, what remains undestroyed is Nārāyaṇa, the inner soul of the universe (*viśvātmā*).'[38] The Varāha Purāṇa states explicitly that Nārāyaṇa is the primary deity of the universe (*ādyo-devaḥ*) and from Him was born Brahmā; and Brahmā in turn caused Rudra.[39] In another statement in the same Purāṇa, it is mentioned that Nārāyaṇa is the Supreme Being and from Him was born *Caturmukha-Brahmā*.[40] The same truth is reiterated by Tirumaḷiśai Āḷvar[41] one of the oldest Vaiṣṇava saints. It cannot be argued that Viṣṇu too is born in the same way, because the scriptural texts and the Purāṇas state that Viṣṇu is eternal (*nitya*) and that no one else other than Him exists in the universe eternally.[42] According to the theory of incarnation, which will be discussed in a separate chapter, the Supreme Being who is eternally existent in the *parama-pada* incarnates Himself out of His own will in many forms for protecting the devotees. In the *Rāmāyaṇa* the following statement is attributed to Brahmā: 'You, who is not subject to *karma* attained the form of Viṣṇu from your original imperishable state for the sake of providing protection to all living beings.'[43] On the basis of these authoritative statements, it is maintained that the three deities—Brahmā, Viṣṇu and Rudra—are neither equal; nor do they together constitute one Reality. For the same reason, Brahmā and Rudra are not higher deities than Viṣṇu. There is no other Reality over and above the three, since Viṣṇu is the Supreme Being and the primary cause of the entire universe.

There are many other statements found in the *Mahābhārata* and the Purāṇas in support of the fact that Brahmā and Rudra, unlike Viṣṇu, are created divine Beings and as such subjected to *karma*, like the individual souls. According to the version of the Epics and Purāṇas, some of these statements are made by these very deities. Thus, Brahmā himself is stated to admit that at the time of creation he was the first to be brought into existence.[44] Similarly, Rudra says both Brahmā and himself were born out of Viṣṇu.[45] In the *Mahābhārata* it is stated repeatedly that all the *devatas* including Brahmā and Rudra worship Vāsudeva.[46] It is also pointed out that Brahmā attained his position and power by worshipping Viṣṇu over a long period.[47] Similarly, Rudra achieved the rulership by performing *sarva-medha yāga*, a sacrifice in which everything including oneself is offered as oblation to the Supreme Being.[48] There are several episodes in the Purāṇas to show that they too are subjected to afflictions and have sought the refuge of Viṣṇu in order to overcome them. One episode which is narrated in the *Mahābhārata* refers to *Caturmukha-Brahmā* who lost the treasure in the form of the four Vedas and got it restored by the grace of Viṣṇu, who took the incarnation of Hayagrīva (the Lord of knowledge) for the purpose. The other episode refers to Rudra, who was cursed by Brahmā because of the offence committed to him by cutting one of his four heads and he got relieved of the ill-effect of the curse only through the help of Viṣṇu. The Āḷvārs and Yāmuna use these Purāṇic episodes to prove the supremacy of Viṣṇu over Rudra and Brahmā.[49] Brahmā and Rudra are regarded as constituting the part of the universal glory (*vibhūti*) of Viṣṇu.[50] They are subordinate deities (*dāsabhūta*) and they carry out their major functions of creation and destruction of the universe respectively with the knowledge and power granted to them by the Supreme Being.[51] Taking all these facts into consideration as revealed in the sacred texts, Vaiṣṇavism claims that Viṣṇu or Nārāyaṇa is the Supreme Deity (*para-devatā*). Thus says the *Mahābhārata*: 'There is no other God higher than Viṣṇu (*na viṣṇoh paramo devaḥ*). The *Harivaṁśa* too states: 'No other deity in the universe is greater than Viṣṇu Nārāyaṇa.'[52] Vaiṣṇavism, therefore, advocates the exclusive worship of Viṣṇu for those who aspire to attain the highest spiritual goal because Viṣṇu alone is capable of granting it.[53] As the *Gītā* clearly points out, the boons granted by other deities are of limited nature as compared to the eternal *Mokṣa* bestowed by Viṣṇu.[54]

Criticisms Against the Theory of Supremacy of Viṣṇu

All these claims made by Vaiṣṇavism may be questioned by the critics. In fact, they have been criticised by the followers of Śaivism. The Śaivites who consider *Śiva* as the Supreme God have written several works to establish the superiority of Śiva over Viṣṇu. There have been serious disputes in the past and even sectarian clashes between the two religions. It is not our intention to arouse the feelings of anyone sect by criticising it or by upholding the religion of anyone sect as superior to the other. Both are important monotheistic religions having certain spiritual and practical values. The fact that they have survived for centuries and are practised even to this day by millions of people all over the country reveals that each religion has its own value and religious significance. However, we shall take up for examination a few criticisms advanced by the critics of Vaiṣṇavism based on the Upaniṣadic texts which *prima facie* appear to lend support to the supremacy of either Śiva or Brahmā as against Viṣṇu and answer them on the lines of the arguments advanced by Rāmānuja and his followers in order to establish the soundness of the Vaiṣṇava theory.

The criticisms against the supremacy of Viṣṇu are based on the statements found in a few Upaniṣads which, *prima facie* uphold either Rudra or Brahmā as a higher deity. The *Atharvaśikha Upaniṣad*, while discussing the question of who is to be meditated upon says: 'The cause is to be meditated upon and *Śambhu*, the Lord of all, to whom belong the universal sovereignty, should be meditated upon in the centre of the heart.'[55] The word 'Śambhu' is commonly equated with *Śiva* or Rudra. In the same Upaniṣad in the preceding sentence it is stated that Īśāna is to be meditated (*dhyāyīta īśānaṁ*). Īśāna is also the designation of *Śiva*. The *Śvetāśvatara Upaniṣad*, while discussing the nature of *Īśvara*, points out that at the time prior to the creation when it was only darkness (*tamas*) which was neither day nor night, when there was neither being nor non-being, only Śiva existed.[56] On the basis of this statement it may be contended that Śiva is the primary cause of the universe. Further, the *Atharvaśiras Upaniṣad* narrates an episode in which the greatness of Rudra is upheld. It reads as follows: Once the *devatās* went to the heaven (*svarga-loka*). There they met Rudra and asked him who he was. In reply he said: 'I alone existed from the beginning, I exist at present and I will be in the future too and that none other than myself is there.' He then entered into the inner-most recess[57] and claimed that he is everywhere. These statements give the impression that Rudra, who alone existed prior to the creation, is the inner soul (*antarātmā*) of all that is created. One more statement appearing in the *Śvetāśvatara Upaniṣad* gives the idea that Lord Śiva is the highest of all and that He is omnipresent (*sarvagataḥ*). It reads thus: 'He (the *Puruṣa*) other than whom there is none that is great, subtle or big, stands firm like a tree in the heaven and He stands alone. By that *Puruṣa* all this is pervaded. That which is superior to him (*tataḥ*) and is formless and defectless is *Bhagavān Śiva*, whose are all the faces, heads and necks, who abides in all hearts and who pervades all and, therefore, all-pervasive. Knowing Him they attain immortality while others are sunk in sorrow.'[58]

There are similar stray scriptural texts which seem to accord a higher place and importance even to Brahmā. In the *Taittirīya Saṁhitā* we have a passage consisting of eight hymns which are reiteration with slight modification of the hymns found in the Ṛgveda.[59] These refer to Hiraṇyagarbha as the cause of the universe. The first hymn says: 'Prior to creation Hiraṇyagarbha existed and that He became the Ruler by creating all the beings. He sustained the physical universe below and also the heavens above. The term Hiraṇyagarbha is generally taken as another name of *Caturmukha-Brahmā*.

One other objection which may be raised against the supremacy of Viṣṇu is that according to a statement of *Atharvaśikha Upaniṣad* all the three deities—Brahmā, Viṣṇu and Rudra—are regarded as having been born. Thus it says: 'All this (the entire universe) including Brahmā, Viṣṇu and Rudra have been caused.[60] If, according to this statement Viṣṇu is brought into existence, He could not be the beginningless, eternal Supreme Being. The *Viṣṇupurāṇa* states that the same one Bhagavān named Janārdana assumes three different forms as Brahmā, Viṣṇu and Śiva for the purpose of creation, sustenance and destruction.[61] This conveys the impression that all the three deities enjoy the same ontological status.

Evaluation of Upaniṣadic Statements Supporting the Supremacy of Śiva

All these statements, taken as they are without the context in which they appear, would no doubt run counter to the thesis that Viṣṇu alone is the Supreme Being. But as Rāmānuja has explained in detail in the *Vedārtha-saṁgraha*, none of these statements when studied carefully with reference to the subject-matter of the concerned Upaniṣadic passage and also its opening as well as concluding sentences, does establish the supremacy of either Rudra or Brahmā. The mere terms such as Śiva, Rudra Śambhu, Īśāna and Maheśvara do not necessarily mean the deity accepted by the Śaivite cult. These terms, unlike the term Viṣṇu or Nārāyaṇa, have several meanings, of which one is also applicable to Viṣṇu. Thus, for instance, Śambhu means etymologically, He from whom happiness is obtained (*śam bhavati asmāt*). The supreme happiness consists in *mokṣa* and the giver of *mokṣa* is Nārāyaṇa. The word in this passage is taken to mean Nārāyaṇa. In the *Mahābhārata*[62] Śambhu is used as synonymous with Nārāyaṇa. The term Īśāna does not necessarily mean Śiva but it would also refer to the Ruler of the universe (*sarvasya Īśānaḥ*) as pointed out in the *Bṛhadāraṇyaka Upaniṣad*. In the Mokṣadharma section of *Mahābhārata Īśāna* is used as a designation for Bhagavān or Nārāyaṇa. Similarly, the term Śiva also means auspiciousness (*maṅgala*) and Viṣṇu being the personification of auspiciousness (*maṅgalānāṁ ca maṅgalam*),[63] the word Śiva stands for Viṣṇu. In the *Viṣṇu-sahasranāma*, this word is used as synonymous with Viṣṇu.[64] The *Taittirīya Nārāyaṇa Upaniṣad* describes Nārāyaṇa as *śaśvataṁ śivam-acyutam*. The term Rudra, though it is commonly identified with Śiva, is also used as synonymous with Viṣṇu. Thus, in *Viṣṇu-sahasranāma*, he is equated with Viṣṇu.[65] In the same way, the word Hiraṇyagarbha is applicable to the Supreme Being, who is the primary cause of the universe. The *Viṣṇu-sahasranāma* uses the word as synonymous with Viṣṇu.[66] From the Vedānta point of view, all terms denote ultimately Nārāyaṇa, either by virtue of its etymological meaning (*avayava śakti*) or on the basis of the principle of final import of the terms (*aparyavasāna-vṛtti*).[67] The important point to be noted is that merely on the basis of the words such as Rudra, Śiva, Śambhu and Hiraṇyagarbha, we cannot conclusively establish that these scriptural statements containing these terms mean any deity other than Viṣṇu. The context in which the statements are made is more important.

Coming to the point of context, Rāmānuja points out that we have to first take into consideration the main purport of all the principal Upaniṣadic texts regarding the ultimate Reality which is accepted as the cause of the universe (*jagat-kāraṇatva*) and which is to be meditated upon for achieving *mokṣa* (*dhyeya-vastu*). Against this background of the central teaching of the Upaniṣads the individual texts which contain stray statements such as the one under consideration are to be interpreted in conformity with the main purport of the larger number of other Upaniṣadic texts. It is well established in the Upaniṣads and the first *adhyāya* of the *Vedānta-sūtra*, that Brahman as the ultimate Reality is the primary cause of the universe and the object of meditation for *mokṣa*. Brahman is Nārāyaṇa or Viṣṇu, according to the *Subāla Upaniṣad*, *Taittirīya Nārāyaṇa Upaniṣad* and the Epics as well as the Purāṇas. In view of it, if we find expressions such as Rudra, Śiva or Hiraṇyagarbha as the cause of the universe, we have to take these terms in the sense of Brahman or Nārāyaṇa. In fact, these terms understood with reference to the context as well as the ephithets used along with them which convey the characteristics of Brahman, mean only Nārāyaṇa. In the words of Rāmānuja, the entire Vedas and the Vedāṅgas (the subsidiary treatises of the Vedas), if they are properly interpreted with the help of the elucidation provided by the sages having an insight into the Vedas and by the adoption of canons of interpretation, declare Hari (Viṣṇu) as the cause of creation, sustenance and dissolution of the universe.[68] The same truth is expressed in *Varāha Purāṇa* in a more emphatic way: 'The main purport of all the Vedas is that *Śripati* or Nārāyaṇa is the Supreme Being; if here and there any other matter is stated, it is intended to establish the same main purport.'[69]

In the light of these general observations, we may examine the individual Upaniṣadic texts referring to the supremacy of Rudra and Brahmā. The statement in the *Atharvaśikha Upaniṣad* refers to Śambhu as the object of meditation. At the beginning of the passage the question is raised as to who is to be meditated upon and in reply, it is said that which is the cause of the universe (*kāraṇaṁ*) is to be meditated upon. Only the Supreme Being, according to Vedānta, is the cause of the universe. The Upaniṣad states that Śambhu, who is *sarvaiśvarya-sampannaḥ* (one who is the over-lord of all) and *sarveśvaraḥ* (one who is the Soveriegn of the universe) is to be meditated. The only deity to whom these two epithets of Supreme Lordship and Sovereignty apply is Nārāyaṇa, as established by *Taittirīya Nārāyaṇa Upaniṣad*. Śambhu, therefore, is to be understood as

Nārāyaṇa and not Rudra. As already pointed out Śambhu also means Viṣṇu. Further, the Upaniṣadic text in question does not say that Śambhu is Kāraṇa, the cause of universe. In fact, Śiva, Brahmā, Indra and other deities, according to the *Nārāyaṇa Upaniṣad* are caused by the Supreme Being and as such they are the glories of *Paramātman* (*vibhūtis*). That which is brought into existence cannot qualify to become a Supreme Being.

An objection may be raised against this conclusion. The preceding Upaniṣadic sentence states that Brahmā, Viṣṇu, Rudra and Indra are all subject to birth and so they are not the cause.[70] How then is Viṣṇu held as the primary cause? The answer to this objection is that the birth of Viṣṇu, unlike that of Brahmā and Rudra, is to be understood in the sense of an *avatāra* or descent of the Supreme Being as one of the deities (*devatā*), out of His own will (*svecchāvatāra*), as in the case of His being born as Rāma to Daśaratha or as *Kṛṣṇa* to Vāsudeva.[71] According to the theory of *avatāra*, which will be discussed in a separate chapter, the incarnation of the Supreme Being in divine or human form, does not amount to a birth due to the influence of *karma*, as understood in the ordinary sense. The Śruti text says: 'Though He is unborn, he takes many births.'[72] Birth here is understood in the sense of *avatāra* or manifestation. Further, the scriptural text also asserts that no one else gives birth to Him nor is there anyone to rule over Him.[73] A similar claim cannot be made in respect of either Śiva or Brahmā because the theory of *avatāra* in their case is not admitted.[74] Besides, the *Nārāyaṇa Upaniṣad* openly says that from Nārāyaṇa, Rudra and Brahmā were born, whereas Nārāyaṇa has no such origin and is beginningless. Nārāyaṇa is not subject to *karma* as *Subāla Upaniṣad* states.[75] As we have already pointed out, there are numerous Śruti and Smṛti texts which speak of the origin of Brahmā and Rudra. The *Mahābhārata*, while answering the questions relating to the creation and dissolution of the universe, states that Nārāyaṇa is the infinite Self, the eternal one and the sages, the manes, the deities and the whole universe consisting of moving and non-moving entities originate from Him.[76] The *Viṣṇupurāṇa* which has been unanimously accepted as an authoritative text for determining the nature of Reality, states explicitly that the universe is originated from Viṣṇu. It adds that *Paramātman* is the supporting ground of all and is the

Supreme Lord. He is sung in the Vedas as well as 'in the vedānta as' Viṣṇu.[77] The same *Viṣṇupurāṇa* in reply to the question as to what is *Para-Brahma,* says that 'The universe originates from Viṣṇu and exists in Him; He is its maintainer and controller.'[78] This is exactly the definition given for Brahman in the *Vedānta-sūtra,* viz., that from which proceeds the origination etc., is Brahman, thereby establishing the identity of Viṣṇu with Brahman of the Upaniṣads. It further states that He is Supreme and He dwells in all and all things dwell in Him and therefore, He is called Vāsudeva, thus identifying Vāsudeva of Bhāgavata religion with Viṣṇu and Brahman. He is the Supreme Brahman, eternal, unborn, imperishable and undecaying. He is free from evil and thus pure. It goes on describing that this Supreme Being is endowed with all auspicious qualities. He is *sarveśvara,* He is *sarvavit,* knower of all, He is *samasta-śaktiḥ,* all powerful. Thus, the *Viṣṇupurāṇa* establishes beyond any shadow of doubt that Viṣṇu who is the same as Brahman is the Supreme Being and He is unborn unlike Rudra and Brahmā, though included in the trinity.

The same *Viṣṇupurāṇa* asserting the supremacy of Viṣṇu makes a statement that Brahmā, Viṣṇu and Śiva are the three names assumed by the same Janārdana by virtue of His three primary functions of creation, sustenance and destruction.[79] This would imply, *prima facie,* that the three deities are of the same status. But this is not so, says Rāmānuja.[80] The expression in the verse 'the same Janārdana' (*eka eva janārdana*) is significant. Its implication is that Janārdana which is another name for Viṣṇu is equated with the three deities and the universe, as is evident by the words used in the verse, viz., that '*He is the very jagat* (*jagacca saḥ*).' The fuller implication of it is brought out in the very next verse which says: The same Lord as the cause of creation creates the creator (*sṛṣṭa*); as Viṣṇu He protects all that is to be protected; and He as the destroyer, dissolves the universe.[81] In other words, Viṣṇu Himself as the Supreme Lord brings forth Brahmā to do the act of creation[82] and both Brahmā as well as what is created by him is equated with the Lord. Similarly, Viṣṇu Himself brings forth Rudra for doing the function of dissolution and both Rudra as well as what is dissolved are equated with the Lord. In the case of Viṣṇu, the third deity, it is a form assumed by Janārdana to look after the protection of what is created. It does not say that Viṣṇu created Viṣṇu as in the case of other two deities. On the other hand, it says Viṣṇu protects all that is to be protected (*pālyaṁ ca pāti*). Its implication is that Viṣṇu as the Supreme Lord manifests Himself in the name of Viṣṇu for the purpose of carrying out the function of protection of the universe. Such an explanation holds good in terms of the doctrine of *avatāra* accepted in respect of Viṣṇu. This truth is made more explicit in a later verse of the *Viṣṇupurāṇa*: 'He (Viṣṇu) alone is what is created and the author of creation; He alone protects and dissolves (the universe) and He is what is protected; Viṣṇu, the greatest Being, the benevolent and adorable, is of universal form as He assumes states of Brahmā, Rudra etc.[83] In brief, Viṣṇu is everything by virtue of His being immanent in all that exists. It is in this sense that *Viṣṇupurāṇa* equates Viṣṇu with the universe including Brahmā and Rudra to signify the fact that He pervades the entire universe.

As regards the statement of the *Śvetāśvatara Upaniṣad* that at the time of creation only Śiva existed (*śiva eva kevalaḥ*), this is to be understood in the light of similar other Upaniṣadic texts relating to the creation of universe, because it is a restatement (*anuvāda*) of what is already said elsewhere (*purovāda*). In the *Subāla Upaniṣad* we have a statement similar to the one in *Śvetāśvatara*. In reply to a question what existed then (prior to creation), it is said in this Upaniṣad that there was neither *sat* nor *asat* nor *sat-asat*. By way of elucidation, it is stated later in the same Upaniṣad that in the beginning (prior to creation) there was nothing that existed but the one Supreme Being, Nārāyaṇa and from Him all these beings in the universe were created. Again in the *Mahopaniṣad* it is categorically stated that at the time of creation only Nārāyaṇa existed and there was neither Brahmā nor Īśāna (Rudra). In the light of these statements the stray sentence appearing in the *Śvetāśvatara Upaniṣad* that Śiva alone existed is to be interpreted in the sense that Śiva is Nārāyaṇa. As said earlier the term Śiva is also applicable to Viṣṇu by virtue of His being the personification of auspiciousness. This interpretation of the text is justified in accordance with the principle adopted in the *Vedānta-sūtra* in explaining the terms such as *ākāśa*, in favour of Brahman. *Ākāśa*, though it generally means ether, the Upaniṣadic text containing this word is interpreted to mean Brahman on the basis of the fact that the characteristics (*liṅga*) attributed to the term in question imply those that are applicable to Brahman.[84]

The statement in the *Śvetāśvatara Upaniṣad* referring to an entity as higher than the *Puruṣa* (*tato yaduttarataraṁ*) has been construed by the critic as an indication of the existence of Śiva as higher than *Puruṣa*.[85] In reply to this Rāmānuja explains that there is no scope to offer such an interpretation if we take into consideration the entire context in which this sentence appears in the Upaniṣadic passage. In the beginning of the passage it is said: 'Knowing Him (*Puruṣa*) one crosses beyond death and that there is no other means.' This indicates that the knowledge of the Reality is the only means for immortality. The next passage begins with the sentence: 'Other than whom there is none that is great' and ends up with the sentence 'By that *Puruṣa* all this is pervaded.' The passage is thus intended to explain the greatness of *Puruṣa* as one beyond all else. Then follows the sentence '*tato yaduttarataraṁ tad-arūpam anāmayam*.'[86] The meaning of this sentence, according to the critic, is that which is other than *Puruṣa* (taking the term *tataḥ* to mean 'other than') is without form and without suffering. Rāmānuja argues that the word *tataḥ* should be taken to mean 'therefore'. That is, because of the facts explained in the earlier sentences, viz., that *Puruṣa* is all-pervasive and His knowledge alone is means to salvation. As a logical conclusion of these facts, it is asserted that the same great *Puruṣa* is formless and defectless and those who know Him will escape death.[87] Thus, the opening declaration is brought to a reasoned conclusion. If we adopt any other interpretation, it would conflict with the opening proposition of the passage. In the light of this explanation, the word Śiva appearing in the passage means Nārāyaṇa, who is the highest Reality. The *Taittirīya Nārāyaṇa Upaniṣad* also describes Nārāyaṇa as Śiva, eternal and imperishable (*śāśvataṁ śivam-acyutam*).

Regarding the statement in the *Atharvaśiras Upaniṣad* which speaks of the greatness of Rudra as one who entered into the innermost recess (*antarādantara-praveśa*), Rāmānuja points out that it has to be understood in the sense that *Paramātman* entered into all beings as their soul. When Rudra speaks that he is omnipresent and enters into the innermost soul, it only implies that *Paramātman* as the inner soul (*antarātmā*) of Rudra is expressing these words. According to the Viśiṣṭādvaita Vedānta

Paramātman, who is the infinite Supreme Being, is all-pervading. As He pervades all beings, sentient as well as non-sentient and as the latter is His body, all terms denote Him. Therefore, the term 'I' expressed by Rudra, represents *Paramātman* as the inner soul of Rudra. In this Vedic episode narrated in the *Atharvaśiras*, Rudra is actually the mouthpiece of *Paramātman* abiding within Rudra. This interpretation is offered on the strength of the principle enunciated in the *Vedānta-sūtra.*[88] The Upaniṣadic text in question does not, therefore, speak of the greatness of Rudra.

Viṣṇu and Brahmā

Regarding the reference to Hiraṇyagarbha or Brahmā as one existing at the time prior to creation mentioned in the Yajus Saṁhitā and also in the Ṛgveda, the term Hiraṇyagarbha does not mean the Caturmukha-Brahmā as popularly understood. The Vedic passage (consisting of eight hymns) related to Hiraṇyagarbha as well as the *uttarānuvāka* of *Puruṣa-sūkta* (comprising of six hymns) are reiterated in the *Taittirīya Nārāyaṇa Upaniṣad*,[89] which is exclusively devoted to prove the supremacy of Nārāyaṇa. From this it follows, that the term *Hiraṇyagarbha* referred to here is applicable to the Supreme Being who is the cause of the universe. If we consider the purport of the eight hymns it becomes evident that Hiraṇyagarbha is the very Supreme Being since the epithets such as *būtasya jātaḥ* (creator of the living beings) *pati* (Ruler of the universe) and *dādhāra* (one who sustains everything) are applicable only to the Supreme Being and not to Hiraṇyagarbha as Caturmukha-Brahmā. Further, the *Śvetāśvatara Upaniṣad* explicitly says that *Paramātman* first created Hiraṇyagarbha[90] and this fact rules out his being the primary cause of the universe. The Nārāyaṇa Upaniṣad also states that Brahmā was born from Nārāyaṇa. As pointed out earlier, the term Hiraṇyagarbha also bears the meaning of Viṣṇu.[91]

Taking all these scriptural and Smṛti authorities, Vaiṣṇavism upholds the theory that Viṣṇu or Nārāyaṇa is the Supreme Being and that Rudra as well as Caturmukha-Brahmā are subordinate deities constituting His glory (*vibhūti*). It is not thus a mere dogma of the Vaiṣṇava cult. This truth is declared emphatically by Sage Vyāsa himself in a significant verse: 'After a very careful examination of all the sacred texts and after repeated investigation into their purport, we come to one obvious conclusion that the deity to be meditated upon at all times is Nārāyaṇa.'[92] 'There is no other deity greater than Viṣṇu.'[93] 'There is no other God higher than Nārāyaṇa.'[94] 'There is no other Being who is higher than Vāsudeva.'[95] Thus all the three deities which are synonymous and represent the Supreme God of Vaiṣṇava religion is the same as the *Para-Brahman*, the ultimate Reality of Vedānta philosophy.

Notes

1. See Chapter 2.
2. The word *Bhagavān* is also used for Īśvara in the Pāñcarātra treatises, the *Viṣṇupurāṇa* and the *Bhagavad-gītā*. The *Bhāgavata* which is one of the Vaiṣṇava Purāṇas, is named after *Bhagavān*.
3. TnUp 28. *nārāyaṇāya vidmahe vāsudevāya dhīmahi, tanno viṣṇuḥ pracodayāt.*
4. Nṛsimhatāpanīya Up. *atha kasmāt ucyate mahāviṣṇuḥ?*
   yasmāt svamahimnā sarvān lokān sarvān devān sarvān ātmanaḥ sarvāṇi bhūtāni vyāpnoti iti tasmāt ucyate mahā-viṣṇur-iti.
5. Nirukta XII.8.
6. AhS LII.52. *vyāpnoti deśakālābhyāṁ sarvaṁ yadrūpato'pi ca;*
   tat paraṁ gaditaṁ sadbhiḥ viṣer-dhātoḥ nirūpaṇāt.
7. Ibid. 42 and 43. *cetanācetanāḥ sarve viśantyeva yataḥ svayam;..*
   ..sa paro gaditaḥ sadbhiḥ viśer-dhātornirūpaṇāt.
8. Ibid. 41. *kāntirnāma guṇaḥ so'yam vaśer-dhātor-nirūpaṇāt....ya iṣyate sadā sarvaiḥ ātmabhāvena cetanā.*
9. VP I.1.31. *viṣṇoḥ sakāśādudbhūtaṁ jagat-tatraiva ca sthitam;*
   sthiti-saṁyama-kartāsau jagato'sya jagacca saḥ.
   VS I.1.2. *janmādyasya yataḥ.*
10. VP I.2.12. *sarvatrāsau samastaṁ ca vasatyatreti vai yataḥ;*
    tataḥ sa vāsudeveti vidvadbhiḥ paripaṭhyate.
    See also VP VI.5.75 & 80. *sarvāṇi tatra bhūtāni vasanti paramātmani;*
    bhūteṣu ca sa sarvātmā vāsudevas-tataḥ smṛtaḥ.
11. TnUp 94. *antar bahiśca tat sarvaṁ vyāpya nārāyaṇaḥ sthitaḥ.*
12. See AhS LII.68.
13. Ibid. LII.64–70.
14. AhS LII.51–54. *nara sambandhino nārā naraḥ sa puruṣottamaḥ;...*
    nara sambandhinaḥ sarve cetanā-cetanātmakāḥ;
    īśitavyatyā nārā dhārya-poṣyatayā tathā;
    niyāmyatvena sṛjyatva-praveśa-bharaṇaiḥ tathā;
    ayate nikhilān nārān vyāpnoti kriyayā tathā;
    nārāścāpi ayanaṁ tasya taiḥ tadbhāva-nirūpaṇāt;
    nārāṇām ayanām vāsaste ca tasyāyanam-sadā;
    paramā ca gatiḥ teṣāṁ nārāṇāṁ ātmanāṁ sadā.

15. For details see RTS XXVII pp. 202-05.
See also *Mumukṣuppaḍi. Sūtras* 95–115.
16. VP III.3.23. *bṛhatvāt bṛhmaṇatvācca tadbrahmety-abhidhīyate.*
See also Chapter 2 p. 52.
17. AhS. LII.60–63.
18. VP VI.5.76. *evameṣa mahān śabdo maitreya bhagavāniti; parabrahmabhūtasya vāsudevasya nānyagaḥ.*
19. Ibid. VI.5.79. *jñāna-śakti-balaiśvarya vīrya tejāṁsy-aśeṣataḥ; bhagavat śabda vācyāni vinā heyair-guṇādibhiḥ.*
20. See Ch. 2 pp. 52-54.
21. While commenting on *Antaryāmi Brāhmaṇa* of BrUp Śaṁkara identifies the *antaryāmin* with Nārāyaṇa.
See SB on BrUp III.3. *ya idrgīśvara nārayaṇākhyaḥ. . . .*
In commenting the term *Viṣṇu* in *Kaṭha* Up he writes: *tadviṣnoḥ vyāpana śīlasya brahmaṇaḥ paramātmanaḥ vāsudevākhyasya paramaṁ prakṛṣtaṁ padaṁ sthānam. . . .*
See SB on KaUp III.9, p. 81.
See SB on BG I.1. *sa ādikartā nārāyaṇo viṣṇuḥ.*
See also SB on BG III.20, IV.35, VIII.15, VII.15, IX.22, XI.9, XV.10.
In interpreting the name *Śiva* appearing in *Viṣṇu-sahasranāma*, Śaṁkara states that Śiva means *Hari* (Viṣṇu), *śivādināmabhiḥ harireva stūyate.* Sureśwara, the direct disciple of Śaṁkara, in his *Vārtika* (commentary on Śaṁkara Bhāṣya) extolls Nārāyaṇa as Paramātman and in support of this view he quotes TnUp, *nārāyaṇāya viśvāya devānāṁ paramātmane; etameva samuddiśya mantro nārāyaṇaḥ tathā.*
22. Yāmuna (A.D. 916–1041) wrote a work entitled *Mahāpuruṣanirṇaya.* It is not extent but it is listed among the works of Yāmuna by Vedānta Deśika. Presumably this treatise must have been devoted to the vindication of the supremacy of Viṣṇu as against the claims of Śaivites. If we assume that this work was compiled about A.D. 950, the rivalry between Śaivism and Vaiṣṇavism would have existed during 9th century.
23. We do not have any authentic information about *Śrikanṭha*, claimed to be the author of *Śrikaṇtha Bhāṣya.* It must have been written by some anonymous person, presumably at a period later than Rāmānuja and Vedānta Deśika (14th century), for the obvious reason that there is no mention of this author or its contents by Vedānta Deśika who has *covered* in his *Tattva-muktā-kalāpa* and other works all the rival schools of thought including Madhva that existed in his time. Neither the followers of Śaṁkara's Advaita nor the followers of Śaiva-siddhānta have accepted the views contained in *Śrikanṭha Bhāṣya.* In a critical evaluation of this work by a scholar of Parakal Mutt, Mysore, undertaken under the title *Śrikaṇtha-samālocana* published in 1963, a view is taken that Appayya Deekṣita himself might have written this commentary under the pseudonym of Śrīkaṇtha to give an appearance of antiquity to the work. In the absence of any authentic evidence, it is difficult to prove whether or not this is true.

24. *Atharvaśikha* Up II.17. *kāraṇaṁ tu dhyeyaḥ.*
25. BrUp III.4.10.
26. ChUp VI.11.1.
27. AIUp I.
28. The *Mahopaniṣad* from which Rāmānuja often quotes is regarded as an authoritative ancient Upaniṣad. Vedānta Deśika upholds its authority on the ground that it is used by Yāmuna as an authoritative text in his *Mahāpuruṣanirṇaya* and also by Yādava Prākāśa, an earlier commentator than Rāmānuja on *Vedānta-sūtras*, in his *Gītābhāṣya* (Chapter VIII) and also by his follower. Its statements are also extolled by the *Mahābhārata*.
   See SR pp. 46-47.
29. *Mahopaniṣad*, *eko ha vai nārāyaṇa āsīt, na brahmā neśāno nāpo nāgniṣomau neme dyāvā-pṛthivī na nakṣatrāṇi na sūryo candramāḥ.*
30. *Nārāyaṇa* Up. *atha puruṣo ha vai nārāyaṇo akāmayata, prajāḥ srajeyeti.* The *Nārāyaṇa Upaniṣad* is different from the *Taittirīya Nārāyaṇa Upaniṣad* (which is part of the *Taittirīya Āraṇyaka*) and it is accepted as an authoritative Upaniṣad by Rāmānuja and his followers. Its contents are also reiterated by the *Mahābhārata* and *Viṣṇupurāṇa*.
31. RB I.1.1, p. 9. Rāmānuja quotes the following statement of Bodhāyana: *saṁhitam-etat śārīrakaṁ jaiminīyena ṣodaśalakṣaṇeneti śāstraikatva-siddhiḥ.*
   See also SD Vāda 3. *karmadevatā paradevatā gocaratayā vibhaktakāṇḍatrayaṁ viṁśatilakṣaṇam-ekam śāstramiti....*
32. SD Vāda 3. "*ante harau tad-darśanāt,*" "*sa viṣṇur-āha hi.*" "*taṁ brahmety-ācakṣate, taṁ brahmety-ācakṣate.*"
   (The concluding *sūtra* is generally repeated twice.)
33. Ibid. *tasya kāṇḍasya upasaṁhāre "ante Harau tad-darśanāt" iti devatākāṣṭām pradarśya, "sa Viṣṇur-āhahi" itisarva devatārādhanānāṁ tatparyavasanāya tasya sarvāntarātmatvena vyāptiṁ pratipādya, "Tam brahmety-ācakṣate....iti tasaiva vedāntavedya-parabrahmatvaupakṣepeṇa upasaṁhārāt sāmānyataśca viśeṣataśca īśvaraḥ prastuta iti tatvavidāṁ saṁpradāyaḥ.*
34. VP I.2.66. *ṣṛṣti-sthityanta-karaṇīṁ brahma-viṣṇu-śivātmikām.*
35. See fn. 29
36. MUp I.1.1. *brahmā devānām prathamaḥ saṁbabhūva.*
   See also SvUp VI.18. *yo brahmāṇaṁ vidadhāti pūrvaṁ.*
37. NUp. *nārāyaṇāt brahmā jāyate; nārāyaṇāt rudro jāyate... .*
38. Mhb II.43.15. *ābhūta-saṁplave prāpte pralīne pṛakṛtau mahān; ekastiṣṭati viśvātmā sa tu nārāyaṇaḥ prabhuḥ.*
39. *Varāha Purāṇa*, 25-26. *ādyo nārāyaṇo devaḥ tasmāt brahmā tato bhavaḥ.*
40. Ibid. 90-93. *paro nārāyaṇo devaḥ tasmāt jātaḥ caturmukhaḥ; tasmāt rudro abhavat....*
41. *Nānmukan Tiruvandādi*, 1. *nānmukanai nārāyaṇan paḍaittān; nānmukanum tānmukamāy śaṅkaranai paḍaittān.*

This Tamil verse means that Nārāyaṇa created the four-headed Brahmā; the four-headed Brahmā created Śaṁkara (Rudra).

42. Mbh. XII.347.32. *nityaṁ hi nāsti jagati bhūtaṁ sthāvara-jaṅgamam; ṛate tamekaṁ puruṣaṁ vāsudevaṁ sanātanam.*
43. *Rāmāyaṇa*, VII.101.26. *tatastvamapi durdharṣaḥ tasmād-bhāvāt sanātanāt; rakṣārthaṁ sarvabhūtānāṁ viṣṇutvam-upajagmivān.*
44. *Rāmāyaṇa*, VIII.104.14. *mahārṇave śayānopsu māṁ tvaṁ pūrvam-ajījanaḥ.*
45. *Harivaṁśa*, III.131.48. *ka iti brahmaṇo nāma īśo' ham sarvadehinām; āvāṁ tavāṅge saṁbhūtau tasmāt keśavanāmavān.*
46. Mhb. XII.350-30. *sabrahmakāḥ sarudrāśca sendrā devā maharṣayaḥ; arcayanti suraśreṣṭaṁ devaṁ nārāyaṇaṁ harim.*
47. *Itihāsa Samuccaya*, I.3.8. *yugakoṭi-sahasrāṇi viṣṇum-ārādhya padmabhūḥ; punaḥs-trailokya-dhātṛtvam prāptavān. . . .*
48. Mbh XII.20.12. *mahādevas-sarvamedhe mahātmā hutvātmānaṁ devadevo babhūva.*
49. *Tiruvāymoli*, IV.10.4. *Stotraratna*, 13.
50. VP I.22.31. *brahmā dakṣā-dayaḥ kālaḥ tathaivākhila-jantavaḥ; vibhūtayo hareretā jagataḥ sṛṣṭi-hetavaḥ.*
51. Mhb XII.359.19. *etau dvau vibudhaśreṣṭau prasādakrodhajau smṛtau; tadā-darśita-panthānau sṛṣṭi-samhāra-kārakau.*
52. *Harivaṁśa*, *nānyojagati devosti visṇoḥ nārāyaṇāt paraḥ.*
53. VDh I.59. *saṁsārārṇavamagnānāṁ viṣayākrānta-cetasām; viṣṇupotaṁ vinā nānyat-kiñcid-asti parāyaṇam.*
54. BG VII.23. *antavattu phalaṁ teṣāṁ tadbhavatyalpamedhasām; devān devayajo yānti mad-bhaktā yānti māmapi.*
55. *Atharvaśikha* Up II.17. *kāraṇaṁ tu dhyeyaḥ; sarvaiśvaryasampannaḥ sarveśvaraḥ śambhuḥ ākāśamadhye dhyeyaḥ.*
56. SvUp IV.18. *yadā tamaḥ tanna divā na rātriḥ na sat na ca asat śiva eva kevalaḥ.*
57. *Atharvaśiras* Up (opening passage). *so antarād-antaraṁ prāviśat.* *Antarād* is taken as the soul within and *antaraṁ* means that which abides in it viz. *Paramātman*; if Rudra can enter the Paramātman, he is greater than the latter.
See RRB p. 474.
58. SvUp III.9-11.
59. *Taittirīya Saṁhitā*, IV.1.8.
See also RV X.121. *hiraṇyagarbhaḥ samavartatāgre bhūtasya-jātaḥ patireka āsīt; sa dādhāra pṛthiviṁ dyām-utemāṁ kasmai devāya haviṣā vidhema.*
60. *Atharvaśikha* Up II.15. *sarvamidaṁ brahma-viṣṇu-rūdrendrāḥ te sarve saṁprasūyante sarvāṇi ca indriyāṇi saha bhūtaiḥ.*
61. VP I.2.66. *sṛṣṭi-sthityanta-karaṇīṁ brahma-viṣṇu-śivātmikām; sa saṁjñāṁ yāti bhagavān eka eva janārdanaḥ.*
62. Mbh (Quoted in Śrutaprakāśikā, I.4.29, p. 197)

iti nārāyaṇaḥ śambhuḥ bhagavān jagatāṁ prabhuḥ;
ādiśya vibudhān sarvān ajāyata yodoḥ kule.

63. Mbh XIII.149.10.
64. *Viṣṇu-sahasranāma*, 4. *sarvaḥ śarvaḥ śivaḥ sthāṇuḥ....* See BGD pp. 152-55 for explanation.
65. Ibid. 13. *rudro bahuśirā babhruḥ.* The term *rudra* is interpreted as one who makes devotees shed tears of joy. See BGD pp. 240-41.
66. Ibid. 44. *hiraṇyagarbhaḥ śatrughnaḥ vyāpto vāyuradhokṣajaḥ.* See also BGD pp. 428-29.
67. See *Śrutaprakāśika*, I.4.29, p. 199.
68. VSa p. 107. *vedavit-pravara-prokta vākyanyāyopabrahmitāḥ; vedās-saṅgā hariṁ prāhuḥ jagat-janmādi-kāraṇam.*
69. *Varāha Purāṇa*, (quoted by Madhva) *mukhyaṁ ca sarva vedānāṁ tātparyaṁ śrīpateḥ paraṁ; utkarṣetu tadanyatra tātparyaṁ syād-avāntaraṁ.*
70. See fn. 60
71. See VSa p. 119. See also TMK III.10.
72. *Puruṣa-sūkta* (Yajurveda recension) 21. *ajāyamāno bahudhā vijāyate.*
73. SvUp VI.9. *na cāsya kaścit janitā na cādhipaḥ.*
74. See *Śrutaprakāśikā* I.4.29, pp. 198-99.
75. Subāla Up VII. *esa sarvabhūtāntarātmā apahatapāpmā divyo deva eko nārāyaṇaḥ.*
76. Mbh XII (quoted in VSa, p. 123) *nārāyaṇo jaganmūrtiḥ anantātmā sanātanaḥ... ṛṣayaḥ pitaro devā mahābhutāni dhātavaḥ; jaṅgamajaṅgamaṁ cedaṁ jagannārāyaṇodbhavam.*
77. VP VI.4.40. *paramātmā ca sarveṣām ādhāraḥ parameśvaraḥ; viṣṇunāma sa vedeṣu vedānteṣu ca gīyate.*
    See also *Harivaṁśa*, III.132.15 (quoted by Madhva)
    vede rāmāyaṇe caiva purāṇe bhārate tathā;
    ādau ante ca madhye ca viṣṇuḥ sarvatra giyate.
78. VP I.1.31. See fn. 9
79. VP I.2.66. See fn. 61
80. See VSa p. 128.
81. VP I.2.67. *sṛṣṭā sṛjati cātmānaṁ viṣṇuḥ pālyaṁ ca pātica; upasaṁhriyate cānte saṁhartā ca svayaṁ prabhuḥ.*
82. According to the Viśiṣṭādvaita Vedānta, Brahman or Viṣṇu as the *antaryāmin* of Caturmukha-Brahmā and Rudra perform the actual creation and destruction respectively of the universe.
    See RB II.4.17. *caturmukha-śarīrakasya parasyaiva brahmaṇaḥ karma devādi vicitra-sṛṣṭiriti....*
83. VP I.2.70. *sa eva sṛjyaḥ sa ca sargakartā sa eva pātyatti ca pālyate ca; brahmādy-avasthābhiḥ aśeṣamūrtiḥ viṣṇuḥ variṣṭho varado vareṇyaḥ.*
84. See VS I.1.23. *ākāśastalliṅgāt* and the commentary of Rāmānuja

thereon. Here the issue raised for discussion is whether the term *ākāśa* used in the *Chāndogya Upaniṣad* refers to the commonly accepted physical ether or to the *Paramātmā*, the Supreme Self. The *prima facie* view is that it refers to the physical element which is to be taken as the cause of the universe. This view is set aside on the ground that *ākāśa* as physical ether is a created entity and cannot be the cause of the universe. It should, therefore, be understood as *Paramātmā*. The word *ākāśa* also means *paramātmā* in the sense that it causes light (*ākāśayati*).

85. See pp. 142-43.
86. SvUp III.10.
87. See VSa pp. 112-13.
88. VS I.1.31. *śāstradṛṣṭyā tu upadeśo vāmadevavat.*

The implication of this *sūtra* is that when Indra said to Pratardana to meditate on him (*māṁ upāsva*), he meant not his soul but the *paramātman* indwelling in him on the strength of the Upaniṣads which declare that *jivātman* is the *śarīra* (body) of *Paramātman*. In the same sense, the sage Vāmadeva asserts that he is Manu, He is Sun etc.... In all such instances, the word 'I' (*ahaṁ*) denotes *Paramātman*. All terms, according to Visiṣṭādvaita, denote ultimately *Paramātman*. In the light of this Vedānta principle, the statement of Rudra in the Atharvaśiras Up. implies the *Paramātman* and not Rudra himself.

89. TnUp I.12. *adbhyassambhūto hiraṇyagarbha ityaṣṭau.*
See RRB for explanation pp. 71-73.
90. SvUp III.4. *hiraṇyagarbhaṁ janayāmāsa pūrvam.*
91. See p. 144.
92. Mbh VII.183.11. *āloḍhya sarvaśāstrāṇi vicāryaca punaḥ punaḥ;*
idaṁ-ekam suniṣpannam dhyeyo nārāyaṇaḥ sadā.
93. Mbh (quoted in RTS VI) *na viṣṇoḥ paramo devo vidyate nṛpasattama.*
94. *Varāha Purāṇa*, 76.48. *Nārāyaṇāt paro devo na bhūto na bhaviṣyati.*
95. RTS VI. 97. *na vāsudevāt paramasti daivatam.*

8

VIṢṆU AND GODDESS ŚRĪ

We have observed in the previous chapter that the Supreme Deity (*paratattva*) in Vaiṣṇavism is designated as *Śriyaḥ-pati* or Viṣṇu as inseparably related to Goddess *Śrī*. *Śrī* is the beloved consort of Viṣṇu (*viṣṇu-patnī*) and the divine couple (*divya-dampatī*) together constitute the ultimate Reality. In the very opening verse of *Śrī-bhāṣya*, Rāmānuja states in a striking way that Brahman is *Śrīnivāsa* implying thereby that the Upaniṣadic Reality is a personal God as associated with Goddess *Śrī*. This doctrine of Goddess '*Śrī*' which constitutes a distinguishing feature of Śrī-vaiṣṇavism is advanced on the irrefutable authority of scriptural texts, the Pāñcarātra Saṁhitās, the Itihāsas, the *Viṣṇupurāṇa* and the hymns of the Āḻvārs. It is very old indeed dating back to the Ṛgveda. The *Puruṣa-sūkta* mentions that *Hṛī* and *Lakṣmī* are the consorts of *Puruṣa*, the Supreme Being. The *Śrī-sūkta*, which is regarded as the *khila-sūkta* of the Ṛgveda, asserts emphatically that *Śrī* is the Sovereign (*Isvarī*) of all living beings.[1] The *Taittirīya Saṁhitā* states explicitly that *Śrī* is *Viṣṇu-patnī* and also the Ruler of the universe (*Īśānā*).[2] There are many other Vedic passages known by the names of *Bhū-sūkta*, *Nīlā-sūkta*, *Medhā-sūkta*, *Śraddhā-sūkta*, *Vāk-sūkta*, *Aditi-sūkta* which speak of the greatness of the Goddess.[3] The *Viṣṇupurāṇa*, accepted by all scholars as the oldest and most authoritative Purāṇa, points out that *Śrī* as the Divine mother of the universe, is eternal (*nitya*), inseparable from Viṣṇu (*viṣṇoḥ anapāyinī*) and all-pervasive (*sarvagataḥ*).[4] We shall, therefore, devote the present chapter for a discussion of this important doctrine of Vaiṣṇavism.

Meaning of the Terms Śrī and Lakṣmī

The term *Śrī* which is regarded by Yāmuna as the most appropriate name for Goddess, is a significant one bearing several theological implications. The Pāñcarātra Saṁhitās offer six etymological meanings of *Śrī*. Taking the root verb *Śru* which means 'to listen' (*Śru śravaṇe*), *Śrī* is the one who listens to the pathetic pleadings of the devotees seeking help,[5] emphasising the quality of easy accessibility (*saulabhya*). Taking the causative form of the verb (*śrāvayati*), *Śrī* is interpreted as the one who causes the Lord to listen to Her words spoken in favour of the devotees. On the basis of the root verb *śṛṅ* which means to serve (*śṛṅ sevāyām*), the Goddess is named *Śrī* because She is always sought for by all individuals (*śrīyate*). She herself approaches the Lord on behalf of the individuals for their redemption (*śrayate*) exhibiting her quality of playing the role of a mediator (*puruṣakāra*).[6] The root verb *Śṛ* also means to 'remove' (*śṛ hiṁsāyām*) and on this basis *Śrī* is interpreted as the one who removes the sins of the devotees who seek Her refuge (*sṛṇāti*). The root *sṛ* has another meaning, viz., to cause expansion (*sṛ vistāre*) and with reference to this, the term *Śrī* is interpreted as the one who promotes good in the universe (*śrīṇāti*).[7]

Lakṣmī is another term which is popularly used to designate the consort of Viṣṇu. This word appears in the later part of the *Puruṣa-sūkta* and also in one of the hymns of Ṛgveda.[8] Yāska, the author of Vedic etymology, offers seven meanings to the term Lakṣmī.[9] In the first place, Goddess is named as Lakṣmī because She was acquired by Viṣṇu as His consort (*lābhād*). Secondly, She serves as an identification mark for Viṣṇu (*lakṣaṇāt*). That is, the eternal association of Lakṣmī with Viṣṇu makes the latter the Supreme Deity as distinguished from other Vedic deities. Thirdly, Lakṣmī is the one who is sought for by all for material prosperity (*lapsyanāt*). Fourthly, She exhibits her identity mark by Her permanent presence in the chest of Viṣṇu (*lānchanāt*). Fifthly, She illumines the whole universe with Her lustre (*laṣate*). Sixthly, Lakṣmī is so-called because of Her everlasting association with Viṣṇu (*lagyate*). Lastly, She is very modest in the sense that though She grants the boons to the devotees, She feels that She has not done enough for them (*lajjate*). These seven interpretations on the basis of the etymological meaning not only bring out the unique virtues of the Divine Mother but also reveal how long before the Christian era the Vedic seers had conceived the concept of a Goddess endowed with rich and well-defined attributes.

The *Lakṣmī Tantra* also offers several interpretations for the term *Lakṣmī* based on the implications of the letters *la*, *kṣa* and *ma*.[10]

Sāyaṇa interprets the term Lakṣmī as the one who possesses all the auspicious qualities (*lakṣaṇavatī*). The commonly accepted, simple definition is that Lakṣmī is the one who shows concern for all living beings (*lakṣayatīti lakṣmīḥ*).

Doctrine of Goddess Śrī

Though *Śrī* or Lakṣmī is accepted by all as the beloved consort of Viṣṇu, her ontological status has become a subject of controversy. The main issues involved are whether Goddess *Śrī* is on par with Viṣṇu, enjoying an equal status and partaking in all the functions of the Lord or whether She, as the consort of Viṣṇu, is a subordinate deity with certain limited functions. These are the two views advanced by the two sects of Vaiṣṇavas known as Vaḍakalai and Tenkalai. Before we consider the controversial issues, we should try to understand the doctrine as expounded by Yāmuna, Rāmānuja and his immediate successors, Kūreśa, Parāśara Bhattar and Nañjīyar.

The earliest extant Vaiṣṇava treatise on Goddess *Śrī* is the *catuḥślokī* (a hymn of four verses) composed by Yāmuna. It has three commentaries written by Periyavācchān Piḷḷai (A.D. 1228) in Tamil, by Vedānta Deśika in Sanskrit (A.D. 1268) and by Nayanārācchān Piḷḷai (son of Periyavācchān Piḷḷai) in Maṇipravāḷa language. Rāmānuja has expressed his views on the status of *Śrī* in the opening passage of *Śaraṇāgati-gadya* (a prose work). He has also referred to the doctrine incidentally in his other works. The *Gadya* has been commented on by Periyavācchān Piḷḷai. Vedānta Deśika and Sudarśana Sūri, the author of the *Śrutaprakāśikā*. Two closest disciples of Rāmānuja, Śrīvatsānkamiśra also known as Kūreśa and Parāśara Bhattar have composed lyrics on Goddess *Śrī*. The work of the former is titled *Śrī-stava* which comprises eleven verses and that of the latter known as *Śrī-guṇaratnakośa* consists of sixty-one verses on the greatness of Goddess Lakṣmī. We have one other important work belonging to the earlier period entitled *Śrī-sūkta Bhāṣya*, a learned and detailed commentary on the *Śrī-sūkta*, the Ṛg-

Vedic passage. This was written by one Nañjīyar[11] also known by such other names as Periya-jīyar, Raṅganātha and Nārāyaṇa Muni. He was born in A.D. 1182 and was the disciple of Parāśara Bhattar as is evident from the opening verse of the *Bhāṣya*. He is referred to by Vedānta Deśika as Periya-jīyar (a respectful name for Nañjīyar) in his *Rahasyatrayasāra* and as Nārāyaṇa Muni in the *Pāñcarātrarakṣā*. It is, therefore, an authoritative work of an earlier period even if it were supposed to be written as some allege, by someone other than Nañjīyar. The above works of the Vaiṣṇava *ācāryas* along with the Vedic statements, the Pāñcarātra treatises, *Viṣṇupurāṇa* and the hymns of Āḻvārs have to be relied on for determining the status of Goddess in Vaiṣṇava theology. We shall first attempt to give the views of Yāmuna, Rāmānuja and his immediate successors.

Views of Yāmuna, Rāmānuja and His Immediate Successors

According to Yāmuna, the beloved consort of Goddess who is rightly described as *Śrī* is *Puruṣottama*, the Supreme Person. In the words of Rāmānuja, *Śrī* is the Divine Queen of the Ruler of all the celestial beings (*devadeva-divyamahiṣī*). Yāmuna also describes *Śrī* as *Lokaikeśvarī*, the Supreme Sovereign of the universe. *Īśvarī* is the feminine word for *Īśvara*. The term *Īśvara* signifies as one who is the Ruler of the universe, as stated in the Upaniṣads[12] and also the controller (*niyantā*) of all. As *Īśvarī*, She too should enjoy the same status as that of the Supreme Lord. Rāmānuja states more explicitly that there is perfect similarity between God and Goddess in all respects, viz., *svarūpa* or essential nature, *rūpa* or divine enchanting personality, *guṇa* or the attributes, *vibhava* or the glory, *aiśvarya* or Lordship and a host of many other auspicious qualities par excellence.[13] In other words, she possesses all the characteristics of the Lord as appropriate to His status (*anurūpa*) and also as liked by Him (*svābhimata*). This one statement of Rāmānuja at the very outset of his *Śaraṇāgati-gadya* has far-reaching philosophical and theological implications regarding the concept of Goddess in Vaiṣṇavism.

Speaking of the *svarūpa* of *Śrī*, She is regarded as eternal (*nitya*), like the Supreme Lord, as *Viṣṇupurāṇa* affirms.[14] She is constituted of knowledge as is Brahman.[15] Like Viṣṇu, She too is all-pervasive, as *Viṣṇupurāṇa* states.[16] Like Bhagavān, Lakṣmī also possesses all the six principal attributes—knowledge (*jñāna*), strength (*bala*), lordship (*aiśvarya*), virility (*vīrya*), power (*śakti*), splendour (*tejas*) and is also free from all kinds of imperfection.[17] Therefore, She is described by Rāmānuja as *Bhagavatī* (feminine of *Bhagavān*).[18] As regards the physical features of the divine personality (*divyavigraha-guṇa*), both Viṣṇu and Lakṣmī are described by the religious texts as possessing a spiritual lustrous body like the colour of gold (*hiraṇyavarṇa*) and with eyes comparable to the freshly blossomed lotus petals (*padmadalā-yatākṣi*).[19] Vālmīki in his *Rāmāyaṇa* describes Goddess Sītā as one possessing a youthful personality, character, physical beauty and dignity equal to that of God Rāma.[20] Regarding *vibhūti* or the property of the Lord comprising the spiritual universe (*nitya-vibhūti*) and the physical universe (*līlā-vibhūti*), Goddess enjoys equal ownership. This point has been brought out in a significant way by Yāmuna in the opening verse of *Catuḥślokī*. Thus, he says: 'The *Ādiśeṣa*, the mythical serpent which serves as the couch and throne for Viṣṇu also belongs to you; the *Garutmān*, the Divine bird which is the vehicle of Viṣṇu is yours; the cosmic matter (*mūla-prakṛti*) constituted of three *guṇas* which functions as a veil (*yavanikā*) by eclipsing the true nature of Reality is also yours; the four-faced Brahmā, Rudra, Indra, Yama, Varuṇa and all other deities together with their wives are your attendants, as they are to Viṣṇu.' The implication of this verse of Yāmuna is that both the physical universe as well as the transcendental spiritual universe are ruled by Goddess *Śrī*. The same truth is emphasised by the scriptural text which says that Goddess who is the consort of Viṣṇu is the Ruler (*Īśānā*) of the entire universe.[21] It is in the same sense that the *Śrī-sūkta* of Ṛgveda also states that *Śrī* is the *Īśvarī* of *sarvabhūtas*. What is intended by these statements is that *Śrī* is the Ruler not merely in the capacity of Her being a consort of *Īśvara* (*Īśvara-patnī*) but also as a Divine Being enjoying equal status with *Īśvara*.[22] The controversy involved in this regard will be discussed later. For the present, we should take note of the fact that both according to Rāmānuja and his predecessor, Yāmuna '*Śrī*' enjoys equal status with Viṣṇu and She possesses *svarūpa*, *rūpa*, *guṇa*, *vibhava* and other great qualities appropriate to Her beloved Lord. Briefly stated, Her glory (*mahimā*) is boundless and immeasurable. Even Her Lord cannot comprehend it in its entirety in the same way as He cannot assess His own greatness.[23]

Though Goddess is equal to Viṣṇu in all respects, She is held in higher esteem by the Vaiṣṇava *ācāryas*. This is due to the fact that She possesses certain motherly qualities such as compassion (*dayā*), the forgiveness (*kṣamā*) on account of which She has a tendency to overlook the offences of the devotees. She also has a tender affection (*vātsalya*) towards all beings like a mother towards her child, by not taking notice of their offences. Above all She has a natural inclination to shower grace (*anugraha*) upon all. Vedānta Deśika describes Her as the personification of grace and as one who never thinks of punishing.[24] The Itihāsas and Purāṇas portray the motherly qualities with numerous mythological episodes. Yāmuna points out that without the grace of *Śrī*, it is not possible to achieve worldly prosperity (*aiśvarya*), blissful experience of the soul (*kaivalya*) and even *mokṣa*.[25] Parāśara Bhattar emphasises Her magnanimity (*udāra-svabhāva*) by pointing out that even after granting the devotees *aiśvarya*, *kaivalya* and *paramapada* in response to a mere prayer expressed through the folded hands (*añjali*), Goddess still feels that She has not given them enough and feels ashamed,[26] reiterating the implication of the term *udārāṁ* (generous character) expressed in the *Śrī-sūkta*.[27]

As compared to the special qualities attributed to Goddess *Śrī*, there are certain unique qualities which exclusively belong to Her Lord. One of these is *daṇḍa-dharatva* or as one who imposes punishment to the individuals committing sins, unlike the Goddess who has a natural inclination to ignore the offences because of Her motherly, compassionate attitude. The most significant role played by *Śrī* as contrasted with that of Her Lord, is to act as an interceder or mediator (*puruṣakāra*) on behalf of the sinners and recommend them to receive His grace. The role of intercession (*puruṣakāratva*) is considered so important that the Tenkalai sect of the Vaiṣṇavas overemphasise this characteristic of Lakṣmī. The controversy related to this issue will be discussed later. This kind of distinction in the relative roles of the Divine couple is made, as Parāśara Bhattar explains, purely by mutual agreement on the same analogy as between the two loving couples chosing a distinctive role for each in the running of a family. This should not be construed as a distinction indicating the superiority of the Lord or the subordinate status of His consort. Both are equal in all respects and both are capable of performing each others role, if they so desire.

As *Viṣṇu-patnī* Goddess is held in Vaiṣṇavism as inseparable from Her Lord at all times and in all states. Thus *Viṣṇupurāṇa* states that *Śrī* is *anapāyinī* or inseparable.[28] Rāmānuja also uses the same expression.[29] Even in the state of dissolution prior to creation, Viṣṇu is associated with Lakṣmī, as the hymn of the Ṛgveda asserts.[30] According to the theory of incarnation the Supreme Being has five forms: *para*, *vyūha*, *vibhava*, *arcā* and *antaryāmī*.[31] *Para* is the state in which God exists as *para-vāsudeva* in the transcendental realm. In this state too He is not separated from *Śrī*.[32] Lakṣmī is also associated with Viṣṇu in all the four *vyūha* manifestations.[33] The *vibhava* forms of God are the various incarnations as Rāma, Kṛṣṇa etc. As the *Viṣṇu-purāṇa* points out, in whatever form God incarnates Himself in the physical universe, Goddess Lakṣmī too takes her birth to be His consort along with God appropriate to the role to be played by Him.[34] In all the *arcā* form, Lakṣmī is ever present in the chest of Viṣṇu. The presiding deity of the Tirumalai (the holy centre in Andhra Pradesh, South India) is known by the name of *Śrīnivāsa*, signifying that the very Divine body of the Lord is the abode (*nivāsa*) for *Śrī*. Nammāḻvār, who is claimed to have had the vision of this Lord of Tirumalai describes graphically that Goddess Lakṣmī is inseparably poised on the Lord's chest, ever saying that She shall not be apart from Him even for a moment.[35] Sage Vālmīki uses the phrase *nitya-śrīḥ*,[36] which implies that Viṣṇu is eternally associated with *Śrī*. Keeping these facts in mind, *Yāmuna* sums up the theological position in the following verse: '(The Śrutis and Smṛtis) declare that your unique splendour and form suited to your Lord are inseparably united with all the form of the Lord such as the state of *Para-Brahman* which is infinite and free from any defects, the states of *vyūha* manifestations which are far more delightful (for the devotees), and many other forms assumed by Him by way of different incarnations at His own pleasure.'[37] He uses the expression *gāḍhopagūḍha* which means that the two are inherently united as inseparable.'[38] Presumably it is in this sense that both *Viṣṇupurāṇa* and Rāmānuja describe the relationship between

Śrī and Her Lord as *anapāyinī* from the ontological standpoint and as *Śriyaḥ-pati* for theological purposes.[39] The fuller ontological significance of this concept will be discussed presently.

Views on the Ontological Status of Śrī in Post-Deśika Period

We have so far presented the doctrine of *Śrī* as developed by Yāmuna, Rāmānuja and his immediate successors. The views expressed by these *ācāryas* on the ontological status of *Śrī* and Her role in the important divine functions are based on the authoritative statements found in the Vedas, Pāñcarātra Āgamas, the *Viṣṇupurāṇa* and the hymns of Āḻvārs. Vedānta Deśika, the most distinguished follower of Rāmānuja, has faithfully subscribed to the views of his predecessors and developed the theories relating to *Śrī* in much greater detail, because these conform, in his opinion, to the accepted tradition. However, in the post-Deśika period the Vaiṣṇava *ācāryas* who owe their allegience to Maṇavālamāmuni, have advanced a few theories which run counter to those of Vedānta Deśika. The doctrine of *Śrī* has thus become one of the major topics of controversy between the two sects and during the last two centuries a few tracts have also been written presenting the arguments and counter-arguments on the status and role of *Śrī*. These arguments are mostly of a doctrinal nature generally arising out of the interpretation of the statements of the ancient *ācāryas*. They do not appear to be of much philosophical significance. However, a few issues which have a bearing on the nature of the Supreme Deity (*paratattva*) as conceived by Vaiṣṇavism needs consideration.

The crucial issue having an ontological implication is whether Goddess *Śrī*, who is inseparable from Viṣṇu, and who also enjoys equality with Him in all respects, is an integral part of the ultimate Reality. There are two views on this question. According to one view held by Vedānta Deśika and his followers, *Śrī* is an integral part of Reality and the divine couple together constitute the *para-tattva*. The basis for this claim is that the scriptural texts, the Pāñcarātra Saṁhitās and the *Viṣṇupurāṇa* declare that *Śrī* is *vibhu* or infinite in character in the same way as Viṣṇu is and She plays an important role in all the functions of the Lord including that of intercession. The other view, maintained by the followers of Maṇavāḷamāmuni contends that

Śrī is not *vibhu* in character but monadic (*aṇu*) like the individual selves and cannot, therefore, become an integral part of Reality. In their opinion if *Śrī* were on par with Viṣṇu, it would militate against the unitary character of the ultimate Reality.

The Theory of Śrī as Subordinate Deity

Before we critically evaluate these views, we may first present briefly the arguments of the Tenkalai school. The main contention is that the Upaniṣads speak of three ontological entities: *Īśvara* or God, *cit* or soul and *acit* or matter. Thus says the *Śvetāśvatara Upaniṣad*: '*bhoktā bhogyaṁ preritāraṁ ca matvā.*'[40] *Bhoktā* refers to the individual self which experiences, *bhogyaṁ* is the world of experience and *preritāra* is the one who controls everything. The question is asked: where does Goddess fit in? She cannot be included in the category of *acit*, because She is a sentient being, whereas *acit* is non-sentient. Nor can She be included in the category of *Īśvara*, because it is stated in the same Upaniṣad that *Īśvara* alone rules both *cit* and *acit* (*īśate deva ekaḥ*).[41] The only alternative left is that Goddess is to be included in the category of sentient souls (*jīva-koṭi*). Besides, the Upaniṣad also asserts that there is no other Being which is either equal to or higher than *Īśvara*.[42] As regards the statements which speak of Lakṣmī as all-pervasive (*sarvagataḥ*), these have to be understood in the sense that She is omnipresent by virtue of either her infinite knowledge (*dharmabhūta-jñāna*) or by the special power She possesses (*śaktivaśāt*).[43] The *jīva* in Viśiṣṭādvaita is monadic in nature (*aṇu*) but it is accepted that its knowledge becomes infinite in the state of *mokṣa*.[44] In the same way, it is contended that though Goddess *Śrī* is *aṇu* in nature, She can be omnipresent by virtue of Her special power. Without accepting this interpretation, if Goddess is treated on par with God, it would inevitably lead to the admission of two Realities (*Īśvaradvitva*), which is against the spirit of Upaniṣadic teaching. Lakṣmī, therefore, though inseparable from Viṣṇu, is the highest among the souls but does not have the same ontological status as the Lord. She is a subordinate deity to Viṣṇu.

Regarding the role of the Goddess, the Tenkalai sect lays such an emphasis on Her function as an interceder (*puruṣakāra-*

tva) as to exclude the power to grant *mokṣa* by Lakṣmī. She is also not regarded as part of the *upāya* or means for *mokṣa*. The basis for upholding this view is that the religious texts including the Pāñcarātra treatises describe Lakṣmī only as an interceder. Theologically, this is an important function[45] because without the mediation of the Divine Mother who has a loving affection to the suffering individuals, it is difficult to approach the Lord directly for refuge. Such a mediation is justified because of the harsh and punishing attitude of God towards sinners. By implication, the one who acts as a mediator pleading on behalf of the devotees, cannot be the giver of *mokṣa*. If She could grant *mokṣa* there would be no need to intercede on behalf of the devotees for this purpose. Further, the Śruti and Smṛti texts declare that God is the sole means of attaining *mokṣa*. The *Muṇḍaka Upaniṣad* says: 'He is the cause-way for immortality.'[46] The *Puruṣa-sūkta* states that there is no way for *mokṣa* other than the knowledge of the Supreme Being.[47] More explicitly the *Gītā* enjoins on all to seek refuge only in Him (*māmekaṁ śaraṇaṁ vṛja*). In none of these texts, there is any mention of Lakṣmī along with God. Besides, one of the requirements for self-surrender is that the aspirant for *mokṣa* should develop an attitude of absolute helplessness by not having anyone as his protector barring *Paramātman*. If Goddess were also involved at the stage of observing self-surrender as a *sādhana*, it would militate against the eligibility requirements of the aspirant for *mokṣa*. Lakṣmī is, therefore, to be regarded as playing only the role of *puruṣakāra*.

The Theory of Śrī as on Par with Viṣṇu

These views of the Tenkalai school have been controverted by the followers of Vedānta Deśika on equally strong grounds. The arguments and counter-arguments do not seem to lead to a finality. However, we may attempt to evaluate these claims in an objective way to determine the correct ontological position of Goddess in Vaiṣṇavism which is sustainable philosophically and logically. In spiritual matters, the Revealed Scripture and Smṛti texts based on it are generally acknowledged as the sole authority for determining the nature of Reality. Logic or *tarka*, though important, can neither prove nor disprove a supernormal object which is beyond our perceptual experience. Logic is to be adopted only to support what is said in the Śruti. This is the stand taken by the author of the *Vedānta-sūtra* for determining the nature of the ultimate Reality and proving the existence of God. The same principle needs to be adopted for deciding the ontological status of Goddess too. Vedānta Deśika has taken such a stand in discussing this issue. He points out by way of a reference to an episode in the *Mahābhārata* relating to a philosophic debate, that it is possible to make weak cases appear strong and strong issues weak by using purely logical arguments.[48] Though it may be possible to prove any selected theory by logical ingenuity, as an honest logician one should submit himself to the authority of Scripture for determining the correct position.[49] In view of this the controversial issue with regard to the ontological status of Goddess *Śrī* is to be decided by resorting to scriptural evidence duly supported by logical arguments. Accordingly, if we go by the scriptural texts, *Viṣṇupurāṇa*, Pāñcarātra Saṁhitās along with the views as expressed by Yāmuna and Rāmānuja in their works, Goddess *Śrī* is infinite (*vibhu*) by virtue of Her essential nature (*svarūpa*) in the same way as Brahman is. As an eternally inseparable consort of Viṣṇu and Sovereign of the universe (*Īśvarī*), She enjoys the same status as Her Lord and constitutes an integral part of Reality.

Scriptural Support for the Theory of Śrī as Vibhu

This conclusion can be substantiated not only on the basis of scriptural evidence but also on logical and philosophical ground. It is no doubt true that there are no scriptural texts which explicitly state that *Śri* is *vibhu* in character. Nor are there any scriptural statements which affirm that She is *monadic* (*aṇu*) in character. However, there are sufficient statements in the Vedas which indicate the infinite character of Goddess. In the *Taittirīya Brāhmaṇa*, a hymn addresses Goddess as '*rāḍasi*, *bṛhatī*, *śrīrasi* ......'[50] *Rāḍasi* means 'you are the sovereign Queen', *bṛhatī* means 'you are infinite' and *śrīrasi* signifies 'you are Goddess of wealth'. The word *bṛhatī* is interpreted on the authority of the *Lakśmī Tantra* as one not conditioned by time, space and another entity, the same meaning as attached to the root *bṛhat* in *Brahma-śabda*.[51] In the *Medhā-sūkta*[52] there is a description of *Medhā-devī* (*Medhā* being another name for Lakṣmī),[53] as *viśvācī* which means as one who pervades the whole universe (*sarva-vyāpī*).[54] In the *Śraddhā-sūkta* (a passage in *Taittirīya Brāhmaṇa*),[55] *Śraddhā-devī* which is also another name for Goddess Lakṣmī, is equated with the universe (*jagat*), in the same way as Brahman is equated with the universe in the *Chāndogya Upaniṣad.* The implication of it is that She is immanent in the entire universe. Another passage of *Taittirīya Brāhmaṇa* known as *Vāk-sūkta*, describes *Vāg-devī* (*vāk* is synonymous with Sarasvatī, who is Lakṣmī) in the words: *anantām-antāt.*[56] This term is interpreted to mean that which is infinite, viz., as one who is not conditioned by space, time and another entity, the same meaning as offered to the term *ananta* in the *Taittirīya Upaniṣad* in respect of Brahman.[57] All these scriptural statements quoted in support of the *vibhutva* of Goddess may be questioned by the critic on the ground that they do not explicitly convey the idea that *Śrī* is *vibhu* by virtue of Her *svarūpa* but, on the other hand, these can be taken as statements glorifying the greatness of *Śrī.* But the issue becomes cleared decisively if we take into consideration the hymn of the *Śrī-sūkta* of Ṛgveda which asserts that Goddess Lakṣmī is the *Īśvarī* or the Supreme Ruler of the entire universe.[58] We have explained earlier the fuller implication of the term *Īśvarī*. On the basis of the root verb *aśu* meaning to pervade (*aśū vyāptau*), *Īśvarī* means the one who pervades everything. It can also mean *niyantṛī* or the one who is the Ruler of all (*īśa aiśvarya*).[59] This particular scriptural text is interpreted by some to mean that Lakṣmī is regarded as *Īśvarī* only in the capacity of Her being the consort of *Īśvara*, who is the actual Ruler of the universe. This cannot be a correct view because two other scriptural statements[60] to which we have referred earlier, state in explicit terms that *Goddess* is *Īśānā*. This description of Goddess as *Īśānā* becomes fully justified only if She is taken as the Sovereign of all beings in the universe, except of course, God. Philosophically, an ontological entity cannot be regarded as Supreme Sovereign unless it is an inner controller of everything (*antarātmā*) by virtue of its all-pervasive character. This truth is borne out by the *Antaryāmi Brāhmaṇa* of the *Bṛhadāraṇyaka Upaniṣad*. Hence *Śrī* is to be accepted as part of Brahman in order to qualify herself to be *Īśvarī* or *Īśānā* The *Viṣṇupurāṇa* which is admitted both by Śaṁkara and Rāmānuja as an authority on the subject of *para-tattva*, asserts without mincing the words that *Śrī* is all-pervasive in the same way as *Viṣṇu* is (*yathā sarvagato viṣṇuḥ tathaiveyam dvijottama*).[61] It may be possible to interpret the word '*sarvagata*' to mean all-pervasive in the sense that *Śrī*, by virtue of Her infinite knowledge or by virtue of Her infinite capacity can be everywhere.[62] This does not appear to be the idea of the sage *Parāśara* since the two adverbs used by him in the verse '*yathā*' and '*tathā*' would not support the view of the critic. *Yathā* meaning '*just like*' applies to Viṣṇu and *tathā* meaning '*in the same way*' applies to *Śrī*. The correct meaning of the verse, if properly understood without a bias is 'Just as Viṣṇu is all-pervasive, in the same way *Śrī* too is all-pervasive.'[63] This meaning gets further supported from another verse appearing in the next chapter of the same Purāṇa which reads: 'You are the Mother of the entire universe and Hari (Viṣṇu), the Highest Deity of all celestial beings, is the Father; this universe comprising the sentient and non-sentient beings is *pervaded* both by you (Goddess) and *Viṣṇu*.'[64] The same truth is reiterated in clear terms by the *Viśvaksena Saṁhitā*, one of the important pāñcarātra treatises. It says: 'The *pervasiveness* by *svarūpa* and *guṇa* is common to both; just as the universe is pervaded by Me (God) both by virtue of My *svarūpa* and *guṇa* (knowledge), the same way everything is pervaded (by Her too). Therefore, She is Supreme Ruler and controller of everything.[65] Taking into consideration all these explanations, there is no room to maintain the view that Goddess *Śrī* is omnipresent only by means of Her infinite power or knowledge. On the other hand, She is *vibhu* in the same way as Viṣṇu is. Although Rāmānuja and his spiritual predecessors Yāmuna and Nammāḻvār did not use the term *vibhu* or *aṇu* to describe the nature of Goddess, it would be obvious from the explanations provided on the basis of the scriptural statements in general and in particular the statement of Sage Parāśara in *Viṣṇupurāṇa*, that it was their intention to regard *Śrī* as *vibhu* and on par with Brahman or *Viṣṇu*. Otherwise, Rāmānuja would not have defined the term Brahman as *Puruṣottama* and equated it with *Śrīnivāsa* or *Śriyaḥ-pati*. The hymns of the Āḻvārs and the ancient classical Tamil literature[66] of pre-Christian era have invariably used the term *Tirumāl* (the Tamil word for *Śriyaḥ-pati*) to describe the Supreme Deity, Nārāyaṇa. The Vedic seers, the reputed sages who have authored the great Epics and Purāṇas, the exponents of the Pāñcarātra treatises, the Āḻvārs and ancient Vaiṣṇava *ācāryas* who have had a deeper insight into the philosophic truth have realized without an element of doubt that God and Goddess are integrally related and the Divine couple constitute the ultimate Reality.[67]

Unitary Character of Reality as Śriyaḥ-pati

Now the question arises relating to the oneness of the Supreme Being. If *Śrī* is *vibhu* and is on par with Viṣṇu, would it not amount to admitting two deities as the Ruler of the universe? Is not such a theory philosophically unsound?

Prima facie this appears to be a valid objection. But when we understand correctly the sense in which the Divine couple are described as constituting one Reality (*para-tattva*) it becomes untenable. There are two explanations for upholding the idea that the Divine couple together constitute the *paratattva*. The first is a philosophical one based on the metaphysical concept of substance and attribute and the theory of *apṛthaksiddhi* or the concept of inseparability admitted in the Viśiṣṭādvaita Vedānta, to explain the oneness of Brahman as a *viśiṣṭa* entity. The second is a theological justification based on the logical principle of *vyāsajya-vṛtti*, the Naiyayika concept according to which a common quality can belong to two entities.

Regarding the first point, the Viśiṣṭādvaita metaphysics maintains that the substance and attribute are distinct but they are inherently related (*apṛthaksiddha*).[68] By virtue of the inherent relationship, the substance as qualified by the attribute is one entity. This is the concept of *viśiṣṭa* or substance as integrally related to its attribute. On the basis of this principle, Rāmānuja has formulated the organic relationship between *Īśvara* and the universe of *cit* and *acit*. The ultimate Reality of Viśiṣṭādvaita Vedānta is Brahman as organically related to *cit* and *acit* (*cid-acid-viśiṣṭa Brahma*). Though the three ontological entities are distinct by virtue of their intrinsic nature, Brahman as a *viśiṣṭa* entity is one even though associated with *cit* and *acit*.[69]

Further, according to the Viśiṣṭādvaita Vedānta Brahman is *satya* or absolute reality, *jñāna* or infinite knowledge and *ananta* or infinite. All the three terms represent the essential characteristics or *asādhāraṇa dharmas* of Brahman. Each one is a distinctive dharma and it is also different from the substrate (*Brahma-*

svarūpa) in which it inheres. In epistemological terms the essential characteristics of an entity are integrally related to the *svarūpa*. The two are *apṛthaksiddha* or inseparable. Brahman and the essential attributes, though distinct as *dharmī* and *dharma*, Brahman as characterised by the attributes is one entity. This is the fundamental concept of Reality in Viśiṣṭādvaita as expounded by Rāmānuja, which is acceptable to all his followers.

The concept of Goddess *Śrī* as an integral part of Brahman is to be understood on the basis of the same metaphysical principle. *Śrī* is admitted in Vaiṣṇavism as an *asādhāraṇa-dharma* or as a unique characteristic of Viṣṇu in so far as She serves as an identity mark to distinguish Viṣṇu from other Vedic deities.[70] As we have explained elsewhere, the *Puruṣa-sūkta* of the Ṛgveda provides the basis for holding this theory. The first part of the *Puruṣa-sūkta* speaks of the ultimate Reality as *Puruṣa*. In order to determine the name of the particular Vedic deity to which the general term *Puruṣa* is applicable, the statement found in the *uttarānuvāka* or the later passage of *Puruṣa-sūkta* in which *Śrī* is specifically mentioned as *patnī*, is adopted as the criteria for deciding the fact that *Puruṣa* is *Śriyaḥ-pati* and that He is the ultimate Reality and not any other deity such as Brahmā, Rudra etc. In view of this the qualification, viz., *śriyaḥ-patitva* is taken by the Vaiṣṇava *ācāryas* as *asādhāraṇa-dharma* or distinguishing characteristic. According to the Viśiṣṭādvaita epistemology, a distinguishing characteristic of an entity should be integrally related to it in the same way as *gotva* (cowness) does to *go* (cow), *prabhā* or luminosity to sun (*prabhāvān*). It is in this sense that the Pāñcarātra Saṁhitās have conceived Goddess Lakṣmī in terms of *śakti* of Viṣṇu.[71] In the same way, Vālmīki in the Rāmāyaṇa describes Goddess Sītā as *prabhā* and God-incarnate Rāma as *prabhāvān* and the two are stated to be inseparable.[72] As already explained, an entity as integrally related to the essential characteristic is one as a *viśiṣṭa* substance. Both *Lakṣmī Tantra* and *Ahirbudhnya Saṁhitā* reaffirm this fact by stating that Brahman is one as inseparably related to Goddess *Śrī*.[73] Parāśara Bhattar a close disciple of Rāmānuja, uses the phrase *antarbhāva* meaning an integral part.[74] In other words though God and Goddess as two sentient beings are distinct deities, they are regarded as constituting one Reality in terms of the integral relationship. As an integral part of Viṣṇu, Goddess

Śrī possesses all the characteristics of Nārāyaṇa such as *svarūpa*, *rūpa*, *guṇa*, *vibhava* etc., as Rāmānuja has stated.

In view of these explanations, the question whether *Śrī* is *aṇu* is not relevant. As an integral part of Viṣṇu, She cannot be anything but infinite (*vibhu*) in character as the *Viṣṇupurāṇa* states (*sarvagataḥ*). The question whether She is a giver of *mokṣa* also does not arise. As part of Viṣṇu, She has the capacity to grant *mokṣa*. This fact is also clearly stated in the *Viṣṇupurāṇa*.[75] As a part of the ultimate Reality, Goddess also partakes in the major cosmic functions of creation, sustenance and dissolution, as the Pāñcarātra Saṁhitās point out.[76]

The theological question whether or not *Śrī* serves as an *upāya* or means at the time of observing *śaraṇāgati* or self-surrender for *mokṣa* does not appear to be relevant. If She is integrally related to Nārāyaṇa as the term *Śrīman-nārāyaṇa* appearing in the *Śaraṇāgati-mantra* signifies, She too is naturally part of the *upāya*. The hymn of the *Śrī-sūkta* explicitly says: 'I surrender to Lakṣmī' and 'I seek Her refuge'. According to the interpretation of Nañjīyar, this hymn implies self-surrender to Lakṣmī as a means to *mokṣa*.[77] The *Gītā* verse which enjoins the observance of the self-surrender to the Lord only (*māmekaṁ śaraṇaṁ vṛja*) is not intended to imply only God without His consort. The *Chāndogya Upaniṣad* states that in the beginning *sat* only (*sadeva*) existed and that it was one only (*ekameva*). These terms *sat* and *eka* are interpreted by Rāmānuja as Brahman qualified with *cit* and *acit* in their unmanifest state. In the same way the terms *māṁ ekaṁ* in the *Gītā* verse are to be understood as referring to the Supreme Lord as integrally related to *Śrī* too.[78]

The admission of *Śrī* on par with Viṣṇu does not also militate against Her major role as an interceder (*puruṣakāratva*) in addition to Her other divine functions. As a feminine deity, *puruṣakāratva* is undoubtedly an important characteristic of *Śrī*, like the other unique motherly qualities such as *vātsalya* or loving disposition and compassion or *dayā*. But these qualities including Her role as mediator should not lower Her ontological status. As explained by Parāśara Bhattar, the division of certain specific roles between the Lord and His consort, is by mutual agreement and as such it does not either enhance the greatness of the one against the other or lower the status of one as against the other.[79] What is arranged by one's own will (*ichhā*) by mutual agreement would not affect the ontological status of the divine couple.

We shall now consider the theological justification for admitting the Divine couple as one *tattva*. It is true that God and Goddess are described in the theological treatises as two distinct deities. They are also worshipped in separate shrines. How then can we justify the two together as one *tattva*?

It may be noted that Goddess in Vaiṣṇavism is not conceived as an independent deity but on the contrary, She is regarded as a dependent Reality. The *Viśvaksena Saṁhitā* describes Goddess as *śeṣa* of Lord (*matśeṣabhūta*).[80] *Lakṣmī Tantra* and *Ahirbudhnya Saṁhitā* which discuss the doctrine of Goddess present the same picture. Nowhere in the Vaiṣṇava religious literature, Lakṣmī is taken as an absolutely independent *tattva*, unlike in Śāktaism. If She were an independent Reality, like God, the objection of two deities constituting one *tattva* stands. But as a dependent Reality, inseparably related to God, the unitary character of *Īśvara* as one *viśiṣṭa-tattva* (Reality) is not affected in the same way as Brahman even though organically related to the universe of *cit* and *acit* remains non-dual. The fact that Goddess is *śeṣa-bhūta* or a dependent deity does not affect Her parity with Viṣṇu and Her being the *Īśvarī* or Sovereign of the universe for two reasons. In the first place, She is not included in the category of individual souls, as the Tenkalai sect believes because there are no scriptural and Smṛti statements affirming explicitly that She is monadic in character and belongs to the *jīva-koti*. On the contrary, there is sufficient justification, as already explained, to regard Her as part of *Īśvara*. Secondly, the *śeṣatva* or the dependent character of *Śrī* is assumed by Her voluntarily out of Her own will with the mutual agreement between the Lord and Herself, as Parāśara Bhattar has indicated. As a consort (*patnī*) of the Supreme Lord, She has chosen to remain *śeṣa-bhūta* to the latter presumably out of respect for the Lord (*aicchika-śeṣatva*).[81] The assumption of a specific characteristic like *śeṣatva* out of one's free will does not affect the intrinsic nature of Her Sovereignty. Thus, for instance, Lord Kṛṣṇa voluntarily chose to become a charioteer for Arjuna and acted as one who was subordinate to Arjuna; but the assumption of such a status out of His free will (*svecchā*), did not in the least affect the Supremacy of God Kṛṣṇa as the Ruler of the universe. The same explanation holds good for the *śeṣatva* of Goddess *Śrī*. These facts have been brought out clearly by the *Viśvakṣena Saṁhitā*. Thus, it says: 'Just as the universe is pervaded by Me by virtue of My *svarūpa* and *guṇa* (knowledge), the same way it is pervaded by Her; She is, therefore, the controller of all (*niyantṛī*) and also the Sovereign (*Īśvarī*). She is subordinate to Me (*mat-śeṣa-bhūtā*); but She is my beloved (*vallabhā*) and therefore, the Ruler of all (*sarveṣāṁ Īśvarī*). The twofold *vibhūti* (the transcendental realm and the physical universe) is the property of both of us.'[82] The same point has also been emphasised in another Pañcarātra Saṁhitā.[83] The implication of all these statements is that Goddess *Śrī* is *Śeṣī* or Ruler for the entire universe excluding Her Lord; whereas God is the Ruler of all including His consort. In other words, both God and Goddess are *Śeṣī* or the Sovereign of the universe except one difference, viz., that the former is the Ruler of all including Goddess, whereas the latter is Ruler of all except God (*ekona śeṣī*). As *Īśvarī* of the entire universe of *cit* and *acit*, She enjoys a higher ontological status than the individual souls (*jīvas*) which are by their very intrinsic nature absolutely dependent beings (*nirupādhika-śeṣatva*).[84] As distinct from individual souls and as sovereign of the universe She is on par with Viṣṇu.

There is no contradiction involved in two ontological entities which are on par in every respect having a common function of the *Lordship* of the universe (*īśitṛtva*). Such a concept of *two-in-one* is not logically untenable. In Indian Logic, we speak of the concept of *vyāsyajya-vṛtti*, which means that a single property or quality belongs to two. Thus, for instance, the concept of relation inheres in both the relata (*ubhaya-niṣṭa*). In the same way, *śeṣitva* can be applicable to both the deities. It is in this sense that we should understand the theory of God and Goddess together constituting one *para-tattva* and not in the sense of *tādātmya* or absolute identity which is philosophically unacceptable. Keeping this truth in mind Śrīrāmamiśra popularly known as Śomāśi Āṇḍān, who is one of the pupils of Rāmānuja describes *para-tattva* of Vaiṣṇavism in the following terms: *ubhayādhiṣṭānaṁ ca ekaṁ śeṣitvam*.[85] The meaning of it is that *śeṣitva* or Lordship which is one inheres in both. That is, *śeṣitva* does not exclusively belong to the Supreme Lord but it equally applies to Goddess Lakṣmī. In other words, the Divine couple (*divya-dampatī*) are the sovereign of the universe.

Theologically *ekatva* or oneness of *para-tattva* can also be explained in a non-controversial way on the basis of the fact that the Divine couple is the object of meditation and self-surrender for *mokṣa* and also for offering divine service in the *paramapada*. This view is acceptable to all the Vaiṣṇavas including those of Tenkalai sect,[86] though there may be difference of opinion with regard to the ontological status of *Śrī*. But philosophically the unity of *para-tattva* would be better justified if we regard Goddess *Śrī* as an integral part of Brahman or Viṣṇu as we have explained by upholding the oneness of the ultimate Reality in the sense of *viśiṣṭa* entity as inseparably associated with Goddess, like *prabhāvān* (sun) and *prabhā* (its luminosity) and also by maintaining the all-pervasive character (*vibhutva*) of *Śrī* as clearly stated in the *Viṣṇupurāṇa*.

Other Theories Regarding Goddess

There are many other theories on the doctrine of Goddess, which appear *prima facie*, to be at variance with the theory we have outlined but we may take up for consideration a few important ones. As we have observed, the Pāñcarātra Saṁhitās describe Goddess as *śakti* or creative energy of Viṣṇu. Some of them maintain the view that Lakṣmī is *prakṛti* (cosmic matter) from which the universe evolves. One school of thought holds the theory that Lakṣmī is the presiding deity of the cosmic matter (*prakṛti-adhiṣṭhātṛī*).[87] According to another theory Lakṣmī is identical with Viṣṇu and the same one Reality assumes feminine form. Vaiṣṇavism does not accept any of these views. Lakṣmī is a sentient Divine Being and She cannot, therefore, be *śakti*. Nor is She the *prdkṛti* because the latter is non-sentient matter. If Lakṣmī is taken as the presiding deity of *prakṛti*, She would be reduced to the position of a minor deity with a status far lower than that of Viṣṇu. This theory would also conflict with the scriptural text which specifically says that Lakṣmī is the Sovereign of the universe (*Īśvarī*). She cannot be regarded as identical with Viṣṇu because the scriptural texts speak of the two as distinct in such terms as *pati* (Lord) and *patnī* (consort).[88]

Vedānta Deśika attempts to reconcile some of these conflicting views with the doctrine held by Vaiṣṇavism by way of offering suitable explanations. The description of Lakṣmī in the Pāñcarātra treatises as *śakti*, *vidyā*, *ahantā*, *sattā* etc., is to be taken in the sense that Goddess constitutes an essential, distinguishing characteristic (*viśeṣaṇa*) of Viṣṇu.[89] Alternatively, She may be regarded as the one who being an inseparable life partner of Viṣṇu, is an impelling force to prompt Him to perform the important divine functions such as creation of the universe.[90] The very concept of *patnī* or wife signifies according to Pāṇini, the one who is associated (with the husband) in all the ritualistic activities.[91] The creation of the universe is a cosmic *yajña* for the purpose of protection of the humanity and Goddess by Her ever presence with Viṣṇu, is a partner in it.[92] It is not necessary that Goddess Herself should actually create the universe by Her will but Her very presence with God would amount to Her taking part in it. Keeping this in mind, Srīvatsānkamiśra, the closest disciple of Rāmānuja states in a poetic way: 'Hari (*Viṣṇu*) looks at the face of *Śrī* and guided by Her gestures, performs the acts of creation, sustenance and dissolution of the universe and also the acts of granting heaven and eternal bliss; if it were otherwise, the sport of creation will no longer offer them the joy.'[93] All these statements emphasise the fact that the Divine Couple (*divya-dampatī*) constitute the one *tattva* as the *viśiṣṭa* entity. As Vedānta Deśika has well summed up, the *dāmpatya* or the everlasting closest association of the divine couple is a permanent feature of the ultimate Reality in Vaiṣṇavism.[94]

The Status of Bhū-devī and Nīlā-devī

Besides Goddess *Śrī*, Vaiṣṇavism accepts two other feminine deities, viz., *Bhū-devī* and *Nīlā-devī* as the consorts of Viṣṇu. The Pāñcarātra Saṁhitās speak of many more feminine deities as aspects of *śakti* such as *Kīrti*, *Śrī*, *Vijaya*, *Śraddhā*, *Smṛti*, *Medhā*, *Dhṛti* and *Kṣamā*.[95] The *Lakṣmī Tantra* mentions eight names as representing different forms of *śakti*.[96] Of these *Śrī* and *Puṣṭi* are stated to be present on either side of Viṣṇu. Vaiṣṇavism regards *Bhū* and *Nīlā* as important deities. There are Vedic passages similar to the *Śrī-sūkta*, speaking the glory of these two deities designated as *Bhū-sūkta* and *Nīlā-Sūkta*.[97] In the post-Rāmānuja period, Bhū-devī who is also known by the name of Godā (in Sanskrit) and Āṇḍāl (in Tamil), has received greater attention. Separate idols of Nīlā are also installed in the Vaiṣṇava temples. In most of the Vaiṣṇava temples, the *utsava-mūrti*, the idol of God used for taking out in procession is invariably found with *Śrī* and *Bhū-devī* seated on either side of it.

The issues to be considered in this connection are: (1) Are these different goddesses distinct from one another? (2) Are they all to be taken as consorts of Viṣṇu? (3) What are their ontological status vis-a-vis Viṣṇu and *Śrī*?

The *Puruṣa-sūkta* of the Yajurveda mentions that *Hrī* and *Lakṣmī* are the consorts of *Puruṣa* who is the same as Nārāyaṇa or Viṣṇu. *Hrī*, according to one interpretation is *Bhū-devī*. In the *Bhū-sūkta* of *Yajurveda Saṁhitā*, *Bhū-devī* is explicitly described as *Viṣṇu-patnī*. She is also named as *Mādhavī*, wife of Mādhava (Viṣṇu) and is claimed to be the friend of Lakṣmī, and also very dear to Viṣṇu.[98]

Regarding *Nīlā-devī* the Vedic passage known as the *Nīlā-sūkta* also describes her as *Viṣṇu-patnī* and that She is the Sovereign of the universe.[99] The *Harivaṁśa* which is an appendix to the *Mahābhārata* presents Nīlā as a Goddess-incarnate to a cowherd by the name of Kumbhaka and that She was offered in wedding to God-incarnate *Kṛṣṇa* for displaying his valour. Āṇḍāl, who is acknowledged as one of the twelve Tamil saints (Āḻvārs) is depicted as the incarnation of Goddess *Bhū-devī* and who through her deep devotion and severe penance got united with Raṅganātha (an *arcā form of Viṣṇu*) at Śrīraṅgam in South India. The *Brahma Purāṇa* refers to her as *acyutavallabhā*, consort of Viṣṇu.

Vedānta Deśika has composed separate lyrics—one for *Śrī* titled *Śrīstuti*, one for Bhū named *Bhūstuti*. He has also composed a separate lyric for Nīlā in the name of *Godāstuti*. From all these accounts it becomes obvious that *Śrī* and *Bhū* are the two distinct consorts of *Viṣṇu*.

As regards the ontological status of these deities, the issue to be considered is whether *Bhū* or *Nīlā* enjoys the same status as *Śrī* or whether they enjoy a lower status than Lakṣmī? If it be the first alternative, the unitary character of Viṣṇu as associated with two consorts having equal status is bound to be affected. This position is not acceptable to Vaiṣṇavism. Therefore, the second alternative is adopted. That is, the two deities such as *Bhū* and *Nīlā* are regarded as two aspects of *Viṣṇu-śakti*, which according to Pāñcarātra Saṁhitās is the very Goddess Lakṣmī.

The Purāṇic episodes also indicate that Bhū and Nīlā are manifestations of Lakṣmī. As we have already explained, Viṣṇu as integrally associated with Lakṣmī is one as a *viśiṣṭa* Reality, even though He may be associated with other consorts. This would amount to the admission of Goddess *Śrī* as the principal consort who is eternally inseparable from Viṣṇu, wheras Bhū and Nīlā are subordinate deities associated with Viṣṇu as His beloved consort. *Śrī* is *vibhu* by virtue of Her intrinsic nature (*svarūpa*) and as such on par with Viṣṇu constituting a single Reality, whereas *Bhū* and *Nīlā* are *omnipresent* by virtue of their infinite knowledge and hence not on par with Viṣṇu. The *Viśvaksena Saṁhitā* supports this view. It clearly points out that *Bhū* and *Nīlā* are not *vibhu* unlike *Śrī* and as such they do not enjoy the same ontological status as *Śrī*. However, both these deities are dear to Viṣṇu and are His consorts.[100]

To sum up, Goddess Śrī is the inseparable consort of Viṣṇu enjoying the same status as Viṣṇu. The other deities—*Bhū-devī* and *Nīlā-devī*, though they are accepted as *Viṣṇu-patnī*, are subordinate deities with restricted role. Bhū-devī and Nīlā-devī are the personification of *kṣamā* or tolerance. Both are worshipped along with Lakṣmī in the form of different manifestations or *aṁśa* of Lakṣmī. The admission of additional consorts for Viṣṇu does not, therefore, affect the unitary character of the Supreme Being.

NOTES

1. *Śrī-sūkta*, 9. *īśvarīṁ sarvabhūtānāṁ tāmihopahvaye śriyam.*
2. *Taittirīya Saṁhitā*, IV.4.12. *asyeśānā jagato viṣṇupatnī.*
3. In Vaiṣṇava parlance, the terms Bhū, Nīla, Medhā, Śraddhā and Aditi denote Goddess Lakṣmī.
   See also VP I.9.119. *tvaṁ siddhiḥ tvaṁ svadhā svāhā sudhā tvaṁ lokapāvanī; sandhyā rātriḥ prabhā bhūtiḥ medhā śraddhā sarasvatī.*
4. VP I.8.17. *nityaiveṣā jaganmātā viṣṇoḥ śrīranapāyanī; yathā sarvagato viṣṇuḥ tathaiveyaṁ dvijottama.*
5. LT L.79. *śrṇomi karuṇāṁ vācaṁ. . . .*
6. AhS L1.62. *śrīyate ca akhilaiḥ nityaṁ śrayate ca paraṁpadam.*
   See also RTS XXVIII p. 220.
7. AhS L1.61. *śrṇāti nikhilān doṣān śrīṇāti ca gunaiḥ jagat.*
8. *Puruṣa-sūkta* (Yajurveda recension) II.6. *hrīścate lakṣmīśca patnyau.*
   See also RV X.71.2. *bhadraiṣāṁ lakṣmīrnihitādhi vāci.*
   See *Sāyaṇa Bhāṣya, bhadrā kalyāṇī nihitā lakṣmīḥ bhavati.*

9. *Nirukta*, IV.9.
10. LT L.62–68.
11. In recent years some Vaiṣṇavas of Tenkalai school have questioned the authorship of *Śrī-sūkta Bhāṣya* by Nañjīyar. But from the internal evidences of the *Bhāṣya* and the references made to it by Vedānta Deśika in his works, there is absolutely no doubt about the *Śrī-sūkta Bhāṣya* being written by Nañjīyar belonging to pre-Deśika period. This fact has been well established by valid arguments by the eminent scholar of 19th century, Śrī Goṣṭīpuram Saumya Nārāyaṇācārya Swāmi. Vide the *Bhūmikā* in Sanskrit and the English Introduction by Sri A. Srinivasa Raghavan to *Śrī-sūkta Bhāṣya* published in 1937.
12. TnUp. *patiṁ viśvasyātmeśvaraṁ.*
    See also BrUp VI.4.22. *eṣa sarveśvara eṣa bhūtādhipatiḥ.*
    See BG XV.17. *yo lokatrayamāviśya bibharty avyaya īśvaraḥ.*
13. *Śaraṇāgati-gadya*, *bhagavan-nārāyaṇābhimatānurūpa-svarūpa-rūpaguṇa-vibhavaiśvarya-śilādy-anavadhikātiśaya asaṅkheya-kalyāṇa-guṇagaṇām..bhagavatīm.*
14. VP I.8.17. *nityaiveṣā jaganmātā....*
15. See LT II.25. *jñānātmakaṁ paraṁ rūpaṁ brahmaṇo mama-cobhayoḥ.*
16. VP I.8.17. *yathā sarvagato viṣṇuḥ tathaiveyaṁ dvijottama.*
    See also LT III.2. *deśāt-kālāt-tathā-rūpāt parichedo na me smṛtaḥ.*
17. See AhS XXI.9. *jñāna-śakti-balaiśvarya vīrya tejaḥ prabhāvatīṁ.*
18. See LT IV.48. *pūrṇaṣāḍguṇyarūpatvāt sāhaṁ bhagavatī smṛtā.*
19. *Śrī-Sūkta*, 1. *hiraṇyavarṇāṁ hariṇīṁ suarṇa-rajata-srajām; candrāṁ hiraṇmayīṁ lakṣmīṁ.*
    ChUp I.6.6. *ya eṣo antarāditye hiraṇmayaḥ puruṣo dṛśyate hiraṇya-śmaśruḥ hiraṇyakeśa ā praṇakhāt sarva eva suvarṇaḥ.*
20. Rāmāyaṇa, V.16.5. *tulya-śīla-vayo-vṛttāṁ tulyābhijana-lakṣaṇāṁ.*
21. *Taittirīya Saṁhitā*, IV.4.12. *asyeśānā jagato viṣṇupatnī.*
    See also *Taittirīya Brāhmaṇa*, III.3.12. *īśānā devī bhuvanasyādhipatnī.*
    The term *īśānā* is interpreted as *svabhāvataḥ niyantrī*, an independent controller of all (ananyādhīneśvarī).
    See SSB p. 4.
22. See SSB p. 43. *ata evātra sarvabhūteśvaratvameva abhipretam.*
23. See *Catuḥślokī*, 2. *yasyāste mahimānamātmana iva tvadvallabho'pi prabhuḥ nālaṁ matum-iyattayā....*
    See also *Śristava*, 8. *devi tvanmahimāvadhiḥ na hariṇā nāpi tvayā jñāyate....*
24. *Yatirāja-saptatiḥ* 2. *anugrahamayīṁ vande nityamajñātanigrahām.*
25. *Catuḥslokī*, 3.
26. *Sri-guṇaratnakośa*, 58.
27. *Śrī-sūkta*, 5. *śriyaṁ loke devajuṣṭāmudārām.*
    See also SSB p. 33. *udārām, "aiśvaryam-akṣaragatiṁ" ityādyukta audārya-guṇavatīṁ.*
28. VP I.8.17. *visṇoḥ śrīranapāyinī.*
29. *Śaraṇāgati-gadya*, *śriyaṁ devīṁ nityānapayinīṁ.*
30. RV X.129.2. *ānīdavātaṁ svadhayā tadekaṁ.*

This passage of Ṛgveda referring to the creation of the universe states that prior to the creation nothing existed except that *one* (Being), *tadekaṁ* with *svadhā*. The word *eka* corresponds to *sat* of *Chāndogya Upaniṣad* and refers to Brahman. The term *svadhā* with which Reality is associated is interpreted as *Lakṣmī*, on the authority of *Viṣṇupurāṇa* which uses *svadhā* as synonymous with Lakṣmi.
See VP I.9.119.
Sāyaṇa interprets *svadhā* as *māyā*. *Māyā*, according to Viśiṣṭādvaita is *prakṛti* and Lakṣmī being the presiding Deity of prakṛti She is implied by the term *svadhā* in this hymn.

31. See Chapter 10 for details.
32. *Laiṅgapurāṇa* (quoted in RTS and GVa) *vaikuṇṭhe tu pareloke śriyā sārdhaṁ jagatpatiḥ; āste visnuḥ. . . .*
See also *Vaikuṇṭha-gadya, śeṣabhoge śrīyā sahāsīnaṁ.*
33. *Harivaṁśa*, 113-64. *eṣa nārāyaṇaḥ śrīmān kṣīrārṇavaniketanaḥ.*
(This refers to Aniruddha, one of the four *vyūhas*) and the term *Śrīmān* implies His association with *Śrī*.
34. VP I.9.142–45. *evaṁ yadā jagatsvāmī devadevo janārdanaḥ;*
avatāraṁ karotyeṣā tadā śrīḥ tatsahāyinī. . . .
viṣṇor-dehānurūpāṁ vai karotyeṣātmanas-tanum.
35. *Tiruvāymoli*, VI.6.10. *ahalakillen iraiyum-enru alarmelmaṅgai urai mārpān*
36. *Rāmāyaṇa*, VI.27.27. *śaṅkha-cakra-dhara-śrīmān. . . .*
śrīvatsa-vakṣā, nitya-śrīḥ. . . .
37. *Catuḥślokī*, verse 4.
This is not the literal translation of the verse but a free rendering of it to make it understandable.
38. VD's *Catuḥslokī Bhāṣya*, p. 22. *dṛḍha-saṁbaddhāni viyogānarhāṇi ityarthaḥ.*
39. See the Introduction to the Īḍu (Muppattiyārāyirappaḍi)—which comprises three sections entitled as Mudal *Śriyaḥpati*, *Iraṇḍāṁ Śriyaḥpati* and *Mūnrām Śrīyaḥpati*.
40. SVUp I.12.
41. Ibid. I.10. *kṣaraṁ pradhānam-amṛtākṣaraṁ haraḥ kṣarātmānau īśate deva ekaḥ.*
42. Ibid. VI.8. *na tat-samaścābhyadhikaśca dṛśyate.*
43. See Viṣṇucitta's commentary on VP I.8.17, p. 48 (The Edition published in 1882 at Madras).
asyāstu śaktivaśāt aṇutvepi tatra sannidhānāt sarvagatatvam uktam.
A much older edition of the *Vyākhyāna* by Viṣṇucitta does not contain this statement. See fn. 63.
44. RB II.3.26.
45. See SVB An entire section in the *Śrī-vacanabhḥṣaṇam* is devoted by Pillailokācārya to the subject of greatness of *puruṣakāratva*.
46. MUp II.2.5. *amṛtasya eṣa setuḥ.*
47. *Puruṣa-sūkta* (Yajurveda recension), 17. *nānyaḥ panthā ayanāya vidyate.*

48. See Mbh II.39.5. *kṛśān-arthān tataḥ kecid-akṛśān tatra kurvate;*
akṛśāṁśca kṛśāṁcakruḥ hetubhiḥ sāstra-niścayaiḥ.
This episode relates to the philosophic debate conducted during the *rājasūya-yāga* of Dharmarāja.
49. See RTS Chapter 5.
50. *Taittirīya Brāhmaṇa*, III.2.20.
51. See LT III.2. *deśāt kālāt tathā rūpāt paricchedo na me smṛtaḥ.*
52. TNUp 129. *medhā devī juṣamāṇā na āgādviśvācī bhadrā sumanasyamānā.*
53. See VP. I.9.119. *tvam siddhiḥ tvam sudhā. . .medhā śraddhā sarasvatī.*
54. See SSB p. 6. *viśvam bhūtajātam añjasā añcantī vyāpya niyacchantī.*
55. *Tait. Brahmaṇa*, II.8.66. *śraddhā devān-adhivaste, śraddhā viśvamidaṁ jagat.*
ChUp. *sarvaṁ khalvidaṁ brahma.*
See also NUp. *nārāyaṇa evedaṁ sarvam.*
56. *Tait. Brāhmaṇa*, II.8.62. *anantām-antāt adhinirmitāṁ mahīm.*
57. See SSB p. 9. *anantām-antāt ityanena deśataḥ kālataḥ vastutaḥ paricchedarahitatvam.*
58. *Śrī-sūkta*, 9. *iśvarīṁ sarvabhūtānāṁ tāmihopahvaye śriyam.*
59. SSB p. 42. *tathā atra sarvabhūta-īśvarīṁ sarvabhūta-niyantṛīṁ, vyāpinīṁ vā.*
60. See fn. 21
61. VP I.8.17. See fn 16.
62. See fn. 43
63. See Viṣṇucitta's commentary on the Viṣṇupūrāṇa, p. 45. (The critical edition edited by Vavilla Anantanarayana Sastry and Vavilla Ramaswamy Sastry and published earlier than 1882 in Telugu script at Madras)
yatheti sarvagato viṣṇuḥ yathā yatsvabhāvāḥ iyamapi tathā tatsvabhāveti, viṣṇoḥ sarvagatatvaṁ satyajñānādi svarūpa kalyāṇa-guṇādīnām atideśaḥ. athavā bhagavān vibhutvena sarvagataḥ iyaṁ ca sarvagatā.
64. VP I.9.126. *tvam māta sarvalokānāṁ devadevo hariḥ pitā;*
tvayaitad-viṣṇunā cāmba jagadvyāptaṁ carā-caram.
The term *jagatvyāpta* implies all-pervasiveness both within and without by virtue of *svarūpa* as in the case of Brahman.
65. *Viśvakṣena Saṁhitā* (quoted in Śrīsūkta Bhāṣya, p. 43).
gunataśca svarūpeṇa vyāptiḥ sādhāraṇī matā; yathā mayā jagadvyāptaṁ svarūpeṇa svabhāvataḥ; tathā vyāptaṁ-idaṁ sarvaṁ niyantrica tathā iśvarī.
66. The ancient Tamil literature of Sangam age known as *Paripāḍal* which belongs to the pre-Christian era speaks of Viṣṇu as *Tirumāl* emphasising the concept of *Śriyaḥ-pati.*
See S. Krishnaswamy Ayyangar: The Religion of the Tamilians in Sangam Age.
67. See LT II.16. *lakṣmī nārāyaṇākhyā-tam-ato brahma sanātanam.*
Also LT XXIV.1. *lakṣmī-nārāyaṇaṁ brahma doṣaśūnyaṁ nirañjanam.*
68. See FVV Ch. 1 for details regarding the doctrine of substance and attribute and the theory of *apṛthaksiddhi.*

69. See NS p. 1. *prakāra-prakāriṇoḥ prakārāṇāṁ ca mitho atyanta-bhede api viśiṣṭaikyādi-vivakṣayā ekatva-vyapadeśaḥ.*
70. RTS XXVII pp. 194-95. *śriyā eva devatāntara-vyāvartakatayā svarūpanirūpakam.*
See also Ramya Jamātṛmuni's *Tattva-dīpa*, p. 32.
71. LT XV.9. *vāsudevaḥ paraṁ brahma nārāyaṇamayaṁ mahat;*
tasyāhaṁ paramā śaktiḥ ahantānandacinmayi.
See also AhS III.24. *śaktiḥ nārāyaṇī divyā sarvasiddhānta sammatā.*
72. *Rāmāyaṇa*, V.21.15. *ananyā rāghaveṇāhaṁ bhāskareṇa yathā prabhā.*
73. LT II.11. *apṛthagbhūta-śaktitvāt brahmādvaitaṁ taducyate.*
AhS III.26. *bhavad-bhāvasvarūpeṇa tattvaṁ ekamivoditau.*
74. See *Sri-guṇaratnakośa*, 28. *tadantarbhāvāt tvām na pṛthagabhidhatte śrutirapi.*
75. VP I.9.120. *ātmavidyā ca devi tvaṁ vimuktiphaladāyinī.*
See also *Taittirīya Brāhmaṇa*, III.3.12. *sa no lokam-amṛtaṁ dadhātu.*
76. LT I.39–40. *eṣā hi sṛjate kāle saiṣā pāti jagattrayam; jagatsaṁharate cānte tattat-kāraṇa-saṁsthitā.*
77. SSB pp. 34-35. *Śaraṇaṁ prapadye-tava-caraṇāravindayoḥ bharanyāsaṁ karomi.*
78. See RTS XXIX p. 253. *ekaṁ jagadupādānam ityuktepi pramāṇataḥ; yathā-pekṣita vaiśiṣṭyam tathā atrāpi bhaviṣyati.*
79. See *Śri-guṇaratnakośa*, verse 34.
80. See fn., 82.
81. See SSB p. 60. *yadyapi bhagavadapekṣayā ubhayoḥ śeṣatvaṁ eka-rūpaṁ vaktavyam, tathāpi devyāḥ sarveśvaratva-pratipādaka śruti-smṛtyādi-bahupramāṇa virodhāt, svataḥ śeṣatvābhāve siddhe, aicchika śeṣatvam-ādāya paryavasyati.*
82. *Viśvakśena Saṁhitā* (quoted by VD in RTS p. 195 and also in SSB p. 43). The available printed edition of this Saṁhitā does not contain these verses.
yathā mayā jagad-vyāptaṁ svarupeṇa svabhāvataḥ;
tathā vyāptaṁ idaṁ sarvaṁ niyantrī ca tathā īśvarī.
matśeṣabhūtā sarveṣāṁ īśvarī vallabhā mama;
asyā mamaca śeṣaṁ hi vibhūtiḥ ubhayātmikā.
83. Quoted in SSB p. 60 and also NS p. 234.
lakṣmyāḥ samasta cid-acit-prapañco vyāpyaḥ tadīśasya tu sā'pi sarvam;
tathāpi sādhāraṇaṁ īśitṛtvam śrī-śrīśayoḥ dvau ca sadaika-śeṣi.
84. See Chapter on Viṣṇu and Jīva.
85. *Ṣaḍarthasaṅkṣepa* (This work is not extant but extracts from it are quoted by Vedānta Deśika).
See NS p. 233. See also fn 83.
86. See *Iḍu* (First introductory section on Śriyaḥpati) p. 90.
"*āśrayaṇa veḷaiyoḍu bhoga veḷaiyoḍu vāśiyara orumithuname uddeśyam.*" The English translation of this statement is: "Both at the time of approaching the Divine Being for self-surrender and also at the time of doing Divine service in *mokṣa*, our goal is only the Divine couple without any distinction."

87. The Madhavas also maintain this view.
88. *Catuḥślokī Bhāṣya*, p. 15. *śrutiśca patyuḥ patnyāśca svarūpabhedaṁ svarasato darśyati.*
    See also *Puruṣa-sūkta, hṛiścate lakṣmīśca patnyau.*
89. NS p. 233. *śaktitvavādastu patnītvādirūpeṇa viśeṣaṇatvābhiprāyaḥ.*
90. Ibid. p. 233. *sṛṣṭyādi-vyāpareṣu samānalīlatayā prerakatvena saha-kāritvābhiprāyā vā.*
91. *Pāṇini Sūtra*, IV.1.33. *patyurno yajña-saṁyoge.*
92. See SSB p. 5: *āśrita-saṁrakṣaṇa-yajñe sahadharmacāriṇī.*
93. *Śrī-stava*, 1. *yasyā vīkṣya mukhaṁ tadiṅgita-parādhīno vidhatte akhilaṁ. . . .*
94. NS p. 233. *śriyā saha tu dāmpatyaṁ śāśvataṁ tata eva tu.*
95. See V. Varadachari: Āgamas and South Indian Vaiṣṇavism, pp. 217-18.
96. LT VIII.25. *lakṣmīḥ, sarasvatī, sarvakāmadā, prītivardhanī, yaśaskarī, śāntidā, ca tuṣṭidā, puṣṭiḥ aṣṭamī.*
97. Both these passages are included in the *Yajurveda Saṁhitā* I.5.12 and IV.4.12.
98. *Bhū-sūkta*, hymn 12. *viṣṇupatnīṁ mahīṁ devīṁ mādhavīṁ mādhava-priyām;*
    lakṣmī-priyasakhīṁ devīṁ namāmy-acyutavallabhām
99. *Taittirīya Saṁhitā*, IV.4.12. *asyeśānā jagato viṣṇupatnī.*
    Though there is no specific mention of the name of *Nīlā* in this passage, Vaiṣṇava tradition holds that it refers to *Nīlā* as *Viṣṇupatnī*.
100. *Viśvaksena Saṁhitā* (quoted in SSB p. 9).
    tathā bhūmiśca nīlā ca śeṣabhūte mate mama;
    svarūpataśtu na tayoḥ guṇato vyaptir-iṣyate.
    Rāmānuja also acknowledges the relative difference between *Śrī* and the other two deities. Thus, he addresses separately *Śrī-vallabha* and *Bhūmi-Nīlā-Nāyaka* in his *Śaraṇāgati-gadya* which implies, as Vedānta Deśika has explained, the degree of difference in their relative status.
    See GaBh p. 114. *nitya-niyata-prādhānya-tāratamya-krameṇa śriyā saha ekāsanasthe devyau tacchāyāsaṅkāśatayā darśyati.*

9

VIṢṆU AND HIS ATTRIBUTES

According to the Viśiṣṭādvaita Vedānta Brahman, the term commonly used in the Upaniṣads to designate the ultimate Reality, is *Puruṣottama*, the Supreme Personal Being, who is essentially free from imperfections and possesses infinite auspicious attributes of unsurpassable excellence. It is the same as the personal God of Religion, who is known in Vaiṣṇava theology by the names of Viṣṇu, Nārāyaṇa, Vāsudeva, Bhagavān, Hari etc. When Reality is conceived as personal Being the admission of certain attributes is inevitable and also logically justifiable. According to the Viśiṣṭādvaita epistemology, a substance, whether it be spiritual or material, is conceivable only in terms of its certain essential qualities. A substance devoid of qualities is a logical myth. God, as a spiritual entity, should, therefore, possess certain attributes. Any sound theological system which believes in the existence of God, should necessarily admit attributes in respect of the Divine Being. What are these attributes according to Vaiṣṇavism and what are their philosophical and theological significance? The Āḻvārs and the Vaiṣṇava *ācāryas* particularly Rāmānuja, have dealt with extensively the various attributes of God. In a broad sense, the hymns of the Āḻvārs is a descriptive narration of the *Bhagavad-guṇas*, the glorious qualities of God. Parāśara Bhaṭṭar has written a compendium under the title *Bhagavad-guṇadarpaṇa* by way of commenting on one thousand names of Viṣṇu (*Viṣṇusahasranāma*). The present chapter is devoted to a discussion of some of these important attributes of God.

The Concept of Svarūpa and Dharma

While discussing the attributes, the Viśiṣṭādvaita epistemology makes a distinction between the essential attributes and the secondary qualities. The essential attributes are those which are unique to a particular object and which constitute its distinguishing characteristics (*asādhāraṇa-dharma*). The nature of an object (*svarūpa*) is determined only in terms of such attributes. It is only on the basis of such characteristics that an object is distinguished from another object. Thus, for instance, a cow is comprehended as cow and not as a horse on the basis of the special characteristic, viz., the dew-lap it possesses, which a horse does not have. This special characteristic is the essential attribute of the cow (*asādhāraṇa-dharma*). Rāmānuja uses the term *svabhāva* for *dharma* as distinct from *svarūpa* or *dharmī*. *Svarūpa* is that which is determined by its essential attributes (*svāsādhāraṇa svabhāvaiḥ nirūpyaṁ dharmī*). *Dharmī* is that which serves as a substrate for attributes. *Dharma* stands for the distinguishing characteristic of an object.[1] In terms of Naiyāyikas the essential characteristic is called *jāti*, a quality which is common to all cows but not found in animals other than cows. The other qualities which the cow possesses such as a colour, the horns, four legs etc., are secondary ones which become known only after the cow with its essential nature is comprehended. The latter type of qualities are, therefore, technically called as *nirūpita-svarūpa-viśeṣaṇa*, that is, qualities which become known after *svarūpa* of the object is comprehended. The essential attributes are called *svarūpa-nirūpaka-dharma*, that is, the attributes which determine or define the essential nature of an object. Devoid of such attributes, an object is inconceivable.[2]

Essential Attributes

As we have observed in an earlier chapter, the essential attributes of Brahman are *satya* or reality, *jñāna* or knowledge and *ananta* or infinite. The term *satya* means, according to Rāmānuja, absolutely unconditioned existence.[3] Brahman is *satyam* in the sense that it exists forever without undergoing any kind of modification (*vikāra*) unlike the non-sentient matter and the bound souls. The term *jñāna* means eternal uncontradicted knowledge.[4] Brahman is *jñānam* in the sense that it possesses knowledge which is never subject to contraction and expansion, unlike our finite knowledge. Brahman is also constituted of knowledge and as such it is essentially spiritual in character. The term *ananta* means that which is not conditioned by space, time and another object.[5] Brahman is *anantam* in the sense that it is omnipresent, it exists all the time and it pervades all other objects. Not only Brahman is infinite but its attributes are also infinite numerically and unsurpassable in excellence. These three attributes which are unique to Brahman reveal its true nature and hence they are regarded as *svarūpa-nirūpaka-dharma*. On the strength of the Upaniṣadic authority, the Viśiṣṭādvaita Vedānta admits two additional essential characteristics in respect of Brahman. These are *ānanda* and *amala*. *Ānanda* means bliss and Brahman is *ānanda* because it is blissful in character. *Amala* means purity and Brahman is *amala* in the sense that it is free from all imperfections (*heyaguṇarāhitya*). The fuller implications of all these *dharmas* are explained in an earlier chapter.[6]

Besides the five essential attributes which determine the nature of *Īśvara* or God, the Vaiṣṇava theology has admitted *Śriyaḥ-patitva* or being the beloved consort of Goddess *Śrī*, as an additional distinguishing characteristic of Viṣṇu or Nārāyaṇa. The basis for accepting this is the *Puruṣa-sūkta* passage of the Yajurveda in which *Puruṣa* or the Supreme Being is qualified by the statement that *Hrī* and *Śrī* are His consorts. The implication of this is that no deity other than Puruṣa Nārāyaṇa or Viṣṇu as the *pati* or consort of *Śrī* is the Supreme Being, thereby distinguishing Him from Rudra, Brahmā and other Vedic deities. In so far as *Śriyaḥ-patitva* serves as a distinguishing characteristic, it is accepted as a unique *liṅga* or identity mark of Nārāyaṇa. As has been explained in an earlier chapter, *Śrī* is inseparable from Viṣṇu, like the Sun is from its luminosity and the two are integrally related. Brahman is, therefore, equated by Rāmānuja with *Puruṣottama*, the highest personal God who is eternally associated with *Śrī* (*Śriyaḥ-pati* or *Śrīman-nārāyoṇa*).

The Six Principal Attributes

Coming now to the other attributes of God, Rāmānuja points out that they are infinite in number. In his words, these are *asaṁkhyeya* or countless. The *Vāmana Purāṇa* offers the example of the precious stones in the ocean. Just as the precious stones in the ocean cannot be counted, likewise the attributes of God are immeasurable.[7] The *Viṣṇupurāṇa* describes Bhagavān as the abode of all auspicious qualities.[8] However, the Pāñcarātra Saṁhitās and the *Viṣṇupurāṇa* uphold six attributes (*Ṣaḍguṇas*) as the most important because these portray the Supremacy of Bhagavān, another name for Brahman. These are: *jñāna* or knowledge, *Śakti* or power, *bala* or strength, *aiśvarya* or Lordship, *vīrya* or energy and *tejas* or splendour. These are the principal attributes and the possession of these make God perfect. *Viṣṇupurāṇa* defines *Bhagavān* as the one who is endowed with these six qualities.[9] We shall first examine each one of these attributes to bring out their philosophical significance.

Jñāna

The term *jñāna* means omniscience or the capacity to know everything at the same time. Nāthamuni explains the term as the capability of having direct vision of everything as it is simultaneously.[10] Unlike our perceptual knowledge, the perception of *Īśvara* is not dependent on the mind and sense organs. His knowledge is also not subject to contraction and expansion. It is eternal (*nitya*) and self-luminous (*svayaṁprakāśa*). It is in this sense that God is described in the *Muṇḍaka Upaniṣad* as *sarvajñaḥ* and *sarvavit* (omniscient).[11] It may be noted that this *jñāna* which is taken as an attribute of *Īśvara* is distinct from *jñāna* which is spoken of as the determinant of the *svarūpa* of Brahman.[12] The former is the attributive knowledge (*dharma-bhūta-jñāna*) of Īśvara, whereas the latter is His *svarūpa-jñāna*. The latter serves as the substrate for the former. It is by means of the *dharmabhūta-jñāna* that *Īśvara* perceives all things in the universe. The *saṅkalpa* or will to create the universe, the showering of grace to devotees (*anugraha*) and dispensation of punishment to the sinners (*nigraha*) are all the modifications of the *dharmabhūta-jñāna*. In accordance with the epistemological doctrine of substance and attribute admitted in the Viśiṣṭādvaita Vedānta, it is justifiable to draw a distinction between *svarūpa-jñāna* and *dharmabhūta-jñāna*. Modifications which take place in the latter are not applicable to the former which remains unchanged (*nirvikāra*), just as the bodily changes do not affect the soul within. The personal God of any theistic system should be omniscient. This is, therefore, the most important attribute of God.

Śakti

The general meaning of the term *śakti* is power. When it is regarded as an attribute of God, it is understood in the sense of *omnipotence.* Like *sarvajñatva* (omniscience), *sarvaśaktitva* (omnipotence) is equally an important attribute of God. A God who is admitted as the creator of the universe, should have the super power to bring forth such a variegated universe. It is a special power inherent in *Īśvara*. In this sense, Vedānta Deśika interprets the word as the power to create the entire universe.[13] The same meaning is upheld by Periyavācchān Piḷḷai.[14] It may also be understood in the sense of the capacity to perform a feat which is impossible for others.[15] This does not mean that anything can be performed by God such as changing blue into red. The correct implication of it is, as Vedānta Deśika has explained,[16] that whatever is free from self-contradiction and whatever is also difficult for others to achieve, the same can be done by God. For instance, sky-flower is a non-existent and it cannot be produced even by God; the creation of the universe is a possibility but it cannot be done by anyone other than God. It is in this sense that God is omnipotent.

Bala

The word *bala* means strength. It signifies the quality by which *Īśvara* supports without any effort everything in the universe, both sentient beings and the non-sentient material world.[17] It is an important attribute of God because He should be able to hold all the created entities such as the heaven, planets, the physical universe etc., in their respective positions. It is in this sense that the *Bṛhadāraṇyaka Upaniṣad* says that Brahman is the causeway (*setuḥ*) that serves as the supporter to keep apart the different worlds.[18] The same truth is reiterated by the *Bhagavad-gitā* and *Viṣṇupurāṇa.*[19]

Aiśvarya

Aiśvarya means lordship. It signifies the quality of controllership of the entire universe by His unchecked freedom.[20] This is a significant attribute because by virtue of this quality God becomes the Supreme Lord (*sarveśvara*). The *Bṛhadāraṇyaka Upaniṣad* describes Brahman as *sarvasya vaśi*, or the controller of all and *sarvādhipatiḥ* or the Lord of all. It also designates

Brahman as *sarveśvara.*[21] By virtue of the possession of this attribute, Viṣṇu is designated as *Īśānaḥ* and *Sarveśvaraḥ* in the *Viṣṇu-sahasranāma.*

Vīrya

Vīrya means energy. As an attribute of God, it signifies the special quality by means of which the Supreme Being remains unaffected by changes (*vikārarahita*) in spite of His being the material cause of the universe, the ground and inner controller of everything.[22] Viṣṇu is, therefore, described as *avikāra*[23] or the one who is not subject to any kind of modification, thereby asserting His transcendental character.

Tejas

The general meaning of *tejas* is splendour. As an attribute of God it signifies the power of self-sufficiency. It is defined as the power which is not in need of any external aids (*anyānapekṣatā*). That is, it is a special power of God by means of which He is able to create the universe without the aid of any other accessories.[24] Except His will (*saṅkalpa*) *Īśvara* as the creator of the universe does not need a body, the sense organs and any other instrument. This point is also affirmed by the *Chāndogya Upaniṣad* when it says that in the beginning there was *sat* only, one only and without any second. What is implied in this statement, according to the interpretation of Rāmānuja, is that Brahman is both the material and instrumental cause and that other than Brahman no other causal agencies are needed for the creation of the universe.[25] The word *tejas* may also be understood in the literal sense of lustre. In that case, as stated in the *Muṇḍaka Upaniṣad,*[26] God is so lustrous that all shining bodies in the universe derive their lustre from Him alone and none of the luminary objects can illumine Him at any time.

Of the six attributes of God outlined above, the first two—*jñāna* and *śakti* are regarded as the most important ones. Any deity which is accepted as the Supreme should necessarily be omniscient and omnipotent. The other four are the different aspects of these two. These six attributes are distinct from the five essential attributes mentioned earlier. While the latter as the distinguishing characteristics of *Īśvara* define the nature (*svarūpa*) of God, the former bring out His Supreme Lordship. These are natural qualities (*svābhāvika*) and transcendental (*para*). In other words, the Supreme Lord should necessarily possess all these six qualities. Hence the Pāñcarātra Saṁhitās accord greater importance to them. The *Ahirbudhnya Saṁhitā* describes Brahman as *ṣāḍguṇya* or as one possessing six qualities.[27]

Secondary Attributes

Coming now to the other numerous secondary attributes of God, (*nirūpita-svarūpa-viśeṣaṇa*), Vedānta Deśika points out that these are all included in the six principal attributes. Just as the whole universe is contained within the body of *Īśvara*, in the same way all other qualities are contained in the six.[28] All these are different aspects of the six qualities. They become manifest as and when the need arises to exhibit them (*āgantava*), whereas the principal six qualities are ever present.[29] Thus, for instance, *jñāna* or omniscience is a permanent *guṇa*, while *sauśīlya* or intimate communion becomes exhibited as and when God is confronted with an ardent devotee. Such secondary qualities, as already stated, are infinite in number. Among these the important ones are highlighted in the Vaiṣṇava treatises for the purpose of understanding the greatness of God by the devotees who seek redemption and protection from God. These have assumed special theological significance because of the religious needs, particularly for the purpose of adopting the self-surrender (*śaraṇāgati*) as a means of salvation. Rāmānuja has enumerated the following nineteen important *guṇas* or the secondary qualities of God. (1) *Sauśīlya* or intimate communion with devotees; (2) *Vātsalya* or tender affection; (3) *Mārdava* or soft-heartedness; (4) *Ārjava* or straightforwardness; (5) *Sauhārda* or friendly disposition; (6) *Sāmya* or equal treatment; (7) *Kāruṇya* or compassion; (8) *Mādhurya* or enchanting beautitude; (9) *Gāmbhīrya* or incomprehensible character; (10) *Audārya* or generosity; (11) *Cāturya* or skilfulness; (12) *Sthairya* or steadfastness; (13) *Dhairya* or courage; (14) *Śaurya* or fortitude; (15) *Parākrama* or valour; (16) *Satyakāma* or ever desired; (17) *Satyasaṅkalpa* or firm resolve; (18) *Kṛtitva* or feeling of having fulfilled the obligation; and (19) *Kṛtajñatā* or the feeling of satisfaction even with the smallest good deed. We shall explain each one of these to bring out its theological significance as pointed out by Vedānta Deśika and Periyavācchān Piḷḷai.

Sauśīlya. The word *śīla* is commonly understood as good conduct. But with reference to God as an attribute, it refers to that virtue by which God, even being the Sovereign of the universe, mixes intimately with the inferior[30] persons. Since such a condescension or communion takes place in a natural way without any motivation, it becomes *suśīla* or gracious in character. It may also mean, as interpreted by Sudarśana Sūri, that virtue of God by which the devotees who approach Him are not made to entertain any fear on the ground that God is the Supreme Being. At the same time, God also does not exhibit His quality of Supremacy so that the distinction between Himself and His devotees is not felt. The best illustration of this *guṇa* (quality) is provided in the episode of *Rāmāyaṇa* related to the meeting of Rāma with Guha, a hunter in the forest. Rāma, hailing from the royal family and enjoying the status of an emperor, embraces with affection Guha, an ordinary hunter living in the forest, when the former meets the latter on his errand to the Daṇḍakāraṇya forest. Similarly, Kṛṣṇa, the incarnate-God, moves intimately with the cowherds of Bṛndāvan. In either case, the Lord does not exhibit even in the slightest degree his own greatness as a Supreme Being but makes the devotees feel the intimate relationship with God. It is an important divine attribute since it establishes an intimate communion between God and His devotees.

Vātsalya. *Vātsalya* means deep affection and as an attribute of God it signifies the loving disposition of the Lord to ignore the defects of those who are to be protected by him.[31] Sudarsana Suri in his *Śrutaprakāśikā* (commentary on *Śrī-bhāṣya*) holds the same interpretation. Thus, he states: '*Vātsalya* means the affection which makes God ignore the defects, as in the case of the mother and the child.'[32] The commonly used example to illustrate this quality is the manner in which a cow licks the newly-born calf out of tender affection unmindful of the dirty matter on its body. On the basis of this analogy it is pointed out that God out of His affection towards the devotees accept them without minding the sinful acts committed by them. The presence of this virtue in God encourages the devotees to seek His refuge without running away from Him out of fear of punishment for their sins.[33] Thus, it constitutes an important attribute of God which makes it possible even for the worst sinners to seek redemption and protection from God. God is, therefore, described as *śaraṇāgata-vatsala*, the one who is kind to the persons seeking His refuge.

Periyavācchān Piḷḷai offers a different definition of *vātsalya*. According to him, *vātsalya* means the acceptance by the Lord the faults of the devotees as good qualities (*guṇas*) because of His affection towards them.[34] An earlier Vaiṣṇava *ācārya*, Aruḷāḷa Perumāḷ Emperumānār, had given expression to such a view, besides the one stated by Vedānta Deśika, on the basis of the analogy of cow and the calf.[35] According to Vedānta Deśika, the definition offered by Periyavācchān Piḷḷai is an exaggerated one.[36] Besides, if God is prepared to accept the defects of the devotees as good qualities, it might encourage the devotees to commit more sins. Realizing the defective character of this explanation, Maṇvālamāmuni, a later *ācārya*, makes a compromise between the two views advanced by the earlier preceptor. The view that the Lord ignores the sins of the devotees applies to the sins committed after one has taken refuge in Him (*śaraṇāgati*). The other view refers to the sins committed prior to *śaraṇāgati*. There are other explanations offered by the later *ācāryas* and the subject has become controversial. In fact, this is one of the eighteen topics leading to the difference of opinion between the two Vaiṣṇava sects. This is purely a subject-matter of textual interpretation and philosophically, it is not of great significance. All that is important for us to note is that *vātsalya* or the quality of showing affection towards devotees is a significant attribute of God. It emphasises the virtue of *kṣamā* or forgiveness on the part of God in respect of His devotees (*kṣamā-kāṣṭā*).[37]

Mārdava. The word *mārdava* literally means softness. As an attribute of God it signifies the quality of not being able to bear the separation from a devotee.[38] It may also imply the lenient attitude taken by God towards the individuals who deserve punishment for the offences committed by them.[39]

Ārjava. *Ārjava* means straightforwardness. It implies being very truthful both in thought, words and action.[40] This creates confidence in the minds of the devotees who approach God for protection.

Sauhārda. The word *suhṛt* means a friend or a well-wisher and *sauhārdam* signifies the friendly disposition of God towards all living beings and also his concern for their well-being (*hitaiṣitvam*). The religious literature, therefore, describes God as a friend of all (*suhṛdaṁ sarvabhūtānām*). If God wills to cause something bad to a few, it is not done on his own wantonly but, on the contrary, it is a dispensation of punishment in accordance with the *karma* of the individual concerned. The inherent character of being a well-wisher to all is not thus affected.

Sāmya. *Sāmya* means equality. As an attribute of God it implies that God treats all devotees as equal without discriminating them on the basis of high or low status due to caste, character and profession. There are numerous episodes in the Purāṇas to illustrate this special virtue of God. In the *Rāmāyaṇa*, Lord Rāma accepts with delight the offering of fruits made by Śabari, a low-caste hermit. Lord Kṛṣṇa in the *Bhāgavata* is worshipped by Mālyavān, a person engaged in the occupation of selling flowers. In view of this, the Lord claims in the *Bhagavad-gītā*[41] that He is impartial to all beings.

Kāruṇya. *Karuṇā* means compassion. *Kāruṇya* as an attribute of God is interpreted as a desire on the part of God to remove the suffering of an individual without any selfish motive.[42] Two other terms which are used as synonymous with *kāruṇya* are *dayā* and *kṛpā*. *Kṛpā* is defined by Vedānta Deśika as the desire to remove the sorrows of others. Both Sudarśana Sūri and Periyavācchān Piḷḷai define it as unbearability of the suffering of others without any selfish interest.[43] It is an important quality of God because it forms the basis for grace. The Vaiṣṇava literature, therefore, describes Supreme Being as *Karuṇā-nidhi* and *Dayā-nidhi*, the one who is the personification of compassion. Vedānta Deśika has composed one hundred and eight beautiful verses on *Dayā* of the Lord. He extolls it to such an extent that all other qualities without *dayā* are regarded as defective.[44]

Some later Vaiṣṇava *ācāryas* belonging to Tenkalai sect define *kāruṇya* as the expression of grief at the suffering of others. That is, compassion or *dayā* means that God himself should feel sorry when His devotees are subjected to grief (*paraduḥkha-duḥkhitvam*). This is not a sound definition, contends Vedānta Deśika. In the first place, this view goes counter to the traditionally accepted concept of *kāruṇya.* Secondly, it is inappropriate to attribute grief to Īśvara. God is untouched by afflictions (*viśokaḥ*). If He expressed grief towards the devotees, as evidenced by the Purāṇic episodes in the state of His incarnations as human beings, it is to be taken as only an *abhinaya* or as mere acting in a drama.[45] Compassion of *Īśvara* is, therefore, to be understood in the sense of His desire to remove the suffering of His devotees without any selfish purpose.

Kāruṇya has an important bearing on the concept of grace (*anugraha*) because it is out of compassion that the Lord showers His grace on the devotees. In this connection an important theological issue arises. If compassion of God is taken as His natural disposition to remove the suffering and do good for the devotees, does God expect some good act on the part of the devotee to deserve His grace? The Vaiṣṇava treatises speak of two types of *kṛpā—nirhetuka* and *sahetuka. Nirhetuka-kṛpā* implies that when God showers His grace on the devotee, it is unconditional in the sense that it does not call for any effort or good act on behalf of the devotee. Thus for instance, a seeker after *mokṣa* does not have to resort to the observance of any spiritual discipline for the purpose since God, who has unchecked freedom and who as an omniscient Being is fully aware of the need of his devotee, should grant *mokṣa* unconditionally out of His compassion. This is the view advanced by the followers of Tenkalai sect. On the contrary, the followers of Vedānta Deśika argue that if God were to grant *mokṣa* without expecting any effort by a devotee, then he would be subjected to the criticism of being partial, since all are equal in God's eyes and there is no scope for discrimination. To overcome this objection, it is contended that dispensation of *kṛpā* towards a devotee is to be linked to some kind of effort or prayer on the part of the devotee. *Kṛpā* is, therefore, conditional or *sahetuka.* Though God is free to do what He chooses, He always looks for some pretext (*vyāja*) in the form of some effort on the part of the devotee, as otherwise He would be open to the charge of arbitrariness. The *Lakṣmī Tantra*, a Pāñcarātra treatise upholds this truth in the following verse: 'Though the Supreme Lord is omniscient and is always compassionate He looks for an excuse to protect because He too has to follow the universally accepted principle.'[46] The relative merits of these two views will be discussed in the chapter on *prapatti,* as this issue has a direct bearing on the observance of self-surrender for *mokṣa.*

Mādhurya. *Madhura* means sweetness and *mādhurya* refers to the enchanting beauty of the Lord which captures the hearts of the devotees and which attracts even the enemies of God, as evidenced in the mythological episodes of Śiśupāla and others.

Gāmbhīrya. This is interpreted as the incomprehensible nature of the grace of God.[47] It is also explained in a different way. Though God is fully aware of the faults of the devotees and their low status as compared to His own, He does not disclose this fact. *Gāmbhīrya* is such an unrevealed grandeur of God.[48] In this sense Viṣṇu though He is omniscient is described as *avijñāṭā* or as one who is not aware of the faults of the devotees.

Audārya. The general meaning of *udāra* is generosity. As a quality of the Supreme Being, it refers to the bountiful character of God who is very keen to grant the boons to the devotees without an expectation of anything in return and also without any regard to the greatness of His gift and smallness of the recipients. Besides, even after granting bountiful gifts, God feels that He has not given enough to His devotees.[49]

Cāturya. The word *catura* means skilful and *cāturya* as an attribute of God refers to His capacity to generate faith in the minds of devotees by dispelling their doubts about the divine power and at the same time by not disclosing to them that He is fully aware of their faults. He does this by revealing His enchanting personality to the devotees so that the latter are induced to meditate on Him and gradually develop the spirit of detachment from the objects of pleasure.[50]

Sthairya. This is a mental quality implying the steadfast character of the divine Being to save his devotees at any cost in spite of their faults being brought to His attention by others. The classic example of this character of the Lord is the determination of God-incarnate Rāma to accept Vibhīṣaṇa, who hailed from the enemy's camp, in spite of the arguments advanced against him by the attendants of Rāma. This truth is brought out in the significant statement in the Rāmāyaṇa pointing out that the Lord will not give up under any circumstances the one who has approached Him for protection with a sincere and friendly attitude.[51]

Dhairya, Śaurya and **Parākramah**. These three are also mental qualities referring to the *courage* of the Lord to fight and destroy the obstacles in the way of the devotees. These are amply demonstrated in the numerous Rāmāyaṇa episodes when God-incarnate is called upon to fight the evil forces such as the demons to protect His devotees. The term *dhairya* signifies the courage with which a solemn vow is taken to save His devotee even long before the actual act of destruction. As an example of it, Vibhīṣaṇa was coronated even before Rāvaṇa was killed. *Śaurya* refers to heroic courage to enter into the camp of the enemies unaided and without any hesitation (*nirbhaya-praveśa-sāmarthyam*). *Parākrama* also means valour to defend oneself and destroy totally the enemies.

Satyakāma and **Satvasaṅkalpa.** *Kāma* means what is desired (*kāmyanta iti kāmaḥ*). It refers to the auspicious attributes and the glory of the Lord which are desired by God and are also aspired by the devotees.[52] As these are of eternal nature, they are regarded as *satyakāma*. God is *satyakāma* because He is endowed with such an eternal glory which the devotees yearn to experience. *Saṅkalpa* means will and *satya* is ever truthful. *Satyasaṅkalpa* as an attribute of God signifies that God's will to grant the *mokṣa* or His will to create the universe is not obstructed. It may also be explained in a different way. *Kāma* in the case of God is His desire to provide protection to the devotees. Such a desire stands unopposed by any other factor. In order to fulfill such a purpose God wills to assume different incarnations. This desire to incarnate Himself also stands unobstructed. God is, therefore, regarded as *satyakāmaḥ* and *satyasaṅkalpaḥ*.[53] The Upaniṣads also describe Him in these terms.[54] Both these attributes, from the standpoint of devotees, are very important because they create an unshakable confidence in their minds that God, who is approached for protection, will definitely grant the desired object.[55]

Kṛtitva and **Kṛtajñatā**. These are two additional qualities attributed to God as distinct from the twelve attributes enumerated above. Both these exhibit the magnanimity of God. *Kṛta* means the helping nature (*upakāra*) and *kṛtitva* is the one who is endowed with it. Its implication is that after fully complying with the request of the devotee, God feels relieved that He has fulfilled His obligation to the devotee[56] and there is nothing more to do in this regard.

God is not required to perform any deed to serve His own purpose. As the *Gītā* says, even the daily obligatory rituals are not binding on Him. The scriptural texts state that He neither becomes great by performing a good deed nor does He become small by doing a bad deed.[57] He is *avāptasamastakāmaḥ*, that is, all His desires are already fulfilled. In spite of it, if he undertakes some activities such as creation of the universe, granting of boons and offering protection to devotees, it is done with the sole purpose of helping others (*paropakāra*) without any selfish motive. In this sense the quality of *kṛtitva* is understood.[58]

Kṛtajñatā is the quality of feeling satisfaction even with one insignificant good act of the devotee and ignore his many other offences.[59] *Kṛtajñatā* may also be interpreted in a different way. Though God has bestowed on the devotees great benefit, He does not take cognizance of it and thinks that nothing has been done to him. There are several Purāṇic episodes to illustrate this quality of God.

We have given a brief account of the five essential attributes which determine the *svarūpa* of the Supreme Deity (*svarūpa-nirūpaka-dharmas*), six principal attributes (*ṣaḍguṇas*), which exhibit the supremacy of the Lord and nineteen other *guṇas* (*nirūpita-svarūpa-viśeṣaṇas*), which are the natural qualities of God useful for the devotees seeking the protection from Him. Though the secondary qualities are countless, Rāmānuja has selected nineteen just to bring out the grandeur of the Supreme Being. The enumeration of these attributes is not to be taken as an imagination of Rāmānuja to depict a majestic picture of personal God accepted as the ultimate Reality. As we have indicated earlier, most of these attributes are formulated on the basis of the Upaniṣadic texts and the statements made in the Pāñcarātra texts and Purāṇas which in turn elucidate the Upaniṣadic thoughts. We find elaborate expression of all these attributes in the hymns of the Āḻvārs who are claimed to have a mystic experience of God. These are, therefore, well established attributes of God and have to be admitted by any sound theistic system which postulates the existence of a personal Supreme Deity. In the case of the Vaiṣṇava theism, which deals with the attributes of God exhaustively and systematically on a rational basis, the concepts expounded are in conformity with the teachings of the sacred texts and as such are authoritative and also meaningful. In view of this Vaiṣṇavism as expounded by Rāmānuja and his followers, repeatedly use the two phrases—*akhila-heyapratyanīka* and *anantakalyāṇaguṇaviśiṣṭa*—whenever it speaks of Brahman or the Supreme Person (*puruṣottama*). According to Rāmānuja, the *Vedānta-sūtra* also refers to this twofold aspect of Brahman (*ubhaya-liṅgatva*).[60]

God and His Divine Body

The God of Vaiṣṇavism is not only a Divine Being endowed with numerous attributes par excellence but He also possesses an eternal, spiritual divine body (*divya-maṅgalavigraha-viśiṣṭa*). Such a bodily form for *Īśvara* is admitted on the authority of numerous scriptural and Smṛti texts. The *Puruṣa-sūkta* of Ṛgveda describes God as a personal Being with thousand heads, thousand eyes, thousand legs[61] (the word thousand in the sense of *ananta* or infinite). The repeated references to the three strides of Viṣṇu in the Ṛk hymns, imply a body for the deity. The hymn of the Ṛgveda also speaks of the Lord as having His eyes in all places, His faces in all directions, His arms in all directions, and His feet in all directions.[62] The *Chāndogya Upaniṣad* says that *Puruṣa* (Brahman) is *Hiraṇmayaḥ* or brilliant like gold with eyes like the freshly blossomed lotus.[63] The Itihāsas and Purāṇas portray God as a personal Being wearing the weapons such as discus (*cakra*), conch (*śaṅkha*), club (*gadā*), sword and bow and decorated with various ornaments.[64] The hymns of the Āḻvārs also emphasise the aesthetic aspect of Divine Being in their mystic outpourings.[65] Based on such descriptive accounts of the Godhead, Rāmānuja in the *Gadyas* presents a vivid and enchanting description of the divine personality of God (*divyarūpa*), His divine ornaments (*divya-bhūṣaṇa*) and His divine weapons (*divyāyudha*). Is there any philosophic justification for accepting a bodily form to Brahman, the ultimate Reality? Would it not be philosophically sounder to conceive Reality as an impersonal Being, as pure *sat*, *cit* and *ānanda*? The Upaniṣads declare that Reality is devoid of hands, feet etc. Does not the postulation of a beautiful personality for the metaphysical ultimate Reality amount to anthropomorphism?

These are important issues for a student of philosophy and need to be examined.

Regarding the metaphysical issue relating to the nature of the ultimate Reality, it may appear sounder, *prima facie*, to conceive it as a pure transcendental Being devoid of attributes and bodily form. But what is transcendental in the strict metaphysical sense cannot have any relation to the universe. Such a Reality cannot be the cause of the universe because creation, protection and dissolution of the universe, the three important functions of primary causal Being as enunciated in the Upaniṣad, need knowledge, power and mental activity in the form of desire or will (*saṅkalpa*) to create. If we attribute these functions to an ultimate Reality, then the latter would invariably become a personal Being endowed with knowledge and divine power. The absolute monist overcomes these difficulties by postulating the concept of *māyā*, a principle to account for the phenomenal appearance of universe and defend the theory of pure undifferentiated Being as the highest metaphysical Reality. But such a theory according to the Viśiṣṭādvaita, is riddled with logical contradictions. Besides, epistemologically the existence of an absolutely undifferentiated entity, whether it be ontological or physical, is an impossibility because all entities in the universe is characterised. Further, a transcendental Being does not meet the religious needs. The main goal of Religion in the context of the Vedānta is the realization of God through the liberation of the soul from bondage by means of *upāsanā* (meditation). The impersonal Being cannot serve the object of meditation. A Reality possessing a bodily form is alone suitable for meditation. Even the Absolutists have to admit in order to meet the needs of religion, a personal God in the name of *Saguṇa Brahman*, but such a divine Being, though it may serve the practical needs of religion, does not enjoy the status of being absolutely real. In view of all these considerations, Rāmānuja has equated Brahman of the Upaniṣads with *Puruṣottama*, a personal God of Religion.

Theological Justification for the Concept of Supreme Personal Being

Regarding the second issue whether such a personal Being is to be conceived in the super human form, the answer to this is provided in a significant Vedic passage known as *Jitante stotram*,[66] which is considered as a *khilasūkta* of the Ṛgveda. The hymn runs as follows: '*Na te rūpaṁ na cākāro nāyudhāni na cāspadam; tathāpi puruṣākāro bhaktānāṁ tvaṁ prakāśase*.' The meaning of this verse, according to the commentary of Vaiṣṇava *ācāryas*,[67] is: 'You do not have any physical qualities such as white or black (*rūpa*); you do not possess any physical organs such as head or legs (*ākāra*); nor are there any weapons or ornaments on you (*āyudha*); nor do you have an abode (*āspada*); nevertheless you manifest yourself with a lustrous bodily form bedecked with ornaments and weapons in an abode (of yours) for the sake of the devotees.' This Vedic hymn has far-reaching implications. From the metaphysical standpoint, the ultimate Reality which is designated as Brahman in the Upaniṣads is eternal, all-pervasive, spiritual Being. It is neither He nor She; it does not possess a bodily form with head, hands or legs (*apāṇipāda*); it is not even comprehensible (*adṛeśyam*) and graspable (*agrāhyam*). It has no birth or death, or decay or growth. But at the same time several Upaniṣads, the Pāñcarātra treatises, Purāṇas etc., give a glorious description of a supreme personal Being having a physical form such as body, complexion, ornaments, weapons, an abode in which He manifests with divine glory. How these two opposite views about the Supreme Being are reconciled? The hymn in question gives the answer and reconciles the two conflicting views. The scriptural texts which deny a bodily form and all its accompaniments, refer to the essential nature of Reality (*divyātma-svarūpa*). In the *svarūpa* of Brahman, like the *svarūpa* of our soul, there is no *rūpa* (colour or shape etc.), nor a physical form with body, head, hands and feet, nor the ornaments and weapons. But nevertheless, the Supreme Being assumes all these out of His own will (*icchā*) purely for the purpose of devotees. If the Supreme Reality remains ever transcendental as an undifferentiated Being, it is not of any use to the devotees. In order to make Himself available to the humanity seeking redemption from bondage, God takes on a physical form and manifests Himself bedecked with ornaments. The mere assumption of a bodily form does not cause bondage to the Divine Being, as in the case of human beings. The body of *Īśvara*, according to the scriptural and Smṛti texts, is not made of the physical elements, as that of human beings, in which case it would be subject to growth and decay. On the contrary, it is made out of the pure *sāttvic* spiritual substance known as *śuddha-sattva* and it is imperishable. The *Viṣṇupurāṇa* says: 'It is immutable (*avikāra*); pure (*śuddha*) and eternal (*nitya*) and always remains in the same form (*sadaikarūpa*).[68] Such a body is assumed by His own will for the sake of the welfare of the humanity.[69] His body is not constituted of the five physical elements.[70] The same *Viṣṇupurāṇa* also says that Hari (Viṣṇu) assumes a body along with ornaments and weapons for the sake of the devotees. The infinite Being does not become finite by conditioning Himself with bodily limitation. Brahman, as Upaniṣad says, is the smallest of all that is infinitesimal; biggest of all that is large.[71] Though He is all-pervasive (*vibhu*) He can still enter into the inner recess of our soul and reside there as an *antaryāmin.* This is the greatness of the Almighty God. He is both transcendent and immanent. He does not, therefore, become a finite Being by assuming a bodily form.

If these facts are borne in mind, the conception of God in the image of super human being should not be construed as anthropomorphism in the ordinary sense of the term. Whether man conceives God in the human form or God Himself manifests in the human form is a moot question to be considered. According to the scriptural evidence, it is God who manifests Himself in a human form. The *Bhagavad-gītā* says: 'In whatever form human beings seek me, I manifest to them in that very form'.[72] The same truth is expressed by Saromuni (also known as Poygaiāḷvār), one of the earliest Vaiṣṇava saints.[73] The doctrine of incarnation (*avatāra*) of God, which will be discussed in the subsequent chapter will make this point more explicit. It is not, therefore, appropriate to bring the criticism of anthropomorphism against the Vaiṣṇava theory of God in the name of Viṣṇu or Nārāyaṇa as expounded by Rāmānuja in his monumental philosophical and theological works.

NOTES

1. For further details of *dharma* and *dharmī* see FVV pp. 26–38.
2. See RTS V.
3. RB I.1.2. *satyapadaṁ nirupādhika sattā-yogi brahma.*
4. Ibid. *jñanapadaṁ nitya asañkucita jñānaikāram.*

5. Ibid. *anantapadaṁ deśa-kāla-vastu-pariccheda-rahitaṁ svarūpam.*
6. See Chapter 2.
7. Vāmana Purāṇa, 74.40. *yathā ratnāni jaladheḥ asaṁkhyeyāni putraka; tathā guṇāśca devasyatu asaṁkhyeyā hi cakriṇaḥ.*
8. VP VI.5.84. *samasta-kalyāṇaguṇātmako asau....*
9. VP VI.5.79. *jñāna-śakti-balaiśvarya-vīrya-tejāṁsyaśeṣataḥ; bhagavat śabda-vācyāni vinā heyairguṇādibhiḥ.*
10. *Nyāyatattva* (quoted by VD in GaBh). *yo vetti yugapatsarvaṁ pratyakṣeṇa sadā svataḥ.*
11. MUp I.1.10. *yas-sarvajñassarvavit yasya jñānamayaṁ tapaḥ.*
12. TUp I.11. *satyaṁ jñānam-anantaṁ brahma.*
13. GaBh p. 111. *sarva-upādānatvātmikā.*
14. GaVa p. 22. *jagadupādāna-śakti.*
15. Ibid. *aghaṭitaghaṭanā-sāmarthyaṁ.*
16. TMK III.77.
17. GaBh p. 111. *śramaprasangarahitaṁ sarvadhārana-sāmarthyam.*
18. BrUp VI.4.22. *eṣa setur-vidharaṇa eṣāṁ lokānām-asaṁbhedāya.*
19. BG XV.17. *yo lokatrayamāviśya bibhartyavyaya īśvaraḥ.* VP VI.4.40. *paramātmā ca sarveṣām-ādhāraḥ parameśvaraḥ.*
20. GaBh p. 111. *avyāhatecchaṁ sarvaniyantṛtvam.*
21. BrUp VI.4.22.
22. GaBh p. 111. *sarvopādānatve sarvadhāraṇe sarvaniyamane'pi vikāra-rahitatvam.* See also GaVa p. 22.
23. VP I.2.1. *avikārāya śuddhāya nityāya paramātmane.*
24. GaBh p. 111. *asvādhīna-sahakārianapekṣatvam.* See also AhS II.61.
25. See VSa p. 31.
26. MUp II.2.11. *na tatra sūryo bhāti na candra-tārakaṁ. . . . tameva bhāntam-anubhāti sarvaṁ tasya bhāsā sarvam-idaṁ vibhāti.*
27. AhS II.53. *ṣāḍguṇyaṁ tat paraṁ brahma sarvakāraṇakāraṇam.*
28. TMK V.97. *ṣāḍguṇyasyaiva kukṣau guṇagaṇa itaraḥ.*
29. Ibid. *aiśāna-jñāna-dharmāḥ katicana niyatāḥ kecid-āgantavaḥ.*
30. See *Śrutaprakāśikā*, I.1.21, p. 245. See also GaVa pp. 22 and 23. *mahato mandais-saha nīrandhrena saṁśleṣa-svabhāvatvam.*
31. GaBh p. 111. *svarakṣaṇīyatayā abhimateṣu doṣatiraskaraṇī prītiḥ.*
32. *Śrutaprakāśikā*, I.1.21, p. 245. *vātsalyaṁ doṣa anādarahetuḥ snehaḥ, yathā mātuḥ putre.*
33. See RTS XXVIII p. 224.
34. GaVa p. 23. Sudarśana Sūri in his commentary on the *Śaraṇāgati-gadya* also states the same view. See GaVa p. 22. *vātsalyaṁ doṣe'pi guṇatva-buddhiḥ.*
35. See *Jñānasāra*, verses 24 and 25.
36. GaBh p. 111. *doṣānāṁ guṇatvena darśanamiti tu ativādaḥ.*
37. See GaVa p. 22. *idaṁ ca kṣmākāṣṭārūpaṁ.* See also GaBh p. 111.

38. Ibid. *āśritavirahāsahatvam.*
39. GaBh p. 111.
40. Ibid. *mano-vāk-kāya-vyāpārāṇāṁ mithaḥ saṁvāditvam.*
41. BG IX.29. *samo'haṁ sarvabhūteṣu.*
42. See GaBh p. 112. *anuddiṣṭa-svaprayojanāntarā paraduḥkha-nirākaraṇecchā.*
43. GaVa p. 22. *svārthānapekṣā paraduḥkha asahiṣṇutā.*
44. *Dayāśataka*, verse 15. *doṣā,bhaveyurete yadi nāma daye tvayā vinābhūtāḥ.*
45. See RTS XXIII p. 153.
46. LT XVII.79.80. *sarvajño'pi hi viśveśaḥ sadā-kāruṇiko'pī san;*
saṁsāratantravāhitvāt rakṣāpekṣāṁ pratīkṣate.
47. GaBh p. 112. *bhaktānugrahavadānyatvādeḥ āmūlataḥ duravagāhatvam.*
48. Ibid.
49. Ibid. *prabhūtaṁ datvā'pi atṛptatvaṁ.*
50. Ibid. *mati-śaṅkāśamana-doṣa-gopanādi-rūpam ajaḍa-kriyātvam.* See also GaVa p. 25.
51. *Rāmāyaṇa*, VI.18.3. *mitrabhāveṇa saṁprāptaṁ na tyajeyaṁ kathañcana;*
doṣo yadyapi tasya syāt. . . .
52. GaBh p. 112. *svena svāśritaiśca bhogyā vibhūtayaḥ.* See also VSa p. 168.
53. GaVa p. 25.
54. ChUp VIII.1.5.
55. GaBh p. 112. *abhimatalābhe nissaṁśayatvaṁ syāt.*
56. GaVa of Sudarśana Sūri, p. 26. *āśritakāryapūraṇena kṛtārthatvaṁ kṛtitvam.*
57. *Taittirīya Brāhmaṇa*, III.12.9. *na karmaṇā vardhate no kanīyān.*
58. GaBh p. 112.
See also BrUp VI.4.22. *sa na sādhunā karmaṇā bhūyān; no evāsādhunā kanīyān.*
59. See *Rāmāyaṇa*, II.2. *na smaratyapakārāṇāṁ śatamapyātmavattayā;*
kathañcidupakāreṇa kṛtenaikeṇa tuṣyatı.
60. See VS III.2.11. *na sthānato'pi parasyo-bhayaliṅgaṁ sarvatra hi.*
61. RV X.90.1. *sahaśraśīrṣā puruṣaḥ sahasrākṣaḥ sahasrapāt.*
62. RV X.81.3.
See also SvUp III.3. *viśvataścakṣur-uta viśvato-mūkho viśvato- bāhuruta viśvataspāt.*
63. ChUp I.6.6.
64. See VP I.22.76. *astra-bhūṣaṇa-saṁsthāna-svarūpaṁ.*
65. See *Tiruvāymoḻi*, III.1.1.
66. *Jitante Strotram*, verse 5.
This passage is referred to in several of the Pāñcarātra treatises and is extolled as a Vedic hymn sung as a prayer to God. It is acknowledged by Periyavaccān Piḷḷai, who has written a commentary on it as a *khilasūkta* of Ṛgveda, that is, a passage belonging to some other *śākhā* (branch) of the Ṛgveda being appended to the extant *Ṛk Saṁhitā.*

67. The explanation offered here is based on the commentary written in Tamil by Puttan Kottam Srinivasacharya Swami.
    See *Jitante Strotram* with commentaries published at Srirangan, 1958.
68. VP I.2.1. *avikārāya śuddhāya nityāya paramātmane; sadaikarūpa rūpāya viṣṇave sarva-jiṣṇave.*
69. Ibid. VI.5.84. *icchāgṛhītābhimatorudehaḥ saṁsādhitāśeṣa jagaddhito yaḥ.*
70. *Varāha Purāṇa,* 31-40 *na tasya prākṛtā mūrtiḥ māṁsa medhosthi saṁbhavaḥ.*
71. TnUp 66. *aṇoraṇīyān mahato mahīyānātmā.*
72. BG IV.11. *ye yathā māṁ prapadyante tāṁstathaiva bhajāmyaham.*
73. *Mudal Tiruvandādi,* hymn 44. *tamar uhandadu evvuruvuṁ avvuruvuṁ tāne.*
    The meaning of this is that in whatever forms the devotees desire, the same bodily forms God assumes.

10

VIṢṆU AND HIS INCARNATIONS

The concept of *avatāra* or incarnation of the Supreme Being in different forms is a unique feature of Vaiṣṇava religion. The central theme of Vaiṣṇavism that Viṣṇu as a benevolent deity is the Saviour of mankind and that He is always ready to extend protection to those who seek His refuge derives its meaning from the doctrine of *avatāra*. We shall, therefore, discuss in the present chapter the different types of *avatāra*, their distinctive features as well as their theological significance.

Vedic Origin of the Concept of Avatāra

At the very outset we should take note of the fact that this doctrine has its origin in the Vedas. It is not a non-vedic theory borrowed from elsewhere and introduced at a later period into Vaiṣṇavism. The hymn appearing in the *Puruṣa-sūkta* states: '(The one) who is not born takes many births.'[1] The implication of this Vedic statement is that the Supreme Being, though He is not subject to normal birth with the physical body, assumes different manifestations for the good of the world.[2] A hymn of the Ṛgveda which is sung for the purpose of invoking Viṣṇu in the sacrificial pillar (*yūpa*), describes: "He comes down decorated with beautiful garments and surrounded by celestial beings and that He becomes great by taking births.'[3] This *mantra* explicitly refers to the ascent of Viṣṇu. The repeated statements in the Ṛgveda about the three strides with which Viṣṇu pervades the three worlds refer to the *Trivikrama avatāra* of Vedic period. The *Taittirīya Brāhmaṇa*[4] states that God who is the father of all chooses His own children (the human beings) as His parents, signifying the secret of the divine descent for the good of mankind. The *Śatapatha Brāhmaṇa* narrates the incarnation of Viṣṇu as fish (*matsya*).[5] The *Taittirīya Āraṇyaka*[6] mentions the *avatāra* of Viṣṇu as tortoise (*kūrma*). The *Taittirīya Brāhmaṇa* gives an episode of *Varāhāvatāra* (incarnation as boar).[7] These versions of the *avatāra* as narrated in the Vedas are somewhat different from those found in the Purāṇas. This variation is due to the fact that there are any number of *avatāras* that have taken place at different epochs in the continuous process of evolution and dissolution of the universe from time immemorial.

The basic theory of *avatāra* as found in the Vedas has been further elaborated in the Āgama treatises and later in the *Mahābhārata* and the Purāṇas. The philosophical and theological significance of *avatāra* has been fully explained in the *Bhagavad-gītā*.[8] This has provided the basis for the detailed formulation of the doctrine by the Vaiṣṇava *ācāryas*.

The Philosophy of Avatāra

Before we go into the details of the different types of *avatāras*, we should understand the theological and philosophical significance of *avatāra*. The term *avatāra* literally means 'coming down' (*avataraṇa*). With reference to God, it signifies the descent of the Supreme Being from His exalted divine abode to a lower level. In a technical sense, it means the manifestation of a deity in different forms.[9] This gives rise to several important questions. (1) In the first place, how can the Supreme Being who is free from all imperfections, who is the Lord of the universe, who is omniscient, who has no unfulfilled desires descend upon the earth as human beings etc.? Birth in the ordinary sense implies being subject to *karma* but God who is a perfect Being is untouched by *karma*. A deity may descend upon earth out of ignorance but God is omniscient. If God were ruled by someone higher than Him, He could have been commanded to descend but He is the Supreme Lord (*sarveśvara*). If God had some selfish desire to be fulfilled He could have come down but He is *avāpta-samasta-kāma*, that is, all His desires are already fulfilled. It may be argued that the descent is for the purpose of protection of humanity but God as *satya-saṅkalpa* [one whose will is paramount) can achieve this purpose by His mere will. Taking all these into consideration, the first issue that arises is whether such a manifestation of God in human form is a real possibility or is it a mere illusory appearance (*mithyā*) like a magical show? If it be real, as Vaiṣṇavism claims, does God take the birth by abandoning His true divine form or by retaining it in full? (3) Thirdly, when God assumes a human body, is such a body made of the physical elements or is it constituted of the spiritual stuff? (4) Fourthly, what causes such a birth? Does the mere will (*saṅkalpa*) of *Īśvara* causes such a birth? Alternatively, does the birth take place as a result of the *karma* in the form of good and bad deeds, assumed by God voluntarily by His own will (*svecchā-parigṛhīta*)? (5) Fifthly, is there any specific time or period when such descents take place? (6) Finally, what is the main purpose of such incarnations? These are the questions which have been raised by Rāmānuja, while commenting on the query of Arjuna posed to Lord Kṛṣṇa in the *Bhagavad-gītā* on the theory of incarnations. An answer to these issues arising from the four significant verses of the *Gītā*,[10] as elucidated by Rāmānuja and Vedānta Deśika will explain the philosophy of *avatāra*.

Regarding the first question, it is pointed out that the *avatāras* of God are not illusory manifestations but real. In other words, it is a fact that God manifests Himself in various forms. That it is real is established on the basis of the reality of the birth of an individual and the several previous births the same individual would have gone through. The birth of an individual is not the beginning and end of it but on the contrary, it is one among a continuous series of births and deaths. This is the basic postulate of Hinduism. If the present birth is not an illusion, the previous ones too would not be unreal.

But there is a fundamental difference between the birth of an individual and that of *Īśvara*. In the former case, it is subject to *karma*, the good and bad deeds of the past, whereas in the latter case, it takes place out of His free will without the influence of *karma*. God is eternal and unborn (*aja*) and as such He is not subject to the normal birth or death due to *karma*. He does not also undergo any modification (*avyaya*). How then *Īśvara* is considered to be born again and again? The answer is that birth of *Īśvara* is to be understood not in the ordinary sense but on the contrary, it is to be taken in the sense of manifestation (*prādurbhāva*), out of His own free will. The body He assumes either as a human being or as any other living being, is made out of the spiritual substance (*śuddhasattva*).[11] When God incarnates Himself as a human being, He does so by retaining His spiritual character along with all His divine qualities. This is possible for God because of His supreme power (*sarva-śakti*) and *saṅkalpa*.[12] Thus says the *Bhagavad-gītā*: 'Though unborn and immortal, and also the Lord of all living beings, I manifest Myself through my own *saṅkalpa* (*ātma-māyayā*) without giving up My spiritual nature.'[13]

In this connection a question may be raised. If God descends to assume a human body, does He not become defiled by the defects common to physical bodies? The answer is given in the negative. If His body were made of the same physical elements as that of the human beings, the objection stands. But it is not so. His body in the *avatāra* stage is constituted of *śuddha-sattva*, the pure spiritual substance, though outwardly it has the appearance of physical body. The spiritual aspect is hidden from the sight of common man. For the Yogis and the ardent *upāsakas*, however, His spiritual form becomes manifest. So, whenever God descends upon earth, He retains His spiritual form along with all the divine qualities.[14] Even in the physical state as an *avatāra*, God possesses all His glorious attributes, as in the state of His *para-rūpa*.

Another important point to be noted in this connection is that all the various manifestations of God in different forms emanate from a part of the spiritual body (*vigrahāṁśa*) of *Para-Vāsudeva*, which is the Supreme transcendental form (*para*) of God.[15] The implication of it is that the different manifestations are not of the very *svarūpa* of God because the *svarūpa* which is infinite in character (*ananta*) cannot have any descent as such and become conditioned by a limited bodily form. On the contrary, it is the transcendental body possessed by God that assumes different manifestations. Here again it is not the entire spiritual body that transforms itself into the body of a particular *avatāra*, in which case it would amount to the physical absence of *Para-Vāsudeva* who exists eternally in His divine realm. The spiritual power (*śakti*) which is limitless, is inherent in God and only a small particle of it emanates as the spiritual body of an *avatāra*. Even this body in *avatāra* stage is capable of assuming an all-pervasive character, though for all practical purposes it appears to be finite like a human body. This accounts for the revelation of the universal nature (*viśvarūpa*) of God to Arjuna by Lord Kṛṣṇa as narrated in the *Bhagavad-gītā*.

Regarding the period of *avatāra*, the answer is that there is no specific time for such an *avatāra*. It takes place as and when a need arises. The need for *avatāra* is linked with the necessity of establishing *dharma* which taken in the broad sense means the cosmic religious order. Whenever *dharma* declines God on His own comes down to earth taking a human form, as in the case of Rāma and Kṛṣṇa, in order to restore the religious order.

What is it that is to be achieved by God by assuming different *avatāras*? In other words, what is the purpose to be served by the *avatāra*? The *Bhagavad-gītā* provides the answer to this question. The purpose from the standpoint of God, is twofold: protection of the ardent devotees of God (*sādhu-paritrāṇa*) and destruction of the evil forces (*duṣkṛt-vināśa*).[16] Here the term *sādhu* does not refer merely to the ordinary devotees or pious persons. On the other hand, it means those persons who are living a strict religious life as enjoined by the scripture, who are dedicated to the exclusive worship of Viṣṇu and who have been craving to have a vision of God without which they are not able to bear their lives even for a moment.[17] God is ready to show His divine form to such ardent devotees. The protection (*paritrāṇa*) of such persons implies the removal of all kinds of obstacles in the way of God-realization and thereby assist them to fulfil their cherished goal. The evil forces also act as an equally strong obstruction for God-realization. The destruction of the evil forces or the enemies in the form of demons is also another purpose of the *avatāra*. Of these two functions—protection and destruction—the former, according to Rāmānuja is of greater importance than the latter. This is due to the fact that destruction of the evil forces can even be carried out by God through His *saṅkalpa* or will without an incarnation, whereas the former needs His physical appearance before the devotees. *Sādhuparitrāṇa* is thus the main purpose of *avatāra*, whereas *duṣkṛt-vināśa* is incidental (*ānuṣaṅgika*).[18] The revelation of God's form to the *upāsakas* or those engaged in *upāsanā* for *mokṣa* helps to promote the devotion to God (*bhakti*) by the direct perception of the object of meditation (*arādhyasvarūpapradarśana*). This is what is implied by the expression *dharma saṁsthāpana* used in the *Gītā* verse. Though the propagation of *dharma* can also be done through the sages, the establishment of *dharma* in the form of manifesting His own divine form needs the *avatāra* now and then in the different epochs.

Types of Avatāra

Against this background of the Philosophy of *avatāra*, the different types of *avatāra* of God must be understood. According to Vaiṣṇavism the Supreme Deity manifests Himself in five forms: (1) *Para*, (2) *Vyūha*, (3) *Vibhava*, (4) *Arcā* and, (5) *Antaryāmi*. The main basis for the fivefold conception of *avatāra* is the Pāñcarātra Saṁhitās. As pointed out earlier there are also scriptural statements referring to the different forms of *avatāra*. According to some Vaiṣṇava *ācāryas*, the opening passage of the *Taittirīya Nārāyaṇa Upaniṣad*[19] refers to the fivefold manifestation of God. The same Upaniṣad also refers to *Puruṣa* Nārāyaṇa as *pañcadhā* or fivefold,[20] implying the five forms of manifestation. We shall.examine each one of these forms in detail.

PARA AVATĀRA

Para is the transcendental form of God existing eternally in the *paramapada*. In a strict sense it is not to be taken as an *avatāra* or descent.. However, in a technical sense it is regarded as *avatāra* in so far as it is the manifested form of the Supreme Being in the *paramapada* to serve a specific purpose. Several scriptural texts[21] as well as the Āgama treatises speak of the existence of God in the transcendental realm to enable the *nityasūris* (eternally released souls) and the *muktas* (souls released from bondage) to offer divine service to the Lord. Brahman, according to the Upaniṣad, is *ananta* or infinite. As transcendental Supreme Being He is *vibhu* or present everywhere and impersonal in character. But such a Being is of no use either for meditation or for offering divine services by the individual souls. Hence the need arises for His manifestation as a personal God.[22] Such a manifestation of the Supreme Being is regarded as *para avatāra* which is known by the name of *Para-Vāsudeva*. The Pāñcarātra Saṁhitās describe Him as one endowed with all the six attributes—*jñāna*, *bala*, *aiśvarya*, *vīrya*, *tejas*, *śakti*—and possessing a spiritual body (*aprākṛta-śarīra*) bedecked with the divine weapons and ornaments and also surrounded by His consorts, divine attendants and released souls.[23]

VYŪHA AVATĀRA

The *vyūha avatāra* is the manifestation of the Supreme Being in four different forms known by the names of Vāsudeva, Saṁkarṣaṇa, Pradyumna and Anirudha.[24] Each *vyūha* is conceived with certain specific attributes and functions such as creation, sustenance, dissolution of the universe and promulgation of spiritual knowledge.

The *vyūha* doctrine has been developed in detail in the Pāñcarātra treatises. The Vedas and Upaniṣads do not make any explicit mention of it, though according to some it is implicit in the first four hymns of the *Puruṣa-sūkta*. The *Ahirbudhnya Saṁhitā* interprets these hymns in terms of the four *vyūhas*.[25] We find adequate description of the *vyūhas* in the *Mahābhārata*, *Viṣṇupurāṇa* and other Vaiṣṇava Purāṇas including the *Bhāgavata*. The *Bhagavad-gītā* which discusses the philosophy of *avatāra* does not refer to it. However, the Vaiṣṇava theology has adopted it as an important doctrine.

In the chapter on God and His attributes, we have mentioned a group of six attributes—*jñāna*, *bala*, *aiśvarya*, *vīrya*, *śakti* and *tejas*—which are inherent in the Supreme Deity. According to the Pāñcarātra system, the possession of these six attributes makes the Supreme Being perfect. These attributes are split up into three pairs of two each and ascribed to each one of the *vyūha* except the first. Thus, Vāsudeva, the first *vyūha* is endowed in full measure with all the six qualities. He is, therefore, regarded as almost the same as Para-Vāsudeva, the Supreme Being. In view af this, some religious literature speak of only three *vyūhas*.[26] Saṁkarṣaṇa, the second *vyūha*, possesses *jñāna* and *bala*; Pradyumna is endowed with *aiśvarya* and *vīrya*, and Aniruddha with *śakti* and *tejas*. This does not mean that these *vyūhas* do not possess the qualities other than what is attributed to them. Since all the *vyūhas* are the manifestations of *Para-Vāsudeva*, who is actually Viṣṇu Himself, each *vyūha* possesses all the six qualities, though two are predominant in each. Further, each *vyūha* is assigned with specific cosmic and moral functions. There are varying accounts in the Pāñcarātra texts regarding the assignment of these functions to each *vyūha*. But according to the commonly accepted view of Vaiṣṇava *ācāryas*,[27] the main purpose of the manifestation as *Vyūha-Vāsudeva*, who is regarded the same as *Para-Vāsudeva*, is to provide an opportunity to the liberated souls to experience the blissful God (*muktabhogya*) and render divine service to Him.[28] He is not, therefore, assigned with either the creative or moral function.

Saṁkarṣaṇa is entrusted with the task of dissolution of the universe and promulgation of *śāstras*. Pradyumna is given the function of creation of the universe and establishment of *dharma*. Aniruddha is assigned with the work of protection of the universe and imparting of the spiritual knowledge. Each *vyūha*, except the first, has thus two functions, a creative and a moral one, that is, one related to the basic functions of creation, sustenance and dissolution of the universe and another one connected with its ethical progress.

What is the justification for such a division of the *guṇas* and the allocation of functions to the three *vyūhas*? According to the Upaniṣad, Brahman is the cause of origin, sustenance and dissolution of the universe. Further, the Purāṇas including the *Viṣṇupurāṇa* have advanced the concept of Trinity—Brahmā, Viṣṇu and Rudra—for the three cosmic functions. Why the three *vyūhas* have to be conceived in order to perform the respective functions? These questions need to be answered to prove the soundness of the theory of *vyūhas*.

Vedānta Deśika has provided an explanation for the attribution of a pair of *guṇas* (*guṇa-niyama*) and the allocation of specific functions to each *vyūha*. In his opinion these have to be understood on the same principle as that adopted for explaining the different *upāsanās* on the same Brahman.[29] There are thirty-two types of *vidyās* or *upāsanās* referred to in the Upaniṣads. Though the object of meditation is the same Brahman, the *upāsanās* are named differently on the basis of the different attributes with which Brahman is to be contemplated. In the same way when a devotee undertakes meditation on a *vyūha* form of God, he focuses his mind on specific divine qualities and God accordingly reveals to the *upāsaka* that form with which the latter desires to intuit the former. Similarly, it is the same *Vāsudeva* who performs different functions by assuming three different manifestations as Saṁkarṣaṇa, Pradyumna and Aniruddha because He is the presiding deity of the *vyūhas* and the controller of all activities.[30]

The Purāṇic concept of three deities as in charge of the three cosmic functions is reconciled with the Pāñcarātra doctrine of *vyūhas* by envisaging two stages of creation (*sṛṣṭi*) sustenance (*sthiti*) and dissolution (*saṁhāra*), viz., *samaṣṭi* or aggregate one and *vyaṣṭi* or diversified one. The *vyūha-Vāsudeva*, who is not different from *Para-Vāsudeva*, the very Brahman of the Upaniṣad, is directly in charge of the *samaṣṭi-sṛṣṭi, sthiti* and *saṁhāra*. That is, He causes the initial process of evolution dissolution of the universe by His *saṅkalpa*, since He is the Supreme Being and controller of the entire universe. As regards *vyaṣṭi-sṛṣṭi* or the creation of the diversified universe, the Caturmukha-Brahmā is brought into existence after the *Brahmāṇḍa* or the cosmic egg is formed. Here again, the same Vāsudeva in the form of Pradyumna enters into the body of Brahmā (*anupraveśa*) and causes the actual creation through him. In the same way, Vāsudeva in the form of Saṁkarṣaṇa enters into the body of Rudra through whom the process of devolution of the universe (*vyaṣṭi-pralaya*) is caused. The task of actual preservation of the universe (*vyaṣṭi-sthiti*) is, however, performed directly by Vāsudeva in the form of Aniruddha. That is, Aniruddha who is an *avatāra* of Viṣṇu performs the function of preservation, whereas two separate deities such as Caturmukha-Brahmā and Rudra are utilized as media for the task of creation and dissolution of the universe.[31] We have explained in an earlier chapter how Viṣṇu included in the Trinity is an *avatāra*, unlike Brahmā and Rudra, who are created beings. The *Viṣṇupurāṇa* also upholds this theory. The Upaniṣads speak of two stages of evolution —*samaṣṭi* and *vyaṣṭi*. The evolution of the *prakṛti* up to the stage of five gross elements is taken as *samaṣṭi-sṛṣṭi*. The creation of the physical universe with all its diversity through the quintuplication (*pañcīkaraṇa*) of the five physical elements is *vyaṣṭi-sṛṣṭi*.[32] The first stage is caused by the Supreme Being, while the second stage is carried out through Caturmukha-Brahmā. The Pāñcarātra treatises which uphold the theory of cosmology in terms of emanation believe in three kinds of creation—*śuddha* or pure, *miśra* or mixed and *aśuddha* or impure.[33] The first one refers to the emanation of the three *vyūhas* and the second covers the intermediate creation with the manifestation of *kūṭastha-puruṣa* (the aggregate of the unmanifested souls who is known as *samaṣṭi-puruṣa* or *Hiraṇyagarbha*[34] and the third corresponds to the Upaniṣadic concept of *vyaṣṭi-sṛṣṭi* or the evolution of the *prakṛti* through all its modifications up to the physical universe. Thus, there is no conflict between the Pāñcarātra theory of *vyūhas* with the cosmic functions and the views of the Vedānta and Purāṇas regarding Brahman vis-a-vis the three deities in charge of the cosmic functions.

In connection with the doctrine of *vyūha*, we have to consider one other aspect which has given room for some controversy. Some of the Pāñcarātra treatises speak of the origin of each of the later *vyūhas* from the preceding one. Thus it is stated: 'From Vāsudeva, who is the primordial cause, the *jīva* in the name of Saṁkarṣaṇa originate; from Saṁkarṣaṇa the *manas* called Pradyumna originates; and from Pradyumna the principle of egoity called Aniruddha comes forth.'[35] Prima facie, this statement gives an impression of the origin *(utpatti)* of *jīva*, which is directly opposed to the Upaniṣadic teaching asserting the eternity of *jīva*. On the basis of it, the author of the *Vedānta-sūtra*, prima facie, questions the authoritativeness of Pāñcarātra system. Assuming this as the final view of Bādarāyaṇa, Śaṁkara in his commentary refutes the validity of Pāñcarātra system, in so far as its philosophical teachings are concerned. Rāmānuja, on the contrary, upholds the authority of Pāñcarātra taking his stand on the fact that the *sūtra* in question does not refer to the final view. He contends that *utpatti* or the origin of *jīva* is not to be taken as the birth of *jīva*. In his opinion, this term in the relevant statement is to be understood in the sense of manifestation (*prādurbhāva*). What the Pāñcarātra system teaches is that the Supreme Brahman, designated as Vāsudeva, out of compassion towards the devotees, voluntarily manifests Himself in a fourfold form, so as to render itself accessible to the devotees. Rāmānuja quotes in support of this view a statement from the *Pauṣkara Saṁhitā*, one of the oldest Pāñcarātra Saṁhitās which enjoins the worship of the four manifestations of Para-Vāsudeva by the devoted Brāhmaṇas. The *Sāttvata Saṁhitā* also affirms that the worship offered to the four manifestations of Vāsudeva is the same as the worship of the Para-Brahman. The Supreme Brahman called Vāsudeva endowed with the six *guṇas* manifests itself into the subtle forms of *vyūha* and the gross forms of *vibhava* and the same Brahman is attained by the devotees through meditation on any of these forms according to one's qualifications with the aid of *karma* (rituals) and *jñāna* (meditation). There are sufficient number of statements in the Pāñcarātra literature which point out that by the worship of each of the *vyūha* in an ascending order one can attain the Supreme Brahman. That is, from the worship of *vibhava* aspect, one reaches *vyūha* and from the worship of *vyūha*, one reaches the Supreme Brahman. Rāmānuja, therefore, concludes that Saṁkarṣaṇa, Pradyumna and Aniruddha are thus the mere bodily forms which the Supreme Being assumes. There is no question of their being born in the ordinary sense, because Śruti declares that though unborn He is born in many ways. These four forms are the manifestations of one Supreme Being out of His free will for the sake of devotees. These statements of Rāmānuja[36] sum up the correct position of the doctrine of *vyūha* according to Vaiṣṇavism.

Some of the Pāñcarātra treatises speak of sub-*vyūhas*. It is believed that from each *vyūha* descend three sub-*vyūhas* (*vyūhāntara*). From Vāsudeva come Keśava, Nārāyaṇa and Mādhava; from Saṁkarṣaṇa descend Govinda, Viṣṇu and Madhusūdana; from Pradyumna manifest Trivikrama, Vāmana and Śrīdhara; and from Aniruddha arise Hṛṣīkeśa, Padmanābha and Dāmodara. Some of these names are common with the names of the *vibhava* manifestations such as Padmanābha, Madhusūdhana, Nārāyaṇa and Trivikrama. The names of Viṣṇu and Nārāyaṇa are also common with the Supreme Deity designated with the same names. It is, therefore, difficult to say whether the twelve sub-*vyūhas* are different from the *vibhava* forms of *Viṣṇu*. As these twelve deities are regarded as presiding deities of the twelve suns ruling each solar month (*dvādaśa ādityas*), they have to be taken as different *vyūha* manifestations. Each deity is described in the Pāñcarātra treatises with a specific complexion and certain ornaments for the purpose of meditation on them.

The *Vihagendra Saṁhitā* speaks of twelve additional *vyūhas*. It says that from *vyūha*-Vāsudeva springs another Vāsudeva, from the latter Puruṣottama, from him Janārdana; similarly, from Saṁkarṣaṇa another Saṁkarṣaṇa, Adhokṣaja and Upendra; from Pradyumna, another Pradyumna, Nṛsimha and Hari; and from Aniruddha another Aniruddha, Acyuta and Kṛṣṇa. These twelve are enumerated after the twelve sub-*vyūhas* and together with the latter, the twenty-four forms (*caturviṁśati-mūrtayaḥ*).[37] No convincing explanation for the further subdivision of the four major *vyūhas* is forthcoming in the Saṁhitās. Presumably, they have been conceived to look after some of the individual functions allotted to the major *vyūhas*.

VIBHAVA AVATĀRA

This is the third type of *avatāra*. The term *vibhava* means manifestation of the Supreme Lord by assuming bodies similar to those of human beings or other living beings.[38] The need and purpose of such *avatāras* have already been explained. The *vibhava avatāra* constitutes the most important doctrine of Vaiṣṇava theology. The Epics and the Purāṇas have highlighted the importance of the various incarnations of Viṣṇu. The number of such incarnations is considered to be infinite (*ananta*).[39] However, the *Sāttvata Saṁhitā* which is the oldest *Pāñcarātra* text, enumerates thirty-nine as important *avatāras*.[40] The same is reiterated by the *Ahirbudhnya Saṁhitā*. The *Viśvaksena Saṁhitā* mentions thirty-six *avatāras*. As there is some difference of opinion among the Saṁhitās regarding the exact number, Vedānta Deśika states that the total number of *vibhavas* is above 30 and below 40.[41] Piḷḷailokācārya puts it at 36 following the *Viśvaksena Saṁhitā*. These *avatāras* are classified under two categories: principal or important ones (*mukhya*) and secondary or subsidiary (*gauṇa*).[42] The difference is based on the fact that the former refers to the direct incarnations (*sākṣāt avatāra*) that is, Viṣṇu Himself with a transcendental body assuming the human form and the latter represents the entry of the divine power into the bodies of the specific individuals. The latter is also called *āveśa avatāra*. *Āveśa* means to get possessed and when an individual becomes possessed of the divine spirit it is taken as *āveśāvatāra*. This is of two kinds: (1) the very spiritual divine body itself can pervade the body of another individual as in the case of *Paraśurāma* (one of the ten Viṣṇu's incarnations), in whom God pervaded his body; (2) the divine power (*śakti*) is infused into the body of an individual to make the latter carry out the extraordinary acts of creation or dissolution of the universe, as in the case of Brahmā and Rudra. Sage Vyāsa, the author of the *Mahābhārata*, is considered to be a case of *aṁśāvatāra*.[43] According to the Vaiṣṇava tradition, the ten Āḻvārs are *anupraveśāvatāras* of God.[44] In the same way, the important Vaiṣṇava *ācāryas* such as Rāmānuja, Vedānta Deśika and others are regarded as the incarnations of either the divine elements or the very Godhead. The basis for this belief is the statement in the Jayākhya Saṁhitā, one of the oldest Pāñcarātra treatises. It says that Nārāyaṇa, the Supreme Being assumes the bodies of human beings in order to uplift the human beings immersed in the ocean of bondage through the aid of *śāstra*, out of His compassion.[45] All the incarnations of God, both direct ones as well as the indirect ones, take place out of His own will (*icchā*) for the purpose of protection of devotees and destruction of evil, as already explained. The bodies assumed during incarnation is of spiritual character and, therefore, they are not defiled by any kind of defects.

The thirty-nine *avatāras*, as enumerated in the *Ahirbhudhnya Saṁhitā*[46] are the following:

1. Padmanābha	21. Rāhujit
2. Dhruva	22. Kālanemighna
3. Ananta	23. Pārijātahara
4. Śaktyātman	24. Lokanātha
5. Madhusūdana	25. Śāntātman
6. Vidyādhideva	26. Dattātreya
7. Kapila	27. Nyagrodhaśāyin
8. Viśvarūpa	28. Ekaśṛngatanu
9. Vihaṅgama	29. Vāmanadeha
10. Kroḍātman	30. Nara
11. Baḍabāvaktra	31. Nārāyaṇa
12. Dharma	32. Hari
13. Vāgīśvara	33. Trivikrama
14. Ekārṇavaśāyin	34. Kṛṣṇa
15. Kamaṭeśvara	35. Paraśurāma
16. Varāha	36. Rāma
17. Nārasimha	37. Vedavid
18. Pīyūṣaharaṇa	38. Kalkin
19. Śrīpati	39. Pātālaśayana
20. Kāntātman	

The origin and nature of each one of these *vibhavas* is shrouded with mysterious mythological episodes. Without going into the details which may be found in the Āgamas and Purāṇas, we will make a few general observations to bring out their significance. The long list of *avatāras* is not given in any chronological order. They have taken place in the remote past (time is infinite according to Hindu Philosophy) at different epochs (*kalpas*). Some of them such as Padmanābha, or the form of Viṣṇu from whose naval the lotus grew and from which Brahmā was born, goes back to the beginning of creation of the universe. The *avatāras* of Viṣṇu as *Ekārṇavaśāyin* or as sleeping on the primeaval waters and *Nyagrodhaśāyin* or Viṣṇu as a boy floating on *nyagrodha* leaf in whose mouth the Sage Mārkaṇḍeya discovered the dissolved universe belong to the period when there was the great deluge after the entire universe was dissolved (*pralaya*). The Vedic Mythology refers to the *Matsya avatāra* or Viṣṇu's incarnation as a fish, *Kūrma avatāra* or incarnation as a tortoise and *Varāha avatāra* or the descent of Viṣṇu as a boar to uplift the earth submerged in water. From the details of the Vedic passages these *avatāras* must have taken place either prior to creation or after the dissolution of the universe. Going by the details furnished by the Purāṇas, the *avatāras* occurred at different *yugas*.[47] The *avatāras* of Vāmana or Viṣṇu as a dwarf to punish the powerful demon-king Bali, and Narasimha, Viṣṇu in the form of man-lion to kill the demon Hiraṇyakaśipu and protect the ardent devotee, Prahlāda, took place in the *Kṛtayuga*. The incarnation of Rāma or Viṣṇu born as the son of the emperor, Daśaratha to kill the demon Rāvaṇa, occurred in *Tretā-yuga*. The *avatāra* of Kṛṣṇa happened in *Dvāparayuga*. Apart from the time factor, what is important to note is that the *avatāras* are not confined to human forms as in the case of Vāmana, Rāma, Kṛṣṇa, Balarāma and Paraśurāma. They cover the animal forms too, such as fish, tortoise, boar, swan (*haṁsa*) and a combination of man and animal, as in the case of Hayagrīva (man with the head of the horse) and Narasimha (man-lion). Even the plant kingdom is chosen for an *avatāra*, as in the case of a crooked mango-tree in the *Daṇḍaka*-forest mentioned in the *Viśvaksena Saṁhitā*. This establishes the fact that all livings beings in the universe which are God's *vibhūtis* or glory are sacred. Though God chooses the human beings and animals as objects for His incarnation, He does not become defiled by His association with them, because, as already explained, He enters into them with His spiritual divine body (*divyamaṅgala-vigraha*) out of His will (*icchā*) and remains unaffected by their defects. We shall discuss this point later.

The Nārāyaṇīya section of the *Mahābhārata* mentions the ten *avatāras* of Viṣṇu, which are popularly known as *Daśāvatāras*. The Vaiṣṇava *ācāryas* have also given due emphasis to the ten *avatāras*.[48] These are *Matsya* or fish, *Kūrma* or tortoise, *Varāha* or boar, *Narasimha* or man-lion, *Vāmana* or the dwarf, *Paraśurāma* or the Kṣatriya king, *Rāma* or the prince of Ayodhya, *Kṛṣṇa* or the son of Vāsudeva, *Balarāma* or the brother of Kṛṣṇa and *Kalkin* or the form of Viṣṇu as riding over a horse (yet to take place at the end of the *Kali yuga*). The mention of these ten is not intended to minimise the importance of other various *avatāras*. As Vedānta Deśika has pointed out, the selection of the ten *avatāras* has been made in order to highlight the distinctive purpose served by each of them. Thus, for instance, *Matsya avatāra* was taken to restore the Vedas, the treasure house of spiritual knowledge; *Kūrma avatāra* was for the purpose of securing the immortal nectar (*amṛta*) for the benefit of *devatās* by churning the ocean; *Vāmana avatāra* was to rescue the three worlds by His pervasion in the form of three strides; *Narasimha avatāra* was for the special purpose of destroying the evil forces and protection of the pious child, Prahlāda from oppression; *Paraśurāma avatāra* was to destroy the haughty kings ruling over the different parts of the earth; *Rāma avatāra* was for the purpose of establishing righteousness in general by the destruction of the wicked forces and in particular to reveal the secret of *śaraṇāgati* as a means of attaining God; *Kṛṣṇa avatāra* was also intended to establish righteousness and also to impart philosophic knowledge through the *Bhagavad-gītā*; *Balarāma avatāra* was to demonstrate the concept of divine service to God (since Balarāma represents the mythic serpent, Ādiśeṣa who renders faithful service to God); The *avatāra* of *Kalkin* which is yet to take place, will be for the purpose of re-establishing the lost *dharma*. Of the ten *avatāras*, the incarnation of God as Rāma and Kṛṣṇa have been accorded greater importance because these two are perfect ideal human beings symbolising the very *dharma*[49] lasted for longer period, unlike the other transitory incarnations such as *Matsya* and *Kūrma*. They have been glorified by the Rāmāyaṇa and *Bhāgavata Purāṇa* with full details of their divine activities and the different ways of providing protection to the pious persons and destruction of evil forces. These two are regarded as *pūrṇa avatāras*. In the Rāmāyaṇa the doctrine of *śaraṇāgati* or self-surrender for attaining *mokṣa* is enunciated fully, whereas in the *Bhāgavad-gītā*, the cream of Upaniṣadic teachings is promulgated. Vaiṣṇavism, therefore, attaches significant importance to these two *avatāras*.

One other important point to be taken note of in this connection is that all these *vibhava avatāras* are similar to an enactment in a drama on the stage. The whole cosmic universe is comparable to a theatrical stage and God appears on it putting on different roles with different costumes and enacts the life drama. Just like the person acting in a drama with either grief or joy, is not affected by it, in the same way God is also not affected by the afflictions to which He is subjected during the incarnation. When Rāma laments the separation from Sītā in the Daṇḍakāraṇya forest after the latter was kidnapped by Rāvaṇa, it was done only to cover up His real divine nature as God and to reveal to others that He too is an ordinary human being. The men of wisdom with deep philosophic insight and the pious sages who have the spiritual vision know the true form of God but for others, He appears in the form of an ordinary human being. This is what is implied in the *Puruṣa-sūkta* text which states that wise men know His origin.[50] In the *Bhagavad-gītā*, Lord Kṛṣṇa says with a sense of regret that the foolish men (men without spiritual vision) insult Him.[51] In another context, He says that one among thousands know His true nature.[52] In order to create a conviction and faith in Arjuna that He is the Supreme Being, Lord Kṛṣṇa reveals His universal form (*viśvarūpa*) by granting him the special yogic power to see His real *svarūpa*. There are numerous such episodes both in the *Rāmāyaṇa*, *Bhāgavata* and other Purāṇas to demonstrate the divine character of the *avatāras*. It would not, therefore, be appropriate to regard the *avatāras* of God as mythological stories written to meet the needs of popular religion. As explained in the *Gītā*, these are the true manifestations of God for the dual purpose of establishing *dharma* and destruction of evil.

Arcā Avatāra

The word *arcā* means the idol of worship (*pujā pratimā*). When God descends in response to our ardent prayers and enters into an idol created by human beings for the purpose of worship, it is considered as an *arcā avatāra*. Idols are generally made of a metal such as gold, silver, bronze and of stone as well as wood according to the choice of the individual devotee on the pattern of any manifested forms of Viṣṇu such as *vyūhas* and *vibhavas* and these are duly consecrated according to the religious rites prescribed for the purpose by the Āgamas. In response to the prayers of the devotees, God who is omnipresent and who has a loving disposition towards His devotees, condescend to be present in those idols by infusing into them His Divinity. The basis for this belief is the statement of the *Sāttvata Saṁhitā,* the oldest Pāñcarātra text, which says that God, by way of assuming a divine body corresponding to the idol made by an individual (*bimba-sadṛśa-vigraheṇa*) enters into it by becoming indistinguishable (*samāgatya*) like water in the milk.[53] When this takes place, the idol becomes sanctified with the divine presence in it (*avatiṣṭhate*). The *Viṣṇu-dharmottara* enjoins that devotees should make an attractive idol of Viṣṇu out of any metal or stone, offer worship to it, prostrate before it, perform religious rites for it and meditate on it; by doing so they become free from all sins.[54] This is the religious significance of the image worship.

Justification for Idol Worship

The idol worship is a very ancient custom which is prevalent in all the cultures of the world. In the primitive societies it was practised in the form of animism and totemism. In more advanced societies it is observed through the worship of a media as symbol of divine power. In Hindu Religion its practice can be traced back to the Vedas. One of the hymns of the Ṛgveda refers to the worship of Viṣṇu.[55] On the authority of this hymn, Sage Marīci, one of the exponents of the Vaikhānasa Āgama, enjoins that Vaiṣṇavas should worship Viṣṇu daily.[56] On the basis of this Vedic authority Sage Śaunaka also extolls the worship of Viṣṇu.[57] One other hymn of the Ṛgveda makes an explicit mention of the worship of idol as a means of God-realization.[58] The hymn states that the *Puruṣottama* who resides in the farthest place manifests Himself in the form of a log floating on the ocean of Sindhu (Indian ocean); it is a divine form and not made by any human being (*apaūruṣeya*) and by offering worship to this wooden image, one will attain the Supreme Being.[59] That this hymn refers to the idol worship is proved by the fact that *Skanda Purāṇa,* while speaking of the greatness of Jagannāth (the presiding deity of the holy place, Puri) elucidates this hymn.[60] It is not, therefore, correct to say that Vedic Religion is primarily concerned with the worship of deities in the form of *yajña* or sacrificial rites in the consecrated fire and that it does not allow the worship of idols. The word *yaj* etymologically means worship of a deity (*yaj devatā pūjāyām*). Worship is done in four ways: *japa* or recitation of mantras, *huta* or offering oblations through the sacrificial fire, *arcana* or offering worship to an image of God and *dhyāna* or meditation. All the four ways of worship have been observed in the Vedic times, according to the capacity of the concerned individual devotee, though more emphasis seems to have been given to *yajña* or *huta*.[61] Even in the performance of *yajña*, the individual divine beings have to be invoked by reciting the appropriate Vedic hymns in a media such as *kuśa* or blade of grass, *kumbha* or a water pot, *agni* or the sacred fire. The consecration of God in an idol prescribed by Pāñcarātra Āgamas through certain religious rites is similar to it. Thus, consecration of an idol with divine spirit and offering of worship to such an idol is not a non-Vedic custom. With the deterioration of the capacity of the human beings to adopt the other harder modes of worship such as *yajña* and *dhyāna* the Āgamas have prescribed the simpler method of image worship and developed this doctrine fully. In fact the worship in the *arcā* form gained prominence in the Āgamas. The hymns of the Āḻvārs singing the glory of the idols in the various Vaiṣṇava temples gave added significance to the temple worship. This explains the development of temples in an increasing way at a later period in the history of Vaiṣṇavism. The importance of the worship of idols in the temples and at homes and the justification for such a practice will be discussed in a separate chapter.

The *arcāvatāra* which constitutes the foundation for image worship is considered more significant than the other incarnations of God. The transcendental form of God (*para-rūpa*) is beyond the approach of human beings since it exists only in the transcendental realm. The *vyūha* forms too are unapproachable to us. The *vibhava* forms have already taken place in the remote past and as such are not available to us at present for direct worship. The presence of God as the indwelling spirit in our heart (*antaryāmin*) though closeby is also beyond the scope of worship because the physical sense organs cannot perceive Him. Thus, the Divine Being present in the form of *arcā-vigraha* is always easily available to us for offering worship. Piḷḷailokācārya has explained by an analogy the five forms of manifestation of God and the unique feature of *arcāvatāra*. The *Antaryāmi* form is comparable to the underground water (*bhūgata-jala*) implying that without the arduous eightfold yoga practice it is not possible to visualise God within, in the same way as the water in the underground cannot be obtained except with hard labour of digging the ground. The *para-rūpa* of God is like the vast stretch of deluge water surrounding the universe (*āvaraṇa-jala*) and as it exists in a realm far remote from the universe, it is absolutely inaccessible to us. The *vyūha* forms are compared to the mythological milky ocean which though exists within the cosmic universe is unapproachable by us. The *vibhava* manifestations are analogous to the seasonal flood water, which comes at a particular time and useful for those living at that time but of no use for others at a later period. Only the persons who were living during the time of the *vibhavāvatāras*, would have worshipped these divine forms but those of the future generations could not do so. The *arcāvatāras* are similar to the water present in the pools of tne river bed and available at all times for a thirsty person. The icons at the temples or at homes in which the divinity is present are easily accessible to every devotee at all times. Hence, the greatness of *arcā* idols is extolled by the Āḻvārs and the Vaiṣṇava *ācāryas*.

The later Vaiṣṇava literature speak of four types of *arcāvatāra*. These are known as *svayaṁvyakta*, *daiva*, *saiddha* and *mānuṣa*.[62] *Svayaṁvyakta* means self-manifest, that is, God on His own manifests Himself in the form of an icon. The idols found in such temples as Śrīraṅgam, Tirupati, Badarikāśrama, Vānamāmalai and Melkote are claimed to be of this category. *Daiva* means those idols which have been consecrated by divine beings. That is, either in response to the prayers offered or sacrifices performed by the divine beings such as Brahmā, God descends on earth in the form of an icon. The idol at Varadarājasvāmi temple at Conjeevaram is claimed to be of this type. The third type is known as *Saiddha*, which means those idols consecrated by sages. That is, in response to the penance (*tapas*) performed by the ardent devotees, God incarnates Himself in the form of an image. There are several Vaiṣṇava temples in South India which are claimed to be of this category.[63] The last one is called *mānuṣa*, or what is consecrated by human beings. To provide an opportunity for the general public to offer worship, temples are constructed and idols made of stone or some other material are installed in them and the same are consecrated by means of rituals prescribed by the Āgamas. Most of the Vaiṣṇava temples of later origin and those which have been coming up in recent years fall under this category. Though every idol duly consecrated is holy and is an *arcā-vigraha* or the incarnation of God, tradition accords greater sanctity to the first three in general[64] and to the *svayaṁvaykta* idols in particular. The mystic saints of South India have sung the glory of the *arcā* idols in the ancient Vaiṣṇava temples in their Tamil hymns portraying their direct experience of God. About 106 religious centres have been referred to by them and these have been regarded as holy places by the Vaiṣṇavas.[65]

The quality of easy accessibility (*saulabhya*) of God in *arcā* form has been the main source of inspiration for the Āḻvārs and the Vaiṣṇava *ācāryas*. God in the *arcā* form is available for worship to all irrespective of the fact whether one is morally meritorious or sinful. Besides, the divine enchanting beauty and glory exhibited in the image which can be felt by the ardent devotee, transform the minds of human beings and elevate them to higher spiritual plane. More than this, as the Smṛti texts assert, the very sight of an *arcā-mūrti* removes all the sins and thereby makes the persons mentally purer and spiritually richer.[66] The *arcā-vigraha* is regarded as *śubhāśraya*. *Āśraya* means the support and *śubha* stands for auspiciousness. The idol is *āśraya* since it serves as a suitable object for *dhyāna* or meditation. It is *śubha* because it can remove the sins of the devotees by virtue of the presence of divinity in it. Another greatness of *arcā* is the spirit of tolerance on the part of God. As the *Bhagavad-gītā* states, whatever offerings are made with devotion to Him, small or big, are accepted as most satisfying.[67] God tolerates even the offences committed to Him by the worshippers (*sarvasahiṣṇuḥ*).[68]

Antaryāmi Avatāra

This is the fifth kind of manifestation of God as indwelling in a subtle form in the inner recess of human hearts for purposes of meditation.[69] The term *antaryāmin* also refers to the indwelling spirit, that is the Supreme Being who is immanent in all sentient as well as non-sentient entities in the universe and who as the inner self, controls everything from within (*niyamayati*), as stated in the *Antaryāmi Brāhmaṇa* of *Bṛhadāraṇyaka Upaniṣad*. In this sense, *Antaryāmin* means the Supreme Being known as Nārāyaṇa.[70] This type of *antaryāmitva* is common to both living beings as well as non-sentient objects in the universe. This is not what is implied when Vaiṣṇavism speaks of *antaryāmi avatāra*. As an *avatāra*, the Supreme Being as residing in the inner recess of heart assumes a subtle divine bodily form (*vigraha-viśiṣṭa*) so as to enable the *upāsaku* to meditate on God. In Yoga system, meditation is twofold—*sālambana* and *nirālambana*. The former type which is the first stage of *samādhi* needs an object that could be visualised, whereas the latter which is next higher stage can be done on a formless entity (*svarūpa*). Before proceeding to the higher stage of *upāsanā*, it is necessary to meditate on a divine *vigraha*.

For such yogis as wish to do the meditation on the divine Being which is present within one's own heart, God, out of love and compassion, takes on a bodily form (*vigraha*). This is the purpose and justification for manifestation of God as *antaryāmin*. This theory is admitted on the strength of the scriptural and Smṛti texts. The *Taittirīya Upaniṣad* refers to the heart as the abode of the Supreme Lord and says that at the centre of it, *Paramātman* resides in a subtle form.[71] It also gives a physical description of *Paramātman* as having the complexion of dark blue (*nīla-megha*) lustre similar to the lightning, very subtle and monadic.[72] In a later passage of the same Upaniṣad, it is stated that the *Paramātman* resides in the heart which is of the size of a person's thumb.[73] The implication of all these statements is that *Paramātman* dwelling in the heart of the *upāsaka* has assumed a spiritual subtle bodily form to enable the yogi to perform the meditation on Him. One of the thirty-two *vidyās* or *upāsanās* laid down in the Vedānta includes *dahara-vidyā*, which according to Rāmānuja is nothing other than the *upāsanā* on the *Paramātman* within one's heart. If it were pure formless or undifferentiated *svarūpa* of Brahman, which is *vibhu* (omnipresent), it will not serve the purpose of meditation for the reason already explained. To meet this purpose, God assumes a bodily form. This is the significance of *antaryāmi avatāra*, which is distinct from all the other kinds of manifestations. This fact has been well brought out by the *Sātvata Saṁhitā* which states: 'For those individuals who have already reached a stage in the *upāsanā* by following the eightfold yoga discipline, and who wish to do further *upāsanā* on the *Paramātman* residing inside the heart, this *Paramātman* as *antaryāmin* becomes the object of meditation.'[74]

To sum up, the doctrine of *avatāra* is not an innovation of later purāṇic period but it is well rooted in the Vedas, though some of its features might have been developed in greater detail in the Pāñcarātra treatises and the *Mahābhārata*. It refers to the fivefold manifestation of the Supreme Lord Viṣṇu also known as Para-Vāsudeva, from the highest transcendental state (*para*) to that of the subtlest state as the indweller in the human hearts (*antaryāmin*). Of the different manifestations, the one in the form of *arcā* or idol of worship is of supreme importance because of the easy accessibility of God to human beings for worship. All these manifestations are real and take place primarily for the protection of the pious ardent devotees of God (*sādhu-paritrāṇa*) and for the establishment of *dharma* by way of destruction of evil forces. There is no particular time factor when such incarnations should occur but it is a continuous process from the time immemorial through the long stretch of infinite time in an endless way. God does not become defiled by His descent to assume the bodies of human or any living beings since such physical forms are taken on out of His pure will and not on account of *karma* and the bodies are constituted of effulgent pure *sāttvik* spiritual substance. Though the incarnations of God appear to ordinary human beings as physical substances with all its defects, they are in fact divine bodies visualized as such by the yogis and pious men of philosophic wisdom and spiritual vision. This is the significance of the Vedic statement which says that God though unborn is born in different ways. Those who know the secret of *avatāra* will attain the highest spiritual goal as asserted by the *Bhagavad-gītā*.[75]

Notes

1. *Puruṣa-sūkta* (Yajurveda recension) II.3. *ajāyaṃāno bahudhā vijāyate.*
2. See VSa p. 131. *ayaṁ tu sarveśvaraḥ..devādiṣu jagadupakārāya bahudhā jāyate.*
3. RV III.8.4. *yuvā suvāsāḥ parivīta āgāt sa u śreyān bhavati jāyamānaḥ.*
4. *Taittirīya Brāhmaṇa*, III.12.55. *pitā putreṇa pitṭṛmān yoni yonau; nā-vedavin-manute taṁ bṛhantam.*
5. *Śatpatha Brāhmaṇa* (Mādhyandina recension), I.8.1.
6. *Taittirīya Āraṇyaka*, I.23.
7. *Taittirīya Brāhmaṇa*, I.1.3.

See also *Taittirīya Saṁhitā* VII.1.5. *taṁ varāho bhūtvā aharat.*
8. BG IV.5–9.
9. See *Viśiṣṭādvaita Kośa*, Vol. I, p. 422. *paramātmanaḥ prādurbhāvaḥ.*
10. BG IV.5–8.
11. The doctrine of *Śudda-sattva* is explained in Chapter 11.
12. VP VI.7.70. *samastāḥ śaktayaścaitā nṛpa yatra pratiṣṭitāḥ...*
See also *Śrutaprakāśikā*, I.1.21 p. 245.
13. BG IV.6. *ajo'pi sannavyayātmā bhūtānām-īśvaro'pi san; prakṛtiṁ svāmadhiṣṭāya sambhavāmyātmamāyayā.*
The word *ātmamāyā* is interpreted by Rāmānuja as *ātma-saṅkalpa.*
14. See RB I.1.21 and also *Śrutaprakāśikā*, pp. 244-46.
15. See *Viśiṣṭādvaita Kośa*, Vol. I, p. 425. *bhagavataḥ avatāravigrahāḥ śuddhasattva-dravyamaya para-vāsudeva-vigrahāṁśa-mūlaḥ.*
16. BG IV.8. *paritrāṇāya sādhūnāṁ vināśāya ca duṣkṛtām; dharma-saṁsthāpanārthāya saṁbhavāmi yuge-yuge.*
17. GB IV.8, p. 135.
18. See TC IV.8, p. 136. *ānuṣaṅgikastu duṣkṛtāṁ vināśaḥ.*
19. TNUp *ambhasya-pāre bhuvanasya madhye nākasya pṛṣṭe mahato mahīyān; śukreṇa jyotiṁṣi samanupraviṣṭaḥ prajāpatiścarati garbhe antaḥ.*
In this statement, *apāre ambhasi* is interpreted to mean Viṣṇu lying in the milky ocean implying one of the vyūhas; *bhuvanasya madhye* is understood as God manifesting in the Sun (*sūrya-maṇḍalavarti*) implying the *vibhava avatāra*; *nākasya pṛṣṭe* refers to the transcendental form (*para-rūpa*); *ṣukṛeṇa jyotiṁsi* is interpreted to mean the idols made of gold etc., in which God is consecrated, implying the *arcā* form; *garbhe antaḥ* is taken to mean the *antaryāmi* form.
See the article by the 42nd Jīyar of Ahobila Matham in the *Nṛsimhpriyā* vol. I issue II p. 34.
20. Ibid. 146 *sa vā eṣa puruṣaḥ pañcadhā pañcātmā.*
See RRB p. 129. *para-vyūha-vibhava-antaryāmy-arcāvatāra lakṣaṇa bhagavatśāstrokta-prakāreṇa vibhaktaḥ pañcānām.*
21. *Puruṣa-sūkta*, (Yajurveda recension) II.2. *ādityavarṇaṁ tamasaḥ parastāt.*
RV VII.100.5. *kṣayantamasya rajasaḥ parāke.*
Taittirīya Brāhmaṇa II.8.9. *yo asyādhyakṣaḥ parame-vyoman.*
22. LT X.10. *trairūpyeṇa jagannāthaḥ samudeti jagaddhite; ādyena para-rūpeṇa...bhaktānugraha-kāmyayā.*
23. Ibid. verse 12–17.
See also *Liṅgapurāṇa*, (Quoted in RTS IV).
vaikunṭhe tu pareloke śriyāsārdhaṁ jagatpatiḥ;
āste viṣṇuracintyātmā bhaktairbhāgavatais-saha.
24. These are the names given to the four *vyūhas* in the Pāñcarātra texts. But Vaikhānsa system which also admits the principle of *vyūha* emanations, uses different names. According to them Puruṣa, Satya, Acyuta and Aniruddha emanate from *Viṣṇu* who is known as *Ādimūrti.*
25. See AhS IIX.5–39. *tatra ādyābhiḥ catasṛbhiḥ cāturātmyaṁ vivicyate.*

26. RTS V p. 92. Vedānta Deśika supports both the views. Śrīvatsānkamiśra also upholds the theory of three vyūhas.
See *Varadarājastava*, verse 16.
27. See *Śrīrangarājastava*. II.39.
See also RTS V and *Tattvatraya*, III.185-88.
28. Ibid. *Ṣāḍguṇyād-Vāsudevaḥ para iti sa bhavān mukta-bhogyaḥ.*
29. TMK III.70. *tattad-vidyāviśeṣa-pratiniyataguṇanyāyataḥ tau tu neyau.*
30. Ibid. *sahyekaḥ sarvasya abhimantā sakala-jagad-vyāprtisu eka kartā*
See also SS. III.70, p. 168.
31. See *Darśanodaya*, p. 227.
32. See Chup VI.3.3. The *trivṛtkaraṇa* which is illustrative of *pañcīkaraṇa* (quintuplication) theory is interpreted as the beginning of the stage of *vyaṣṭi-sṛṣṭi*. The evolution of *prakṛti* up to the five elements is *samaṣṭi-sṛṣṭi.*
See SS I.17. See also FVV pp. 321-22.
33. See for details Otto Schrader's Introduction to Pāñcarātra and Ahirbudhnya Saṁhitā Chapter II.
34. Ibid. p. 70 and LT VII.11.
35. See *Parama Saṁhitā* (quoted by Rāmānuja in RB, II.2.39).
See also SB II.2.42.
36. RB II.2.41.
37. See Otto Schrader: Introduction to Pāñcarātra and Ahirbudhnya Saṁhitā p. 49.
38. See *Yatīndramata-dīpikā*, p. 136. *vibhavo nāma tattad-sajātīya rūpeṇa āvirbhāvaḥ.*
39. *Tattvatraya*, sūtra 189.
40. *Sāttvata Saṁhitā*, XII.66.
41. See RTS V. p. 92.
42. *Tattvatraya*, sūtra 189.
43. VP III.4.5. *kṛṣṇadvaipāyanaṁ vyāsaṁ viddhi nārāyaṇaṁ prabhum.*
44. *Viṣṇu-dharmottara*, 108-50 (quoted by VD in RTS p. 70).
pūrvotpanneṣu bhūteṣu teṣu teṣu kalau prabhuḥ; anupraviśya kurute yatsamīhitamacyutaḥ.
45. *Jayākhya Saṁhitā*, (quoted in RTS p. 70). *sākṣān-nārāyaṇo devaḥ kṛtvā martyamayiṁ tanum; magnān-uddharate lokān kāruṇyāt śāstra-pāṇinā.*
46. AhS V.50–56. *vibhavāḥ padmanābhādyāḥ triṁśacca nava caiva hi.*
See LT XI.19–25. *triṁśacca aṣṭau ime devāḥ padmanābhādayo matāḥ.*
47. The word *yuga* means the age of the universe. According to Hindu Mythology, there are four *yugas—kṛta, tretā, dvāpara* and *kali*. The duration of each is said to be respectively 1,728,000, 1,296,000, 864,000 and 432,000 years of men.
48. See VD's *Daśāvatāra Stotra.*
The ten *avatāras* generally acknowledged by the Vaiṣṇavas do not include the Buddhāvatāra. Buddha, as the founder of Buddhism in vogue, is not an *avatāra* of Viṣṇu. If some later Purāṇas speak of him as an avatāra, it is regarded by the Vaiṣṇavas as an interpolation.

49. See Rāmāyaṇa, *Ramo vigrahavān dharmaḥ*.
See also Mbh III.71.123. *Kṛṣṇaṁ dharmaṁ sanātanam.*
50. *Puruṣa-sūkta* (Yajurveda recension) II.3. *tasya dhīrāḥ parijānanti yonim.*
51. BG IX.11. *avajānanti māṁ mūḍhā mānuṣīṁ tanum-āśritam.*
52. BG VII.3. *manuṣyāṇāṁ sahasreṣu...kaścin-māṁ vetti tattvataḥ.*
53. *Sāttvata Saṁhitā*, VI.22. *bimbākṛtyātmanā bimbe samāgatya avatiṣṭhate.*
See also Poygai Āḻwār's *Mudal Tiruvandādi*, hymn 44.
"*tamar uhandadu evvuruvum avvuruvum tāne.*"
The meaning of this Tamil verse is: In whatever form the devotees desire, God assumes a body in that very form.
See also BG IV.11. *ye yathā māṁ prapadyante tāṁstathaiva bhajāmy ahaṁ.*
54. VDh 103–16. *surūpāṁ pratimāṁ viṣṇoḥ prasannavadanekṣaṇām; kṛtvātmanaḥ prītikarīm suvarṇa-rajatādibhiḥ; tāmarcayet tāṁ praṇamet tāṁ yajet tāṁ vicintayet; viśatyapāsta-doṣastu tāmeva brahmarūpiṇīm.*
55. RV I.155.1. *pravaḥ pāntam-andhaso dhiyāyate; mahe śūrāya viṣṇave ca arcata.*
56. *Vimānaracana Kalpa*, p. 503. *tasmāt viṣṇu arcanam-eva dvijaiḥ aharahaḥ kartavyam-iti vijñāyate.*
57. See PR, II p. 115.
śaunako'haṁ pravakṣyāmi nityaṁ viṣṇvarcanaṁ param; pravaḥ-pāntam-andhasodhi ity-ardharca-vidhānataḥ.
58. RV X.155.3. *ado yad-dāru plavate sindhoḥ pāre apūruṣam; tadārabhasva durhaṇo tena gaccha parastaram.*
59. See Sāyaṇa's commentary, vol. VIII, p. 626.
The word *ārabhasva* is interpreted as *ālambasva*, *upāsva*, which means to offer worship; *parastara* is explained as *atiśayena taraṇīyaṁ utkṛṣṭaṁ vaiṣṇavaṁ lokaṁ*, that is, the supreme abode of Viṣṇu to be attained by devoted worship.
60. *Skanda Purāṇa* (Vaiṣṇava Khaṇḍa). *kṣirodārṇava madhye hi śvetadvīpe hi talpake; yaḥ śete yoganidrāṁ tāṁ mānayan puruṣottamaḥ ...tan-madhyastho hi ayaṁ vṛkṣaḥ caitanyādhiṣṭitaḥ suraḥ; svayaṁ utpatitaḥ sindhoḥ salīle sattva-puruṣaḥ; bhogān bhoktuṁ trilokasthān dāru-varṣma janārdanaḥ.*
61. See RV VIII.19.5. *yaḥ samidhā ya āhutī yo vedena dadāśa marto agnaye, yo namasā svadhvaraḥ.*
This hymn acknowledges the *yajña* performed through a *mental act* as equivalent to the actual sacrifice performed in the sacred fire by faggots (*samit*) and recitation of *mantras*.
See also Chapter 13, p. 262.
62. See *Yatīndramata-dīpikā*, p. 139.
63. The *sthalapurāṇas* or the narrative accounts maintained by the concerned individual pilgrim centres explain the origin of the idols in these temples. Most of these narrations are included in the Purāṇas and *upa-purāṇas*.

64. *Pārameśvara Saṁhitā, viśeṣeṇa svayaṁvyakte divya siddhepi cārṣake...*
65. Two more holy centres—the mythological milky ocean and the *paramapada* are added to these to make a total number of 108 Vaiṣṇava religious centres (*Divya-deśa*).
66. *Sāṇḍilya Smṛti* (quoted by VD in RTS XV).
apiṭhān-mauliparyantaṁ paśyataḥ puruṣottamam; pātakānyaśu naśyanti kiṁ punastu upapātakam.
See also *Pauṣkara Saṁhitā*, I.31.32.
sandarśānād-akasmācca puṁsāṁ...kubhāvaśca nāstikatvaṁ layaṁ vrjet.
67. BG IX.26. *patraṁ puṣpaṁ phalaṁ toyaṁ yo me bhaktyā prayacchati;*
tadahaṁ bhaktyupahṛtam-aśnāmi prayatātmanaḥ.
68. *Śri-raṅgarājastava*, verse II.74.
See also *Tattvatraya*, Sūtra 200.
69. See NS p. 237. *hṛt-padmakarṇikā-madhyagatasya antaryāmiṇaḥ parasya viśeṣataḥ sūkṣma antaryāmyavatāraḥ.*
See also RTS V and *Tattvatraya*, sūtra 198.
70. See SB on BrUp V.7.3.
71. TNUp 101. *tasyāḥ śikhāya madhye paramātmā vyavasthitaḥ.*
72. Ibid. *nīlatoyadamadhyasthā vidyullekheva bhāsvarā.*
73. Ibid. 128. *aṅguṣṭamātraḥ puruṣo aṅguṣṭaṁca samāśritaḥ.*
Here the word *anguṣṭamātra puruṣa* is to be understood as referring to the heart in which *Paramātman* resides in a subtle form.
See RRB p. 118. *anguṣṭa-parimāṇa-hṛdayam-āśritaḥ.*
74. See *Sāttvata Saṁhitā* II.7 (quoted by VD in RTS),
aṣṭāṅgayoga-siddhānāṁ hṛdyāganiratātmanām;
yoginām-adhikārasyād-ekasmin hṛdayeśaye.
75. BG IV.9. *janma karma ca me divyam-evaṁ yo vetti tattvataḥ;*
tyaktvā dehaṁ punarjanma naiti māmeti so'rjuna.

11

VIṢṆU AND NITYA-VIBHŪTI

In the earlier chapters we have referred to the concepts of *nitya-vibhūti* and *śuddha-sattva* or pure spiritual *sattva* quality. *Nitya-vibhūti* is admitted as one of the six metaphysical categories of the Viśiṣṭādvaita Vedānta. Several theories of Vaiṣnava theology such as the divine body of the Supreme Being, the incarnation of God in human or other forms, the divine service by the released souls and the existence of an eternal abode of God are all based on the concept of *śuddha-sattva*. It thus constitutes an essential doctrine of Vaiṣnavism and a proper understanding of it is, therefore, called for. We shall examine it in the present chapter.

Definition of Nitya-vibhūti

What is *nitya-vibhūti*? Vedānta Deśika defines it as a substance constituted of pure *sattva*, while it is different from the cosmic matter comprising the three *guṇas*.[1] It is also defined as a substance constituted of pure *sattva*, while being self-luminous.[2] According to these definitions, the first essential characteristic of *nitya-vibhūti* is that it should be constituted of pure *sattva*. *Sattva* generally refers to one of the three qualities of cosmic matter, viz., *sattva*, *rajas* and *tamas*. *Prakṛti* and all its material products are always characterized by these qualities (*guṇas*) in varying proportion. It is not this *sattva* quality that is referred to by the term of *śuddha-sattva* of *nitya-vibhūti*. On the contrary, it refers to a different type of *sattva* which is regarded as absolutely free from the tinge of *rajas* and *tamas*. This would mean that there are two types of *sattva—śuddha* which does not possess even in the slightest degree *rajas* and *tamas* and *aśuddha* which is associated with *rajas* and *tamas*.[3] The *prakṛti* and all its evolutes is characterised by the latter, whereas the pure *sattva* consists of the former. This brings out the second characteristic of *nitya-vibhūti*, viz., that it is other than *prakṛti* comprising three *guṇas* (*triguṇa-*

dravya-vyatirikta). It is, therefore, characterised as *svayaṁprakāśa* or self-luminous to emphasise the spiritual character of *śuddha-sattva* as contrasted with the material substance (*jaḍa-prakrti*). It thus follows that *nitya-vibhūti* is spiritual substance (*ajaḍa dravya*) constituted of pure *sattva* quality.

In Vaiṣṇava treatises the term *nitya-vibhūti* is applicable to the eternal, transcendental universe (*aprākṛta deśa-viśeṣa*) as distinguished from the physical universe which is named as *līlā-vibhūti*. In Vaiṣṇava terminology, the word *vibhūti* means divine wealth or glory (*aiśvarya*).[4] In other words, all that belongs to the Supreme Lord is His *vibhūti*. That which exists eternally as His glory is named *nitya-vibhuti*. This is the transcendental spiritual universe in which the *paramapada*, the Supreme abode of God is located. The physical universe which is also His property is termed *līlā-vibhūti* to signify the fact that it is created as His play ground for His own pleasure.[5] In Vaiṣṇavism, the Supreme Being is the Lord of both the realms (*ubhaya-vibhūti-nātha*).

In Vaiṣṇava literature the terms *nitya-vibhūti* and *śuddha-suttva* are generally used as synonymous, because all that exists in the realm of *nitya-vibhūti* is made of *śuddha-sattva*. In a technical sense the two are distinct because the former is applicable to a transcendental universe, whereas the latter refers to the pure *sattva* quality.

Proof for Existence of Nitya-vibhūti

Does such a transcendental universe exist? What is the justification for admitting it? The only proof for the existence of *nitya-vibhūti* is as in the case of God, the Revealed Scripture. There are numerous scriptural as well as Smṛti texts which speak of such a realm. It is on the basis of an unquestionable authority of the sacred texts that Vaiṣṇavism has adopted the doctrine of *nitya-vibhuti*. The *Puruṣa-sūkta* says: 'I know that Supreme Being who resplendent like the Sun, exists far beyond the physical universe'.[6] The expression *tamasastu pāre* or beyond *tamas* (*prakṛti*) in this statement is taken to mean the existence of a transcendental realm. The hymn of Ṛgveda states: 'He who lives beyond this *rajas* (cosmic universe)'.[7] There are other scriptural texts speaking of the existence of the Supreme Being in the *parama-vyoma* or the highest heaven which is a reference to the *nitya-vibhūti*.[8] The *Ṛk* hymn on Viṣṇu explicitly mentions by name the *paramapada* (the highest abode) of Viṣṇu which the enlightened seers always see.[9] As we have explained elsewhere, the fact that the *Sūris* (eternally free souls) see such a place all the time, indicates its eternal character. The Smṛti texts also lend support to this theory. Thus says *Viṣṇupurāṇa*: 'Those who are yogins, who meditate on Brahman continuously with undivided devotion attain the Supreme abode, which the enlightened seers always see.'[10] The *Mahābhārata* is more specific about the transcendental realm which is described as divine, eternal, immeasurable, incomprehensible, primordial and knowable only through scripture.[11]

The Nature of Nitya-vibhūti

According to the Viśiṣṭādvaita, *nitya-vibhūti* is infinite in so far as its upper limit is concerned. As regards the lower limit, it does not extend beyond the cosmic universe (*prakṛti*) constituted of three *guṇas*.[12] As the *Puruṣa-sūkta* states, the physical universe covers only a small part (*pāda*) of Viṣṇu's *vibhūti* (glory). *Pāda* or part implies as explained in the *Gītā*, that the physical universe is brought forth from a small particle of God's infinite energy.[13] But the rest of His glory permeates the entire higher region.[14] On the basis of this, one of the Pāñcarātra Saṁhitās describes that the realm of God known as *Vaikuṇṭha*, is infinitely extensive (*anantayāma*) and that the infinite glory of the Lord (*tripādāṁśa*) manifests itself in the *nitya-vibhūti*. The *prakṛti* or cosmic matter is also *vibhu* and *ananta* (spatially immeasurable) according to Viśiṣṭādvaita but nevertheless it does not cover the *nitya-vibhūti* since the latter is declared by the sacred texts as existing beyond *prakṛti*.

Though it is self-luminous, it is categorised as *acetana* or non-sentient, as distinct from *Īśvara* and *jīva*, which are *cetanas* or sentient beings. This is a peculiar classification adopted by the Viśiṣṭādvaita Vedānta. *Cetana*, in this system means that which is a substrate or subject of knowledge (*caitanya-viśiṣṭa*). Knowledge (*jñāna*) as well as *nitya-vibhūti* taken as a *dravya* (substance) are *acetanas* because they are not the subjects of knowledge. That is, they only reveal the objects like light but they do not know the objects thus revealed as in the case of *jīvas* because they do not possess knowledge as a quality.

This leads to the question whether what is *acetana* or non-sentient can be self-luminous (*svayaṁprakāśa*)? The answer is given in the affirmative. According to the Viśiṣṭādvaita epistemology, the function of knowledge is to reveal something and while it reveals, it does not require the aid of another knowledge to reveal it. This is the meaning of *svayaṁprakāśatva* or self-luminosity. However it is not *jaḍa* or an inert object, in which case it would not be able to reveal the objects. *Svayaṁprakāśatva* and *ajaḍatva* (spirituality) are not opposed to each other. *Jñāna* and *nitya-vibhūti* are regarded as self-luminous in order to bring out the fact that they are not material but are essentially spiritual in character.

Even among the Viśiṣṭādvaitins, some have taken the view that *śuddhasattva* is *jaḍa* or material and not spiritual in character. The reason for holding this view is that in some Pāñcarātra treatises the *nitya-vibhūti* and the objects existing in it are described to be of the same nature as God; since God according to the followers of Pāñcarātra is constituted of six attributes such as knowledge, *nitya-vibhūti* too should comprise all the six qualities. But such a view, they argue, does not sound good since that would amount to equating *śuddha-sattva* with a sentient being. Hence they contend that *nitya-vibhūti* is to be taken as *jaḍa*.

Vedānta Deśika does not agree with this explanation. The sacred texts declare that *Īśvara* is of the essence of *jñāna*. The *vigraha* or the bodily form of such a Being cannot be made of anything other than pure *sāttvic* substance. If it were made of material substance, it would be subject to change and decay. Therefore, it is appropriate to accept that *śuddha-sattva* is of the nature of knowledge implying that it is purely spiritual in character. The Pāñcarātra texts describe *śuddha-sattva* not only of the nature of knowledge (*jñānātmaka*) but also as self-luminous.[15]

If as a spiritual entity it is self-luminous, the question arises for whom it reveals itself? The released souls which are omniscient in the state of *mokṣa*, can apprehend it even if it is not self-luminous. The embodied souls do not cognise it in anyway since it is transcendental. What is the purpose of its being self-luminous? In reply to this objection Vedānta Deśika explains that it is not necessary that what is self-luminous should necessarily be the object of cognition. *Īśvara* is self-luminous but He is not perceived by us as such. In the same way *śuddha-sattva* can remain self-luminous, whether or not it is the object of cognition.

The *dharmabhūta-jñāna* which is an essential attribute of the self (*jīvātman*) does not manifest itself during the state of deep sleep because it does not then experience any object; nevertheless, it does not cease to be self-luminous. In the same way *śuddha-sattva* is not cognised by us during the state of bondage but it can still remain self-luminous by virtue of its intrinsic character.

The Concept of Paramapada

The Pāñcarātra Saṁhitās and the Vaiṣṇava treatises present a highly attractive account of the abode of Viṣṇu known as *paramapada* or *vaikuṇṭha-loka*. It consists of beautiful castles with towers, halls with thousand pillars etc., and also laid out with enchanting flower gardens, trees, streams, lakes etc. Thus, the *Kauśītakī Upaniṣad*[16] mentions the existence of a lake named *ara*, a river by the name *viraja* and a tree known as *tilya* and an impenetrable residence. *Chāndogya Upaniṣad* speaks of two seas *Aṛa* and *Ṇya* and a lake named *Airammadīya* in the *Brahma-loka*. It also describes the city of Brahman as *aparājita* (unconquerable) and refers to a golden hall built for the Lord.[17] Another scriptural text says: 'In that mansion constructed with one thousand pillars, there lives the Lord of all the devatas'. The *Mahābhārata*, *Viṣṇupurāṇa* and other Vaiṣṇava Purāṇas contain references to the *paramapada*. The hymns of Nammāḻvār describe vividly the way the individual souls soon after release from bondage are received with warm welcome by the celestial beings (God's personal attendants) at the entrance of God's mansion. Presumably based on these ideas Rāmānuja in his prose work named *Vaikuṇṭha-Gadya*, gives a highly picturesque description of the *vaikuṇṭha-loka* using such expressions as are beyond anybody's imagination. Following the same line of thought, Vedānta Deśika excells Rāmānuja in presenting a graphic account of the ascent to the abode of God in his *Paramapada-sopāna*, a work written in Maṇipravāḷa language (Sanskritised Tamil prose). A non-Vaiṣṇavite student of Philosophy may feel that these are imaginative statements meant to extoll the importance of Viṣṇu's abode. A question, therefore, arises as to whether these are facts or fiction created to meet certain theological needs.

The doctrine of *nitya-vibhūti* and the concept of *śuddha-sattva* which are accepted by Vaiṣṇava theology on the authority of scriptural and Smṛti texts including Pāñcarātra treatises provide sufficient justification for the admission of a higher divine abode with all its paraphernalia. According to the Viśiṣṭādvaita Vedānta, the ultimate Reality of Philosophy is a personal Supreme Being (*Puruṣottama*) which implies a concept of God with a body (*vigraha*). An impersonal God or an undifferentiated pure Being without any form (*nirākāra*) does not serve the purpose of meditation and worship by the devotees. Besides, such a transcendental Being cannot have relation to the universe and the individual souls. The *vigraha* or body assumed by the personal Supreme Being for the benefit of the universe and devotees, should be, as we have explained earlier, of spiritual character as otherwise a body constituted of five elements is subject to constant change and decay. Further the individual souls (*jīvas*) according to the Viśiṣṭādvaita Vedānta, are infinite in number and also eternal. Even in the state of *mokṣa,* they do not lose their individuality and remain ever in their true form as omniscient, blissful, pure, spiritual monads enjoying the full glory of God. Besides the released souls, Viśiṣṭādvaita admits on the authority of the scriptural texts the existence of a category of souls known as *nityas* or those who are eternally free. These souls, like the permanent attendants of God perform divine service as part of their duty without any selfish motive. According to the Upaniṣads the souls released from bondage can also assume bodies, if they so desire, to perform certain divine activities at the command of the Supreme Lord either in the higher regions or in the physical universe in the form of incarnated beings. Even the Supreme Being descends to the earth assuming the form of human or other living beings for the sole purpose of re-establishing *dharma,* to protect the *sādhus* and incidentally, punish the wicked persons. The bodies assumed by God during His incarnations cannot be considered material since they would be subject to destruction or decay. God is always a perfect Being untouched by birth, old age, death, *karma* and suffering (*apahatapāpma, vijaraḥ, vimṛtyuḥ*) as the Upaniṣads state. In view of these considerations, the doctrine of *nitya-vibhūti,* or the transcendent spiritual realm constituted of *śuddha-sattva* or spiritual substance stands justified.

The kind of descriptive account of the highest divine realm (*paramapada*) may be somewhat exaggerated. But it has a religious significance in so far as it stimulates in the *mumukṣu* a strong desire for the attainment of supreme spiritual goal (*mokṣa*). *Mokṣa* in Viśiṣṭādvaita is a positive concept. It refers not merely to the total liberation of a soul from bondage but it also leads to a blissful state of existence enjoying in full measure the glory of Brahman (*paripūrṇa-brahmānubhava*) leading to the *kaiṅkarya* or service to God. *Bhakti* or *prapatti* is enjoined as the means to attain that state. In order to enable an individual to develop a desire for *mokṣa* and promote the practice of *bhakti-yoga*, the Vaiṣṇava *ācāryas* seem to have presented a vivid descriptive account of the glory of God and His abode. Thus, in the introductory opening verse of *Vaikuṇṭha-Gadya*, Rāmānuja states: 'I am presenting the precious topic of *bhakti-yoga* as gathered from the works of Yāmuna'.[18] Commenting on this verse, Vedānta Deśika points out, that it is intended to instruct the disciples to contemplate the glory of Bhagavān as a goal in itself. Periyavācchān Piḷḷai adds further that the narration of the divine realm to be attained, the glory of its Lord to be experienced and the consequential performance of divine service to be performed therein are all intended to create an interest in the minds of the listeners.[19]

In order to be fair to the orthodox Vaiṣṇavites who take the description of *vaikuṇṭha* by Rāmānuja as factual, a different explanation is possible. God in Vaiṣṇavism is the Supreme Lord (*Sarveśvara*) endowed with *jñāna* (omniscience), *śakti* (omnipotence), *bala* (strength) and many other attributes par excellence.[20] If such a Supreme Being can create a wondrous physical universe of variegated character by mere *saṅkalpa* or will without any other aid. He should be able to create by His very *saṅkalpa* a spiritual universe with the best of all objects of pleasure (*bhogopakaraṇa*) for His own benefit. One need not, therefore, question the validity of the descriptive account of *paramapada*, the abode of God. Whether a critic accepts this explanation or not, the three *Gadyas* of Rāmānuja, both in terms of the beauty of their language and depth of thought, have deep aesthetic and emotional appeal for the devotees of Viṣṇu.

Immutable Character of Śuddha-sattva

In this connection a question is raised whether the entities made of *śuddha-sattva* in the transcendental universe are eternal and remain unchanged for all the time? The physical universe comes into existence at a point of time when it is evolved from the primordial cosmic matter and it also ceases to exist in its manifested form when it is dissolved at a particular point of time. It also undergoes modification continuously (*satata-vikriyā*), though the basic causal substance (*prakṛti*) is not totally destroyed. Evolution is only unfolding of what exists in an unmanifest form and dissolution is returning to the original state from the manifested form. This is a continuous and never ending process. The question may be raised whether such an evolution and consequent change apply to *nitya-vibhūti* also which in a sense is a universe, though spiritual in character?

The *nitya-vibhūti* is a *dravya*, one of the six metaphysical categories (*padārtha*) admitted in the Viśiṣṭādvaita system. *Dravya* is defined as that which has states or modification. *Nitya-vibhūti* is also eternal but as a substance, it has modifications. The abode of God (*paramapada*) made of pure *sāttvik* substance is also *nitya* (eternal) and so also all the mansions, pavillions, pleasure gardens created for His own use. The body assumed by *Īśvara* in the *paramapada* known as *para-Vāsudeva-vigraha* is also *nitya*.[21] But those bodies of *Īśvara* taken out of His own *saṅkalpa* (will) during the various manifestations and also those assumed by the individual souls residing there are not all eternal. Some of the products of *nitya-vibhūti* need not be permanent in character, though they are made out of *śuddha-sattva*. The permanent and non-permanent character of the products in *nitya-vibhūti* depends on the kind of *icchā* or *saṅkalpa* of *Īśvara*. His *saṅkalpa* is of two kinds: one known as *nityecchā*, that is the will of God to make certain things endure eternally, such as the individual souls; and *anityecchā*, that is, the will of God to create things for limited duration. The body (*vigraha*) that God has assumed in His own abode bedecked with ornaments and certain weapons, in which form He is known as *Para-Vāsudeva* is permanent like God's *svarūpa*, because of His *nitya-saṅkalpa*. On the other hand, the bodies assumed by God during His various incarnations right from *vyūha* manifestations to the *antaryāmi* form, last for the duration of that *avatāra* since He takes a *saṅkalpa* accordingly. In the same way, the bodies assumed by the released souls as well as *nitya-sūris* for performing certain specific functions in response to the desire of the Lord are not eternal because these are caused by the *saṅkalpa* of the individual souls for a limited duration.

This principle applies to the products found in *nitya-vibhūti*. Depending upon the will of God, they may be for a limited duration or forever.

Two objections may be raised against this view. The first objection is that according to the Vedānta, what exists in the beginning prior to creation is *sat* or Brahman only, as *Chāndogya Upaniṣad* states. If this position is accepted, where is the room for the existence of *nitya-vibhūti* besides *sat*? Secondly, we come across concepts such as evolution or modification of *śuddha-sattva* in the form of such products as mansions, pavillions, gardens, lakes etc. We also hear of the names of evolutes such as *ākāśa*, *prāṇa*, *indriyas*, *pañca-bhūtas*, attributes of elements etc. Since these concepts imply change or modification, how then can *śuddha-sattva* be regarded as *nitya*?

Regarding the first objection, Vedānta Deśika replies that the *nitya-vibhūti* falls outside the purview of the universe intended to be created by *Īśvara*.[22] As the scriptural texts emphatically refer to the existence of an eternal abode of Viṣṇu and also the existence of eternally free souls (*nityasūris*) in a supra-mundane realm, the Upaniṣadic statement in question is to be understood as referring to the creation of the physical universe that is contemplated by Brahman and not the region of *nitya-vibhūti*. This is evident from the fact that the word '*idam*' or (this) in the statement implies that the universe which is to be created by the will of God, is that one which was in an unmanifest state without name and form after dissolution and the same to be made manifest with name and form after creation. This interpretation is supported by another Upaniṣadic text which explicitly says: 'This universe was in an unmanifest state and the same will be made manifest.'[23] In this statement the universe referred to is the physical one and not the transcendental realm which does not need to be evolved out of *prakṛti*. If such an interpretation were not accepted, then the creation of universe would be inconceivable, because according to the theory of causality, what is brought into existence as an effect is from something which already exists in either a potential or subtle form. All the schools of Vedānta including the absolute monist such as Śaṁkara has to admit the presence of either *māyā* or *śakti* along with Brahman prior to the creation.

Regarding the second objection, it is argued that the kind of modification to which *śuddha-sattva* is subjected is different in nature from what obtains in the material world. In the latter case, the evolution which is a continuous process from one state to another and constant is due to the variation in the three *guṇas*—*sattva*, *rajas* and *tamas*—and they are not, therefore, of permanent character; whereas in the region of *nitya-vibhūti* the modification takes place from one spiritual substance to the other with the least amount of change and the products as such remain permanent without being subject to further modification or decay in accordance with the *saṅkalpa* of *Īśvara*. As already explained, *Īśvara* wills that the objects made out of *śuddha-sattva* should remain so for a limited time only, whereas if His *icchā* or *saṅkalpa* is that it should be of permanent nature, it will remain so. The concepts such as *ākāśa*, *śarīra* and *indriyas*, *gandha* (odour), *rasa* (taste), etc., may be the same in name only but what holds good in respect of the entities in physical universe does not apply to those existing in *nitya-vibhūti* since the latter are wholly spiritual or supra-normal constituted of pure *sattva*. Thus, for instance, the *ākāśa* of physical world is not the same as *ākāśa* of spiritual realm. The former, to use a technical word, is *prākṛta* or material made out of three *guṇas* of *prakṛti*, whereas the latter is *aprākṛta* or non-material (spiritual) made out of pure *sattva*. Similarly, the physical body of human and other living beings in the physical universe is *prākṛta* constituted of the five elements (*pañcabhūta*), while those assumed by the *Paramātman* and *jivātman* in *nitya-vibhūti* are *aprākṛta*. An idol of metal used for worship is a mere piece of metallic sculpture fit for display in a museum, whereas the same kind of idol when duly consecrated and installed after the prescribed religious rites becomes an *aprākṛta-vigraha*, a pure spiritual entity fit for worship. This is the significance of the concept of *śuddha-sattva* which constitutes an important theory of Viśiṣṭādvaita religion and which provides logical justification for several of its theological doctrines.

Notes

1. NS p. 235. *triguṇadravya-vyatiriktatvesati sattvavattvam.*
2. Ibid. *svayaṁprakāśatve sati sattvavattvam.*
   Two more definitions are offered but their implication is the same as the above.

3. See NS p. 247. *tat dvidhā, śuddham-aśuddhaṁ ca iti.*
4. See *Darśanodaya*, p. 208. *aiśvaryaṁ hi vibhūti padārthaḥ.*
5. Ibid.
6. *Puruṣa-sūkta* (Yajurveda recension) 16.
vedāhametaṁ puruṣaṁ mahāntamādityavarṇaṁ tamasastu pāre.
7. RV VII.100.5. *kṣayantamasya rajasaḥ parāke.*
See also *Taittirīya Brāhmaṇa* II.2.9.
8. *Taittirīya Brāhmaṇa*, II.8.9. *yo asyādhyakṣaḥ parame vyoman.*
See also TNUp 2. *tadakṣare parame vyoman.*
TUp I.ii. *yo veda nihitaṁ guhāyāṁ parame vyoman.*
9. RV I.22.20. *tadviṣṇoḥ paramaṁ padaṁ sadā paśyanti sūrayaḥ.*
See also VSa p. 163.
10. VP I.6.39. *ekāntinaḥ sadā brahmadhyāyino yoginaśca ye;*
teṣāṁ tu paramaṁ sthānaṁ yattat- paśyanti sūrayaḥ.
11. Mbh XVI.5.27. *divyaṁ sthānam-ajaraṁ ca aparameyaṁ.*
durvijñeyaṁ cāgamairgamyamādyam...
12. NS p. 235.
13. BG X.42. *viṣṭabhyāhamidaṁ kṛtsnam-ekāṁśena sthito jagat.*
See also VP I.9.53. *yasyāyutāyutāṁśāṁśe viśvaśaktiriyaṁ sthitā.*
14. See *Puruṣa-sūkta*, 3. *tripādasya amṛtaṁ divi.*
Here *tripād* means the eternal transcendental form of the Supreme Being (*amṛtaṁ rūpaṁ*).
15. See NS p. 235.
Also TMK III.62.
16. *Kauṣītakī* Up I.22.26.
17. ChUp VIII.8.5.
18. See *Vaikuṇṭha-Gadya*, *ādāya bhakti-yogākhyaṁ ratnaṁ sandarśayāmyaham.*
19. See GaVa p. 152.
20. See VP VI.7.70. *samastāḥ śaktayaścaitā nṛpa yatra pratiṣṭitāḥ.*
21. See *Pauṣkara Saṁhitā* I.38 (quoted by VD in RTS IV p. 82)
nitya-siddhe tadākāre tat-paratveca pauṣkara...
See also VP I.2.1. *Sadaikarūparūpāya.*
22. See TMK III.61. *sṛṣṭeḥ prāg-ekamevetyapi nigamavacaḥ*
sṛyakṣyamāṇa-vyapekṣam.
23. BrUp III.4.7.

12

VIṢṆU AND JĪVA

We have already presented the philosophic doctrine of *jīva* or the individual self as enunciated in the Viśiṣṭādvaita Vedānta based primarily on the teachings of the Upaniṣads, *Vedānta-sūtra* and *Bhagavad-gītā*.[1] According to the Vedānta, *jīva* is essentially an eternal spiritual entity (*ajaḍa-dravya*), whose essence is constituted of *jñāna* (knowledge). As *jñāna-svarūpa* it is sentient in character as contrasted to a material object and self-revealing (*svayaṁ-prakāśa*). It is the knower or the subject of knowledge (*jñātā*), the agent of action (*kartā*) and it experiences both pleasure and pain (*bhoktā*). It is monadic in character (*aṇu*), unlike *Īśvara*, who is all-pervasive (*vibhu*). It is distinct from *Īśvara* but is inseparably related to the latter like an attribute is inherent in the substance. In the words of the *Vedānta-sūtra*, *jīva* is an *aṁśa* (integral part) of *Paramātman*, the term *aṁśa* being understood in a technical sense as that which is always supported (*ādheya*), controlled (*niyāmya*) and dependent (*śeṣa*). Based on these philosophical teachings Vaiṣṇavism has developed a few distinctive theories of *jīva* which are of theological significance. We shall examine them in the present chapter.

Types of Jīva

Jīvas which are infinite in number are classified into three categories—*baddha*, *mukta* and *nitya*.[2] *Baddha* means one who is bound. These are the souls which are caught up in bondage in the form of continuous cycle of births and deaths from a beginningless time due to the influence of *karma*. *Karma* means merit and sin (*puṇya-pāpa*) caused by the good and bad deeds respectively of an individual in the past lives. As *karma* is variegated in character, the lives that the individual souls assume with physical bodies are of various types ranging from the highest celestial being such as Caturmukha-Brahmā to the lowest living organism such as a germ. As long as a soul is bound, it continues to pass through the numerous births and deaths until it is finally liberated from it by means of spiritual discipline (*sādhana*) as laid down by the scriptural texts.

Mukta means one who has become free from bondage. These are the individuals who as a result of some extraordinary merit become the object of God's grace and who consequently aspire to be liberated from bondage. For this purpose they pursue the path of spiritual discipline as enjoined by scripture and by the grace of God, they are released totally from the shackles of *kurma* and attain liberation (*mokṣa*) leading to the enjoyment of the bliss of God forever without a return to the mundane existence.

The *nityas* are the blessed souls who have never had bondage at any time and who ever exist as eternally free souls in the transcendental realm of God engaged in the divine service solely for the pleasure of God. The divine serpent, Ādiśeṣa, the divine bird, Garuḍa and the divine angel, Viśvakṣena are the examples of *nityas*. The basis for admission of such a category of souls in Vaiṣṇavism is the scriptural text. Thus *Puruṣa-sūkta* says: 'There (in the realm of God) deities in the name of *sādhyās* exist from time immemorial'.[3]

All the three types of *jīvas* are intrinsically of the same nature, viz., they are of the essence of knowledge (*jñāna*), purity (*amala*) and bliss (*ānanda*). They are also eternal, that is, they do not have any origin in the form of birth and destruction in the form of death. In respect of their intrinsic nature (*svarūpa*) the souls are neither celestial beings (*devas*), nor human beings, nor animals nor trees; but the distinction between one individual and the other is, however, made on the basis of the type of the physical bodies they assume on account of the *karma*.[4] What is common to all of them, besides the essential nature of *jñāna*, *ānanda* and *amalatva* is that they are subordinate to *Paramātman* (*paramātmanaḥ śeṣaḥ*).[5] The Vaiṣṇava theology has given added emphasis to this characteristic feature of *jīva* and developed the concept of *śeṣatva* with all its theological implications. In fact the term *jīva* is defined as that which is a spiritual entity, while dependent on God.[6] On the basis of this definition, *jīva* is distinguished from *Īśvara* who, though a sentient being (*cetana*) is all-pervasive (*vibhu*) and also the Supreme Lord (*śeṣī*); it is also differentiated from material entities as the latter, though dependent on God for their existence (*śeṣa*), are not sentient in character.

The Concept of Seṣatva

The concept of *śeṣatva* or subordination is not a novel idea introduced by Vaiṣṇava theology. It is in fact evolved out of the concept of *śarīra* or body referred to in the *Antaryāmi Brāhmaṇa* of *Bṛhadāraṇyaka Upaniṣad*. The famous passage in this Upaniṣad has described all the entities in the universe, both non-sentient as well as sentient, starting from the five physical elements and culminating in the soul as the *śarīra* of *Paramātman*. The term *śarīra* is defined by Rāmānuja,[7] in order to make it applicable to all the twenty-two entities enumerated in this Upaniṣadic passage, as that substance which is wholly supported and controlled by a spiritual Being and that which exists as entirely dependent on that Being. In other words, all sentient and non-sentient entities including the *jīvas* constitute the *śarīra* or body of *Īśvara* in the technical sense that the former are wholly dependent on the latter for their existence; they are completely controlled by *Īśvara* and they subserve the purpose of the Supreme Being. Three concepts are used to explain the organic relationship that exists between Brahman and the universe of *cit* and *acit*. These are: *ādhāra-ādheya* (the sustainer and the sustained), *niyantā-niyāmya* (the controller and the controlled) and the *śeṣi-śeṣa* (the Supreme Lord and the dependent). *Jīva* in relation to Paramātman is *ādheya, niyāmya* and *śeṣa*. It is out of this threefold character of the concept of *śarīra* that the Vaiṣṇava theology has formulated the theory of *jīva* as *nirupādhika-śeṣa*.

Implications of the Concept of Nirupādhika-śeṣatva

This concept has several implications. Ontologically, it signifies that the very existence of *jīva* is absolutely dependent on the *svarūpa* as well as the *saṅkalpa* (will) of *Īśvara*. In other words, it does not have an independent existence. This position is comparable to the epistemological theory of substance and attribute. An attribute, though distinct from substance, cannot exist by itself except as inherent in the substance. An independent existence of an attribute devoid of a substance is inconceivable since the two are inseparably related. In the same way *jīva* which is an *aṁśa* or an integral part of *Īśvara* derives its existence (*sattā*) from *Īśvara*. That it endures eternally (*sthiti*) is also due to the fact that *Īśvara* wills that it should be so. Further, all the activities of *jīva* (*pravṛtti*) are controlled by *Īśvara*. As the scriptural text says,[8] *Īśvara* who is immanent in the *jīvas* controls all their activities. This would mean that the capacity to think and act is given by *Īśvara*, as the *Vedānta-sūtra* asserts. It is in this sense that *jīva* is dependent on God.

From the theological standpoint, *śeṣatva* has a different significance. The fact that *jīva* is wholly dependent on *Īśvara* for its every existence implies that no one else other than *Īśvara* can be the supporter of *jīva* (*ananyādhāra*). In other words, *jīva* is supported exclusively by the Supreme Being. Further, such a dependence is not conditioned by any other factor. A servant, for instance, is dependent on his master but this kind of dependence is regulated by the former's service to the latter for monetary benefit. The servant does not depend always on the master since such a relation can be terminated at the choice of either at any time. In the case of the Supreme Lord and the *jīva*, it is not so. It is unconditional which means that the relationship between the two is a natural and permanent one, not being influenced by any external factors. This is the significance of the term *nirupādhika*.

From the teleological point of view, the question arises as to what is the sole purpose of the existence of *jīva*. If the *jīva* is absolutely dependent on God without any freedom of its own, what is the important purpose to be fulfilled by it? According to Vaiṣṇavism, the *jīva* is *parārtha*, that is, it exists not for its own sake but for the purpose of *Īśvara*. The entire universe consisting of both sentient souls and non-sentient matter is intended to provide joy to the Supreme Lord similar to an object of sport. A beautiful garden created by an individual does not derive any pleasure for itself but on the contrary, it provides delight to its owner. A sweet fruit in a tree does not get any benefit for itself but it causes joy to the person who eats it. In the same way, the souls as well as the material world are regarded as beneficial to the Lord. It follows from this view that an individual soul has no other goal to achieve than serving *Īśvara*. God-realization is the supreme goal or *summum bonum* of one's life. *Jīva* is, therefore, regarded as *ananya-prayojana* or the one who has no other goal to achieve than the Supreme Being. Since it is absolutely dependent on God, it does not also have any other refuge than the

Supreme Being. It is, therefore, considered as *ananya-śaraṇa* or one who has no refuge other than God. Elaborating the same idea, the *jīva* is described as *ananya-rakṣyatva* or one who has no protector other than God, with all its implications that at all times, at all places and in all ways the *jīva* is being protected by *Īśvara* (*sarvatra-sarvadā-sarvaprakāra-rakṣyatvaṁ*).[9]

Just as Īśvara is the only goal to be achieved by the *jīva*. He is also the sole means or *upāya* for attaining Him. In Vaiṣṇavism, God is regarded both as the goal (*upeya*) and the means (*upāya*). He is *upeya* because He alone is to be attained as the supreme goal of life (*puruṣārtha*). He serves as the *upāya* because the ultimate success in the observance of the spiritual discipline in the form of *upāsanā* (meditation) or *prapatti* (self-surrender) is achieved by His grace. In view of this the *jīva* is regarded as *ananyopāya* or the one not having any other means to adopt for *mokṣa* than God.

Jīva as Viṣṇu-dāsa

The Vaiṣṇava theology regards *jīva* as *Viṣṇu-dāsa* that is, an individual is a subservient person to Viṣṇu. Though this concept is not different from the concept of *paramātma-śeṣa* mentioned earlier, the former is more meaningful than the latter. The word *śeṣa* is a general term which is applicable to all that exists in the universe other than God. It covers both the sentient souls as well as non-sentient material objects. The word *dāsa* is more specific and applies exclusively to living human beings as well as celestial beings.[10] Only they have the capacity to worship God and seek redemption. In order to establish a closer religious communion with God they regard themselves as *dāsas* or servants of God. More important than this, by the submission of an individual with all humility to the Almighty, he would be able to shed the egoism. The feelings of I-ness (*ahaṁkāra*) and mineness (*mamakāra*) which are the natural mental traits caused by lack of philosophic wisdom, are the real enemies of human beings aspiring for spiritual progress. These are unethical traits causing obstruction to the realization of the existence of a higher Divine power. Hence all religions emphasise the need to forsake the egoistic tendencies and develop the ethical virtue of humility with faith in the Supreme Being in order to attain the higher spiritual goal. The concept of *dāsatva* as developed by Vaiṣṇavism is intended to promote the spiritual progress by way of realizing through philosophic knowledge that as individuals they are humble before God and that they should, therefore, submit themselves as subservient beings to the will of God. A person who develops this kind of mental attitude with the utmost faith and unshakable conviction that God is the sole protector and that he is a humble being like a doll in His hands does not have to be affraid of anything. Such a mental disposition gains added significance in the context of the self-surrender to God seeking liberation from bondage. The term *namaḥ* used in the esoteric *mantras*, which ordinarily means salutation, has the deeper implication of negating this kind of egoism (*na-mama*).

The Concept of Bhāgavata-śeṣatva

The concept of *dāsatva* has been further expanded by Vaiṣṇava theology to include the subordination not merely to Viṣṇu but also to His consort, as well as to His devotees known as *bhāgavatas*. The subordination of *jīva* to the divine couple is justified by the doctrine accepted by Vaiṣṇavism that *Śriyaḥ-patiḥ* or the Supreme Being as integrally related to *Śrī* constitutes the ultimate Reality. As *Lakṣmī Tantra* points out, Lord Viṣṇu as associated with Goddess Lakṣmī is the saviour (*rakṣaka*) for all.[11] The Kaṭha Śruti while interpreting the letters *a, u* and *ma* of the word 'oṃ' which is known as the *praṇava* or the mystic syllable, explicitly states that the letter *a* stands for Viṣṇu, the Sovereign of the universe, the letter *u* means Lakṣmī who was lifted by Viṣṇu when the former as a presiding deity of the universe was immersed in water; the letter *ma* implies that the *jīva* is a *dāsa* of the divine couple.[12]

The extension of *śeṣatva* of *jīva* to the *Bhāgavatas* is a distinctive contribution of Vaiṣṇavism. The subordination to Godly men does not merely mean that one should show respect to them but he should also render services to them (*kaiṅkarya*). The justification for the worship of the *Bhāgavatas* is provided by Vaiṣṇavism on the authority of the religious texts which enjoin the worship of God's devotees as a religious duty which will please God. Thus, says the *Pādmottara Purāṇa*: 'Of all the forms of worship the one offered to Viṣṇu is the best; but even superior to this is the worship offered to the devotees of Viṣṇu'.[13] The *Mahābhārata* states: 'I (*paramātman*) have great affection to those who are devoted to my devotees; therefore, one should offer service with devotion to them'.[14] There are several such statements in the *Mahābhārata* and the Purāṇas.[15] It is stated in the Gītā that the devotees of God are very dear to Him.[16] We can also find a philosophical justification for the worship of *Bhāgavatas*. According to the Viśiṣṭādvaita Vedānta, God is immanent as *antaryāmī* in all living beings and the worship offered to them ultimately goes to the God within. The *Vedānta-sūtra* and the statement in the *Mahābhārata* support this theory. According to the *Vedānta-sūtra*, the *upāsanā* enjoined on Indra is interpreted to mean *upāsanā* on the *Paramātman* who is the *antarātmā* of Indra and not Indra's soul. The *Mahābhārata* says: 'Those who worship the manes, the *devatas*, the Brāhmaṇas and the fire (*agni*) worship only *Viṣṇu* who is the *antarātmā* of all these.'[17] Taking all these facts into consideration, Vaiṣṇavism maintains that the *jīva* is a *dāsa* to the devotees of Bhagavān Viṣṇu (*bhāgavata-śeṣa*). The Vaiṣṇava treatises as well as the hymns of Āḻvārs have extolled the service to Bhāgavatas as the greatest religious act of a Vaiṣṇava. To emphasise its importance, they even go to the extent of commending that a true Vaiṣṇava should accord the highest respect and devotion even to the person of the lowest caste as long as he is a true devotee of Viṣṇu. We will discuss the subject of *Bhāgavata-kaiṅkarya* or service to Bhāgavatas in a later chapter.

Freedom of the Soul

In this connection we may examine an important ethical issue relating to the freedom of the soul. If an individual is absolutely dependent on God and if all his mental as well as physical activities are controlled by the latter, does he have any freedom at all to act on his own? If not, is he then responsible for the good or bad deeds he performs? The concept of *nirupādhika-śeṣatva* as conceived by Vaiṣṇavism gives the impression that the *jīva* is almost similar to a lump of earth without any freedom of its own. In that case it would not be subject to the scriptural commands requiring observance and non-observance of certain acts. If an individual is not subject to the moral dictates of the *śāstra*, he would not also be subject to *karma* in the form of merit and sin, which cause the bondage involving the cycle of births and deaths. Then there would be no need to seek redemption of sins from God for obtaining final liberation. We have examined this issue in the chapter on the 'Nature of Individual Self' and given an explanation as provided by the Vedānta. We will consider here the answer offered by Vedānta Deśika from the theological point of view.[18] The dependence of *jīva* on *Paramātman* (*pāratantrya*) does not affect the freedom of an individual to respond to the dictates of the sacred texts. In fact, it is helpful to him to obey the laws. If the individual self enjoyed unchecked freedom like *Īśvara*, he would not be subject to any external commands. If he were a non-sentient material object like a piece of stone, the commands have no meaning. If he were a sentient being like an animal, he would not be fit to obey the orders, because of the incapacity to understand the ethical laws. Fortunately, *jīva* is a human being endowed with the mental capacity to think and also the physical ability to function. As the Upaniṣads and the *Vedānta-sūtra* point out, an individual self is the knower (*jñātā*), the doer (*kartā*) and the enjoyer (*bhoktā*). The ethical codes laid down by the sacred texts are meaningful only in his case. Though an individual may be dependent on *Īśvara,* he has freedom to respond to the commands of the sacred texts since he has been gifted by God with the intellectual and physical powers. In other words, God has granted to every individual the innate capacity to think (*citśakti*) and the physical ability to function (*pravṛtti-śakti*) with the freedom to follow His commands. Nevertheless, the *jīva* is a dependent being (*paratantra*) only in the sense that the capacity to think and act is derived from the unchecked freedom of the Supreme Lord. As stated in the *Vedānta-sūtra*, the *kartṛatva* or doership of *jīva* is caused by *Paramātman* because it is stated so in the Śruti and Smṛti texts.[19] As *kartā* or the agent of action, the *jīva* is also *bhoktā* or the enjoyer of the result of action in accordance with one's own deeds of the past lives. As explained earlier, the *jīva* is *kartā* in the sense that it is the substrate (*āśraya*) for effort (*kṛti*). Effort is caused by a desire to do an act. It is, therefore, a mental modification or an *avasthā* of *jñāna*. It is not to be confused with the actual physical activity which follows subsequent to the desire to do an act. As the *jīva* is only the *āśraya* for the *kṛti*, the change involved in the physical activity does not affect its *svarūpa.* The same explanation holds good for *jīva* being the *bhoktā. Bhoga* is an experience in the form of pleasure and pain, which are different states of *jñāna.* As the *jiva* is an *āśraya* for such states of experience, it is regarded as *bhoktā* or enjoyer of pleasure and pain.

The fact that the action of *jīva* is controlled by *Paramātman* does not affect the individual freedom. If *jīva* had no freedom to act, the scriptural injunctions enjoining duties to be performed by the individual will have no significance. This is not so. As we have explained in an earlier chapter, a distinction is drawn between the initial action of an individual and his subsequent activity. In all human effort, the individual initially wills to do a thing. To this extent he is free to do what he desires. Based on this initial action, the subsequent activity which follows it is approved by *Īśvara*. By according such an approval, Īśvara prompts the individual to proceed further (*paramātmā tadanumatidānena pravartayati*).[20] If it were not so, the Vedic injunctions in this regard would become meaningless. Even though *Īśvara* gives his approval to the activity initiated by an individual, He does not become the *kartā* or the doer. He is only a *kārayitā* or one who causes the *jīva* to act.[21] The real *kartā* is the individual concerned. It is in this sense that *Īśvara* is considered to be the controller of human action and to this extent the human freedom of an individual, though he is *paratantra*, is not affected.[22]

The *śeṣatva* or *dāsatva* is a permanent characteristic of the *jīva*. If this be so, it would follow that the character of subordination endures even in the state of *mokṣa*. But according to the scriptural texts, when the *jīva* becomes totally liberated from *karma*, it becomes a free individual (*svatantra*) and also omniscient. The *jīva* in the state of *mokṣa* attains the status of equality with *Īśvara*, according to the *Muṇḍaka Upaniṣad*.[23] How then the *jīva* which by its very *svarūpa* is a dependent being is considered equal to *Īśvara* who, on the contrary, enjoys supreme freedom? Another question which is raised in this connection is: how such a dependent *jīva* can be regarded as *svatantra* or a free soul in the state of *mokṣa*, as Śruti text claims?[24]

Regarding the first question, Vedānta Deśika answers that the Upaniṣadic text which speaks of equality between the *muktātmā* (the liberated soul) and *Īśvara* is in respect of the blissful experience (*bhogamātra*) as *Vedānta-sūtra* states.[25] There is a fundamental difference between *jīva* and *Īśvara*. The latter is the cause of the universe (*jagat-kāraṇa*), which is the unique characteristic of *Īśvara*, whereas the former does not have such a power to create the universe. In a weighing scale a piece of gold and a lump of poisonous substance may be found to be of the same weight but the two are not equal in every other way. In the same manner, the *śeṣatva* of *jīva* is not affected even in the state of *mokṣa*, though it becomes equal to *Īśvara* in respect of *jñāna* and *ānanda*. A fuller discussion of the equality of *jīva* with *Paramātman* is given in the chapter on the Nature of *mokṣa*.

Regarding the second question, it is explained that *jīva* is the body (*śarīra*) or *aṁśa* of *Paramātman* in a technical sense as established by the *Antaryāmi Brāhmaṇa*. As a *śarīra* of *Paramātman*, *jīva* continues to be dependent on *Paramātman* even in the state of *mokṣa*. The intrinsic nature of *jīva* as *paratantra* does not change with the attainment of liberation. The change is only in respect of the physical body caused by *karma* which ceases to exist. *Jīva* is free only in the sense that it is no more subject to *karma*. *Dāsatva* or subordination caused by the influence of *karma* leads to suffering and it is undesirable. But *dāsatva* to *Īśvara* arising as a result of the very *svarūpa* of *jīva* does not cause any affliction and in fact it is most desirable in so far as *jīva* has freedom to do any kind of divine service that it chooses in accordance with the wishes of the Lord.[26] Such a *dāsatva* in the state of *mokṣa* does not conflict with the freedom that the soul enjoys in the state of *mokṣa* to do divine service.

Bondage of the Soul and its Removal

We have so far discussed one important theological concept of *jīva* as *nirupādhikaśeṣa* of *Īśvara* with all its implications. We shall now examine another aspect of *jīva* referring to its intrinsic capability of attaining the blissful state of existence enjoying the *Brahmānanda* and consequently the rendering of divine service in the state of *mokṣa*. This is known as *niratiśayānanda-yogyatva* and *aśeṣa-kaiṅkaryaikaratitva*. It means that *jīva* has the intrinsic capacity to experience divine bliss par excellence and to perform all divine service. Both these are important concepts in Vaiṣṇava theology since they justify the possibility of bondage and the need of its removal. The *jīva*, as we have already explained, by virtue of its intrinsic character is essentially of the nature of knowledge, bliss and purity. The religious literature compares it to the precious gem (*kaustubha*) worn by Viṣṇu on his chest, implying that it is sacred and dearest to God. It is described variously as a boy (*kumāra*), as a son (*putra*), as a disciple (*śiṣya*), as a dependent (*śeṣa*) and as the servant (*dāsa*) of God. It should have been on par with the eternally free souls (*nityasūris*) enjoying the divine glory and perform service to God in the transcendental realm. How then such a *jīva* deserving to enjoy the godly status remains a fallen individual devoid of the supreme happiness and caught up in the cycle of numerous births and deaths? The answer to this question is that all this is due to the sheer ignorance of its true nature. The ignorance which is termed as *avidyā* refers to the mistaking of non-self (the physical body) as self (*anātmani ātmabuddhiḥ*) and the delusion of oneself as a free individual (*svantrātmabhrama*) thereby denying the existence of a higher power that controls all our destiny. The origin of *avidyā* is inexplicable and it is, therefore, treated as beginningless (*anādi*). In other words, the association of *avidyā* with *jīva* does not occur at any particular point of time and hence it is regarded as beginningless like the continuous flow of the water in a stream. This is similar to the analogy of seed and sprout. Whether seed came first or the sprout came first is inexplicable. The process goes on indefinitely from time immemorial.

Is it possible at all that such a *jīva* which is intrinsically pure should be subjected to ignorance causing the deprivation from attaining its true status? The answer is given in the affirmative. This point is explained on the analogy of a young prince who was lost in the jungle while the king was on a hunting errand. The child who was picked up by a hunter and brought up in a different environment adopted the mode of life of the hunter and thereby got deprived of the knowledge of his right to ascend the throne. In the same way, the *jīva* too out of ignorance of its true nature stands denied of its divine status.

Though bondage caused by *avidyā* has no beginning, it has an end. There is an escape from this miserable condition of *jīva*, as there is an escape for the prince from the life of the hunter. In the case of the prince, some sages living in the jungle accidentally recognise the boy by his external appearance as one belonging to the royal family and taking pity on him, endeavour to get him out of this situation by training him in such appropriate manner as to make the boy realize his true nature and eventually arrange to get him reunited with the king. In the case of the individual *jīva*, who is caught up in bondage, some pious men chance to come across him and through his parents, impart to him the knowledge of the true nature of the self thereby creating an interest in the religious pursuits. Such an individual in whom a general interest in religion is kindled, will secure a qualified preceptor through whom he will be able to acquire philosophic knowledge leading to the observance of the prescribed spiritual discipline for attaining *mokṣa*. The acquisition of an *ācārya* or preceptor is not accidental. It happens as a result of *sukṛta* or merit acquired by the individual in some previous birth and also by the grace of God. God showers his grace on a particular individual on the basis of the specific merit acquired by that person, as otherwise He would be open to the criticism of partiality. There are six factors which cause the acquisition of a right preceptor by an individual. These are: the natural friendly disposition of God to save mankind; the merit acquired by an individual accidentally; on the basis of such a merit, the showering of God's grace on him; the right religious attitude of a person without any hatred towards God and His glory; and lastly the accidental acquaintance with pious Godly men and dialogue with them.[27] This is the manner in which an individual soul which is caught up in the ocean of bondage from time immemorial gets an opportunity to escape from it and attain the realm of God to enjoy the eternal unsurpassable happiness.

Only such individuals as have acquired the right philosophic knowledge and developed a detachment towards the worldly pleasures which are of transient character and consequently a yearning for the attainment of God are regarded as *mumukṣus*. The word *mumukṣu* means one who desires to be liberated from bondage. Such a desire does not spring in everybody. It comes to those who, after proper study and understanding of the Vedānta have realized that life in this universe is full of suffering as *Viṣṇu Purāṇa* points out.[28] Even the celestial happiness such as the life in *svarga* is of transitory character as compared to the bliss in the realm of God. The so-called worldly pleasures are short-lived, unstable, preceded by physical suffering, mixed with grief, lead to grief, cause further delusion and stand opposed to the happiness to be derived by meditation on Godhead.[29] With a fuller realization of these facts a *mumukṣu* should develop a sense of total detachment from all worldly things and devotion to God.[30] This is known as *vairāgya*. Only such an individual as developes the *vairāgya* is fully qualified to seek *mokṣa* and he is the genuine *mumukṣu*.

Obstacles for Attainment of Supreme Goal

It may be relevant to take note of the factors which constitute the obstacles for the attainment of the highest spiritual goal (*prāpti-virodhi*) as outlined in the Vaiṣṇava treatises. The major obstacles is the combination of *avidyā, karma* and *vāsanā*. *Avidyā* in this context, as already explained, stands for ignorance of the true nature of the self. It refers to the mistaking of the physical body for self and thinking oneself as independent (*svatantra*) without being aware of one's absolute dependence on *Īśvara*. *Karma* refers to merit (*puṇya*) and sin (*pāpa*). The performance of a good deed causes *puṇya* and the performance of what is prohibited by sacred text leads to *pāpa*. *Puṇya* and *pāpa* in Vaiṣṇavism refer to the pleasure and displeasure of God (*anugraha* and *nigraha*). The word *vāsanā* means the latent impression generated both by *karma* as well as *avidyā*. That is, by doing a deed, good or bad, one develops an innate tendency to do the same thing again and again. *Avidyā* or ignorance causes attachment to the body. Thus, *vāsanā* prompts a person to do the deeds, good and bad, causing *puṇya* and *pāpa* respectively. These in turn generate ignorance (*avidyā*). As a result of ignorance, one again indulges in deeds prohibited and thereby intensify the sins. This in turn, will cause bondage in the form of being born again. In this way, it goes on like a wheel with chain reactions. The primary factor which is responsible for this kind of involvement in the continuous bondage is the displeasure of God (*nigraha*) incurred continually from time immemorial by disobedience of God's commands.[31] As a punishment for it, God causes the soul to be associated with the physical body, mind and sense organs and makes the individual soul become a slave to the body and sense organs. The punishment imposed by God may take different forms depending upon the magnitude of the sin. A soul may take birth in lower forms of life such as animals, insects etc., in which case there is absolutely no chance of acquiring any kind of philosophic knowledge. Even if one were lucky to get a birth as a human being it is possible that he is misled by the wrong teachings of the atheists. If one can escape it, he may be influenced by wrong knowledge which like a magical curtain hides the true nature of Reality and causes greater attachment to worldly pleasures. By repeatedly committing religious offences, one is dragged into the cycle of births and deaths. It is possible for some individuals to acquire Vedic knowledge but they may be tempted to aspire for celestial happiness in the form of *svarga* by worshipping the lower deities and thereby deprive themselves of the opportunity of attaining *mokṣa*. Even those who undertake meditation (*upāsanā*) may not achieve the supreme spiritual goal. *Upāsanā* is of different kinds, depending on the type of object to be meditated. A person may meditate on *prakṛti* (cosmic matter), or the lower deities such as Indra or on one's own self. Though all such *upāsanās* give certain types of higher spiritual powers, they do not lead to *mokṣa*. Even the state of *kaivalya* which is the goal of meditation on the self, falls short of *mokṣa*.[32] Thus, the *bhagavan-nigraha* or the displeasure of God incurred by the repeated commitment of sins can prevent a person from achieving the liberation from bondage (*mokṣa*). Only the most fortunate soul which comes under the purview of *bhagavadanugraha* or the grace of God is capable of achieving it. It is difficult to find out who is such a fortunate person to be blessed or who is the unfortunate one not to be blessed. The only remedy to overcome the greatest obstacle in the way of attaining *mokṣa* is, as Rāmānuja has emphatically stated, to seek the refuge or protection of Viṣṇu, the Supreme Deity by means of total self-surrender (*tasya ca vaśīkaraṇaṁ tat śaraṇāgatireva*).[33] This is the crux of the Vaiṣṇava religion. We shall discuss this theory in detail in the subsequent chapter.

Notes

1. See Chapter 3.
2. Piḷḷailokācārya adds two more categories of souls: *mumukṣus* or souls which desire liberation and *kevalas* or the souls that are interested in attaining the state of *kaivalya*, a place where without rebirth they enjoy the bliss of the individual self.
   See *Arthapañcakam*, pp. 41-42.
3. *Puruṣa-sūkta* (Yajurveda recension), 18.
   te ha nākaṁ mahimānaḥsacante;
   yatra pūrve sādhyāḥ santi devāḥ.

The words *sādhyāḥ devāḥ* are interpreted as *nitya-sūris* who already exist eternally in the *nāka* (the eternal abode of God).
See also RV I.22.20. *tad viṣṇoḥ paramaṁ padaṁ sadā paśyanti surayaḥ.*
In this hymn the word *sūrayaḥ* is taken to mean the eternally existent souls (*nitya-sūris*).
See Chapter 1 p. 9.

4. See VP II.13.98. *pumānna devo na naro na paśuḥ na ca pādapaḥ. śarīrākṛtibhedāstu bhūpaite karmayonayaḥ.*
5. See RTS I. *jñānānandamayastu ātmā śeṣohi paramātmanaḥ.*
6. Ibid. V. p. 86. *svataḥ śeṣatve sati cetanatvam.*
7. RB II.1.9.
   See Chapter 2, p. 60.
8. *Taittirīya Āraṇyaka*, III.11.21. *antaḥ praviṣṭaḥ śāstā janānāṁ sarvātmā.*
   See also BG XVIII.61.
   īśvaras-sarvabhūtānāṁ hṛd-deśe arjuna tiṣṭati;
   bhrāmayan sarvabhūtāni yantrārūḍhāni māyayā.
9. RTS XXVII p. 208.
10. See *Īśvara Saṁhitā* (quoted by VD in RTS). *dāsabhūtāḥ svatas-sarvehyātmānaḥ paramātmanaḥ.*
11. LT XXVIII.14. *lakṣmyāsaha hṛṣīkeṣo devyā kāruṇya-rūpayā; rakṣakaḥ sarvasiddhānte vedānteṣu ca gīyate.*
12. *Kaṭha Śruti* (referred to in Vaiṣṇava treatises but is not extant).
    akāreṇa ucyate viṣṇuḥ sarvalokeśvaro hariḥ;
    udhṛtā viṣṇunā lakṣmīḥ ukāreṇocyate tathā.
    makārastu tayoḥ dāsaḥ iti praṇava lakṣaṇam.
13. *Pādmottara Purāṇa*, XXIX.81. *ārādhanānāṁ sarveṣāṁ viṣṇorārādhanaṁ param; tasmāt parataraṁ proktaṁ tadīyārādhanaṁ param.*
14. Mbh XIV.116.23. *mama madbhakta-bhakteṣu prītirabhyadhikā bhavet; tasmāt madbhaktabhaktāśca pūjanīyā viśeṣataḥ.*
15. See RTS XVI pp. 126-27.
16. BG VIII.18. *sa ca mama priyaḥ.*
17. Mbh XII.355.24. *ye yajanti pitṛn devān brāhmaṇān sahutāśanān; sarvabhūtāntarātmanaṁ viṣṇumeva yajanti te.*
18. See *Virodha-parihāra*, pp. 372-73.
19. VS II.3.40. *parāttu tat-śruteḥ.*
20. RB II.3.41.
21. See RTS XXIX p. 255.
22. See FVV pp. 201-02 for further details on this subject.
23. See MUp 3.1.3. *nirañjanaḥ paramaṁ sāmyamupaiti.*
24. ChUp VII.25.2. *sa svarād bhavati.*
25. VS IV.4.21. *bhogamātra sāmyāt.*
26. See SD Vāda 37. *ātmatattvavidāṁ puṁsāṁ yaddāsyaṁ lāsyakāraṇam.*
27. See RTS I. *īśvarasya ca sauhārdaṁ yadṛcchāsukṛtaṁ tathā; viṣṇoḥ katākṣam-adveṣam-ābhimukhyaṁ ca sātvikaiḥ. saṁbhāṣaṇaṁ ṣadetānihyācārya-prāptihetavaḥ.*
28. VP I.17.69. *sarvaṁ duḥkhamayaṁ jagat.*

29. See RTS VII p.102 All sensual pleasure are subjected to these seven limitations: *alpatva, asthiratva, duḥkha-mūlatva, dūḥka-miśratva, duḥkhodarkatva, viparitābhimānatva* and *svābhāvikānanda-viruddhatva.*
30. Ibid. (quoted from *Bārhaspatya Smṛti*).
paramātmani yo rakto virakto aparamātmani.
31. See RTS IV p. 83.
32. See Chapter 5 fn. 29 p. 119.
33. RB I.4.1.
See also BG XVIII.62 *tameva śaraṇaṁ gaccha.*

13

PRAPATTI AS MEANS OF ATTAINMENT OF VIṢṆU

Prapatti as a direct means (*upāya*) to attain *mokṣa* is a distinctive doctrine of the Vaiṣṇava theology. According to the Viśiṣṭādvaita Vedānta, *bhakti-yoga* and *prapatti-yoga* are the two important *sādhanas* (means) for achieving the supreme spiritual goal (*parama-puruṣārtha*). While the Upaniṣads have laid more emphasis on *upāsanā*, which is the same as *bhakti-yoga*, the Vaiṣṇava treatises have accorded greater prominence to *prapatti*. Both have been sanctioned by the Śruti and Smṛti texts and they have been advocated as alternative means for *mokṣa* intended for two different categories of individuals with different capacities and conditions of eligibility. As explained in an earlier chapter, *bhakti-yoga* is a rigorous discipline and is restricted to certain class of individuals. On the other hand, *prapatti* is recommended as an easier path intended for all without any restriction of caste, creed and status of individuals. In view of this, the Vaiṣṇava *ācāryas* right from the time of Nāthamuni have given preference to *prapatti* and advocated it as the easier means of *mokṣa*. *Prapatti* has, therefore, assumed significance in Vaiṣṇavism. We have dealt with *bhakti-yoga* in the Philosophy section and we shall now examine the doctrine of *prapatti*.

Meaning of the Term Prapatti

The term *prapatti* is derived from the root words *pra-pad*; *pad* means to move and *pra* implies in the best manner. In the context of *upāya*, the term implies total self-surrender to God as the sole refuge. A more appropriate Sanskrit term for *prapatti* is *ātma-nikṣepa* or *bharanyāsa*, that is, to place the burden of the protection of the self in the care of God. It is also known as *śaraṇāgati*, or seeking God as the sole refuge.

Antiquity of the Doctrine

Before we go into the details of the nature of *prapatti*, we should take note of the fact that this doctrine is very old having its roots in the Vedas. There are numerous statements in the Ṛgveda referring to the basic principle of *śaraṇāgati*, viz., that an individual pleading his inability to achieve a desired object seeks with fervent prayer the help of a divine power. The famous *Ṛk* hymn addressed to *Agni*[1] which is reiterated in the *Īśāvāsyopaniṣad* states: 'O Agni, lead us along the auspicious path to prosperity, O God, who knowest the means of attainment, remove all the obstacles coming in our way; we shall offer unto Thee salutation with the expression of *namaḥ*.' According to the interpretation of Vedānta Deśika, *Agni* in the hymn refers to the Supreme Being as its *antarātmā* and the word *namaḥ* signifies the act of self-surrender to God.[2] Another hymn states explicitly that the person who offers prayer with the expression of *namaḥ* (implying self-surrender) is to be regarded as one who has performed a good sacrifice (*sodhvaraḥ*) almost equivalent to the formal sacrifice done in the consecrated fire by offering the faggots (*samit*) along with the recitation of the *mantras*.[3] The interpretation of this hymn in favour of self-surrender (*ātmanyāsa*) is upheld by the *Ahirbhudhnya Saṁhitā*.[4] The Vedic seers were fully conscious of the fact that none other than the Divine Being is capable of protecting man from the ocean of bondage.[5] God is regarded as a dear friend and near relative of all human beings.[6] He is compared to the non-leaky boat that can safely take persons from one shore to the other, through the turbulent waters of life.[7] The Vedic seers have, therefore, sought in all their prayers the grace of God for achieving their desired objectives.

The Upaniṣads have given expression in clearer terms to *prapatti* as a means of *mokṣa*. Thus, the *Śvetāśvatara Upaniṣad* says: 'I as an aspirant of *mokṣa* seek refuge in that effulgent God who creates Brahmā first and who verily delivers to him the Vedas, etc.'[8] The *Taittirīya Nārāyaṇa Upaniṣad* extolls *nyāsa* (*prapatti*) and enjoins that the self is to be surrendered to Brahman with the *praṇava mantra*.[9] The *Kaṭhavallī Śruti* which is not extant but frequently referred to by Vedānta Deśika and other Vaiṣṇava *ācāryas*, contains the secret *mantra* known as *dvaya* which enunciates the essence of *śaraṇāgati* (self-surrender).[10]

The Itihāsas, Purāṇas and the Pāñcarātra Saṁhitās uphold the observance of *śaraṇāgati* as the direct means of attaining not only *mokṣa* but whatever an individual desires. The *Rāmāyaṇa* is regarded by the Vaiṣṇava *ācāryas* as a *Śaraṇāgati Śāstra* or a sacred work expounding the *śaraṇāgati-dharma.* The *śaraṇāgati* observed by Vibhīṣaṇa, seeking the refuge of Rāma is cited as a classic illustration of *prapatti.* In the *Mahābhārata* and *Bhāgavata Purāṇa* there are several episodes glorifying *śaraṇāgati.* In the *Bhagavad-gītā* which is part of the *Mahābhārata*, Lord Kṛṣṇa enjoins Arjuna to observe *śaraṇāgati* as a last resort for attaining God, if other harder paths of yoga such as *bhakti-yoga* is found difficult. The verse on this subject which appears in the concluding portion of the *Gītā* is upheld as an important *mantra* (*carama-śloka*)[11] by the Vaiṣṇavas enunciating *prapatti* as an alternative means to *mokṣa.* The *Lakṣmī Tantra* and the *Ahirbhudhnya Saṁhitā*, two older and important Pāñcarātra treatises extensively deal with the various aspects of *prapatti.* In fact, Vedānta Deśika and other Vaiṣṇava *ācāryas* have drawn mostly from these two works while expounding the doctrine of *śaraṇāgati.* The hymns of the Āḷvārs have emphasised the importance of *prapatti.* Nammāḻvār, who is regarded as the leader of *prapannas* (*prapanna-jana-kūṭhstha*) has set an example by himself performing *prapatti* at the feet of Lord Śrīnivāsa, the presiding deity at Tirumala Hills. Both Yāmuna, in his *Stotraratna* and Rāmānuja in his *Śaraṇāgati-gadya* have done the same thing and shown to the Vaiṣṇavas the need and importance of *śaraṇāgati* as a direct means to *mokṣa.* Vedānta Deśika, the illustrious follower of Rāmānuja has contributed several independent works written both in Sanskrit and Maṇipravāḷa language, expounding in great detail, the various feature of *śaraṇāgati* and defended it against all possible criticisms in his *Nikṣeparakṣā* and *Rahasyatrayasāra.* Piḷḷailokācārya, the leader of the Tenkalai sect of Śrīvaiṣṇavas and his predecessor, Periyavācchān Piḷḷai have also upheld the doctrine of *prapatti* as taught by Yāmuna and Rāmānuja. Thus, the observance of *prapatti* as a means to attain *mokṣa* or any other desired goal is a Vedic practice and has been in vogue from ancient times. Right up to the time of Nāthamuni, it was preserved as a secret doctrine and its knowledge was imparted orally by the qualified preceptors to the deserving pupils. It was only in the post-

Rāmānuja period that the doctrine was expounded with all its details in written works for the benefit of future generations.

Bhakti versus Prapatti

We have explained in an earlier chapter how an individual is caught up in the ocean of bondage and how he develops a desire to escape from it. Such an individual is called *mumukṣu* or the one who desires to attain *mokṣa*. The only way to get over the major obstacle standing in the way of liberation is to seek the grace of God by self-surrender, as the *Gītā* says.[12] Though an effort is needed to achieve a goal, the grace of God is far more important for success in one's effort. There are two ways by which the grace of God may be secured. One is the loving meditation on God (*bhakti*) and the other is self-surrender to Him (*śaraṇāgati*). Thus, it is stated: 'It is only either by means of intense *bhakti* or by means of *prapatti* that it is possible to attain God.'[13] Keeping this in mind Vedānta Deśika also asserts that *bhakti-yoga* and *prapatti* are the two important means to secure the grace of God.[14] The implication of all these statements is that *bhakti* and *prapatti* observed by an individual do not by themselves give salvation. On the other hand, they serve the purpose of securing the grace of God which actually causes the final liberation. The philosophy of *sādhana* is based on this twin principle of divine grace and human endeavour. We shall discuss this point later.

Though *bhakti-yoga* and *prapatti* are laid down as two alternative means for attaining God, Vaiṣṇavism has accorded greater importance to *prapatti*. According to both Rāmānuja and Vedānta Deśika, it is not possible to attain *mokṣa* without observing *prapatti* in some form or the other.[15] The implication of it is that even those who resort to *bhakti-yoga* as means to *mokṣa*, have to observe *prapatti* as a subsidiary (*aṅga*) to *bhakti-yoga*. The purpose of the observance of *prapatti* in their case is to seek the grace of God in order to overcome the obstacles standing in the way of commencement of *bhakti-yoga* and also for successful completion of it. In the case of those who resort to the path of *prapatti* as direct means to *mokṣa*, *prapatti* can secure the result through the grace of God without the need to follow *bhakti-yoga*. In view of this, Vedānta Deśika classifies *prapatti* into two categories: *sadvāraka-prapatti*, that is *prapatti* as a subsidiary means to *bhakti-yoga* and *advāraka-prapatti*, that is, *prapatti* serving as a direct means to *mokṣa*. They are also called *aṅga-prapatti* in the sense that *prapatti* is the subsidiary means and *aṅgi-prapatti* or *prapatti* as the principal means. All the aspirants for *mokṣa* are in a broad sense *prapannas* or the individuals resorting to self-surrender. Both are also *bhaktas* or devotees of God in a broad sense, because both have to develop devotion to God in order to secure His grace.[16] *Bhakti* is a general term which means love towards God (*mahaṇīyaviṣye prītiḥ*). An individual who wishes to undertake *prapatti* should be deeply devoted to God. Even after he has observed it, he needs *bhakti* to perform the divine service (*kaiṅkarya*) which is a moral duty for a *prapanna*.

Though *bhakti* and *prapatti* are interrelated, they are two distinct but alternative *upāyas* for *mokṣa*. This is justified on the basis of the principle followed in the Vedānta in connection with the different *vidyās* or kinds of meditation. The Upaniṣads speak of several types of *upāsanās* such as *dahara-vidyā*, *sad-vidyā*, *madhu-vidyā*, *vaiśvānara-vidyā* etc. They are called by different names because of the difference in the description of the object of contemplation, viz., Brahman in terms of its different attributes. Each *vidyā* is, therefore, distinct from the other.[17] However, the goal to be achieved in all these *upāsanās* is the same, viz., attainment of Brahman. In view of this, the *Vedānta-sūtra* states that various *vidyās* are alternative means to *mokṣa* to be adopted by the individuals in accordance with their mental disposition and capacity.[18] According to the author of the *Śrutaprakāśikā* and also Vedānta Deśika, the thirty-two *vidyas* prescribed by the Upaniṣads include *nyāsa-vidyā* which is the same as *prapatti* or *bharanyāsa*.[19] *Prapatti* is, therefore, distinct from *bhakti-yoga* and the two are laid down as alternative means to *mokṣa* since they aim to achieve the same goal.

The most important point of difference between the two *upāyas* (means) is that *bhakti-yoga* is a rigorous discipline, whereas *prapatti* is the easiest method to attain salvation. Would it be appropriate to regard a rigorous discipline and an easy method as alternatives (*vikalpa*) for the same goal? The answer is offered in the affirmative on the ground that they are prescribed for two different categories of individuals with different eligibility requirements (*adhikāri-bheda*). A person who takes recourse to *bhakti* should acquire philosophic knowledge and should go through the discipline of *karma-yoga* and *jñāna-yoga* leading to the direct intution of self (*ātmāvalokana*). *Karma-yoga* consists in the strict observance of the religious rituals prescribed by the sacred texts purely for divine pleasure without any selfish motive. *Jñāna-yoga* refers to constant meditation on the individual self until it leads to the direct vision of the self. After successful completion of *jñāna-yoga*, the person should embark on *bhakti-yoga*. *Bhakti-yoga* involves unceasing meditation on God until the person is able to perfect it to the extent of reaching a stage of God-realization similar to the perceptual vision of God.[20] This is to be practised not only for the life time but to be continued in a subsequent life until all the obstacles in the form of *prārabdha-karma* which stands in the way is totally eradicated leading to the final goal. This implies that the aspirant should have the patience to brook delay. The practice of *bhakti-yoga* is also restricted to the person's born in the three higher castes.

Prapatti, on the contrary, does not require the observance of *karma-yoga* and *jñāna-yoga* as preliminaries. Nor is there any restriction on the basis of caste. It is open to all irrespective of caste, creed and status. Even the person born in the lowest caste and the worst sinner are eligible for it.[21] Besides, it is to be observed only once in the form of absolute self-surrender at the feet of God, with all humility, faith and the realization of one's utter incapacity to adopt any other means of *mokṣa*. The *prapanna* does not have to wait for another life to attain *mokṣa* but he can get it at the end of the present life as soon as the *prārabdha-karma* or the *karma* which has already begun to give result is eradicated by enduring it. It is thus considered to be an easier path to be adopted for *mokṣa* for those who are incapable of doing *bhakti-yoga* and who are also keen to attain *mokṣa* either at the end of the present life or even sooner. *Upāsanā* or *bhakti-yoga* enjoined in the Upaniṣads is meant for those who have the capacity and eligibility to perform it and who have the patience to wait until the goal is achieved. The sages like Vyāsa observed *bhakti-yoga*. In the present epoch, persons do not possess that kind of ability to do severe penance and hence the Vaiṣṇava *ācāryas* have adopted the path of *prapatti* as a practical means of salvation. This also has Vedic sanction.

As stated in the *Bhagavad-gītā*,[22] *bhakti-yoga* can confer only one of the four desired objects—worldly lordship (*aiśvarya*) which has been lost, worldly prosperity to be newly acquired (*arthārthi*), *kaivalya* or the state of blissful self-experience, and *mokṣa* or liberation from bondage. These are the four categories of individuals who practise *bhakti-yoga* to attain one of the four results which are granted by God who as the giver of fruits corresponding to our prayers. In other words, *bhakti-yoga* can help to achieve any of these four goals including *mokṣa*. In the same way, *prapatti* too, can confer, through the grace of God, any of these desired goals including *mokṣa*.[23] The basis for this claim is that the all-merciful, omnipotent God whose grace is secured is capable of conferring all the desired objects.[24] Thus, *prapatti*, though it is a simple and easier method for obtaining God's grace can secure all the desired objects including *mokṣa*, the highest *puruṣārtha*.

Siddhopāya and Sādhyopāya

Though *bhakti* and *prapatti* are enjoined by scripture as alternative means to be adopted by a *mumukṣu*, God is the actual direct means (*upāya*) for it. As we have observed earlier, it is the grace of God that plays a major role in securing *mokṣa*. In a correct sense God is the primary cause of *mokṣa* for an individual. The *Muṇḍaka Upaniṣad* states that Brahman is the causeway for attaining the eternal state (*amṛtasya eṣa setuḥ*).[25] The *Kaṭha Upaniṣad* points out that *Paramātman* can be attained only by those on whom He confers His grace (*yamevaiṣa vṛṇute, tena labhyaḥ*).[26] In view of this God is described as *siddhopāya*. *Siddha* means one who has been in existence even prior to the observance of the *sādhana* and since the ever existing God is Himself the principal cause for attaining Him, He is *siddhopāya*.[27] If God is the *upāya* for *mokṣa*, where is the need for *bhakti-yoga* and *prapatti*? Why do we have to undertake them? The answer is that *bhakti* and *prapatti* are required to secure the grace of God. As we have explained earlier, the individual souls have been deprived of the enjoyment of the blissful Brahman in the state of *mokṣa* due to the beginningless karma which stands in the way of attaining God. The removal of this obstacle is possible only by the grace of God. *Bhakti-yoga* and *prapatti* serve the purpose of winning the grace of God. These are, therefore, described as *sādhyopāya*, that is, the means to be observed for attaining God.[28] *Sādhya* means what is to be accomplished by human effort and *sādhyopāya* implies that *bhakti* or *prapatti* is to be accomplished by individuals in order to earn the grace of God. There are two kinds of cause: primary (*pradhāna*) and accessory (*sahakāri*). God is the primary cause of salvation in so far as He, through His grace helps an individual in his endeavour to attain *mokṣa*. *Bhakti* and *prapatti* are the accessory cause for *mokṣa* since they serve as the basis for the all-compassionate God to confer His grace and remove the obstacles standing in the way to attain Him. If God were to shower His grace on an individual without any kind of effort on his part He would be open to the criticism of arbitrariness. Hence *bhakti* and *prapatti* are enjoined by Śruti as *upāyas* to invoke the grace of God. A few objections raised by the critics against the need of human endeavour in the form of observing *prapatti* as a discipline to seek *mokṣa* will be discussed later after we have considered the nature and different features of *prapatti*.

Conditions of Eligibility for Prapatti

An individual who adopts the path of *prapatti* for *mokṣa* is required to fulfil two important conditions of eligibility, besides the general qualification such as a yearning for *mokṣa* (*arthitva*) and basic knowledge of the nature of *prapatti* along with the capacity to follow it (*sāmarthya*). The two special requirements are: (1) *ākiñcanya*, that is absolute inability on the part of the individual to adopt any other *upāya* for *mokṣa* such as *bhakti-yoga* aided with *karma-yoga* and *jñāna-yoga* (*upayāntara-sāmarthyābhāva*). (2) *ananya-gatitva*, that is, not to aspire for any goal other than *mokṣa* (*prayojanāntara-vaimukhya*). The second condition implies that the aspirant for *mokṣa* should not seek refuge in any other deity than the Supreme Being for the obvious reason that *mokṣa* cannot be granted by other deities. Both these conditions should be fulfilled by the aspirant to become eligible to adopt the path of *prapatti* as direct means to *mokṣa*.[29] Both Yāmuna and Rāmānuja have emphasised this point by imposing on themselves these qualification in their ardent prayer for *śaraṇāgati*.[30] With the fulfilment of these two conditions, any person, irrespective of caste, creed and status can become qualified to observe *prapati* for *mokṣa*.

Components of Prapatti

Regarding the nature of *prapatti*, it is essentially a kind of ethico-spiritual discipline comprising six components (*ṣaḍaṅga-yoga*) analogous to the *aṣṭāṅga-yoga* or the eightfold discipline of Yoga system. The *Ahirbhudhnya Saṁhitā* describes it as a sixfold discipline (*ṣaḍvidhā śaraṇāgatiḥ*).[31] The *Lakṣmī Tantra* while defining *ātma-nikṣepa*, which is also known as *nyāsa* and *śaraṇāgati*, speaks of five components (*nyāsaḥ-pañcāṅga-saṁyu-taḥ*).[32] There is, however, no conflict between the two views. In the former statement, the principal act of self-surrender (*ātma-nikṣepa*) is combined with its five subsidiaries, whereas in the latter statement the two, *aṅga* and *aṅgi*, are separately mentioned. The six components of *prapatti*, as explained by Vedānta Deśika on the basis of the Pāñcarātra treatises,[33] are:

(1) *Ānukūlya-saṅkalpa*, that is, a determined will on the part of the aspirant to perform only such acts as would please God.
(2) *Prātikūlya-varjana*, that is, to refrain from acts which would cause displeasure to God.
(3) *Kārpaṇya* or the feeling of humility arising from the helplessness of an individual in resorting to other means of salvation.
(4) *Mahā-viśvāsa* or the absolute and unshakable faith in God as the sole protector.
(5) *Goptṛtva-varaṇa* or to make a request to God seeking His protection.
(6) *Ātma-nikṣepa*, that is, entrusting the burden of protecting the individual self to the care of God.

Each one of these constitutes an important component of *śaraṇāgati* and bears ethical and theological significance. The first two *aṅgas*—*ānukūlya-saṅkalpa* and *prātikūlya-varjana*—have ethical significance as they involve right conduct by way of strictly obeying the commands of the Lord. The sacred texts have prescribed the religious acts to be performed by an individual and prohibited certain activities from which he should refrain. These are like the commandments of God[34] and by strictly following the dictums of the *śāstra* one incurs the pleasure of God and by doing the prohibited acts, one incurs His displeasure. As the individual is absolutely subservient to the Supreme Lord, it becomes imperative for him to please God by doing the right thing and avoiding His displeasure by refraining from the prohibited acts.

The third *aṅga—kārpaṇya* or humility is an important mental trait to be developed by the aspirant for *mokṣa.* It is actually an outcome of the two eligibility conditions we had referred to earlier, viz., the feeling of utter helplessness in adopting any other means for *mokṣa* and having the conviction that no one other than the Supreme Being can protect a person. It also implies absence of pride (*garva-tyāga*). Such an humble attitude on the part of an individual truly arouses the compassion of God.

The fourth *aṅga—mahāviśvāsa* or unshakable faith in God as the only saviour is the most important part of *śaraṇāgati.* Such a conviction enables an aspirant to perform *prapatti* without entertaining any doubt regarding its effectiveness to secure *mokṣa* for him. Even after its performance, it helps him to live in peace for the rest of the life without entertaining any doubt regarding the attainment of *mokṣa.* The Vaiṣṇava *ācāryas* have laid greater emphasis on the development of such a faith as otherwise *prapatti* will be ineffective.

The fifth *aṅga—goptṛtvavaraṇa,* implies that the individual who seeks liberation should make a formal request to God to grant him *mokṣa.* A question is raised whether such a request is to be made to God on the ground that the omniscient and all-compassionate God should by Himself be able to know the mind of the aspirant and grant him what he yearns for even without his asking for it. Vedānta Deśika takes the view that this is against the general principle, viz., that one grants the desired object only when it is asked for. If God does not bestow other human goals such as *dharma, artha* and *kāma* unless these are requested for, *mokṣa,* the highest human goal, cannot also be granted to the aspirant unless the latter requests for it. As *Lakṣmī Tantra* points cut,[35] though God is omniscient and also compassionate, He looks forward to a formal request by the aspirants for protection. This is because God rules the universe in accordance with certain accepted principle and He too should conform to it in the matter of offering protection to an individual as otherwise He would be open to the charge of discrimination. In the case of granting *mokṣa* which is the highest *puruṣārtha*, it becomes all the more necessary to make a request for it as an important part of *prapatti*.

The sixth part—*ātma-nikṣepa* or the act of surrendering the self to the care of God is the principal component of *prapatti* (*aṅgi*). We will explain the fuller meaning and significance of it later.

All the five requirements outlined above constitute the essential constituents (*aṅga*) of *śaraṇāgati* and have to be complied with by an aspirant for *mokṣa* at the time of performing *prapatti*. If any one of these accessories is absent, *prapatti* will be incomplete and will not lead to the desired goal. In other words, *ātma-nikṣepa*, which is the principal part (*aṅgi*) of *prapatti* should invariably be connected with the five accessories. It is in this sense *nyāsa* or *ātma-nikṣepa* is described as *pañcāṅga-saṁyutaḥ* or closely connected with five components. There are numerous episodes in the Itīhāsas and Purāṇas narrating the observance of *śaraṇāgati* by the celestial deities (*devatās*), the sages, human beings of all kinds and even living beings of lower order such as animals. In all these cases, a careful study of the episodes reveal that *śaraṇāgati* includes either implicitly or explicitly all the five accessories. The *śaraṇāgati* observed by Vibhīṣaṇa seeking the protection from Rāma, as narrated in the Rāmāyaṇa is a classic example of complete *śaraṇāgati*.[36] Even in our ordinary experience, we can find all the features of *śaraṇāgati* when the help of another person is sought to protect some valuable material. Thus, for instance, when a person who has in his possession a valuable article wishes to hand it over to the care of another capable individual, since he himself is unable to take care of it, he should entertain good feelings towards the latter, he should not displease him in anyway, he should have utmost trust in him, make a request to him with all humility to protect it and then hand over the article to him. When such a procedure has been gone through with utmost confidence in the protective power of the capable individual, the owner of the valuable article can remain carefree. The same principle applies to the *śaraṇāgati* done at the feet of God with faith and conviction and with the compliance of all the five requirements. Because of its practicability, effectiveness and sure result in short time, *prapatti* has been extolled by the Vaiṣṇava *ācāryas* as the best means of *mokṣa*.

Meaning and Significance of Ātma-nikṣepa

What is *ātma-nikṣepa* or self-surrender which is regarded as the principal component (*aṅgi*) of *prapatti*. The sacred texts which advocate *śaraṇāgati* enjoins that one's self is to be placed in the care of God (*svātmanaṁ mayi nikṣipet*).[37] The individual self (*ātman*) is not a commodity like an ornament one wears. It is, on the contrary, a spiritual entity and cannot as such be handed over to God for protection. Besides, *jīva* according to the Viśiṣṭādvaita Vedānta, is absolutely dependent on God and it is His property. As an individual dependent on God and not having any freedom of his own, how can he hand over his soul to God? If the product which does not belong to one is to be handed over to another as if it were his property, would it not amount to some kind of cheating? All these questions need a satisfactory answer for a proper understanding of the concept of *ātma-nikṣepa*.

It is true that the self is not a physical commodity and the question of its being handed over to God for protection does not arise. *Ātma-nikṣepa* does not imply such a transfer from one to the other. On the contrary, its implication is something different. The individual, caught up in bondage from a beginningless time due to *avidyā* or ignorance, had assumed that the self belongs to him and that he enjoys full freedom, thereby developing a sense of egoism. After gaining philosophic knowledge through a preceptor regarding the true nature of the self and its relation to *Paramātman*, he realizes that the self is absolutely dependent on God, that it is the property of the latter and that he has no right or capacity to take care of it. With this realization of the true nature of the self, he regrets over the wrong notion he had harboured so far and with all sincerity he pleads before God that the self does not belong to him, that it is God's own property, that he has no power to take care of it and that whatever pleasure is derived from the feeling of its protection also belongs to God. *Ātma-nikṣepa* or self-surrender is thus a specific mental state (*mati-viśeṣa*) qualified by the three important notions: (*a*) that the self is not mine but the property of God, (*svarūpa-samarpaṇa*); (*b*) that its protection is the responsibility of God (*bhara-samparpaṇa*) and (*c*) that the happiness derived from its protection is that of God (*phala-samarpaṇa*). Along with such a mental attitude, the individual seeking *mokṣa* should pray to God formally requesting Him to accept the responsibility of protecting his soul. This is the implication of *ātma-nikṣepa* or the surrendering the self to the care of God. Vedānta Deśika has expressed this truth in one verse: 'My self, the responsibility of protecting it, the fruit of its protection is not mine; it is that of Śrīpati (God); it is in this manner that a wise person should surrender himself to God.'[38] Thus states the *Ahirbhudhnya Saṁhitā*: 'Self-surrender (*śaraṇāgati*) is a mental notion accompanied with an ardent prayer addressed to God that He alone should serve as the *upāya* for the individual to attain *mokṣa*.'[39] A similar explanation is offered by Bharata Muni who says: 'When it is found impossible to achieve a desired object by other means, a request made (to God) with an unshakable faith that God alone is *upāya* along with the mental act of surrendering the self to the care of God is *prapatti* or *śaraṇāgati*.'[40] The fuller implication of this statement is made more explicit by Vedānta Deśika in the following verse: 'When an individual finds himself incapable of achieving the desired object either by his own effort or by the help of anyone else, he places that responsibility of securing it for him on another person who is capable of getting it for him. This is done with a formal request in the following words: 'This desired object should be accomplished for me by you without my making any effort hereafter on my part. This kind of specific thought (*mati-viśeṣa*) accompanied with an ardent prayer along with the act of surrendering one's self to the care of God is *prapatti* or *bharanyāsa*.'[41]

The act of self-surrender presupposes the renouncement of threefold egoism, viz., (*a*) that he is the agent of action (*kartṛatva-tyāga*); (*b*) that it belongs to him (*mamatā-tyāga*) and (*c*) that the fruit of the act is for himself (*phala-tyāga*). The feeling that the self is not the agent of action arises from the realization of the fact that the doership or the capacity to act is only given to him by God. The notion that the act of self-surrender does not belong to him comes from the awareness that it is caused by the grace of God. The notion that the enjoyer of the fruit of the self-surrender is not himself comes from the understanding that, the act of self-surrender to be observed by the aspirant is only a pretext (*vyāja*) and that *mokṣa* is actually made possible by God's grace which is primarily responsible for it. In addition to the realization of these three factors, the act of self-surrender should be accompanied with the compliance of five requirements stated earlier as *aṅgas* or components of *prapatti*. The *ātma-nikṣepa* or self-surrender performed with all these requirements along with the prayer as explained earlier (*prārthanāpūrvaka-bharanyāsa*) is considered as *sāṅga-prapatti* or complete *prapatti* which alone serves as a direct means for *mokṣa*.

Naḍādur Ammāl, the spiritual preceptor of Vedānta Deśika has summed up the features of *sāṅga-prapatti* in a simple way in the following sentences which are quoted by Vedānta Deśika in support of his view.[42] 'I have been caught up in bondage (*saṁsāra*) by performing prohibited deeds that cause Thy (God) displeasure; from now onwards, I will do such acts as would please Thee; I will also refrain from acts which cause displeasure to Thee; I have made up my mind to seek only Thee as the means; be Thou my *upāya*; hereafter, I have no further responsibility for either the removal of what is evil or in the attainment of what is good.'

Types of Prapatti

There are different types of *prapatti* depending upon the mode of its observance. One can observe it by the recitation of the prescribed prayer with the help of a qualified preceptor (*ācārya*). This is known as *uktiniṣṭha*. Alternatively, one may do it through the medium of an *ācārya*, who on behalf of the concerned individual performs *śaraṇāgati* in the prescribed manner. This is known as *ācārya-niṣṭha*. There are also other modes of observance and the prescribed ritualistic procedure varies from one sect to the other even among the Śrīvaiṣṇavas. But whatever procedure is followed, it is definite, according to the Vaiṣṇava theology, that the attainment of *mokṣa* is assured. Once it is done there is no need to pursue any other spiritual discipline for the purpose of *mokṣa*. The aspirant can than feel himself as a *kṛtakṛtya* or a person who has done his duty and he can live in peace for the rest of his life without any fear of rebirth and engage himself in divine service for the pleasure of

God. The pattern of life a *prapanna* is expected to live and his duties will be dealt in a later chapter.

The role of an *ācārya* is important in this matter since an aspirant seeking *mokṣa* needs to be initiated with the preaching of the requisite *mantras* and imparted with the basic knowledge of the Vaiṣṇava doctrines. The importance of an *ācārya* for a Vaiṣṇava disciple is so great that a section of Vaiṣṇavas regard the love and worship of an *ācarya* (*ācāryābhimāna*) as one of the subsidiary means to *mokṣa*.[43] The role of an *ācārya* in Vaiṣṇavism is outlined in a separate chapter.

Unlike *bhakti-yoga* which is a lifelong process, *prapatti* as a means to *mokṣa* is to be performed only once. This is compared to the function of a clever archer who shoots the arrow at the target in a moment. Thus, says the *Muṇḍaka Upaniṣad*: 'The *praṇava* (syllable *aum*) is the bow; one's self is the arrow; Brahman is the target of it; it is to be hit with concentration of mind; thus, the self becomes united with it like the arrow (with its target).'[44]

Controversial Theories Regarding Prapatti

Some questions have been raised by the followers of Tenkalai sect regarding the necessity of compliance with all the five accessories and the observance of the principal act of self-surrender (*ātma-nikṣepa*). Thus, they contend that the Supreme Lord who is compassionate, who is ready to protect anyone who approaches Him as a refuge irrespective of his status either as a sinner or virtuous, should not expect the compliance with these accessories. Secondly, any religious minded person who has studied the sacred texts and grasped the teachings contained therein, would have developed general faith in *śāstra* and apart from it, there is no need to insist on unshakable faith (*mahāviś-vāsa*) as a separate subsidiary requirement for self-surrender.

These doubts are set aside by Vedānta Deśika. The main authoritative source of information for determining the details of *prapatti* is the Pāñcarātra treatises. These texts have stated explicitly that *nyāsa* or *śaraṇāgati* is a sixfold discipline comprising five components and one principal act (*aṅgi*).[45] As already pointed out even in the case of our common experience, a person seeking protection from another capable person needs to fulfil all these requirements. In view of these considerations the five accessories including the absolute faith are to be admitted as essential prerequisites for *prapatti*.

Regarding the nature of *prapatti*, it is maintained by some Vaiṣṇavas that the mere faith in God as the sole means of *mokṣa*, is itself *prapatti* and that there is no need to observe self-surrender as a separate act. The basis for upholding such a view is the statements of the learned preceptors who equate *prapatti* with *viśvāsa* or faith.[46] Vedānta Deśika does not agree with this view. The definition of *prapatti* offered by Bharatamuni makes it very clear that a formal prayer to God along with an unshakable faith expressed in the words 'Thou should be my sole means for *mokṣa*' followed by the act of surrendering one's self to the care of God is the proper *śaraṇāgati*.[47] The Pāñcarātra treatises have also laid down that the act of self-surrender should also be associated with the fulfilment of five requisites. In view of this it is not correct to assert that mere prayer with faith is *prapatti*. It is, on the contrary, one of the five prerequisites and not itself the principal act (*aṅgi*). The statements which refer to the equation of *prapatti* with *viśvāsa* have to be taken in the sense that they are intended just to highlight the importance of *faith* as an essential accessory of *prapatti*. The teaching of Rāmānuja in the *Vaikuṇṭha-gadya* regarding the procedure to be followed for self-surrender makes this point clear.[48]

There is another theory which believes that the actual knowledge of relationship of the individual self to the Supreme Being (*śeṣatva-jñāna*) by itself constitutes *prapatti*. According to Vaiṣṇavism, the soul as a dependent entity exists for the pleasure of God and it is, therefore, the responsibility of the latter to take care of the former. It is contended that a mere realization of this truth and constant remembrance of it should serve the purpose of securing the liberation and there is no need to observe *śaraṇāgati* as a separate act.

This view is dismissed by Vedānta Deśika on the ground that a mere knowledge of the relation of soul to God cannot lead to *mokṣa* in the same way as the knowledge derived from the scriptural texts (*vākyārtha-jñāna*) cannot become a direct means to *mokṣa*. The philosophic knowledge about the soul and God is no doubt useful to create a deep interest in the pursuit of a proper method to realize the spiritual goal but that by itself cannot bring liberation from bondage. Hence the scriptural texts enjoin additional spiritual disciplines to be scrupulously followed by the aspirants for *mokṣa*.

There are a few other controversial views regarding the doctrine of *prapatti*. These have arisen in the later part of the post-Rāmānuja period as a result of the sectarian differences between the followers of Vedānta Deśika and Piḷḷailokācārya. These are generally related to the different interpretations offered by the two sects on the words of the esoteric *mantras* and on some of the statements made by Āḷvārs, Yāmuna and Rāmānuja. The discussion of these disputes is beyond the scope of the present book which aims to present objectively the basic doctrine of Vaiṣṇavism as developed on the basis of ancient authoritative sources. However, a few important points which have a direct bearing on the doctrine of *prapatti* will be taken up for examination.

Justification for Prapatti as Direct Means to Mokṣa

The first point which needs consideration is whether *prapatti* which appears to be easy to observe as compared to the lifelong rigorous practice of *bhakti-yoga*, can serve as a means to *mokṣa*, even though it might have been enjoined by Śruti and Smṛti texts. This doubt regarding the efficacy of *prapatti* as a means to *mokṣa* does not arise if we understand the philosophy of *sādhana* and the true nature of *Paramātman*. As we have explained earlier, the doctrine of *prapatti* is based on the concept of God's grace and intimate relation of *jīva* to *Paramātman*, as *śeṣa* and *śeṣī*. God according to sacred texts is *sarva-rakṣaka*, one who is willingly ready to redeem all *jīvas*. He is *śaraṇāgata-vatsala*, one who has a natural loving disposition to those who seek His refuge; He is *sahaja-suhṛt*, friendly towards all by nature.[49] Besides these divine qualities, He is *sarvajña*, omniscient, *sarvaśaktimān*, omnipotent and *satyasaṅkalpa* or one whose words of assurance to the devotees never go false. On the other hand, the individual soul belongs to *Īśvara* and by virtue of its intrinsic nature it has the potential right and capacity to enjoy the bliss of Brahman. All that stands in its way to attain the spiritual goal is the accumulated *karma* from beginningless time and it is to be overcome by securing the grace of God by the observance of either self-surrender or *upāsanā*. If we bear in mind all these facts and in particular, the special qualities of God mentioned above, there should be no room for doubt as to whether God would ever respond to our sincere and ardent prayer seeking *mokṣa*. *Prapatti*, as we have explained, is total self-surrender with an ardent prayer and with an unshakable faith in God as the saviour to accept the responsibility of saving the soul. This point has been brought out clearly in the final teaching imparted to Arjuna by Lord Kṛṣṇa in the *Bhagavad-gītā* in the following significant verse: *sarvadharmān parityajya māmekaṁ śaraṇaṁ vṛja*; *ahaṁ tvā sarvapāpebhyo mokṣayiṣyāmi ma śucaḥ.*[50] The implication of this verse, as interpreted by Vaiṣṇava *ācāryas*, is that when an aspirant for *mokṣa* is incapable of observing the path of *bhakti-yoga* along with *karma-yoga* and *jñāna-yoga*, he should surrender himself to God. The all-compassionate and all-powerful God will redeem him from all the sins standing as obstacles to *mokṣa*. The aspirant does not have to grieve any more with regard to the attainment of the goal. The same truth is emphasised in the *Rāmāyaṇa* when God-incarnate Rāma assures Vibhīṣaṇa with protection when the latter sought unconditional refuge of the former. The verse which is acclaimed by the Vaiṣṇavas as a *mantra* conveying the *śaraṇāgati-dharma* runs as follows: *sakṛdeva prapannāya tavāsmīti ca yācate*; *abhayaṁ sarvabhūtebhyao dadāmyetat vṛtaṁ mama.*[51] The meaning of this verse is: 'That individual who has surrendered himself to God only once with the pleading that he is to be protected, to him God assures complete protection and this is a vow taken by Him.[52] There are numerous such episodes in the Epics and Purāṇas depicting the importance of *śaraṇāgati* for achieving the desired goals including *mokṣa*.[53] If we go by the teachings of these sacred texts, *prapatti* as an easy and sure means of *mokṣa* is unquestionable.

The Theory of Nirhetuka-kṛpā Versus Human Effort

In this connection a question is raised whether the all-compassionate, omnipotent God who wields unchecked freedom to do what he chooses makes the act of self-surrender mandatory on the part of an aspirant to grant him *mokṣa*. The assumption behind this query is that the grace of God should flow freely towards the devotees without expecting an effort on their part as in the case of the spontaneous flow of the mother's milk to the newly-born infant. This kind of unconditioned compassion is called in Vaiṣṇava terminology *nirhetuka-kṛpā* as compared to the *sahe-*

tuka-kṛpā or showing compassion in response to some good act done by the devotee. The issue involved here is spontaneous God's grace versus conscious human effort to secure it.

This subject has assumed a controversial character in the post-Rāmānuja period and it constitutes one of the points of difference between the two sects of the Vaiṣṇavas. The Tenkalais emphasise the operation of grace as not conditioned by human endeavour in the form of observance of *prapatti* as a *sādhana* for *mokṣa*, because that would be a reflection on the absolutely natural character of free-flow of grace and also God's unchecked freedom. God is reputed to be the very treasure of *karuṇa* or compassion (*karuṇā-nidhi*). *Kāruṇya*, as we have explained earlier, means, according to this school of thought, the keen desire to remove the suffering of others without any selfish motive.[54] If this be so, the expectation of the observance of a *sādhana* by an afflicted individual for the purpose of *mokṣa* is unwarranted. If God were to grant it only in response to the *sādhana*, there would be no need for *kṛpā*. Against this view a question may be raised: if God were to protect an individual without expecting an effort on the part of the latter, why was such a protection not given much earlier? The answer to this, as given by the Tenkalais, is that it is an exclusive privilege of God since He is absolutely free to do what He likes at any time that He chooses. That is, whenever God desires to bestow *mokṣa* on an individual, He will do so at His pleasure. In support of this contention, the *Muṇḍaka Upaniṣadic* text is quoted which states that whomsoever God chooses, that person will attain God.[55] On this account, *upāsanā* and *prapatti* which have been enjoined by the scriptural texts as means to *mokṣa*, would not become invalid since they serve the purpose of qualifying an aspirant for *mokṣa* by making him realize that without God's grace human endeavour will not secure *mokṣa*. According to this school of thought *mokṣa* is not a goal to be won by effort but it should come as a gift of God out of His grace. If the Supreme Being Himself is both *upāya* (means) and *upeya* (goal) the idea of separate *sādhana* for seeking His grace amounts to self-contradiction.

The above theory is controverted by Vedānta Deśika and his followers. The main point of criticism is that the denial of human effort as a requisite condition of redemption would amount to arbitrariness on the part of God. In other words, if God were to release an individual from bondage without any endeavour on his part, the latter should have become free long time ago. If it be said that the release takes place later at a particular point of time due to the mere pleasure of God, God would be inevitably subject to the arbitrariness and cruelty. In order to avoid this criticism, it is necessary to admit, contends Vedānta Deśika, that God showers His grace only on those who become qualified for it by observing the prescribed *sādhana* or other religious acts sanctioned by the sacred texts.[56] In other words, the grace of God is dependent on human endeavour. It does not flow automatically to one who has been passive. Even in the illustration of mother and the infant, flow of mother's milk may be natural but nevertheless, the child is required to suck it, which involves some effort.[57] The need for human effort to receive God's grace does not negate the importance of God's *kṛpā*. On the other hand, it emphasises the fact that in order to make *kṛpā* or compassion operative, a valid excuse is called for on the part of an individual so that God escapes the criticism of being partial and cruel (*vaiṣamya nairghaṇyadoṣa*). The *bhakti* or *prapatti* to be observed by the aspirant for *mokṣa* as enjoined by the sacred texts are intended to serve the purpose of *vyāja* or a pretext for God to shower His grace. Even such opportunities to observe a spiritual discipline to earn God's grace are actually provided by God. They are not granted arbitrarily to a selected few but, on the contrary, they are given only to those individuals by God in response to some *sukṛta* or good meritorious deed performed even unintentionally either in the previous lives or in the present life. As a universal principle, God's grace comes forth necessarily in response to one's good *karma*, as otherwise He would be open to the charge of discrimination. This is the philosophy of grace and in the light of it, *bhakti* or *prapatti* are needed to earn it. As observed earlier, *bhakti* or *prapatti* by itself does not directly confer *mokṣa* because it is a non-sentient activity. The main cause of liberation is God's grace. It is the *pradhāna-hetu* or principal cause, whereas *bhakti* or *prapatti* is *sahakāri-kārnaṇa* or accessory cause. If we understand this distinction between the two types of cause, there would be no conflict between the *nirhetuka kṛpā* upheld by Tenkalai sect and *sahetuka-kṛpā* as explained by Vedānta Deśika. *Kāruṇya* or *kṛpā* which is the basis for showering grace serves as a common cause for several other purposes.[58] It is responsible for the very creation of the universe, for the sustenance of all that is created by God, for providing a body, sense organs, intellect etc., to human beings, for providing suitable opportunities for them to pursue *sādhana* for *mokṣa*, for removing the obstacles coming in the way of attaining *mokṣa*, for serving as the very means or *upāya* in the case of the *prapannas*, for blessing them to do divine service and many such things. Vedānta Deśika uses the expression *pradhāna-sāmānya-nidāna*[59] which means an important general cause. This view does not, therefore, deny the operation of God's *nirhetuka-kṛpā*. But, in order to become an object of such an unlimited *Kṛpā* an individual has to exercise his mental faculties and general capacity granted by God. Such a human effort which is fully justifiable, becomes the *sahakāri-kāraṇa* or the accessory cause for generating the operation of the unlimited *kṛpā* of God and its flow in the form of *anugraha* or grace towards a particular individual. In this sense the *nirhetuka-kṛpā* becomes *sahetuka-kṛpā*. Thus, the concept of *vyāja* bridges the so-called dualism between the two. Both are important and are complementary.

The need for the observance of *prapatti* as an act of self-surrender to attain *mokṣa* is also questioned on the basis of the absolute dependent character of the individual soul. According to Vaiṣṇava theology an individual is absolutely a dependent being and has no freedom of his own to function independently. He is comparable to a tool in the hands of God. In the first place, as in the case of an infant which does not have to make a request to the mother to feed it, it looks inappropriate that an individual should plead before God for protection and adopt for this purpose a *sādhana*, as if rendering some service in return for a reward. Secondly, if he has no freedom of his own, there would be no justification to enjoin the observance of *prapatti* for the purpose of *mokṣa*. It would also be against the very nature (*svarūpa*) of the individual self to undertake the act of self-surrender or *upāsanā*, which amount to self-effort (*svaprayatna*). As a subservient being he has no right to make an endeavour.

The above objections are based on a misconception of the concept of the dependence of *jīva* (*pāratantrya*). As we have explained in the earlier chapter, the *jīva* though dependent on God for its existence (*sattā*), is also an agent of action (*kartā*). As an agent of action, it has freedom to function. Otherwise, the commands of the sacred text would be meaningless. In view of this, the observance of the act of self-surrender seeking protection, as enjoined by the sacred texts, is not inappropriate. Even though the Supreme Lord regards the *jīva* as His own and knows its needs as the mother understands her child. He has to look forward to some kind of an excuse for extending His favour to do it in order to avoid the arbitrariness on His part. The initiative taken by an individual in accordance with his good *karma* to observe either the act of self-surrender or meditation, is not against his *svarūpa*, because such good acts do not either annihilate the *jīva* or even cause any undesirable results to him. *Śeṣatva* or dependence of an individual on God truly implies that he would have been a non-entity but for God, that he possesses nothing of his own other than what has been endowed to him by God and that he does nothing for himself except for the pleasure of God. It involves the notion of forsaking the egoism in the form of *I*, *my* and *mine*. As *Swāmin* or Lord of the souls, God is always ready to take care of His property for His own sake and pleasure as and when an opportunity is provided by the initiative of the *jīva*. As explained earlier, the act of self-surrender includes these three notions: *svarūpa-samparpaṇa*, the convinced feeling on the part of the individual that the soul is not his but of God, *bharasamarpaṇa* or the thought that the responsibility of protecting the soul is that of God, *phala-samparpaṇa* or the conviction that the pleasure derived from such protection is that of God. This philosophic truth is expressed beautifully in one verse by Vedānta Deśika: '*svamin svaśeṣaṁ svavaśaṁ svabharatvena nirbharaṁ; svadatta-svadhiyā svārthaṁ svasmin nyasyasi māṁ svayaṁ.*'[60] The meaning of the verse is: 'O Lord, I am your dependent (*sva-śeṣa*); I am controlled by you (*svavaśaṁ*): You have endowed me with the capacity to think; You have enabled me to know your nature; You Yourself have made me surrender myself to You for Your own pleasure with the responsibility of protecting it and getting rid of that burden from me.' The verse connotes the height of self-renunciation and utter humility of an individual. This is the inner secret of *śaraṇāgati* and if this is properly understood, the doctrine of *prapatti* accepted by Vaiṣṇavism as a direct means to *mokṣa* stands fully justified.

Notes

1. RV I.189.1. *agne naya supathārāye asmān viśvāni deva vayunāni vidvān; yuyodhyasmajjuhurāṇameno bhūyiṣṭāṁ te nama-uktiṁ vidhema.*
   See also *Iśa* Up 18.
2. See VD's commentary on *Iśa* Up 18.
   Also RTS XXVII p. 200.
3. RV VIII.19.5. *yaḥ samidhā ya āhutī yo vedena dadāśa marto agnaye; yo namasā svadhvaraḥ.*
4. See Ahs XXXVII.37. *samit-sādhanakādīnāṁ yajñānāṁ nyāsam-ātmanaḥ; namasā yo akarot deve sa svadh - vara itiritaḥ.*
5. RV VIII.66.13. *na hi tvadanyaḥ puruhūta kaścana.*
6. RV I.75.4.
7. RV X.63.10.
8. SVUp VI.18. *yo brahmāṇaṁ vidadhāti pūrvaṁ, yo vai vedāṁśca prahiṇoti tasmai; taṁ ha devam-ātmabuddhi-prakāśaṁ mumukṣur-vai śaraṇam-ahaṁ prapadye.*
9. TNUp 147.8. *tasmānnyāsameṣāṁ tapasām-atiriktamāhuḥ . . . brahmaṇe tvā mahasa om-ityātmānaṁ yuñjīta.*
   See also Ahs XXXVII.36. *yāni niśreyasārthāni coditāni tapāṁsi vai; teṣāṁ tu tapasāṁ nyāsam-atiriktaṁ tapaḥ śrūtaṁ.*
10. See RTS XXVII p. 218.
11. See fn. 55 on p. 120.
12. BG VII.14. *māmeva ye prapadyante māyāmetāṁ tarantī te.*
    BG XVIII.62. *tameva śaraṇaṁ gaccha sarvabhāvena bhārata.*
    See also RB I.4.1. *tasya ca vaśīkaraṇaṁ tat śaraṇāgatireva.*
13. RTS XXIX p. 234 (quoted from a Pāñcaratra treatise)
    bhaktyā paramayā vā'pi prapattyā vā mahāmate;
    prāpyo'ham nānyathā prāpyo mama kaiṅkarya-lipsubhiḥ.
14. RTS XXIII p. 159. *bhakti-prapatti-pramukhaṁ tadvaśikārakāraṇam.*
15. See VSa p. 79. *eteṣāṁ saṁsāra-mocanaṁ bhagavat-prapattimantareṇa nopapadyate.*
    See also RTS VIII p. 105. *prapannād-anyeṣāṁ na diśati mukundo nijapadaṁ.*
16. See RTS VIII p. 103.
17. VS III.3.56. *nānā śabdādibhedāt.*
18. VS III.3.57. *vikalpo-aviśiṣṭaphalatvāt.*
19. See *Śrutaprakaśikā*, *akṣara-vidyādikā iti ādi-śabdena'nyāso vivakṣitaḥ.*
    See also *Adhikaraṇa-sārāvalī*, verse 385.
    See also TMK II.31.
20. Rāmānuja uses the expression *darśana-samānākāra.* The implication of it is that the vision of God one gets during the perfected state of *bhakti-yoga* is not the same type as that obtained in the state of *mokṣa.*

Perfect vision is possible only after the soul is disembodied. What one gets in the form of a vision during meditation is just a glimpse of God for a short duration. Such a visual experience is, therefore, regarded as something similar to *darśana* or vision of God.

See also Chapter 5, pp. 102-03.

21. See *Sanatkumāra Saṁhitā* (quoted in RTS XXIV p. 160),
kuyoniṣvapi sañjāto yassakṛt śaraṇaṁ gataḥ;
taṁ mātāpitṛhantāramapi pāti bhavārtiha.
22. BG VII.16.
23. RTS VII p. 105.
24. VP I.12.76. *sarvaṁ saṁpadyate puṁsāṁ mayi dṛṣṭipathaṁ gate.*
See also VP I.12.79. *kiṁ vā sarvajagatsṛṣṭaḥ prasanne tvayi durlabham.*
25. MUp II.2.5.
26. KaUp I.2.23.
27. RTS XXIII p. 159. *samastapuruṣārthānāṁ sādhakasyadayānidheḥ;*
śrīmataḥ pūrvasiddhatvāt siddhopāyamimaṁ viduḥ.
See also RTS XXIII p. 160. *svaprāpteḥ svayameva sādhanatayā joghuṣyamāṇaḥ śrutau . . .*
28. Ibid. p. 159 *bhakti-prapatti-pramukhaṁ tadvaśikārakāraṇam;*
tattat-phalārthi-sādhyatvāt sādhyopāyaṁ vidur-budhāḥ.
29. See RTS X p. 108.
See also Ahs XXXVII.30. *ahamasmi aparādhānām-ālayo akiñcano agatiḥ.*
30. *Stotraratna* 22. *akiñcano ananyatatiḥ śaraṇya tvatpādamūlaṁ saraṇaṁ prapadye*
Śriraṅgagadya, *anantakāla-samīkṣayāpyadṛṣṭa-santāropāyaḥ.*
31. Ahs XXXVII.28.29. *ānukūlyasya saṅkalpaḥ prātikūlyasya varjanam;*
rakṣisyatīti viśvāso goptṛtva-varaṇaṁ tathā;
ātma-nikṣepa-kārpaṇye ṣaḍvidhā śaraṇāgatiḥ.
32. LT XVII.75. *nikṣepāparaparyāyo nyāsaḥ pañcāṅga-saṁyutaḥ.*
33. RTS XI p. 110.
See also LT XVII.66–73.
34. VDh. VI.31 (quoted by VD in RTS XVII p. 131).
śrutiḥ smṛtiḥ mamaivājñā yastām-ullanghya vartate;
ajñā-ccedī mama drohī madbhakto'pi na vaiṣṇavaḥ.
35. LT XVII.79–80. *sarvajño'pi hi viśveśaḥ sadā kāruṇiko'pi san;*
saṁsāratantravāhitvād-rakṣāpekṣāṁ pratīkṣate.
36. See RTS XI pp. 111-12.
See also the *Abhayapradānasāra*, a work in Maṇipravāḷa language written by Vedānta Deśika which expounds in detail the fuller significance of *śaraṇāgati* of Vibhīṣaṇa to substantiate this doctrine.
37. *Sātyaki Tantra* (quoted by VD in RTS XII p. 114).
38. *Nyāsa-daśaka*, verse 1. *ahaṁ madrakṣaṇabharo madrakṣaṇaphalaṁ tathā; na mama śrīpaterevetyatmānaṁ nikṣipedbudhaḥ.*
39. Ahk XXXVII.31. *tvamevopāyabhūto me bhaveti prārthanā-matiḥ;*
śaraṇāgatirityuktā sā deve asmin prayujyatām.

40. Bharata Muni statement (quoted by VD in RTS XXVIII and Pillailokacarya in his Rayasyagranthas

    ananyasādhye svābhiṣṭe mahāviśvāsapūrvakam;
    tadekapāyatā-yācñā prapattiḥ saraṇāgatiḥ.

    The word *yācña* means prayer (*prārthanā*) and fuller implication of it, as explained by Vedānta Deśika, is an ardent prayer along with the act of surrendering one's self to God.

    See GaBh p. 107. *prārthanāpūrvaka-bharanyāsātmakatva-siddhirityeṣā dik.*
41. See the opening verse in RTS XII p. 114.
42. See RTS XII p. 116.
43. See *Arthapañcakam*, p. 48.
44. MUp II.4.
45. See fn. 31 p. 284 ante.
46. See RTS XXIV p. 161. *nārāyaṇaṁ salakṣmīkaṁ prāptuṁ taccaraṇadvayayam; upāya iti viśvāso dvayārthaḥ śaraṇāgatiḥ.*
47. See fn. 40 above.
48. Vaikuṇṭha-gadya, *mām-aikāntikātyantika-paricarya-karaṇāya parigṛhṇiṣva iti yācamānaḥ praṇamya ātmānaṁ bhagavate nivedayet.*

    The words '*ātmānaṁ bhagavate nivedayet*' imply that the self is to be offered or surrendered to God.
49. See SVUp III.17. *sarvasya śaraṇaṁ suhṛt.*
50. BG XVIII.66. See RTS XXVIII and *Mumukṣuppaḍi* for fuller explanation of all the theological implications of this verse.
51. *Rāmāyaṇa*, VI.18.31.
52. See *Abhayapradāna sāra*, Chapter VIII for detailed interpretation of the verse.

    See also *Taniśloki.*
53. The classical examples of *śaraṇāgati* are those observed by the devoted child Prahlāda for protection from the torture of his demon-father, Hiraṇyakaśipu; Draupadi, the devoted wife of Arjuna for escaping from the insult caused to her in the open assembly; the *kākāsura* (the demon assuming the body of a crow) for protection of his life; the mythical elephant (*Gajendra*) for saving it from the attack of a crocodile; the mythical serpent (*bhujaṅgama*) from destruction etc.

    See *Abhītistavaḥ*, verse 19.
54. *svārtha-nirapekṣa-viśiṣṭam para-duḥka-nirākaraṇa-prāvaṇyam.*
55. MUp III.3. *yamevaiṣa vṛṇute tena labhyaḥ tasyaiṣa ātmā vivṛṇute tanūm svām.*

    See also KaUp II.23.
56. See RTS XXIII pp. 152-53.
57. Ibid., p. 156.
58. RTS XXIII p. 154. *kāruṇyaṁ anugrahattukku asādhāraṇam.*

    It means that *kāruṇya* is an essential cause for showering grace on an individual.
59. Ibid.
60. *Nyāsadaśakam*, verse 3.

14

VIṢṆU AS SUPREME GOAL OF LIFE

The central theme of Vaiṣṇavism is that Viṣṇu as the saviour of suffering humanity, is both the means (*upāya*) and the goal (*upeya*). He is the *upeya* because what is aspired for by the devout Vaiṣṇava is the divine service (*kaiṅkarya*) to Viṣṇu in the state of *mokṣa*. He is the *upāya* since the success in the spiritual endeavour laid down by the sacred texts for *mokṣa* is achieved only through His grace. The Vaiṣṇava treatises which have prominently brought out these facts describe Viṣṇu as *siddhopāya* which means that an ever-existent benevolent deity serves as the means of *mokṣa*, the *summum bonum* of human endeavour. *Prapatti* and *upāsanā* are described as *sādhyopāya* or the *sādhana* to be accomplished by the aspirants seeking *mokṣa* to earn Viṣṇu's grace. We have already discussed in detail the nature of *upāsanā* and *prapatti* in the earlier chapters. We have also considered the nature of *mokṣa* as enunciated in the Vedānta. We shall now examine the theological aspect of *mokṣa* involving divine service (*kaiṅkarya*) in Viṣṇu's abode (*paramapada*).

The Concept of Mokṣa as Divine Service

According to the Upaniṣadic teachings, *mokṣa* is the liberation of the soul from bondage leading to a complete and comprehensive experience of Brahman in a supra-mundane realm. As true philosophers the Upaniṣadic seers stop with the description of *mokṣa* as *Brahma-prāpti*, attainment of Brahman or *Brahmānubhava*, experience of Brahman. The Vaiṣṇava theology goes a step further to conceive it as not merely a vision of Brahman but as *kaiṅkarya* or service to the Supreme Deity. Thus, Rāmānuja prays in his *gadyas*, to grant him *nitya-kaiṅkarya* in *mokṣa*. The later Vaiṣṇava treatises have placed greater emphasis on this aspect of *mokṣa*. The important issue we have to consider in this connection is whether such a view of *mokṣa* is philosophically justified?

According to the Viśiṣṭādvaita Vedānta, *jīva* is essentially of the nature of *jñāna* (knowledge). It also possesses *jñāna* as an essential attribute. It is through this *jñāna* that *jīva* experiences objects outside it. This *jñāna*, which is known as *dharmabhūta-jñāna* as distinct from the *jñāna* as its very *svarūpa* (*dharmi-jñāna*), is finite in scope due to the influence of *karma* but with the removal of bondage the same knowledge becomes infinite in its scope. That is, *jīva* whose knowledge was eclipsed in the state of bondage becomes omniscient in the state of *mokṣa*. It, therefore, becomes possible for *jīva* to have a full and comprehensive vision of God in *mokṣa*, which was denied to it during bondage. The functions of *jīva* were also restricted in the state of bondage due to the influence of *karma*. With the eradication of *avidyā* which is the cause of bondage, *jīva* becomes free to act and move freely according to its desire by its own will (*saṅkalpa*).

Jīva as a spiritual monad is absolutely dependent on *Paramātman*. Its very existence (*sattā*), its knowledge and its power to function as the agent of action (*kartṛtva*), are all derived from the *svarūpa* and *saṅkalpa* of *Īśvara*. Its sole existence is to serve the purpose of God. It is, therefore, regarded as *śeṣa*, a subservient being of *Paramātman* who is the Supreme Lord (*śeṣī*). According to the Vaiṣṇava theology, *jīva* is absolutely and unconditionally a dependent being on God (*nirupādhika-śeṣa*) and it is its inherent character to render appropriate service (*kaiṅkarya*) to its master (*swāmin*) at all times, at all places and in all states (*sarvadeśa sarvakāla sarvāvasthā*) purely for the pleasure of God. The *dāsatva* or subordination of *jīva* to *Paramātman* does not cease with its attainment of the state of *mokṣa*. The ontological relationship between *jīva* and Brahman as *śarīra* and *śarīrī*, body and soul, is eternal since both the relata are eternal in character. Hence even after the total removal of bondage of *jīva* and its attainment of Brahman, it continues to exist as a distinct spiritual entity but as a dependent being (*śeṣa*) on the *Paramātman*. *Kainkarya* or rendering appropriate service to God becomes a spontaneous act of *jīva* as its inherent character and a pleasant duty.[1] Such a subordination and servitude do not constitute a bondage to the individual as in the case of servitude arising out of certain obligations to a master for material gains. The latter type of servitude may be regarded as undesirable but servitude performed out of pure love and devotion to God as a part of one's inherent character (*svarūpa*) for the pleasure of the Supreme Lord is most desirable.

Further, the soul needs a physical body and the sense organs to perform services to God in the state of *mokṣa*. As we have explained earlier such a body assumed by *jīva* out of its *saṅkalpa* is made of a spiritual substance, unlike the body constituted of the five physical elements by the influence of *karma* and it does not, therefore, cause bondage to *jīva*. The concept of *śuddha-sattva* and the justification for its acceptance is explained in an earlier chapter.

Thus, five points emerge out of the Upaniṣadic teachings about the nature of *jīva* and its liberation from bondage.

1. *Jīva*, after the release from bondage regains its omniscience and full freedom of action.
2. *Jīva* continues to remain a distinct spiritual monad as absolutely dependent on Brahman even in the state of *mokṣa*.
3. *Jīva* as subservient being to *Paramātman* possesses the inherent character to render service to God at all times for divine pleasure.
4. Servitude to God as the very *svarūpa* of *jīva* is a source of delight rather than grief.
5. The body put on by *jīva* in the state of *mokṣa* is constituted of spiritual substance and caused by its *saṅkalpa* and it does not cause bondage to *jīva*.

If we take these five factors which are supported by the scriptural texts, the concept of *mokṣa* as service to the Supreme Lord, Viṣṇu in His abode stands fully justified. Philosophically, *mokṣa* means attainment of Brahman or the experience of the blissful Supreme Deity. The concept of *kaiṅkarya* is not, therefore, mentioned in the *Vedānta-sūtra* and the commentary on it by Rāmānuja. But the fact that Bādarāyaṇa supports the theory of soul assuming a body in the state of *mokṣa* allows implicitly the possibility of rendering service to God in *Brahma-loka*. Rāmānuja, who is also a theologian, presumably takes this clue and develops the concept of *kaiṅkarya* to Supreme Deity in the

Paramapada. Thus, he prays to God to grant him *nitya-kaiṅkarya*, everlasting divine service. Theologically, *mokṣa* also implies divine service as an outflow of the intense love for God. When *jīva* becomes so enchanted with the beautitude of the Supreme Deity in the state of *mokṣa*, it is prompted spontaneously out of its love for God to render some divine service to the Lord.[2] Vedānta Deśika, therefore, describes the nature of *mokṣa* as *paripūrṇa-brahmānubhava* culminating in *kaiṅkarya* which follows out of divine love as a result of the blissful experience of Brahman.[3] If we understand this causal relationship between Brahman-realization and *kaiṅkarya*, there is no conflict between the concept of *mokṣa* as developed in the Vedānta and that advanced by the Vaiṣṇava theology. The negative concept of *mokṣa* as cessation of bondage for *jīva* becomes more meaningful by conceiving it in a positive way as enjoyment of the blissful Brahman. The latter concept becomes further enriched spiritually by adding to it the idea of performance of service to the Supreme Deity by the released souls purely out of love and for the divine pleasure.

Nature of Kaiṅkarya in the State of Mokṣa

Kaiṅkarya or offering service to God is an essential religious duty of a devotee of Viṣṇu (*Vaiṣṇava*). It is laid down as an obligatory duty for a Vaiṣṇava because an individual as a *Viṣṇu-dāsa* or subservient being to Viṣṇu, is morally obliged to render some service or the other to his Lord which pleases Him most. The details of the nature of *kaiṅkarya* and its religious significance will be discussed in a separate chapter. For the present it may be noted that *kaiṅkarya* enhances the value of life and makes it happier too. The performance of religious duties laid down by the sacred texts takes the form of *kaiṅkarya*, if these duties are carried out without any selfish motive purely for the pleasure of God (*bhagavat-prīti*). In the same way, even social and ethical duties performed in the spirit of *niṣkāma-karma* as advocated by the *Bhagavad-gītā*, would be regarded as *kaiṅkarya*. The concept of *kaiṅkarya* is thus an essential part of religious life. The same idea is extended to the role of *jīva* in the state of *mokṣa*. In a broad sense, the *kaiṅkarya* to be rendered to God by a devotee, whether in the transcendental realm or in the physical world, is basically the same and it serves the same purpose of causing pleasure to God. The only difference lies in the fact that an individual in the state of *mukti* has a direct intuition of the *Paramātman* and His glory in all its aspects, whereas in the state of bondage he performs his divine service on the basis of the love towards God developed out of the knowledge derived from the study of the religious texts. In fact some Vaiṣṇava *ācāryas* extoll the *kaiṅkarya* done in the physical world to God manifested in the *arcā* form as beautiful idols in the temples. The spiritual delight derived from such services is of unique type and often indescribable in words except the experience of inner joy of the devotee similar to the experience of God by the mystics. In view of it the Vaiṣṇava *ācāryas* have expressed a preference to the *kaiṅkarya* in this life.[4]

The Vaiṣṇava treatises provide details of the types of Godly services one can perform according to one's capacity. It may range from the highest act of construction of a temple to the simplest job of fetching flowers for the worship of God. We do not come across such details regarding the *kaiṅkarya* in the *Paramapada* by the released souls. Nor is it possible to know these details since the types of services with which we are familiar in the empirical world may not be comparable to those in a transcendental world which is beyond our comprehension. What is relevant from the theological point of view is that whatever act is performed by an individual soul it should conform to the wishes of the Supreme Lord and pleasing to Him. *Jīva* has no desire of its own. It is totally submissive to the wishes of God and whatever it does even on its own initiative is actually what is prompted by God who is the inner controller of all *jīvas* including the released souls. It is also not obligatory that all souls should engage themselves in the act of divine service. A soul may be contented with the mere vision of God which itself is a kind of divine service. In view of this, the *Vedānta-sūtra* holds the view that the assumption of a body by a *jīva* is purely optional.[5] It may put on such a body temporarily to perform a particular act of service prompted by *Paramātman*. It may remain without a body purely as a spiritual *monad* shining with its knowledge and experiencing the unsurpassable joy arising from the vision of God. This is the theological significance of *mokṣa* as divine service.

According to the Vaiṣṇava theology *kaiṅkarya* or service in the state of *mokṣa* is to be offered to the divine couple (*mithuna*). That is, the released soul renders its service to Viṣṇu as associated with Goddess *Śrī*. We have observed in an earlier chapter that Ultimate Reality of Vaiṣṇavism is *Śriyaḥ-pati*, Viṣṇu as integrally related to His consort. We have also noted that the Supreme Deity resides in *Vaikuṇṭha*, the transcendental realm, along with *Śrī* and other hosts of eternal souls known as *nityasūris*.[6] In conformity with this doctrine, Vaiṣṇavism describes the goal of human life as *Śrīman-nārāyaṇa* or *Śriyaḥ-pati*, implying the service to the divine couple.

Such a concept of *mokṣa* naturally presupposes the existence of an appropriate *spatial* realm to enable the God to stay in a particular place and also to give an opportunity for the released souls to render the act of worship or perform meditation. God by His *svarūpa* is infinite (*ananta*) that is, not conditioned by space or time. He is everywhere. But such a *svarūpa* does not serve the purpose of religious aspirants. It, therefore, becomes a necessity for God for the sake of the devotees to assume a finite form with a divine body and also condition Himself to a limited space. In the same way the *jīva*, though monadic, is partless (*niravaya*). It will have to assume a body and sense organs to render divine service. In view of these considerations, Vaiṣṇava theology has formulated the doctrine of *nitya-vibhūti* along with the theory of *paramapada*.

The Nature of Paramapada

The justification for the admission of the *nitya-vibhūti* and the concept of *paramapada* by Vaiṣṇavism has already been discussed in an earlier chapter. We are concerned here with the considera-tion of the nature of *paramapada* and the spiritual path leading to it. The term *paramapada* bears three meanings. It refers to the very *svarūpa* of Brahman or Viṣṇu since that is the goal of life to be attained (*parama-prāpya*).[7] *Viṣṇupurāṇa* uses the word in this sense.[8] It also refers to the very *svarūpa* of *jīvātman*, that is, *jīva* in the state of *mokṣa* when it is totally dissociated with the physical body. As the state of *jīva*-hood free from bondage is also a desirable thing to be attained for the enjoyment of the eternal bliss of Brahman, it is appropriate to call it *paramapada*. The most commonly used meaning of *paramapada* is the supreme abode of Viṣṇu. The hymn of the Ṛgveda refers to such an eter-nal place of Viṣṇu.[9] It is in this sense that most of the Vaiṣṇava treatises generally use the word, because that is a place to be attained by all the aspirants seeking *mokṣa*. It is not possible to experience the unsurpassable bliss of Brahman unless *Viṣṇu* conditions Himself with the physical and spatial limitation out of His free will for the sake of devotees. Such a place in which the Supreme Being manifests Himself with a divine body with all the splendour is called *paramapada*. In Vaiṣṇava terminology, it is called *Vaikuṇṭha-loka* or *Viṣṇu-loka*, the abode of Viṣṇu. It is also designated as *parama-vyoma*, the highest heaven. It is the same as *Brahma-loka* referred to in the *Chāndogya Upaniṣad*. It is not the *svarga-loka* or heaven as popularly understood as the place of the celestial beings. Nor is it the *satya-loka* of Caturmukha-Brahmā or any other *loka* of other Vedic deities because all these places are not eternal. The phrases such as 'kingdom of God', 'The Highlands of the blest', do not convey the significance attached to *paramapada* or *vaikuṇṭha-loka* of Viṣṇu. As *Viṣṇu-purāṇa* states, it is the Supreme abode, highest of all, which can only be attained by the Yogins who meditate on Brahman constantly with undivided devotion and which is always seen by the enlightened seers.[10] As the *Mahābhārata* describes, it is the spiritual realm which is ageless, immeasurable, incomprehensible, primordial and knowable through Scripture.[11]

Spiritual Ascent to Paramapada

The *Kauṣītakī Upaniṣad* gives a fairly detailed account of *paramapada*, also called *Brahma-loka* and the ascent to it. The other Upaniṣads speak of the path to *mokṣa* designated as *arcirādi-mārga*. The Pāñcarātra treatises too refer to the description of *vaikuṇṭha*. Nammāḷvār in the Tiruvāymoḷi gives a graphic account of the ascent of the soul to the realm of *Paramātman*. Based on these authoritative sources Rāmānuja presents in the *Vaikuṇṭha-gadya* a detailed and picturesque account of *Vaikuṇṭha* and the manner in which the *jīva* after release enters it. Following this, Vedānta Deśika presents in his *Paramapada-sopāna*, a work written in Maṇipravāḷa language, a superb account of the ascent of the *jīva* to *paramapada*, step by step in the manner of a piligrim's progress, starting with the acquisition of philosophic knowledge right up to the entry into the majestic abode of Viṣṇu. All these descriptions may be taken literally to satisfy the aspirations of the devout religious minded persons for whom they provide a source of inspiration and an incentive to strive for the spiritual progress. Alternatively, they may be understood symbolically as portraying the spiritual progress of the soul caught up in bondage. In either way, they have theological significance in so far as they provide a logical justification to the doctrine of *mokṣa* which is an essential feature of all the orthodox systems of Indian Philosophy in general and Vedānta in particular.

Without going into the details of the artistic imagery, we may take note of the important points regarding the spiritual ascent of the soul to *paramapada* as described by Vedānta Deśika.[12] It consists of nine stages or steps:[13] (1) *viveka* or philosophic knowledge, (2) *nirveda* or repentance, (3) *virakti* or non-attachment, (4) *bhīti* or fear of bondage, (5) *prasādana* or grace of God, (6) *utkramaṇa* or exit of the soul from body, (7) *arcirādi* or the path of ascent, (8) *divyadeśa-prāpti* or entry into the divine abode and (9) *parāpti* or actual attainment of Supreme Deity. The first five stages refer to the gradual spiritual progress of the soul, while it is associated with the living physical body. The latter four cover the spiritual march of the soul after it is disembodied. The first four steps are verifiable from our experience, whereas the other five have to be accepted on the authority of the sacred texts. We shall briefly explain the significance of each stage.

As a first step the aspirant for *mokṣa* should acquire a clear philosophic knowledge about the true nature of Brahman, the individual self (*jīvātman*) and their inherent relationship. This kind of discriminatory knowledge known as *viveka* comes to him through the guidance of a qualified preceptor and it provides an insight into the nature of the supreme goal of life. Such a knowledge about Reality and in particular, the reflection over the condition of the *jiva* passing through the cycle of births and deaths from a beginningless time causes a deep sense of remorse over the loss of all earlier opportunities to get over it. This is known as *nirveda*, a sincere repentance born out of proper philosophic knowledge. The *nirveda* leads to *virakti*, a sense of detachment towards worldly pleasures which cause further bondage and also towards celestial happiness in the form of attaining the *svarga* and other higher realms because these too cause rebirth to the soul in the mundane existence. *Virakti* helps the aspirant to develop a yearning for the everlasting supreme happiness in the form of eternal enjoyment of the bliss of Brah man. At the same time he develops fear too (*bhīti*) when he ponders over the consequences of rebirth and the suffering in hell if final liberation is not obtained. This induces him to seek the ways and means of attaining the supreme goal by adopting either the path of *bhakti* or *prapatti*. When he reflects over the hardships involved in the practice of the arduous *bhakti-yoga*, he realizes that only through the grace of God (*prasādana*) he can ever hope to achieve *mokṣa*. The *bhakti* and *prapatti* which are enjoined as means to *mokṣa* are instrumental to secure the grace of God.

The first four steps—*viveka, nirveda, virakti, bhīti*—which are preparatory in character lead the aspirant to seek the grace of God (*prasādana*) through the observance of either the prescribed *bhakti-yoga* or *prapatti*. Through the grace of God all the karma in the form of *puṇya* and *pāpa*, acquired in the past lives will cease to operate (*vināśa*) at the very commencement of the spiritual discipline, as the Upaniṣad states.[14] What remains is the *prārabdha-karma* or the *karma* which has already begun to give its result in the form of the present life and experience of suffering and happiness. This has to be endured till the end of the present life in the case of the *prapanna* and through one or more lives in the case of the person practising *bhakti-yoga* until it is totally eradicated. As regards the *karma* in the form of merit and demerit acquired during the present life after the commencement of the *upāsanā* or *prapatti*, this is of two types: those done unintentionally (*abudhipūrvaka*) and those performed intentionally (*buddhipūrvaka*). The former does not affect the aspirant due to the influence of the spiritual discipline and grace of God. The latter does affect him and hence he has to get rid of it by means of either prescribed expiatory rituals or by enduring the consequences of it during this life or in the next. In the case of the aspirant adopting *prapatti*, he has prayed to God at the time of self-surrender to grant him *mokṣa* at the end of the present life and in view of it, he will experience the effects of merit or demerit in some form or the other in this very life. In either case, both types of aspirants, being the objects of the special grace of God are ready to receive the gift of *mokṣa* to be granted by the all-compassionate *Paramātman* soon after death when the soul becomes disembodied.

Next comes *utkrānti* or the exit of the soul from the body, the sixth step and the beginning of the actual march to the *paramapada* from the physical world. The *Chāndogya* and *Praśna Upaniṣads*[15] give a descriptive account of the process of the dissolution of the body and the manner in which the soul leaves the body. On the basis of this authority it is believed that at the time of death the released soul withdraws from the gross state of the physical body to the subtle state and ascends to the highest spiritual realm through the path of *arcirādi*. The dissolution of the body is not destruction (*laya*) but a gradual process of involution which is effected by the indwelling *Paramātman*. The order in which it takes place is that the *svarūpa* (the subtle essence) of conative organs and five cognitive organs enter into mind (*manas*), and *manas* into *prāṇa* (vital breath) and *prāṇa* along with all the eleven sense organs becomes combined with the *jīvātman*. The *jīva* then gives up the gross physical body and becomes associated with a subtle body (*sūkṣma-śarīra*) constituted of the five subtle elements.[16] This is the process of withdrawal of the soul from the physical body soon after death, as warranted by the Upaniṣadic teachings. From the centre of the heart emanate 101 *nāḍis* (subtle arteries) and of these one leads up to the crown of the head. This is known as *suṣumnā-nāḍi* or *Brahma-nāḍi* in the yogic language. The soul of the aspirant who has performed *upāsanā* or *prapatti* for *mokṣa*, is made to depart the body by the grace of God through this *nāḍi*. As the *Vedānta-sūtra* points out, the gate of exit is illumined by the indwelling *Paramātman* and the *jīva* soars itself gloriously through the *brahma-nāḍi* to the higher realm following the course of the rays of Sun.[17]

After *utkrānti* comes the ascent of the *jīva* through a long divine path known as *arcirādi*, passing through the different realms of celestial beings who hail the released soul with joy and warm reception. Both the Upaniṣads and *Vedānta-sūtras* give a full account of this.[18] According to Rāmānuja who has attempted to reconcile the conflicting views on the subject, the path of the celestial deities comprises the following in order: *jyotis* or flame, *ahas* or the day, *śuklapakṣa* or the bright fortnight of lunar month, *uttarāyaṇa* or the bright half of the year when the sun travels northward, *saṁvatsara* or the year, *vāyu* or air, *āditya* or sun, *candra* or moon, and *vidyut* or the lightning accompanied by Varuṇa, Indra and Prajāpati. Flame, day etc., do not refer to the physical entities but to the deities presiding over these entities. They are known as *ātivāhikas* those who serve as guides en route to *paramapada*. These deities are commanded by God to be guides to the *jīva* proceeding to *mokṣa*. The presiding deity of *vidyut* is known as *amānava* or *mānasa*.

The next step in this spiritual progress of *jīva* is the entry into the transcendental spiritual realm (*divyadeśa-prāpti*) soon after crossing the cosmic universe. In this final stage of the soul's spiritual march, it is led by the *amānava-puruṣa* who is regarded as an eternal super-divine being unlike the other celestial cosmic deities, to the frontiers of the abode of god. The transcendental spiritual realm is far beyond the cosmic world of space-time (*prakṛti-maṇḍala*) consisting of seven spheres (*āvaraṇasaptaka*): (the mundane world), (*aṇḍa*) the world of water (*jala*), the world of fire (*agni*), the world of ether (*ākāśa*), the realms of *ahaṁkāra* (egoism) and of *mahat* (the two evolutes of cosmic matter) and finally the sphere of *prakṛti* (cosmic matter). The first milestone of the frontier of *Parmapada* to which *jīva* is taken is the sacred river known as *Viraja* which marks the boundary line between the transcendental realm of Brahman and the empirical realm of the bound souls. By taking a plunge in the river of immortality, the *jīva* before reaching the other shore of the river, is able to cast off the subtle body (*sūkṣma-śarīra*) by its *saṅkalpa*. It then becomes totally purified and on arrival at the other shore, it is transfigured with a spiritual body (*aprākṛta-śarīra*) fit to approach *Paramātman*. The process of transfiguration is explained metaphorically as *brahmālaṁkāra*, decoration in the divine way, *brahmagandha*, bearing divine odour and *brahmatejas*, possessing divine lustre.[19] The religious texts give a picturesque account of how the soul is received with joy and hospitality by hundreds of divine damsels, implying the greatness of the *muktātmā*, the released soul which has been able to reach the final spiritual destiny by herculean task after passing through countless births and deaths from a beginningless time.

After the entry into the frontiers of *Paramapada*, the *jīva* has reached its final destination which marks the highest spiritual goal, viz., *parabrahma-prāpti* or the attainment of Lord Viṣṇu. Rāmānuja has given a vivid descriptive account of *Paramapada* in his *Vaikuṇṭha-gadya*. It is a very extensive spiritual world of a unique kind beyond human imagination, always shining with spiritual light and surrounded with most enchanting lakes, streams and gardens filled with blooming flowers and creepers. Such a description may look imaginative but it stands justified, as we have explained earlier, if we bear in mind the fact that the Supreme Lord who can create a wondrous universe should be able to create a beautiful place for His own stay appropriate to His unsurpassable divine glory. The *Kauṣītakī Upaniṣad*, therefore, speaks of Brahman as enthroned on a golden couch (*Paryaṅka*) located in a beautifully decorated hall. *Paramātman*, who is the very personification of beauty, manifests Himself bedecked with ornaments and weapons, seated with His consorts and surrounded with His eternal divine attendants such as Ananta, Garuḍa, Viśvaksena etc. The *jīva* which intuits for the first time *Paramātman* with all His full splendour is overwhelmed with joy. *Paramātman* too who has been wanting the *jīva* to come out of the bondage and be reunited with Him feels extremely delighted to see the released *jīva* right before Him. He receives it with deep affection, blesses it wholeheartedly with the boundless and glorious opportunity of ever enjoying His bliss and rendering Him *kaiṅkarya* at all time and in all ways. Thus, the attainment of the Supreme Deity Viṣṇu and performance of divine *kaiṅkarya* for Him eternally in His own abode is the highest spiritual goal (*parama-puruṣārtha*) of *Vaiṣṇavism.* As Rāmānuja has well demonstrated by his own observance of *prapatti* for *mokṣa* in his *Śaraṇāgati-gadya* and *Śrīraṅga-gadya* and taught the same to others in his *Vaikuṇṭha-gadya*, every Vaiṣṇava should aspire for this spiritual goal and pray always for the eternal *kaiṅkarya* (*nitya-kaiṅkarya*) of Viṣṇu in *Paramapada.*[20]

NOTES

1. See SD Vāda 37. *yaddāsyaṁ lāsyakāraṇam.*
2. See *Śaraṇāgati-gadya*, 2. *bhagavadanubhavajanita anavadhikātiśaya-prītikārita . . . nitya-kaiṅkarya-prāpty-apekṣayā . . .*
3. See RTS XXII p. 147. *kaiṅkaryaparyanta-paripūrṇa-brahmānubhava.*
4. See Vedānta Deśika's *Varadarāja-pañcāśat*, 49. *satyaṁ śape vāraṇaśailanātha vaikuṇṭhavāse'pi na me abhilāṣaḥ.*
5. VS IV.4.12.
6. See fn. 23 on p. 229.
7. See VSa pp. 164-65.

8. VP I.22.53. *viṣṇvākhyaṁ paramaṁ padam.*
9. See p. 9 chapter 1.
10. VP I.6.39. *ekāntinaḥ sadā brahmadhyāyino yoginaśca ye;*
teṣāṁ tu paramaṁ sthānaṁ yattat pasyanti sūrayaḥ.
11. Mbh XVI 5.27. *divyaṁ sthānaṁ ajaraṁ ca aprameyaṁ. . . .*
durvijñeyaṁ ca āgamaiḥ gamyamādyam.
12. See *Paramapada-sopāna*, I-IX.
13. Ibid. (opening verse), *viveka-nirveda-virakti-bhītayaḥ prasādahetu utkramaṇa arcirādayaḥ; prakṛtyatikrānta-padādhirohaṇaṁ parāptirityatratu parvaṇāṁ kramaḥ.*
14. ChUp IV.14.3 and V.24.3.
See also VS IV.1.13.
15. *Praśna* Up III.9. See also VS IV.2.1–4.
16. See VS IV.2.5. BrUp VI.4.5.
17. See ChUp VIII.6.5.
Also VS IV.2.17. *raśmyanusārī.*
18. See ChUp IV.15.5 and VIII.6.5.
BrUp VIII.2.15 and VII.10.1.
Also *Kausītakī Up* I.21 and VS IV.3.2 and 3.
There is another path known as *dhūmayāna* or the path of smoke through which the souls not destined for *mokṣa* pass. They go only to *Candraloka* and from there to heaven. After enjoying the fruit of the merit, they again come back to earth and go through rebirth in some form or the other.
See *Kauṣītakī* up I.9–12.
19. *Kauṣītakī* Up I.34.
See also RTS XXI.
20. *Śaraṇāgati-gadya, nitya-kiṅkaro bhavāni.*
See also *Śrīraṅga-gadya, bhagavantaṁ nitya-kiṅkaratāṁ prārthaye.*
See *Vaikuṇṭha-gadya, ātyantika-paricaryā karaṇāya parigṛhṇīṣva iti yācamānaḥ praṇamya, ātmānaṁ bhagavate nivedayet.*

PART IV

RELIGIOUS DISCIPLINE OF VAIṢṆAVISM

15

RELIGIOUS DISCIPLINE OF VAIṢṆAVISM

In the earlier parts of the book we have presented the philosophical and theological doctrines of Vaiṣṇavism. The philosophical theories as enunciated in the Upaniṣads provide the foundation for the development of theological doctrines. The philosophy and religion of Vaiṣṇavism are complementary and the two together constitute one single system of philosophy of religion representing two different aspects. As a monotheistic religion, Vaiṣṇavism lays equal emphasis on a specific ethical and religious way of life aimed at the attainment of the highest spiritual goal. It comprises the cultivation of certain ethical virtues and performance of certain important religious duties. It is this practical aspect that gives a distinction to the Vaiṣṇava religion and it is far more important than its philosophy. We shall, therefore, attempt in this chapter to outline the important features of the Vaiṣṇava way of life.

The Role of Ācārya in Vaiṣṇavism

One of the essential requirements for a Vaiṣṇava in order to lead a religious life is to have a well qualified *ācārya* or *guru* (a spiritual preceptor). The term *ācārya* implies: (*a*) one who acquires philosophic knowledge by the study of sacred texts; (*b*) who by way of imparting the same to others makes them adopt the religious life as laid down by the *śāstra*; and (*c*) he himself strictly follows the same.[1] The word *guru* means one who removes ignorance of philosophic knowledge.[2] An individual who aspires for *mokṣa* or final liberation from bondage needs the blessings and the spiritual guidance of a preceptor. A Smṛti text points out that a person may be a sinner of the worst kind or one may be the most meritorious but both of them would achieve *mokṣa* only through the guidance of an *ācārya*.[3] It is, therefore, essential for a *Vaiṣṇava* seeking *mokṣa* to have a preceptor. The Upaniṣad also enjoins that one should approach a proper *guru* in order to comprehend the philosophic truth.[4] The reason for emphasising the need to acquire a preceptor is that true philosophic knowledge and a deeper understanding of the inner meaning of the philosophical truths with conviction cannot be obtained by self-study of Vedānta. It has to be imparted by a suitably experienced and qualified teacher. Only such knowledge as obtained through the teachings of a *guru* will be useful for practising the *sādhana* laid down by the Vedānta for achieving the spiritual goal.[5] Being connected with a *guru*, one should show him the utmost respect. It is laid down as an important moral obligation that one should worship an *ācārya* in the same way as one worships God (*devamiva ācāryam upāsīta*).[6] The *Kaṭha śruti* says: 'An individual who has the utmost devotion in God and who in the same way shows equal respect to his *guru*, will be able to comprehend all philosophic knowledge.'[7] It is, therefore, absolutely necessary for a spiritual aspirant to show the utmost devotion to his *guru* and speak about his glory. Failure to do so leads to the decay of his spiritual knowledge.[8]

Qualification of an Ideal Ācārya

The scriptural text has laid down certain qualifications to become entitled as a *guru*. The *Muṇḍaka Upaniṣad* states that he should be a *śrotriya*, one well-versed in Vedānta and *Brahma-niṣṭha* or one who has realized the true nature of Brahman. Vedānta Deśika elaborates this by mentioning fourteen qualifications for an *ācārya*. These are: acquisition of good and sound philosophic knowledge imparted through a succession of the learned preceptors (*sat-saṁpradāya-siddha*); having an undisputed clear, decisive knowledge (*sthiradhīsiddha*); free from sins and afflictions (*anagha*); well-versed in the Vedas and its subsidiaries (*śrotriya*); having deep, unshakable faith in Brahman or God (*Brahma-niṣṭha*); possessed of *sāttvic* quality, that is, mentally alert and well-disposed towards others (*sattvastha*); truth-speaking (*satya-vāca*); living a life in accordance with the ways laid down by one's religion and the holy men (*samayaniyatayā-sādhuvṛttyā-sameta*); free from show, jealousy etc. (*dambhāsūyādi mukta*); having control over the objects of sense organs (*jita-viṣayagaṇa*); friendly towards all (*bandhu*); compassionate towards all living beings (*dayālu*); helping the erring disciples to follow the right track (*skhālitye-śāsitāra*); and wishing the welfare of oneself and others as well (*svaparahita-para*). These are the fourteen qualities according to Vedānta Deśika, that an *ācārya* should possess. An aspirant for *mokṣa* should approach such an *ācārya* for initiation and instruction in philosophic knowledge.[9]

What has been sketched above gives an idea of what an ideal *ācārya* should be. It is not an easy task, and it may be impossible in the present day to find one possessing all these virtues. Even in the matter of coming into contact with a proper *ācārya*, the grace of God is needed. According to Vedānta Deśika, there are six factors which are responsible for the acquisition of a suitable *ācārya*. These are: the friendly disposition of God, the good deeds done by a person even accidentally, the grace of God showered on one at the time of birth, development of faithful attitude towards God and sacred texts, coming into contact even casually with pious religious minded persons and conversation with them.[10]

Guru-paramparā in Vaiṣṇavism

According to Vaiṣṇavism the Supreme Lord, Nārāyaṇa is the first and foremost of all *ācāryas* (*prathama-guru*). He is the *guru* of the entire world but He himself does not have any preceptor.[11] According to tradition He taught the Vedas to Caturmukha-Brahmā and the latter in turn to his sons and others. He disseminated Vedic knowledge through the great sages such as Nārada, Parāśara, Śuka and Śaunaka. He incarnated Himself as Matsya, Hayagrīva, Nara, Nārāyaṇa and Kṛṣṇa and revealed the philosophic knowledge. It was by His grace that *Vyāsa* promulgated the great epic, the *Mahābhārata* and the *Vedānta-sūtra*.[12]

Vaiṣṇava tradition claims a long lineage of *ācāryas* commencing from the Supreme Being right up to the *guru* of an individual. An orthodox Vaiṣṇava who is seeking spiritual knowledge should pay homage to the long succession of *ācāryas* starting from his own right up to the *Paramātman*. This practice is not a mere convention but on the other hand, it is enjoined on the authority of scripture.[13]

Leaving out the divine beings, the principal *ācāryas* who have been included in the spiritual lineage as commonly accepted by the Śrīvaiṣṇavas of both sects are: Nammāḻvār, also known as Ṣaḍagopan (one of the twelve Āḻvārs), Nāthamuni, Ālavandār,

Rāmānuja, Vedānta Deśika (according to the Vaḍakalai sect) and Maṇavālamāmuni (according to the Tenkalai sect).

In between Rāmānuja and Vedānta Deśika the important spiritual descendants are: Piḷḷān, Viṣṇucitta, Varadācārya also known as Naḍādūr Ammāl, Appuḷḷār and Vedānta Deśika (A.D. 1268-1369). The spiritual lineage acknowledged by the followers of Maṇavālamāmuni includes: Embār, Parāśara Bhattar, Nañjīyar, Nampiḷḷai, Vadakkuttiruvīdipiḷḷai, Periyavāccānpiḷḷai, Piḷḷailokācārya, Śrīśaileśa and Maṇavāḷamāmuni. Both Vedānta Deśika and Maṇavālamāmuni have had a long line of spiritual successors. The biographical accounts of these *ācāryas* are contained in the *guruparaṁparas* or the geneaology of preceptors maintained by the concerned religious institutions and the individual families.

We should take note of the great importance accorded to the place of an *ācārya* in Vaiṣṇava religion. It is a universal practice common to all religions to show respect to the teacher by a disciple. But the special feature of Vaiṣṇavism is the emphasis it places on worshipping not merely one's own *ācārya* but the entire lineage of *ācāryas* (*ācārya-santati*) right up to God who is the first *ācārya* (*prathama-guru*) from whom the spiritual knowledge emanates. There is a *tanian* or a single stanza pertaining to every preceptor. This is generally composed in Sanskrit by the first disciple of the preceptor. According to the Vaiṣṇava tradition the *tanian* of one's own *ācārya* and also those of his spiritual predecessors right up to *Paramātman* are to be recited by a Vaiṣṇava both at the time of initiation into Vaiṣṇavism by the prescribed sacraments (*pañca-saṁskāra*) and also at the time of undertaking Vedānta study. Such recitation of *tanians* at the time of religious acts signifies the importance of worship of the spiritual preceptors and also the acknowledgement of gratitude that a Vaiṣṇava owes to the great service rendered by them to the community by way of preserving and disseminating the sacred knowledge through which alone one can hope to attain salvation.

Sacraments in Vaiṣṇavism

The Vaiṣṇava theology has laid down a fivefold sacrament known as *pañca-saṁskāra* as an essential requirement for an individual to become fully qualified as a Vaiṣṇava. In a broad sense, any individual who is a devotee of Viṣṇu is a Vaiṣṇava.[14] The distinctions of caste, creed, learning and social status of individuals have no bearing on being a Vaiṣṇava.[15] That caste is not a bar on becoming a Vaiṣṇava is evident from the fact that one of the twelve Vaiṣṇava saints, Tiruppāṇāḻvār was born in the lowest caste. The *Garuḍa Purāṇa* mentions that a true *bhakta* or devotee of Viṣṇu is to be respected even if he belonged to another creed (*mleccha*).[16] Vaiṣṇavism is a broad-based universal religion which has kept its doors open to all.

In order to qualify oneself to become a fit person to worship Viṣṇu, one is required to go through the prescribed initiation ceremony to be conducted by a qualified preceptor. The sacrament known as *pañca-saṁskāra* comprises five simple ceremonies: (1) *tāpa*, or wearing the mark of the conch and discus, the two weapons of Viṣṇu, on the left and right shoulder blades of the initiate; (2) *puṇḍra* or applying on the forehead the mark in the shape of Viṣṇu's feet; (3) *nāma* or naming the initiate as *Viṣṇu-dāsa*; (4) *mantra* or imparting the esoteric Vaiṣṇava *mantras*; and (5) *ijyā* or formal instruction of the mode of worship of God.

A few lines of explanation on each ceremony will bring out its spiritual and religious significance. Of these five, *tāpa* is the most important because in the absence of it an individual will not become a qualified *Vaiṣṇava* to recite the esoteric *mantras* and perform the formal worship of Viṣṇu (*Viṣṇu-pūjā*), which is an obligatory daily religious duty of a Vaiṣṇava. The word *tāpa* means heating and as a *saṁskāra* or sacrament it implies the branding on the two shoulder blades, the mark of Viṣṇu's conch and discus by using the heated pieces of metal (made of either silver or copper) engraved with conch and discus. There are certain preliminary rituals in the form of *homas* to be performed in the consecrated fire by the preceptor or his representative. The purpose of this ritual is to purify the body and mind of the individual who in token of his having become a Viṣṇu devotee should bear permanently on his body the symbol of Viṣṇu's *śaṅkha* and *cakra*. The reason for choosing these two symbols of Viṣṇu is that the conch represents the auspiciousness, whereas the discus stands for the spiritual energy that wards off evil. This apart, there are numerous scriptural texts as well as the statements of Pāñcarātra Saṁhitās and Purāṇas which enjoin the wearing of the marks of these two symbols. Thus says the

Mahopaniṣad: 'The Brahmin should bear the discus on the right arm and the conch on the left.'[17] The *Bāṣkala Saṁhitā* of the Ṛgveda also points out that the learned (Vaiṣṇava) must wear the mark of the sanctifying conch and discus on the upper part of the arms in order to cross the ocean of bondage.[18] Many other scriptural texts are quoted by Vedānta Deśika in support of this ancient practice.[19] There are numerous statements in the Purāṇas too advocating this practice.[20] The *Mahābhārata* which refers to the Pāñcarātra system known by the name of *sātvata-vidhi*, mentions explicitly that God is to be worshipped by persons of all castes who have obtained the marks of identity such as *śaṅkha* and *cakra* (*kṛtalakṣaṇaḥ*).[21] The Pāñcarātra Saṁhitās too emphasise the necessity of bearing the marks of Viṣṇu's *cakra* and *śaṅkha* as an essential requirement in performing the worship of God.[22] Based on such authoritative sources Vaiṣṇavism has advocated the observance of the sacrament of *tāpa*.

A small section of Vaiṣṇavas who are the followers of the *Vaikhānasa-sūtras*, which is another branch of the Āgamas, does not observe the formal practice of *pañca-saṁskāra* because it is not prescribed in their treatises. They, however, believe that a child during the eighth month of pregnancy of the mother, gets marked with the conch and discus by Lord Nārāyaṇa Himself and in view of it no separate ritual need be observed. The followers of the Pāñcarātra system scrupulously go through this initiation ceremony, as otherwise they are deemed to be disqualified to offer worship to God. This practice of *pañca-saṁskāra* has been made an obligatory rite for all Vaiṣṇavas and is being followed since Rāmānuja's time as an essential purificatory sacrament. According to his biography Rāmānuja himself went through the *pañca-saṁskāra* which was conducted by his guru, Perianambi.

The next important ceremony as a part of the fivefold sacrament is *puṇḍra*. *Puṇḍra* which is an abbreviated form of the word *ūrdhva-puṇḍra*, means the wearing on the forehead the symbolic mark in the shape of the feet of Viṣṇu with white clay. Though it is a common practice among the Vaiṣṇavas including those who are not initiated, to wear the creed mark as a daily routine, the formal ceremony of applying it on the face and other selected parts of the body, twelve in all is observed at the time of the initiation. An orthodox Vaiṣṇava is expected to wear the *dvādaśa* (twelve) *puṇḍras* with the chanting of the names of the twelve incarnations of *Vyūhas*. The significance of wearing the *ūrdhva-puṇḍra* with the chanting of the names of Bhagavān is to purify the body.[23]

There is no unanimity among the Vaiṣṇavas in the manner in which the creed mark is put on. In fact, this religious custom which is of little philosophical significance has led to some conflict between the two primary sects of Vaiṣṇavas—the Vaḍakalais and Tenkalais. The former group wear the *puṇḍra* in the shape of a single foot of Viṣṇu in the 'U' shape with a curve formed at the bottom of the forehead right above the nose. The latter group put on the mark in the 'Y' shape symbolizing two feet of Viṣṇu with a separate mark on the nose symbolizing the pedestal for the feet to rest. Both the sects, as followers of Rāmānuja, use the soft white clay selected from select places considered holy. It is drawn vertically in two parallel columns leaving some space in between and at the centre a red or yellow vertical line is drawn with the powder made of turmeric. We do not have any historical evidence to prove when this distinction of wearing the *puṇḍra* in two different ways arose, though the followers of the two sects trace its origin to the time of Rāmā-nuja. According to the scriptural and Smṛti texts and in particular, the Pāñcarātra treatises, *ūrdhva-puṇḍra* is to be put on by every devotee soon after a bath in the morning.[24] The Smṛti texts mention in general terms that it should be in the shape of a flame, (*varti-dīpākṛti*) the leaf of the bamboo (*veṇu-patrākṛti*), a flower bud or shape of Viṣṇu's feet (*Hari-pādākṛti*). It is difficult to say in which particular shape Rāmānuja and his immediate followers were wearing the *puṇḍra*. While introducing the observance of *pañca-saṁskāra* as an obligatory rite for a Vaiṣṇava, Rāmānuja must have emphasised the practice of wearing a *puṇḍra* by every Vaiṣṇava to prove his allegiance to Vaiṣṇava *saṁpradāya*. Presumably, at a later period when the rift between the two sects became increasingly pronounced on the basis of certain doctrinal differences the changes in wearing the *puṇḍra* in two different styles would have come into vogue for identifying the respective followers. The sectarian bias was unfortunately manifested by marking the *puṇḍra* even on the idols, the temple walls and towers, the vehicles and the mounts of the images.[25] As observed earlier, the shape of the *ūrdhva-puṇḍra* has really no philosophic significance. In conformity to the scriptural and Smṛti injunctions it is to be put on by every devoted Vaiṣṇava since the religious ceremony performed without it is not considered fruitful.[26] In recent years due to the influence of modern way of life, the practice of wearing it has practically disappeared, particularly among the younger generation. However, an orthodox Vaiṣṇava should necessarily put on the *puṇḍra* as otherwise, he would not be qualified on religious ground to perform the divine worship and any other religious ceremony.[27]

Nāma or giving a name to the disciple is the third part of the fivefold *saṁskāra*. This is a simple and formal symbolic ritual. The disciple is named as *viṣṇu-dāsa* (*servant of Viṣṇu*) to signify the fact that with his initiation into the Vaiṣṇava-hood he is made to realize that he is subservient to Viṣṇu. It is also customary to name the initiate as *Rāmānuja-dāsa* to emphasise the fact that he has become a follower of Rāmānuja. Another justification for naming the initiate as *Viṣṇu-dāsa* is that a devotee of Viṣṇu is not to be addressed by either the name of his birthplace or the family surname but, on the contrary, he is to be identified as a *Viṣṇu-dāsa*.[28] Thus, it is customary even today among the orthodox Vaiṣṇavas to introduce oneself to another Vaiṣṇava as a *dāsa* (*daso'haṁ*) and not by his real name.

The remaining two ceremonies of *pañca-saṁskāra* are also simple but formal in character. An esoteric *mantra* which is preserved as a secret treasure is to be orally transmitted by the preceptor to a deserving disciple. In the ancient days, a *mantra* was never put in writing. It was kept secret and orally imparted from a teacher to a pupil. The *mantras* containing a few mystic syllables or words are spiritual in character pregnant with philosophical implications. The chanting of such *mantras* associated with the names of Lord Nārāyaṇa, Viṣṇu, Vāsudeva etc., are supposed to secure the grace of God, through which one's sins are removed and thereby liberation of the soul from bondage is secured. In view of the spiritual value of the *mantras*, the initiation ceremony is adopted for the purpose of imparting them to the deserving disciple by a qualified *ācārya*. This custom is strictly followed by the Vaiṣṇavas even to this day.[29]

The last part of the *pañca-saṁskāra*, viz., *ijyā* is also similar in character to the imparting of *mantra* and intended to serve the same purpose. In *ijyā*, which is also called as *yāga*, the essentials of the mode of actual worship of God in the form of an icon or *sālagrāma* (a kind of stone obtained from Gandak river in Nepal in which it is believed that the Divine Being is ever present) are taught. The daily worship of God is an obligatory religious duty of a Vaiṣṇava and it is but proper that a disciple is initiated to it by formal instruction by an *ācārya*. Thus, all the five ceremonies of initiation are interlinked. Without *tāpa*, *ūrdhva-puṇḍra* and the eligibility to recite the sacred *mantras*, a Vaiṣṇava is not qualified to conduct the formal worship of God either at home or in the temple. *Pañca-saṁskāra*, therefore, occupies an important place in Vaiṣṇava religion.

Daily Religious Duties of Vaiṣṇavas

A true *Vaiṣṇava* is required to dedicate himself to the worship and service for Viṣṇu throughout the day right from the early morning to the midnight. The Pāñcarātra Saṁhitās have divided the day into five parts and laid down a specific religious routine to be observed by a devoted Vaiṣṇava at each time of the day.[30] This fivefold religious routine is known as *pañcakāla-prakriyā*. This comprises: (1) *abhigamana* or morning prayer, (2) *upādāna* or collection of the requisite materials for worship, (3) *ijyā* or formal worship of God, (4) *svādhyāya* or recitation and study of sacred texts, (5) *yoga* or contemplation on God. We will presently explain each of these. Rāmānuja has included the essential features of the fivefold routine in the treatise known as *Nitya-grantha* written by him in Sanskrit. Based on this, one of his immediate successors, Śrīraṅganārāyaṇācārya also known as Vaṅgivamśeśvara has written a work under the title of *Āhnika-kārikā* giving details of the various religious rituals including the five religious duties to be observed by a Vaiṣṇava. Vedānta Deśika in his *Pāñcarātrarakṣā* has defended the observance of the daily routine as prescribed by the Pāñcarātra Saṁhitās taking note of all the known criticisms. There are two independent works written on the subject by later Vaiṣṇava *ācāryas* under the title of *pañcakāla-prakāśikā* and *pañcakāla-kriyādīpa*.

Before we go into the details of the daily religious routine, we should take note of the fact that the scriptural and Smṛti texts in general and the *Dharmaśāstra* treatises in particular have enjoined numerous other religious duties broadly classified as *nitya* and *naimittika karmas* to be performed by every individual according to his caste and stages of life (*varṇāśrama-dharma*). These rituals include among others prayers, *japa* (chanting of *mantras*), *homa* or sacrifice in the consecrated fire, worship of God, offering certain oblations to the celestial deities etc. As we have explained in the chapters on *Bhakti-yoga* and *Prapatti*, the performance of these *karmas* laid down by scriptural and Smṛti texts are mandatory for every aspirant for *mokṣa.* As Rāmānuja has observed, they are never to be given up under any circumstances (*na tyajeyam kathañcana*) since these are the commands of God. The Vaiṣṇava *ācāryas* have codified these religious duties under the title of *āhnika* or good deeds to be performed daily.[31] The *Āhnika-kārikā* to which we have referred, is devoted to this subject-matter. There are several other treatises of similar kind written by Vaiṣṇava *ācāryas.* The *pañcakāla-prakriyā* of the Pāñcarātra system is formulated from out of the religious duties prescribed by the Smṛti texts and fitted into the daily life of a Vaiṣṇava to be observed at five specific times of the day as a form of dedication of one's life to the service of Viṣṇu. From this it follows, as Vedānta Deśika has explained, that those who live a life according to the dictates of Śruti and Smṛti are not to give up the fivefold religious routine of Pāñcarātra system. Similarly, those who strictly follow the dictates of Pāñcarātra are not permitted to abandon the religious duties of *Dharmaśāstra.* To illustrate this point, the performance of *sandhyā* or the morning prayer is an obligatory religious act and a Vaiṣṇava following the fivefold *kriyā* should necessarily observe it because without *sandhyā* the individual is not qualified to do the worship of God. Thus, there is no conflict between the religious duties laid down by the Pāñcarātra system and those by the Smṛti texts. The two go together. That is, the fivefold religious routine of Pāñcarātra is to be carried out along with the other prescribed religious duties laid down by sacred texts in accordance with one's *varṇa* (caste) and *āśrama* (stages of life).[32]

The *abhigamana* is the first religious act to be performed in the morning. The word literally means going towards God.[33] It implies that a Vaiṣṇava after he has completed the bath and the morning prayer (*sandhyā*), should enter the place of worship, either in a temple or in one's own home, offer either a formal worship to God or recite the prayer after duly prostrating before the God. It is customary among the Śrīvaiṣṇavas to recite the *Śaraṇāgati-gadya* composed by Rāmānuja at this time since it contains the essential features of *śaraṇāgati* or self-surrender. The main object of this simple religious act in the morning time is to seek the grace of God for carrying out successfully the rest of the divine service during the day.

The second daily religious duty of a Vaiṣṇava is *upādāna* which means collection of flowers, fruits and requisite materials needed for the worship of God. This time of the day known as *upādāna*, which follows immediately after the *abhigamana* is most appropriate for acquiring not merely the fruits and flowers but other food items including money needed for buying the requisite products. If one does not have to go in search of money or food items, he can engage himself during this period in the study of Vedānta or any allied treatises. It is a common custom among the orthodox Vaiṣṇava preceptors to teach Vedānta during this time when the pupils are mentally alert to grasp the philosophic knowledge. If one is not competent to undertake philosophic study, he can utilize the time for rendering some kind of services in the temple. The details of the divine service (*kaiṅkarya*) and its significance will be dealt with separately.

Ijyā is the third and most important religious duty of a Vaiṣṇava. It refers to the actual worship of God. It is known as *Bhagavad-yāga* in Pāñcarātra Saṁhitās. Since the formal worship is to be done daily in the forenoon, after completing the first two routines, this period is called *ijyā-kāla*. On the authority of the scriptural and Smṛti texts, the daily worship of Viṣṇu is enjoined as a *nitya* or mandatory religious act.[34] Taking its stand on the hymn of the Ṛgveda, the Vaikhānasa system also upholds the daily worship of Viṣṇu.[35] The *Vyāsa Smṛti* states that there is no other Vedic deed more meritorious than the *ārādhanā* of Viṣṇu.[36] The Smṛti texts go to the extent of saying that it is sinful to take food without performing the daily worship (*pūjā*) of God.

The procedure for worshipping God is elaborate and the details are given in the *Nitya-grantha* of Rāmānuja based on the Pāñcarātra treatises. The works on *āhnika* also contain the details. According to Vaiṣṇava tradition, the method of *Bhagavadārādhanā* or worshipping God is to be learnt from a qualified preceptor after the individual is duly initiated by the prescribed sacrament. This condition is imposed in order to maintain the sacred character of the *mantras* which are to be used in the mode of worship. Without going into the details of the procedure, we may take note of the essential features of worship. The first requirement is the maintenance of physical and mental purity of the worshipper for which certain preliminary purificatory acts are prescribed. The idol of God is to be approached with a feeling of devotion and a sense of fear towards the Holy.[37] There are six stages which mark the mode of worship. In the first stage known as *mantrāsana*, the worshipper offers himself and all his belongings to God and seeks His blessings and permission to commence the worship. He offers to God *arghya* or water with a spoon or small vessel as a token of washing the hands of the deity, *pādya* or water in the same manner to wash the feet and *ācamanīya* or water in the same way for sipping as an internal purification. These are symbolic methods of receiving an elderly respected person and the same kind of respectful offerings are made to the deity too. In the second stage known as *snānāsana*, a holy bath is given to the idol with the recitation of *Puruṣa-sūkta*. The third stage called *alaṁkārāsana* is intended to decorate the idol with clothes, flowers and ornaments. During this stage, the sandal paste (*gandha*), incense (*dhūpa*) and *dīpa* or waving of light either by burning a piece of camphor or cotton wick dipped in oil are offered. At this time *arcana* or the offering of *tulasī* (basil) leaves and flowers is done with the recitation of Vedic *mantras*, the selected passages from the sacred works and the names of Viṣṇu (*nāmāvalī*), specially the names of twelve *vyūha* manifestations of Viṣṇu. In the fourth stage named *bhojyāsana*, offering in the form of cooked food is made to the idol. In the next stage known as *mantrāsana* God is presented with fruits and betel leaves and also camphor light. The Lord is also adored with the recitation of the concluding hymns of the *Tiruppāvai* (a Tamil composition of Āṇḍāl, one of the twelve Tamil saints) and the opening hymn of Periyāḻvār's *Tiruppallāṇḍu*, which is a benediction for Lord's glory to continue forever. The sixth and the final stage which is called *Paryaṅkāsana* is intended to put back the idol to rest. After concluding the worship, the devotee is required to prostrate himself before God, circumambulate and with utter humility seek forgiveness of all the sins committed.

The mode of worship outlined above is what is generally prescribed for observance at home. The object of worship may be an idol of (some form of) Viṣṇu which is duly consecrated or it may just be a special stone in the shape of a round black pebble known as *sālagrāma* which is collected from the sacred river Gandak in Nepal. According to the Purāṇas, God is ever present in such stones. As they need no consecration, unlike the icons they are preferred for worship at the homes of Vaiṣṇavas as a symbol of God. The worship of God at home is to be performed by all Vaiṣṇavas irrespective of the caste including women. In the case of those who are not eligible to recite Vedic *mantras*, they can adopt non-Vedic or *tāntrik mantras*.

The method of worship to be performed at the temples are somewhat different from what obtains at homes and are also very elaborate. Not all persons are permitted to do the *pūjā* at temples. In the case of the temples following the *Vaikhānasa* system, only those born in the family of the Vaikhānasa temple priests can do the *pūjā*. As regards the temples adopting the Pāñcarātra method, the temple priests have to get themselves qualified for worship by undergoing a formal initiation ceremony known as *dīkṣā*. The daily worship of Viṣṇu at home is however an imperative for every devoted Vaiṣṇava.

We now come to the fourth daily religious duty, viz., *svādhyāya* which means study of sacred texts. There is a long interval between the conclusion of the midday rituals and sunset. This time is to be utilized by engaging oneself in useful activities. In the case of a devout Vaiṣṇava who is dedicated to the service of Viṣṇu, the best way of spending the time is to engage himself in either reading the sacred works such as the *Rāmāyaṇa* or any other religious texts. If one is not competent to do it, he may listen to discourses given by others on the subject. If there are other domestic duties to be executed one is not prohibited from attending to them.

The fifth and final duty comes after completing the evening prayers and dinner before one goes to rest. This part of the day is called *yoga*. What is implied by *yoga* is that one should contemplate on God until he actually goes to sleep. At that time the individual should bring himself to feel that his self is resting in God.[38]

The *pañcakāla-prakriyā* or the fivefold daily religious routine prescribed for the Vaiṣṇavas is a rigorous discipline. The primary objective of it is to make a devoted Vaiṣṇava, for whom service to Viṣṇu is the major preoccupation of life, engage himself in purposeful religious activities throughout the day. Orthodox Vaiṣṇavas did follow the discipline scrupulously in the past and also in the present century until the last few decades. With the rapid changes in the social and economic conditions of the society, it has become impracticable to lead such a rigorous religious life, even if one desires to do so. We should however, take note of what the ideal way of life of a true Vaiṣṇava is. Keeping the idea in mind a devoted Vaiṣṇava may endeavour to follow at least in spirit the religious practices to the extent possible with faith and sincerity.

There are many other important religious practices which are easy to follow by Vaiṣṇavas even under the compulsions of present-day style of living. We may take note of these. The *Bhāgavata Purāṇa* mentions nine modes of worship of *Viṣṇu*. These are: *śravaṇa* or listening the glory of Viṣṇu, *kīrtana* or singing the glory of the Lord, *smaraṇa* or constantly remembering His greatness, *pāda-sevana* or service to God, *arcana* or offering worship to God's image, *vandana* or prostrating before God, *dāsya* or developing the feeling of subordination to Supreme Being, *sakhhya* or developing a friendly disposition towards God and *ātmanivedana* or surrendering oneself to God.[39] These are easier methods of worshipping God. They do not require any preparatory and purificatory religious ceremonies, unlike the *Bhagavad-ārādhanā* except deep love to God. Of all these, *Kīrtana* or the singing the names of God is the easiest which can be followed even by laymen. The same is known as *bhajana* in popular language and is performed everywhere by groups of devout Vaiṣṇavas. The recent Vaiṣṇava movement of the Kṛṣṇa Consciousness in the West which has adopted among others the *bhajana* as a form of mass worship is a case in point. When Vaiṣṇavism of Rāmānuja spread in other parts of India *bhajana* became a popular method of adoration of Viṣṇu by the masses. Even today it is the most popular form of participation by the masses all over India. The *Mahābhārata* extolls *saṁkīrtana* as the best mode of worship of Viṣṇu in the *kaliyuga*. It states that by merely chanting the name of Nārāyaṇa one becomes free from all afflictions.[40] The sage Bhīṣma declares that the mere chanting of the three names, Acyuta, Ananta and Govinda, which are like medicine, one is relieved of all illness.[41] One of the Āḷvārs states that a mother who names her child as Nārāyaṇa will not go to hell. The *Viṣṇu Purāṇa* points out that expressing God's name even unconsciously removes all sins.[42] There are any number of such statements in the religious literature extolling the greatness of *nāma-saṁskīrtana* as the best form of worshipping God. The justification for this belief is that God who is known to be *stava-priyaḥ* will be pleased with the singing of His glory.[43]

Kaiṅkarya for Bhagavān

Vaiṣṇavism has developed two types of worship of God in which any member of the society can participate and derive the same spiritual benefit as one would get from the performance of formal religious worship. These are known as *Bhagavat-kaiṅkarya* or service to God and *Bhāgavata-kaiṅkarya* or service to Godly men. The concept of *kaiṅkarya* to which we have referred in an earlier chapter, is a universal one and is prevalent in some form or the other in all religious systems. It however gets an added emphasis in Vaiṣṇavism with philosophical and theological justification. This concept is developed in Vaiṣṇavism on the basis of the doctrine of the ontological relation of *jīva* or the individual self to *Paramātman* or God. As we have fully explained earlier, the *jīva* by its very nature is a *śeṣa* or absolutely dependent on God who is Supreme Lord (*śeṣin*). It exists for the pleasure of God and as a subservient being (*dāsa*) it is the intrinsic duty of an individual to serve God at all times (*sarvakāla*) and in all ways (*sarvāvasthā*). On the basis of this doctrine, the *kaiṅkarya* or service to God is ordained on *jīva* both during the states of bondage and *mukti* purely for the pleasure of God.

Against this philosophic background, every deed in a broad sense becomes a *kaiṅkarya* if the same is done purely for the pleasure of God without any selfish motive. Vaiṣṇavism has adopted the concept of *niṣkāmakarma* advocated in the *Bhagavad-gītā* and made it an integral part of every religious act. Thus, at the commencement of any religious act—whether it be a simple chanting of prayer, or the formal worship of God or an act of giving charity (*dāna*) or an act of giving away one's daughter in wedding (*kanyā-dāna*), the individual performing it is required to say in the form of a *saṅkalpa* (declaration) that he is doing it purely for the pleasure of God (*Śrīmannārāyaṇa-prītyarthaṁ* or *Bhagavat-kaiṅkaryarūpaṁ*). In addition to the *saṅkalpa*, the orthodox Vaiṣṇavas say at the commencement of a *karma* with sincere faith that the very Supreme Being caused it (*svayameva kārayati*). Similarly, at the conclusion of the *karma*, they repeat that it was got accomplished with the grace of God (*svayameva kāritavān*).[44] The implication of it is that the individual is a tool in the hands of the Almighty and whatever he does is not for his selfish purpose but for the pleasure of God. This is the height of renouncement of the ego (*ahaṁkāra*) and the notion of *mine* (*mamakāra*). A service done in this spirit removes the sins by earning the grace of God and thereby gradually leads one to the attainment of God which is the highest goal of human life.

Though any religious act can be taken as *kaiṅkarya* in the sense explained above, Vaiṣṇavism as a way of life has advocated certain religious activities as specific types of *kaiṅkarya* in a technical sense. These are mostly related to the various services in the temples. Any service done in a temple ranging from the simplest act of bringing flowers to the highest task of construction of a temple, is a *kaiṅkarya* for God. There is a variety of such services that one can render in a temple. To name a few, lighting the oil lamp, offering flowers, waving the fan before the deity, bringing water from the river or pond for Lord's worship, arranging food offering for God, taking out the deity in procession, recitation of songs or hymns about God, prostration before God, going round the temples, cleaning of the floor of the temples and many such acts. All these are regarded as *kaiṅkarya*. According to one's capacity and choice any one of these acts performed with devotion is bound to earn the grace of God. Irrespective of one's caste or social status, everyone can easily participate in such pious activities. Though the concept of divine service is old prevalent from prehistoric times, *kaiṅkarya* as a form of worship of God was introduced with added emphasis by Rāmānuja, who was the foremost reformer of Vaiṣṇavism. The sole consideration of Rāmānuja in doing so was to involve millions of illeterate men and women in some kind of divine worship. In view of it, he encouraged his followers to engage themselves in temple activities. From the biographical account of Rāmānuja we have clear evidence of how he promoted temple worship and also introduced the reforms in the mode of worship in accordance with the Pāñcarātra system. The three major and oldest Vaiṣṇava temples at Śrīraṅgam and Conjeevaram (both in Tamil Nadu) and Melkote (in Karnataka) follow even to this day the mode of worship introduced by Rāmānuja in the eleventh century. He encouraged the Vaiṣṇavas living in and around those temples to involve themselves in divine-service and allocated specific duties to different families. The other Vaiṣṇava temples have followed the same practice. This accounts for the development of the temple towns as centres of religion and culture with a large number of residential houses built around the outer temple walls. We can notice this development in a remarkable way at Śrīraṅgam. The Vaiṣṇavas in the ancient days considered themselves as fortunate to have had an opportunity to do some kind of service in a temple without any monetary benefit. A true *kaiṅkarya,* it is believed, is that which is done not for monetary gain but as a source of divine pleasure.

Kaiṅkarya for Bhāgavata

Along with the divine service, Vaiṣṇavism has developed the concept of *Bhāgavata-kaiṅkarya* or service, to Godly men. In fact, the latter is regarded as of greater importance than the former. As we have explained earlier, the basis for this belief is that the true devotees of Viṣṇu are dearest to God and any service rendered to them is most pleasing to God. The *Pādmottara Purāṇa* says: 'Of all the types of worship, the worship to Viṣṇu is great; greater than that is the service to Godly men.'[45] It further adds that even by neglecting the worship of God if one offers worship to Godly men, God becomes supremely pleased with him and showers His grace on him.[46]

The hymns of the Āḻvārs, the elaborate commentaries thereon and the later Vaiṣṇava treatises extoll the *Bhāgavata-kaiṅkarya* as an essential requirement and the greatest virtue of a Vaiṣṇava. The author of the *Īḍu* regards service to God's devotees as central to the behaviour of a Śrīvaiṣṇava.[47]

Who is a *bhāgavata* and what is the *Bhāgavata-kaiṅkarya*? The word *bhāgavata* is derived from the term *Bhagavān.* The word *Bhagavān*, which is very commonly used in the Pāñcarātra Saṁhitās, means the Supreme Being or God who is endowed with the six essential attributes as *Viṣṇupurāṇa* explains.[48] In a general sense the worshippers of *Bhagavān* are called *bhāgavatas.*

All Vaiṣṇavas in a broad sense irrespective of caste are *bhāgavatas* because they are all worshippers of Viṣṇu as the Supreme Deity. In a technical sense a *bhāgavata,* as stated in the *Mahābhārata*[49] is one who has full knowledge of the nature of Bhagavān and the doctrine of Vyūhas, and one who strictly follows the fivefold religious duty. In view of this the religion propounded in the Pāñcarātra system is named Bhāgavata religion and the followers of this religion were acknowledged as *bhāgavatas.* The same are also called *sātvatas* because they worship Bhagavān Vāsudeva and their religion is known as *Sātvata* religion which is the same as Bhāgavata religion. They include both Brāhmaṇas as well as non-Brāhmaṇas.[50]

Kaiṅkarya in a general sense means a service (*sevā*) rendered to others. In the context of the Bhāgavata cult, any kind of a service rendered to a devotee of Viṣṇu is also *bhāgavata-kaiṅkarya.* The Vaiṣṇava treatises do not make mention of any specific type or types of services to be rendered to a *bhāgavata* except that whatever is done should be in conformity with the dictates of the sacred texts (*yathā-śāstram*). That is, the services offered to a devotee should be within the ambit of the ethical and religious code laid down by the *Śāstra.* Then only it would be pleasing to God.[51] In this context even a respectful attitude towards a devotee of Viṣṇu can be regarded as a *kaiṅkarya.* Contrarily, an unfriendly disposition or hatred towards a devotee amounts to an offence to a *bhāgavata* (*bhāgavata apacāra*). In a technical sense, *kaiṅkarya* refers to the assistance rendered with devotion to a *bhāgavata* in the form of manual services, providing food, clothing, shelter and helping him in other ways to carry on his religious activities. A service done to one's own *ācārya* is also a form of *bhāgavata-kaiṅkarya* and in fact, it is a nobler service than the other two. An *ācārya* too is a *bhāgavad-bhakta.* As he is easily accessible, it is far more important to serve him than going in search of a *bhāgavata.*[52] The importance of a *kaiṅkarya* to an *ācārya* has been exemplified by Madhurakavi Āḷvār in his classic eleven Tamil hymns[53] portraying the devotion of a Vaiṣṇava to his *guru.* The association of a Vaiṣṇava with *bhāgavatas* is itself considered an act of religious merit. The author of the *Iḍu,* while commenting on the hymn of Nammālvār[54] referring to *keśavan tamar* (Viṣṇu's devotee) points out that God gives salvation to the *bhaktas* (Vaiṣṇavas) if only they associate with *bhāgavatas.*

Such is the importance attached to *bhāgavata-kaiṅkarya* in Vaiṣṇavism.

Other Types of Kaiṅkarya

Rāmānuja has recommended five kinds of services which may be brought under the category of *kaiṅkarya* to be performed by the Vaiṣṇavas depending on one's capacity and convenience. According to tradition, these were the last words uttered by Rāmānuja for the benefit of his pupils at the time of his death.[55] According to him, a Vaiṣṇava should not worry about his after-life since he has been assured of *mokṣa* with the performance of self-surrender to God. Nor should he worry about his present life since that will go on in accordance with his past *karma.* He should, therefore, engage himself to the extent possible in one of the five services. The first and the most important one in the opinion of Rāmānuja, is to study the *Śrī-bhāṣya*, the learned commentary on the *Vedānta-sūtra* and propagate the teachings contained therein. Secondly, if a person is not competent to do the first task, he should engage himself in listening to the teachings contained in the Tamil hymns of the Āḷvārs and impart the same to others. Thirdly, if a person is not able to do it, he can undertake the services at the holy temples in the form of arranging for the offer of food stuffs, flowers, lighting of lamps etc. If a person cannot perform any of these services for the temples, it is suggested that as a fourth type of *kaiṅkarya*, he may chant the sacred secret *mantra* (*dvaya*) along with contemplation on its inner philosophic meaning. Even if this cannot be done, it is advised, as the fifth easy type of service, that one should spend the time in the company of a devout Vaiṣṇava.

It may be observed that in the opinion of Rāmānuja the acquisition and propagation of philosophic knowledge are nobler services for a Vaiṣṇava. These need a good knowledge of Sanskrit and Tamil and learning in other *Śāstras.* Only a small number of intellectuals can undertake them. The majority of the Vaiṣṇavas who are laymen but devotees of Viṣṇu are, therefore, to be occupied with the temple services. Contemplation on the meaning of the *mantra* is open to all but here again some amount of intellectual power to grasp its philosophic significance is needed. The illiterate masses, who embrace Vaiṣṇavism have to be provided with an opportunity to serve Viṣṇu. Keeping this in mind, Rāmānuja, with his magnanimous and compassionate attitude towards the suffering humanity and with the sole purpose of uplifting the lower classes of the society, advocated the service to Godly men which is the easiest method of divine worship.

Vaiṣṇava Dharma

We have so far dealt with the important religious duties of a Vaiṣṇava as laid down in Vaiṣṇava tradition. Most important than the observance of religious duties, Vaiṣṇavism emphasises the need to cultivate certain ethical virtues to be a true Vaiṣṇava. This is called the *Vaiṣṇava dharma.*

The *Mahābhārata* states that philosophic knowledge would be fruitful only if it helps an individual to develop good character (*śila*) exemplified in daily conduct (*vṛtta*).[56] The word *śīla* or character implies cultivation of ethical virtues (*ātmaguṇa*) and the term *vṛtta* or conduct means religious mode of life (*sadācāra*). Another ancient saying points out that the study of the philosophical works is intended to secure *śama*,[57] mental tranquillity. Knowledge which does not lead to good conduct is futile.[58] These general observations equally hold good for religion. A mere formal observance of certain religious duties without developing good character is not of any significance. The philosophic knowledge is an essential requisite for developing a desire to seek liberation from bondage. But such a knowledge acquired either from the study of the sacred texts or from hearing the essentials of the Vedānta from a qualified preceptor should lead to the religious pursuit which should, at the same time, reflect itself in one's character and conduct.

Every religion emphasises the importance of leading a moral life. A religious person is expected to develop ethical virtues such as faith in God, honesty, integrity, compassion towards others and proper social behaviour. *Satya* or truth-speaking and *ahiṁsā* or non-injury to other living beings are the fundamental ethical concepts of Hinduism, Buddhism, Jainism and all other religions. These are all *common dharmas* (*sāmānya-dharma*) accepted by Vaiṣṇavism too. But there are other special values—social, ethical and spiritual which have been advocated by Vaiṣṇavism and the cultivation of these values gives a distinctive character to a Vaiṣṇava.

From the religious standpoint, the most important *Vaiṣṇava dharma* is the development of an unshakable faith that only Viṣṇu as the Supreme Being (*paratattva*) is the saviour (*rakṣaka*). This would imply that as a true Vaiṣṇava, he should not worship any deity other than Viṣṇu. The Vaiṣṇava treatises, particularly the hymns of Āḻvārs and the elaborate commentaries thereon, repeatedly emphasise this principle. Tirumaṅgai Āḻvār goes to the extent of saying that he would not associate himself with those who worship other deities.[59] This view should not be construed as dogmatism because it arises from the philosophic doctrine of ultimate Reality in Vaiṣṇava theology, namely Viṣṇu is the Supreme Deity and He alone is capable of bestowing *mokṣa*, the highest spiritual goal. The emphasis laid on the exclusive devotion to Viṣṇu does not amount to a condemnation of other deities such as Śiva. According to an ancient saying mentioned in the *Matsya Purāṇa*,[60] the Sun-God is to be worshipped for health, the fire-God (*Agni*) for wealth, Śiva for knowledge and Viṣṇu for *mokṣa*. This is perhaps an ideal set-up which accords importance to the four Vedic deities. As *mokṣa* is the supreme human goal, greater importance is given to the worship of Viṣṇu. However, a Vaiṣṇava should show veneration to other deities too since they constitute the *vibhutis* or glory of Viṣṇu. Viṣṇu as all-pervasive (*vibhu*) and inner controller of all that exists in the universe is the *antarātmā* of other deities also as stated in the *Mahābhārata*.[61] The *Gītā* also reiterates that the worshippers of other deities with devotion only worship the Supreme Being (Viṣṇu).[62] A true Vaiṣṇava should understand this philosophic truth and accordingly, he should develop the spirit of tolerance for other religious faiths and respect the deities of other cults. A true spirit of toleration is the greatest virtue of a religious minded Vaiṣṇava.

The adoration of Viṣṇu also implies the need of showing utmost respect to the God's devotees (*bhāgavatas*). As we have explained earlier, the devotees of Viṣṇu are dearest to God and any kind of service or worship offered to them amounts to the worship of Viṣṇu Himself. An offence committed towards them is most sinful and causes the utmost displeasure to God. A Vaiṣṇava should refrain from committing sins in respect of both *bhagavān* (*bhagavad-apacāra*) and *bhāgavatas* (*bhāgavadapacāra*).

Along with this spirit of toleration, a Vaiṣṇava should

develop compassion towards all other living beings in general and fellow-Vaiṣṇavas in particular. The author of the *Īḍu* holds the view that it is an important trait of a Vaiṣṇava to consider the sorrows and sufferings of others as his own. It is the duty of every Vaiṣṇava to feel sorry for the suffering inflicted on a fellow-Vaiṣṇava. In the same way, he should also feel happy at the thought of any good that may happen to another Vaiṣṇava. As a criteria for determining whether or not one is a Vaiṣṇava, it is pointed out that if a person sincerely feels pity on account of the suffering caused to another, he may consider himself as a devotee of God. If, on the contrary, he does not show sympathy to the sufferings of others, he distances himself from God. Thus, it is important for a Vaiṣṇava to feel the joys as well as the sufferings of others as his own.[63]

Besides *dayā* or compassion, a Vaiṣṇava should cultivate a few other ethical virtues. These are *satya* or truthfulness, *ārjava* or integrity, *dāna* or benevolence, *ahiṁsā* or non-violence and *anabhidhyā* or not coveting the property of others. These qualities are regarded as *kalyāṇa* or noble virtues.[64] Though they have been laid down as preliminary ethical requirements for practising *bhakti-yoga*, they are essential qualities of every devotee of Viṣṇu. Of all these, *satya* is the most important. *Satya* in the ordinary sense means speaking the truth. This is a common quality to be cultivated by all honest people. But its connotation here is even wider. *Satya* is defined as cherishing the welfare of all living beings (*bhūtahita*). According to Vaiṣṇavism, Viṣṇu is all-pervasive and He abides in all living beings as their *antarātmā*. As all the souls are the *aṁśa* of Viṣṇu, a Vaiṣṇava should look upon all individuals as not only equal but also should wish for their welfare. Under no circumstance he should cherish any ill-will or hatred towards others. Even if a Vaiṣṇava is insulted or abused by another individual, he should keep himself calm unperturbed by it. Such an attitude is possible because he should realize that the insulting remarks made against him do not in anyway apply to the *svarūpa* of the self (*ātman*). The soul is distinct from the body and whatever criticisms are levelled against a person these are applicable to his physical being. He should not, therefore, feel disturbed. On the contrary, he should feel sorry for the critic since the latter is acting under the influence of ignorance and commits sin. The

Mahābhārata points out that a person who abuses another individual takes on himself the sins of the latter.[65] The *Viṣṇu-purāṇa* says that when persons hate one another, a pious individual should express sympathy towards them because of the fact that they are acting out of ignorance.[66] Further, according to the Vaiṣṇava philosophy, all souls are absolutely dependent on *Paramātman* and all their actions are prompted by the latter. If one commits a sin against a pious individual, the latter should feel that the former has been prompted to do so by God and should regard it as a sort of punishment for his previous *karma*. With this realization the pious Vaiṣṇava, instead of hating the sinner, should develop a sense of joy that his *karma* has been removed to that extent by such a punishment. The assumption here is that one's *karma* is to be removed either by enduring its effect or by undergoing a punishment inflicted on him by God.

A true Vaiṣṇava should also develop a sense of fearlessness. The greatest fear of a human being is death. According to Yoga system all living beings have an instinctive fear of death. How is it possible for anyone to be free from it? The Vaiṣṇava philosophy upholds that God is the saviour of mankind (*sarvarakṣaka*) and one who has surrendered himself at His feet, is sure to be protected by Him. According to the doctrine of *prapatti* an individual who has observed self-surrender as a means to *mokṣa* is assured of salvation soon after death. If one develops a deep faith in this philosophy, there is no need to fear death. An ancient saying points out that true devotees of God who have sought His refuge should welcome death in the same way as one treats his dearest guest.[67]

Mental equanimity is an important virtue to be cultivated by a Vaiṣṇava. The worry over the means of livelihood such as food and shelter generally causes mental disturbance. A Vaiṣṇava should avoid it and this is possible for him if he realized the truth that fortune or misfortune comes to one in accordance with one's past *karma*. The *Mahābhārata* points out that an individual who has been sitting passively is blessed with unexpected fortune, while another, despite serious and repeated efforts, may not get even a morsel of food.[68] If one is not destined to get something, he will not have it despite his efforts. According to Vaiṣṇava philosophy everything happens in accordance with God's will on the basis of past *karma*. There is no need for one to worry about his livelihood because it is already ordained to him at the time of birth.[69] This theory should not be taken as fatalism. It is intended to emphasise the fact that one should endeavour to obtain one's needs without undue worry within the framework of moral codes and enjoy life with self-contentment. As *Gītā* advocates, a person with equanimity of mind neither grieves over the suffering caused to him nor he delights over the happiness that comes to him.[70] The same point is emphasised in the *Mahābhārata.* The happiness and unhappiness revolve one after the other like a wheel. When a person gets happiness he should not feel too delighted over it; same way if one faces unhappiness, he should not regret for it.[71] All that is expected of a devoted Vaiṣṇava is to fear the possibility of committing a sin either to God or the *bhāgavatas* and live in peace unmindful of happiness and suffering and perform the divine service to the extent possible with the conviction that he is a servant of Viṣṇu (*Viṣṇu-dāsa*).

Apart from the cultivation of the ethical virtues, the way in which a Vaiṣṇava conducts himself in the society is equally important. Vaiṣṇavism has laid certain broad principles for the guidance of a Vaiṣṇava who has become a *kṛtakṛtya* or one who has already accomplished the primary duty of seeking refuge of God for *mokṣa.* Though there is no need to worry about his after-life a Vaiṣṇava as a member of the society has the social as well as religious obligations to fulfil. We have already considered his religious duties. Regarding his attitude towards the members of society, he should regard all individuals as equal and show the utmost kindness towards all living beings. Besides these general principles which are binding on all members of the society irrespective of their creed, a Vaiṣṇava has a special role to perform. According to Vedānta Deśika, the members of the society are classified not on the basis of caste or social status but on the basis of their attitude towards religion. From the standpoint of Vaiṣṇava religion, those who have faith in this religion are of one category. They are regarded as persons who are favourable to a Vaiṣṇava. The second category of persons are those who have hatred towards Viṣṇu. They are regarded as enemies of God and are unfavourable individuals. There is a third category of individuals who do not belong to either of the groups and these are indifferent people who constitute the common folks caught up in bondage (*saṁsāri*). A Vaiṣṇava should look upon the first category of persons with a sense of delight and cultivate friendly association with them. As regards the second category of persons, he should try to avoid their company. With regard to the third category of individuals, he should remain indifferent towards them. If possible, he should try to uplift them by offering suitable guidance. If they do not respond, he should express pity on them rather than condemn them. If a Vaiṣṇava transgresses this code of conduct, he would be not only failing in his duty but also will incur the displeasure of God. That is, if a Vaiṣṇava disregards the devotees of God, he will incur the wrath of the Supreme Being for whom they are the dearest. Similarly, if he cultivates friendly contacts with the enemies of God instead of avoiding their company for money or satisfaction of sensual pleasures, he would be causing displeasure to God. The cultivation of friendship with the common folks who are indifferent to religion is also a reflection on the character of a Vaiṣṇava. An individual who is wedded to Viṣṇu and in whom he has sought refuge should not care for material gains or sensual pleasures which are against Vaiṣṇava *dharma*. The *Śāṇḍilya Smṛti* asserts: 'One should not under any circumstances and even in critical times, accept any gifts, not even a penny, from an unchaste woman, a eunuch, an outcaste or an enemy.'[72] The *Viṣṇu-dharmottara* says: 'Those who remain blind to the defects of others, who act as eunuch in respect of the wives of others, who behave like dumbs in the matter of accusations of others, are very dear to God.'[73] Such a code of conduct which may sound rigid is intended to guide a Vaiṣṇava to live a pious life.

Universal Character of Vaiṣṇava Ethical Values

The ethical values advocated by Vaiṣṇavism have universal appeal. The greatest man of our time, Mahatma Gandhi was so attracted by these values that he adopted as part of his daily prayer the famous song known as *Vaiṣṇava janato* composed by Narasimha Mehta (a Gujarati poet of 15th century) enshrining the Vaiṣṇava values. The contents of the song are worth noting.

He is the true Vaiṣṇava who knows and feels
  Another's woes as his own.

Ever ready to serve, he never boasts.
He bows to everyone and despises no one,
Keeping his thought, word and deed pure.
Blessed is the mother of such an one.
He Reverences every woman as His mother.
He keeps an equal mind and does not
Stain his lips with falsehood; nor
Does he touch another's wealth.
No bonds of attachment can hold him.
Ever in tune with Rāma-*nāman*, his body
Possesses in itself all places of pilgrimage.
Free from greed and deceit, passion
And anger, this is the true Vaiṣṇava.[74]

A similar devotional song composed by Guru Arjuna (1565-1605), the fifth Sikh Guru, extolls the Vaiṣṇava ethical ideals. It says:

He is a true Vaiṣṇava on whom God's favour has slighted,
Who dwelleth apart from worldly entanglements
And performeth right actions without seeking a reward for them
Such a Vaiṣṇava lives a life of true piety;
He seeketh no gain from any good deed he doeth,
But setteth his heart only on the Lord's service and the singing of the Lord's praises;
And with his body and his mind remembereth ever the Lord,
And hath compassion upon all living creatures
He holdeth fast to the Lord's Name and inspireth others to meditate on it,
Nanak, such a Vaiṣṇava attains to the supreme state.[75]

We can find the echo of such statements emphasising the religious and ethical values in almost all the world religions. However, the distinctive feature of *Vaiṣṇava dharma* lies in the fact that it is based on its central philosophy that Viṣṇu, the Supreme Being, prevades the entire universe as enunciated in the Upaniṣads.[76] A Vaiṣṇava should, therefore, love all human beings, treat them as equal and hate none. He should live with peace of mind and lead an humble pious life dedicating himself to the service of God and His devotees. Such a way of life will bring him not only happiness in this world but an everlasting bliss in the other world.

Notes

1. *Yājñavalkya Smṛti* (quoted in RTS).
   ācinoti ca śāstrārthān ācāre sthāpayatyapi;
   svayam ācarate yasmāt tasmāt ācārya ucyate.
2. *gu śabdastu andhakārasyāt ru śabdaḥ tannirodhakaḥ.*
3. According to the mythological episodes, a king named Kṣatrabandhu was a worst sinner; another pious person known as Puṇḍarīka was reputed for his unsurpassed merit. But both were able to achieve *mokṣa* through the guidance of sage Nārada.
4. MUp I.2.12. *tadvijñānarthaṁ sa gurumeva abhigacchet.*
5. ChUp IV.9.3. *ācāryāddhaiva vidyā viditā sādhiṣṭāṁ prāpat.*
6. See TUp I.11. *ācārya devobhava.*
7. *Kaṭha Śruti* (referred to by VD ir the *Guruparaṁparā-sāra*)
   yasya deve parābhaktiḥ yathā deve tathā gurau;
   tasyaite kathitāhyarthāḥ prakāśante mahātmanaḥ.
8. See *Guruparaṁparā-sāra, guruṁ prakāśayet dhīmān mantraṁ yatnena gopayet;*
   aprakāśa-prakāśābhyāṁ kṣīyete sampadāyuṣī.
9. *Nyāsaviṁśati*, verse 1.
10. RTS See ch. 12 fn. 27 p. 259.
11. VP V.1.14. *mamāpyahilalokānāṁ guruḥ nārāyaṇo guruḥ.* (The second word *guru* is to be read as *aguruḥ*; not having a guru.)
12. According to tradition, sage Vyāsa is an incarnation of God (*anupraveśāvatāra*) and he is the author of both the *Mahābhārata* and *Vedānta Sūtra.*
13. See *Guruparaṁparāsāra.* The scriptural authority referred to here is found in *Rahasyāmnāya Brāhmaṇa* which states:
   sa ca acarya-vaṁśaḥ jñeyeyaḥ ācāryāṇām asau asau iti ābhagavattaḥ..
14. The term *Vaiṣṇava* means one who is connected with Viṣṇu (*viṣṇu-sambandhavān*). In this sense the definition becomes too wide which will include every individual in so far as Viṣṇu is immanent in all. In order to make it more specific the term is interpreted as one who is devoted to Viṣṇu and has realised that he is a *dāsa* or subservient to Viṣṇu (*viṣṇu-sambandha-jñāna-rasikavān*).
15. See *Nārada-sūtra*, 72. *nāsti teṣu jāti vidyā rūpa kula dhana kriyādi bhedaḥ.*
16. *Garuḍa Purāṇa*, 219.7. *bhaktiraṣṭavidhāhyeṣā yasmin mlecche'pi vartate...saca pūjyaḥ.*
   Mleccha is one who does not conform to Hindu ideals.
17. *Atharvaṇa Mahopaniṣad* (quoted by Vedānta Deśika in SR p. 43).
   dakṣiṇe tu bhuje vipro bibhṛyādvai sudarśanam;
   ṣavye tu śaṅkhaṁ bibhṛyāditi brahmavido viduḥ.

18. See SR p. 43. *prate viṣṇo abjacakre pavitre janmāmodhiṁ tartave carṣaṇīndrāḥ; mūle bāhvordadhate...*
19. Ibid.
20. Ibid. pp. 58-59.
21. Mbh VI 66.39 and 40. *brāhmaṇaiḥ kṣatriyaiḥ vaiśyaiḥ śūdraiśca kṛta-lakṣaṇaiḥ; arcanīyaśca...sātvataṁ vidhimāsthāya.*
22. *Pārameśvara Saṁhitā*, XV.962-65.
23. See *Vāmana Smṛti* (Quoted in SR p. 63),
    rakṣārtham-aghanāśārthaṁ maṅgalārthaṁ ca bhāmini;
    dhārayedūrdhva-puṇḍraṁ tu śirasā aharniśaṁ sadā.
24. See SR pp. 60–63.
    See also *Dakṣa Smṛti* (Quoted by VD in SR),
    snātvā lalāṭe tilakaṁ mṛdā kuryād-atandritaḥ
    homapūjādi-samaye sāyaṁ prātaḥ samāhitaḥ;
    ūrdhava-puṇḍradharo vipro bhavet śuddho na cānyathā.
25. The *Kriyādhikāra* (a Vaikhānasa treatise) enjoins this practice on the temple walls and utensils used for worship.
26. See *Bhārgava Smṛti* (Quoted by VD in SR p. 63). *sarve bhavanti viphalā ūrdhva-puṇḍraṁ vinā kṛtāḥ.*
27. See *Pārāśarya Saṁhitā* (quoted by VD in SR p. 63),
    nirūrdhva-puṇḍrastu bhavenna kadācidapi dvijaḥ;
    vaiṣṇvaśced-viśeṣeṇa sarvakarmāṇi nārhati.
28. See *Viśvaksena Saṁhitā* (Quoted by VD in RTS XX p. 137),
    ekānti vyapadeṣṭavyaḥ naiva grāmakulādibhiḥ.
    viṣṇunā vyapadeṣṭavyaḥ tasya sarvam sa eva hi.
29. The three important *mantras* which are generally imparted by the preceptor to his disciple at the time of *pañca-saṁkāra* are known as *Mūla-mantra*, *Dvaya* and *Carama-śloka*. The first contains the name of Nārāyaṇa, the second refers to the self-surrender and service to Śrīman-nārāyaṇa and the third covers the need of the self-surrender to God for *mokṣa*.
    For details see *Rahasya-traya-sāra* (Chapters XXVII-XXIX) and *Mumukṣuppaḍi* and the *Rahasya-granthas*.
30. See *Jayākhya Saṁhitā*, XXII.68.
    ekasyaiva hi kālasya vāsarīyasya nārada;
    āprabhātaṁ niśāntaṁ vai pañcadhā parikalpana.
31. See *Śrīvaiṣṇavasadācāra-nirṇaya*, p. xxvii.
    āhnikaṁ nāma ahni bhavam saccaritram.
32. See PR p. 108. *kālapañcaka-vibhāgena abhigamanopādāna ījyāsvādhyāyayogarūpa bhagavatsevanaṁ sva-varṇāśrama-jāti guṇa-nimittādi-niyatadharma-sacivaṁ bhagavad-dharma-niṣṭhānāṁ sarveṣāṁ samānam.*
33. Ibid. p. 109. *abhigacchet jagadyoniṁ taccābhigamanaṁ smṛtam.*
34. See PR p. 115. *nityaṁ caitat vaiśvadevādivat bhagavat-samārādhanam, "nityam-ārādhayet harim-iti" vacanāt.*

35. See fn 57 p. 231.
36. *Vyāsa Smṛti*, II.42. *na viṣṇu ārādhanāt puṇyaṁ vidyate karma vaidikam.* See also *Pādmottara*, XXIX-81. *ārādhanānāṁ sarveṣāṁ visṇoḥ ārādhanaṁ param.*
37. See *Śāṇḍilya Smṛti*, IV.31. The examples given are the loving mother treating a son, one approaching an intoxicated elephant with fear and a person meeting the youthful king (with devotion and fear).
yathā yuvānaṁ rājānaṁ yathāca madahastinam ... yathā ca putraṁ dayitaṁ tathaiva upacaret harim.
38. See *Dakṣa Smṛti*, (Quoted by VD in PR p. 118).
sarvopādhi-vinirmuktaṁ kṣetrajñaṁ brahmaṇi nyaset; etat dhyānaṁ ca yogaśca...
39. *Bhāgavata*, VII.5.23.
śravaṇaṁ kīrtanaṁ viṣṇoḥ smaraṇaṁ pādasevanaṁ;
arcanaṁ vandanaṁ dāsyaṁ sakhhyam ātma-nivedanam.
40. Mbh *saṁkīrtya nārāyaṇa-śabdamātraṁ vimuktaduḥkhāḥ sukhino bhavanti.*
41. VDh 43.12. *acyutānanta-govinda-nāmoccāraṇa-bheṣajāt;*
naśyanti sakalā rogāḥ satyaṁ satyaṁ vadāmyaham.
42. VP VI.8.9. *avaśenāpi yan-nāmni kīrtanāt sarva pātakaiḥ vimucyate.*
43. See *Viṣṇu-sahasranāma, stavyaḥ stavapriyaḥ*
44. The *sātvika-tyāga* in a formal way is not observed by the Vaiṣṇavas of Tenkalai sect. But since all religious acts are done by them with the sole purpose of *kaiṅkarya* for *Bhagavān* (*Bhagavat-kaiṅkarya-rūpa*), *sātvika-tyāga* is implied in the *saṅkalpa.*
45. *Pādmottara Purāṇa*, XXIX.81.
ārādhanānāṁ sarveṣāṁ viṣṇoḥ ārādhanam param;
tasmāt parataram proktaṁ tadīyārādhanaṁ param.
46. *svārādhanaṁ vihāyapi svabhaktān arcayanti ye;*
tebhyaḥ prasannaḥ bhagavān siddhim-iṣṭam prayacchati.
47. *Īḍu*, VIII.10.3.
48. VP VI.5.79. See Chapter VII p. 134.
49. See Mbh XIV.118.33. *dvādaśākṣara-tatvajñaḥ cāturvyūhavibhāgavit;*
acchidra-pañcakālajñaḥ satu bhāgavataḥ smṛtaḥ.
50. The word *sātvata* does not refer to a particular clan or to persons of lower community as some scholars believe. It denotes the Pāñcarātra system (*sātvata-śāstra*) and their followers. *Sat* means Brahman and those who believe in it or worship Him are *sātvatas.*
sat satvam brahma, tadvantaḥ sātvatah
sātvikā brahmavidaḥ teṣām idam karma śāstram vā sātvatam.
tat-kurvāṇa ācakṣaṇo vā sātvikāḥ.
51. See *Rahasyaratnāvalihṛadayam*, p. 42.
52. Ibid. p. 43.
53. See *Kaṇṇinum-śirattāmbu.*
54. *Tiruvāymoli*, II.7.4.
55. See RTS XVII p. 129.
56. See Mbh II5.117. *śīlavṛtta-phalaṁ śrutam.*

57. *Itihāsa Samuccaya*, 17.37. *śamārthaṁ sarvasāstrāṇi vihitāni maṇiṣibhiḥ.*
58. RTS VII p. 102. *anarthaṁ pāṇḍityaṁ dharmavarjitam.*
59. See *Periya Tirumoḻi* VIII.10.3. *mattramor daivaṁ uḷadenru iruppāroḍu uttrilen.*
60. See *Matsya Purāṇa*, 67.41. *ārogyaṁ bhāskarādicchet dhanamicchet hutāśanāt; iśvarāt jñānamanvicchet mokṣamicchet janārdanāt.*
61. See Mbh XII.345.15. *ye yajanti pitṛn devān brāhmaṇān sahutāśanān; sarvabhūtāntarātmanam viṣṇumeva yajanti te.* See also VS I.1.29 and I.1.31.
62. BG IX.23. *yetvanya-devatābhaktāḥ yajante śraddhayānvitāḥ te'pi māmeva kaunteya yajantyavidhipūrvakam.*
63. See *Iḍu*, VII.10.8. See also K.K.A. Venkatachari; Śrivaiṣṇava Maṇipravāla pp. 30-31.
64. See RB I.1.1. *satya ārjava dayā dāna ahiṁsā anabhidhyāḥ kalyāṇāni.*
65. Mbh XIV 110.64. *śapyamānasya yatpāpaṁ śapantamadhigacchati.*
66. See VP I.17.82. *baddhavairāṇi bhūtāni dveṣaṁ kurvanti cet-tataḥ; śocyānyaho atimohena vyāptāniti maniṣiṇā.*
67. See *Itihāsa Samuccaya*, VII.38. *kṛtakṛtyāḥ pratikṣante mṛtyuṁ priyamiva atithim.*
68. See Mbh XII.359.15.
69. *Parāśara Gita* (quoted by VD in RTS XIV p. 120) *nāhāraṁ cintayet prājño dharmamevānucintayet; āhāro hi manuṣyāṇāṁ janmanā saha jāyate.*
70. BG IV.22 and II.38.
71. Mbh XII.175.3. *na sukhaṁ prāpya saṁhṛṣyet duhkhaṁ prāpya na saṁjvaret.*
72. *Śāṇḍilya Smṛti*, III.18. *kulaṭā ṣaṇḍapatita vairibhyaḥ kākiṇīmapi; udyatāmapi grahṇīyāt nāpadyāpi kadācana.*
73. VDh, 76.22. *pararandhreṣu jātyandhāḥ paradāreṣu apuṁsakāḥ; parivādeṣu ye mūkāḥ te ativa dayitā mama.*
74. The English translation is taken from P.N. Srinivasachari, *The Philosophy of Viśiṣṭādvaita*, p. 569.
75. Translation from the *Sacred Writings of the Sikhs*.
76. *Īśa Up* 1. *īśāvāsyamidaṁ jagat.* See also *Viṣṇupurāṇa* II.12.38. See fn. 22 on p. 97.

16

CONCLUSION

In the preceding chapters we have presented the fundamental doctrines of Vaiṣṇavism, both philosophical as well as theological, based on original sources. In the first chapter we have outlined the historical development of Vaiṣṇava religion with a view to showing how this religion having its roots in the Ṛgveda, the oldest religious literature of the world, has evolved itself in successive stages into a well formulated monotheistic system in the hands of Rāmānuja and other eminent *ācāryas* who have contributed extensive scholarly works. In the first part of the book (Chapters 2 to 6), we have covered the philosophy of Vaiṣṇavism as enunciated in the Upaniṣads and the *Vedānta-sūtra* in order to establish the fact that the Vaiṣṇava theology has a positive philosophical foundation. In the second part of the book (Chapters 7 to 14), we have given a comprehensive account of the important theological doctrines of Vaiṣṇavism in order to provide a deeper insight into the Vaiṣṇava theology in all its aspects. In the concluding part of the book (Chapter 15) dealing with Religious Discipline of Vaiṣṇavism we have outlined the pattern of life of an ideal Vaiṣṇava and the ethical virtues to be cultivated by him.

The main objective of the book has been to present in a single volume a comprehensive account of the philosophy and theology of Vaiṣṇavism as far as possible in a coherent manner as it developed over a period of centuries. Though a comparative and critical study of this religion with other monotheistic religions would have enhanced the value of the book, it has not been attempted for two reasons. In the first place, such a study would involve a detailed discussion of the doctrines of other religions and it would not be possible to do full justice to the subject in a single treatise without the risk of running into great length. Secondly, it would be more appropriate to provide an accurate and authentic account of a single religion and leave it to the readers to judge its merit. However, the relevant criticisms against some of the theories and a few controversial issues have been discussed in their appropriate places to evaluate the soundness of the doctrines. Since it would be redundant to go over them again in this chapter, it may be useful to recapitulate in the concluding chapter a few important points that give a distinctiveness to this monotheistic system.

The first important point is that Vaiṣṇavism has its roots in the Vedic religion as all its essential tenets are found in the Ṛgveda. As we have observed in the chapter on the historical development, the *Ṛk Saṁhitā* refers to Viṣṇu as the Supreme Deity and that Viṣṇu is associated with Goddess Lakṣmī (*Sriyaḥpati*); secondly, that Viṣṇu incarnates Himself in many forms for the protection of the humanity and that Viṣṇu as a benevolent Deity is the giver of bounty to His devotees including salvation; thirdly, that Viṣṇu has an eternal abode (*paramapada*) and that devoted worship of Viṣṇu leads to higher spiritual goal. Both Śaivism and Śāktaism which are the two living monotheistic religions and which have been in existence from ancient times, cannot make such a positive claim. In the first place, the terms *Śiva* and *Śakti* as understood by these religious cults are not mentioned anywhere in the Ṛgveda. The concept of *Rudra* in the Ṛgveda, on the basis of which the concept of Śiva is developed in the post-Vedic period, has none of the characteristics attributed to Śiva as the supreme benignant deity. In the same way the *Ṛk Saṁhitā* nowhere makes any mention of a female deity as an independent Supreme Goddess. *Umā*, the wife of a Vedic deity, referred to in the Ṛgveda does not overshadow her male consort. The names such as Rudrāṇī and Bhavānī, which are derivates do not imply the existence of an independent powerful Goddess.'

Even if we concede that Rudra, Paśupati, Indrāṇī, Bhavānī, Umā and Aditi mentioned in the *Ṛk* hymns provide the basis for the conception of the deities of these two cults at a later period, it is difficult to trace the roots of the essential tenets of these religions in the Ṛgveda. As we have observed in the Introduction, the ancient Śaivites themselves maintain the view that their religious teachings are developed primarily on the Śaiva Āgamas which were revealed by God Śiva and not so much on the Vedas.[2] The same is the case with Śāktaism whose doctrines and religious practices are formulated on the basis of Śākta Āgamas. Though Vaiṣṇavism too makes use of the Vaiṣṇava Āgamas, there is this fundamental difference, viz., that these Āgamas—both the Vaikhānasa and Pāñcarātra—are of Vedic origin.[3] We have observed that the Vedic Religion is basically monotheistic with the belief in the existence of one Supreme Being.[4] If this view is accepted, then Vedic Religion cannot be anything other than Vaiṣṇavism as Viṣṇu among all other Vedic deities pre-eminently fulfills the criteria laid down in the Vedānta for determining the nature of Ultimate Reality or the Supreme Lord (*Īśvara*) of Religion. We have established this fact with sufficient arguments substantiated by the Ṛgvedic hymns as rightly interpreted by the ancient Vedic commentators such as Yāska and exponents of Vedānta such as Śaṁkara, Rāmānuja and Madhvā.[5]

As important as being Vedic in origin, Vaiṣṇavism is also a well-developed theological system with a philosophic foundation. Its theological doctrines are clearly traceable to the Upaniṣads and the *Vedānta-sūtras*. As we have explained in the Introduction, Vaiṣṇavism is a Philosophy of Religion. To use a Western terminology, it is Natural Theology or Religio-philosophy as distinct from Revealed Theology which is generally based on a set of dogmas and beliefs. If the older, major Upaniṣads such as *Īśa*, *Kaṭha*, *Taittirīya*, *Chāndogya* and *Bṛhadāraṇyaka* contain acceptable philosophical theories, then the Philosophy of Vaiṣṇavism too, which is the same as Viśiṣṭādvaita Vedānta founded on these Upaniṣads as expounded by Rāmānuja, should be regarded as a sound philosophy. In part I of the book we have outlined the philosophical theories of Vaiṣṇavism as enunciated in the Vedānta. That Viśiṣṭādvaita Vedānta is essentially a philosophical system and not a mere theology and that it is even a better philosophical system than that of Śaṁkara is established by Vedānta Deśika in his *Tattva-muktā-kalāpa* and my book *Fundamentals of Viśiṣṭādvaita Vedānta* written on the basis of this classic.[6]

The Vaiṣṇava religion has no doubt taken material from the Epics, selected Purāṇas and the Tamil hymns of Āḻvārs for expounding its doctrines. But this would not affect its value as a religio-philosophical system because the teachings of the Epics etc., are in consonance with those of the Vedas and the

Upaniṣads. This post-Vedic religious literature categorised as Smṛti texts as distinct from Śruti texts, are taken as *upabrāhmaṇas* or those which elucidate what is already contained in the Vedas and Upaniṣads. In so far as the Smṛti texts are not in conflict with the Śruti texts they are a valid source of knowledge and the material drawn from them lend additional support to the Vedic teachings. We have shown in the concerned chapter how each one of the theological doctrines of Vaiṣṇavism is an outgrowth of the philosophical concept found in the Vedānta and how the same has been further expanded with the support of the Smṛti texts.

We may now evaluate a few theological doctrines to bring out their distinctive character. Coming to the central doctrine of Viṣṇu as the Supreme Deity (*para-tattva*), it may be observed that whatever God or Goddess is accepted as the Supreme Being, that deity should fulfill the criteria for the Ultimate Reality of philosophy or the Supreme Personal God of religion. According to the Vedānta, the Ultimate Reality is that metaphysical entity which is the cause of origin, sustenance and dissolution of the universe. It is called Brahman in the Upaniṣads. According to the Hindu religious schools of thought, the important criteria for determining the supremacy of a deity is that it should be the sole creator and protector of the universe. It is generally conceived in terms of a personal God or Goddess possessing such characteristics as omniscience, omnipotence and omnipresence. These characteristics can be attributed to any deity which is to be regarded as the Supreme Being. The three theistic schools—Vaiṣṇavism, Śaivism and Śāktaism—use the names of Viṣṇu, Śiva and Goddess Śakti respectively to denote their highest Divine Being. Theoretically, any deity with any name can be claimed as identical with the metaphysical Ultimate Reality known as Brahman and also as the Highest God or Goddess of that religious cult. Which view is logically and philosophically tenable is the main issue to be considered.

In the Indian context, the Revealed Scripture which covers the Vedas and Upaniṣads, is the final authority for resolving the issue concerning the super-normal spiritual entity. This is an accepted view of all orthodox Hindu schools of thought. Logic is not ruled out but it is adopted to support what is said in the Scripture for the obvious reason that logic cannot conclusively either prove or disprove a super-normal theory. If we accept that Śruti supplemented with logic is the most valid source of knowledge (*pramāṇa*), the theory that Viṣṇu is the Supreme Deity of Religion and that He is also the same as the Ultimate Reality of the Upaniṣads has a better chance of acceptability than the theories of other religious cults.

Viṣṇu, Nārāyaṇa and Vāsudeva are the names which are commonly used to denote the Supreme Deity of Vaiṣṇavism. We have observed in Chapter 7 that these terms are not mere names of a cult God but, on the other hand, connote the distinctive characteristics of a Supreme Deity. Both the etymological meanings of these terms as well as the teachings of the whole gamut of sacred texts from the earliest Ṛgveda to the *Mahābhārata* and the *Viṣṇupurāṇa* support this conclusion.

We have pointed out in Chapter 2 how Rāmānuja has equated Nārāyaṇa with Brahman of the Upaniṣads by adopting the Mīmāṁsā principle of interpretation. This equation of Viṣṇu or Nārāyaṇa with Brahman provides the concept of a perfect Godhead endowed with every conceivable auspicious attributes and free from any kind of defect. Chapter 9 on Viṣṇu and His Attributes will reveal how convincingly the God of Vaiṣṇavism is presented. The numerous attributes of God and the manner in which these are justified by the Vaiṣṇava *ācāryas* on the authority of the scriptural and Smṛti texts as well as the mystic experience of Āḻvārs, provide the conception of an ideal personal Divine Being. It is not an anthropomorphic concept but a theory that draws sustenance from the spiritual insight of many sages and mystics who are claimed to have intuited God in His true form.

The doctrine of Goddess, which is an important feature of theistic systems, is a distinctive contribution of Vaiṣṇavism. The worship of Goddess in some form or the other is an ancient religious practice which is prevalent both among primitive tribes as well as among civilised ancient communities. The idea of a divine power as the protector of human beings either as father or mother, has given rise to the concept of Goddess as Divine Mother. In the more developed theistic schools of thought, we come across a well formulated doctrine of Goddess. While most of the theistic religious sects accept the theory of Goddess, the ontological status accorded to Her varies from one school to another. From the philosophical point of view, the ontological status of Goddess with which we are concerned here is far more important.

There are three ways of conceiving this theory:

(1) Goddess as a primordial energy or *Śakti* is the Supreme Being.
(2) Goddess as the consort of God with a subordinate status as a higher soul.
(3) Goddess is inseparable from God and the divine couple enjoying equal status constitute the Supreme Reality.

Each theory has its own merits and defects. It will suffice to make a few brief observations to say how the theory advanced by Vaiṣṇavism as discussed in the Chapter on Viṣṇu and Goddess *Śri* is philosophically sound.

The first theory which is upheld by Śāktaism accords supreme importance to Goddess and relegates God to a subordinate position. According to this school of thought, Brahmā, Viṣṇu and Śiva, the three principal deities of the Purāṇas are all the creations of *Śakti.* What is created cannot be the Ultimate Reality. Besides, if *Śakti* is taken as primordial *energy*, it cannot be a sentient Being, endowed with knowledge (*jñāna*) and power (*śakti*) to perform the cosmic functions of creation and protection of the universe. It has to be a personal Deity. Some of the Śākta sects have done so by naming Śakti as Kālī, Durgā and Devī. In that case, the highest deity becomes a personal Goddess, supported only by the Śākta Āgamas without any connection with the main philosophical teachings of the Upaniṣads regarding the nature of the Ultimate Reality.

The second theory is advanced by a large number of both Vaiṣṇava and Śaiva theistic sects. Among the Vaiṣṇava sects, the Madhavas and the Tenkalai Śrīvaiṣṇavas hold the view that Goddess who is named as Lakṣmī is a consort of Viṣṇu (*Viṣṇu-patnī*). Ontologically, She cannot be on par with Viṣṇu but holds a subordinate status as a higher soul (*cetana*). Some of the later Śaivite sects have accepted Goddess in the name of *Pārvatī* as the consort of Lord Śiva without according to Her an equal ontological status with Śiva. The Śaiva-siddhānta developed at a later period in South India regards the Goddess as the creative energy of Śiva (*Śiva-śakti*). Even the Vaiṣṇava Āgamas such as

Ahirbudhnya Saṁhitā and *Lakṣmī Tantra* which have given a prominent place to *Lakṣmī* present the view of Goddess as *śakti* of Viṣṇu (*Viṣṇu-śakti*) and the two are inherently related like the *prabhā* (luminosity) and *prabhāvān* (sun). The merit of all these theories lies in maintaining the unitary character of God as one, independent Supreme Being. The major defect of the theories is that Goddess as subordinate deity cannot be on par with God and enjoy the status as *Īśvarī* or the Sovereign Ruler of the universe as stated by the scriptural texts,[7] having a role in the important divine functions such as creation and protection of the universe. Besides, *śakti* as an attribute is non-sentient in character and it cannot have any function of its own except as an instrumental cause to be operated by the intelligent Lord, who is the *Śaktimān* or the possessor of *śakti*.

According to the third theory, Goddess is a distinct Divine Being but as an inseparable consort of God, She enjoys an equal ontological status with God and the Divine couple together constitute the *para-tattva* in the name of *Śrīman-nārāyaṇa* or *Śriyaḥ-pati*. This is the view advanced by Vaiṣṇavism as expounded by Rāmānuja and as further developed by his illustrious successor, Vedānta Deśika. Though Viṣṇu and His consort, Lakṣmī are two distinct deities, the Divine couple function together as the Supreme Ruler of the universe (*śeṣī*) and partake in all the important divine functions such as creation and protection of the universe. As we have explained in the Chapter 8, this theory finds justification in the teachings of the sacred texts.

The doctrine of *avatāra* or incarnation of Viṣṇu in different manifestations constitutes another important contribution of Vaiṣṇavism. No other theistic religion has accepted this theory. Even Śaiva-siddhānta, which is the closest parallel to Vaiṣṇavism, does not believe in the incarnation of *paśupati*. Both Śaivism and Śāktaism speak of different forms of Śiva and Devī with different appellations of the same deity but not incarnations as Vaiṣṇavism believes. In Christianity, Christ is regarded as the son of God but this concept does not conform to the idea of God Himself descending in a human form. Even if such a view is conceded, it does not sound reasonable to say that there can be one and only incarnation. Most of the theistic schools abhor the idea of incarnation of God as human or other living beings as it would amount to defilement of God being associated with the defects of a physical body. If we understand properly the philosophy of *avatāra* as expounded in Vaiṣṇavism on the authority of the scriptural texts and the *Bhagavadgītā*[8] and also the concept of *śuddha-sattva* admitted by Viśiṣṭādvaita,[9] there is no room for such doubts.

In any sound theistic system which believes in the existence of personal God as the redeemer and saviour of mankind, endowed with the attributes of omniscience, omnipotence, omnipresence and compassion, the theory of His incarnation is a logical corollary. We have discussed fully the philosophy of *avatāra*, its main purpose and its need in the Chapter on Viṣṇu and His Incarnation. An all-compassionate God, who is always willing to protect His devotees, should be easily accessible to them for worship and meditation. If He ever remained in His exalted Divine abode as a transcendental Being, it would not serve the purpose of the devotees. The pious individuals, saints as well as mystics, yearn to have a vision of Him. Such a craving is not a mental aberration but a natural instinct of human being who is under intense religious fervour. A benevolent God should be able to reveal His divine form. This is the significance of *sādhu-paritrāṇa*, protection of the pious individuals, mentioned in the *Bhagavad-gītā* as the main purpose of *avatāra*. The destruction of the evil forces (*duṣkṛt-vināśa*) which is the other objective of *avatāra* is only incidental because such a function can be performed by the will (*saṅkalpa*) of God without His physical presence. God is no doubt omnipresent. His *svarūpa* is *ananta*, infinite both spatially and temporally, as the Upaniṣad states. Such a presence without a concrete physical form will not serve the purpose of worship or meditation. Meditation in the initial stages needs a concretised divine object. Even those religions which do not accept idol worship, do have some kind of symbol for worship. With the acceptance of the *avatāra* theory, an idol or image, when duly consecrated with the prescribed rituals, becomes a spiritual object befitting worship and meditation. The *arcā* form, which is one of the five types of *avatāra* accepted by Vaiṣṇavism, provides a more acceptable theological basis for image worship than symbols devoid of such significance.

The most significant contribution of Vaiṣṇavism lies in its

advocacy of the doctrine of *prapatti* or the absolute surrender of the self to the care of God as the easiest means of salvation; it is open to all irrespective of caste, creed, sex or social status of individuals. Though the basic concept of seeking divine grace for obtaining our desired objects is commonly accepted by all theistic religions, the credit of developing it into a doctrine of spiritual discipline for liberation from bondage (*mokṣa*) goes to Vaiṣṇavism as expounded by Rāmānuja. We have explained how this doctrine stands well justified on the basis of the scriptural and Smṛti texts.[10]

Religion in its broadest sense is a way of life leading to a higher spiritual goal. If we evaluate Vaiṣṇava religion in terms of the practical mode of life that it advocates, one dominant concept stands out as worthy of universal acceptance, namely, loving devotion to one Supreme Being who is the controller of the universe and who is immanent in all sentient beings and non-sentient entities. By naming that Supreme Deity as Viṣṇu or Nārāyaṇa by emphasising the exclusive worship of that one God, Vaiṣṇavism may, on the face it appear as a dogmatic cult. But it is not so, if we bear in mind the fact that the term Nārāyaṇa or Viṣṇu is not a mere name of a cult God but it connotes all the essential characteristics of the Ultimate Reality of philosophy or the personal God of a religion.

The concept of God as omnipresent (*vibhu*) is undisputed in Indian philosophy. By giving Him a name and a form, He does not become a sectarian cult deity. The Ṛgveda, the oldest extant religious literature in the world, uses the expression *sat* for the Supreme Being. So too the *Chāndogya Upaniṣad* describes the Ultimate Reality as *sat* or Brahman. It is neither He nor She; it does not have any physical form (*nirākāra*). But for purposes of worship, God Himself manifests in a bodily form to serve the needs of the devotees.[11] The name by which we refer to God is, therefore, secondary for a true religious aspirant or a metaphysician. In view of this, Vaiṣṇavism emphasises the fact that to whomever worship is offered, it will ultimately reach that one Supreme Deity who is the *antarātmā* or the indwelling self of all deities. If we take note of this significant teaching, which is the crux of Vaiṣṇava philosophy, there need be no room for any sectarian disputes. There is only one God, who is Supreme Ruler (*Īśvara*) and all that exists in the universe—the sentient beings and non-sentient entities—are His *vibhūti* or glories. As God is immanent in all human beings, all are to be respected as equal. In the eyes of God, there is no distinction between one individual and the other. As the famous Sanskrit poet, Bhartṛhari states, for those who have a broad religious outlook, the whole universe is one family (*udāra caritānāṁ tu vasudhaiva kutuṁbakam*).

On the basis of this philosophy, Vaiṣṇavism lays greater stress on the cultivation of ethical virtues than on formal religious observances. Among the ethical virtues, it advocates love and compassion towards all living beings, avoidance of hatred towards others, tolerance of other faiths and looking upon all individuals as equal. It was this aspect of the ethical teachings of Vaiṣṇavisṁ that attracted the attention of the greatest man of our time, Mahatma Gandhi who adopted the famous song, *Vaiṣṇava janato . . . .*, extolling the universal brotherhood as part of his daily prayer.[12]

To conclude:

Vaiṣṇavism is the most ancient Vedic religion developed on the authority of the Upaniṣads, Āgamas, Epics, Purāṇas and the hymns of the Āḻvārs.

It is a religion founded on the philosophical concepts enunciated in the Vedānta.

It is a religion in which the nature of Supreme Deity is well defined and identified with the Ultimate Reality of Metaphysics, thereby bridging the gulf between Religion and Philosophy.

It is a religion in which the concept of Goddess is clearly formulated and given a proper ontological status.

It is a religion which has expounded the philosophy of *avatāra*.

It is a religion which advocates an easy way of attaining the higher spiritual goal.

It is a religion which preaches ethical and religious values having universal appeal.

Notes

1. See R.G. Bhandarkar, *Vaiṣṇavism, Śaivism etc.*, p. 203.
2. See Introduction, . xxviii.
3. See Chapter 1, p. 15.

4. Ibid., pp. 3-7.
5. Ibid., pp. 7-12.
6. See FVV Chapter 12.
7. See Chapter 8, fn. 1 and 2, p. 178.
8. See Chapter 10.
9. See Chapter 11.
10. See Chapter 13.
11. See Chapter 9, pp. 200-202.
12. See Chapter 15, p. 328.

GLOSSARY

abhayam: assurance of protection.
abheda: non-difference.
abhigamana: approching God; first of the five religious duties to be observed by a Vaiṣṇava.
abhimata: as liked by oneself.
abhyāsa: repeated practice.
acetana: non-sentient.
acit: non-sentient matter; primordial cosmic matter (*Prakṛti*).
adhiṣṭhāna: substratum; objective basis for illusion.
advaita: non-dualism; system of Vedānta associated with Śaṁkara.
agni: fire; consecrated fire.
aham: ego; the notion of 'I'.
ahamartha: entity denoted by the notion of 'I'; the individual self.
ahaṁkāra: egotism; an evolute of cosmic matter.
ahas: the day.
aikya: identity; oneness.
aiśvarya: lordship; one of the six principal attributes of God.
ajaḍa: non-material; spiritual.
ajñāna: ignorance; absence of knowledge.
amala: pure; free from defects.
amānava: the presiding deity of the lightning who guides the soul to *mokṣa*.
amṛta: immortal.
aṁśa: a part; an integral part of a complex whole; an essential and inseparable attribute of a substance.
aṁśin: that which is the substrate for the attribute; Brahman as organically related to *cit* and *acit*.
ananta: infinite; that which is not conditioned by space, time or another entity; a distinguishing attribute of Brahman.
anantayāma: immeasurable.
ananya: non-distinct.
ananya-śaraṇa: not having any other refuge than God.

ananyopāya: not having any other means than God.
anapāyinī: inseparable.
anavasāda: a mental state unaffected by afflictions.
aṇḍa: the primordial egg out of which Brahmā, the creator of the cosmic universe springs.
aṅga: subsidiary; a component.
aniṣṭa: undesirable.
añjali: folded hands.
antaḥkaraṇa: internal sense organ; mind.
antaryāmin: the inner controller; the immanent Supreme Self.
antarātmā: the indwelling Self; the Paramātman who is immanent in all beings.
antarikṣa: sky; mid-region.
aṇu: monad; atomic.
anuddharṣa: tranquillity of mind.
anugraha: grace of God.
anukūla: agreeable.
anumāna: inference.
anumantā: one who accords approval; God.
anuvāda: restatement.
apacāra: offence; improper conduct.
apahata-pāpmā: free from evil.
apara: lower; a dependent reality.
aparokṣa: immediate; direct.
aparyavasāna-vṛtti: the connotation of a term denoting ultimately God.
apauruṣeya: not ascribed to human author.
aprākṛta: non-material; made of spiritual substance.
apṛthaksiddha: inseparability; integrally related as substance and attribute, body and soul.
arcā: idol of worship; incarnation of God by entering into the idols chosen by devotees.
arcana: a mode of worship; offering flowers to God with recitation of His names.
arcā-vigraha: icon worshipped at the temples or homes.
arcirādimārga: the path of the divine beings leading to *mokṣa*.
arthapañcaka: five major topics of Vaiṣṇavism; the treatise dealing with five topics.

asādhāraṇa-dharma: the distinguishing characteristic; an essential attribute.
aṣṭādaśa: eighteen.
aṣṭāṅga-yoga: the eight-fold discipline of yoga.
audārya: generosity; an attribute of God.
avasthā: a state of modification.
avatāra: descent of God; incarnation of God.
avayava: part; component.
avāptasamastakāma: one whose desires are already achieved without obstruction; God.
avidyā: ignorance; the cosmic principle which is the cause of the world illusion.
avikāra: not subject to modification; unchangeable.
avyaya: immutable, eternal.
ayana: ground; basis.
ācamana: sipping of water for inner purification.
ācāra: conduct; observance of prescribed religious rites.
ācārya: a teacher; a spiritual preceptor.
ādhāra: supporter; the ground of the universe.
ādheya: the supported; that which is sustained by the Supreme Being.
āgama: Revealed Scripture; the treatises dealing with the modes of worship of God and matters relating to temples.
āhnika: daily religious observances.
ālvār: one who is deeply immersed in God's experience; the Vaiṣṇava saint of South India.
ākāra: physical form; image.
ākāśa: ether; space.
ākiñcanya: state of helplessness.
ānanda: bliss; blissful; an essential attribute of Brahman.
ānuṣaṅgika: incidental.
ārādhanā: worship of God.
ārjava: straight-forwardness.
āspada: abode.
āśrama: four stages of life; an hermitage.
āśraya: locus; basis.
ātivāhikas: the deities commanded by God to serve as guides to the soul on its march to *mokṣa*.
ātman: the self; the individual soul.

ātma-guṇa: ethical virtues.

ātma-nivedana: surrendering one's self to God.

ātma-nikṣepa: placing the burden of protection of the soul to the care of God with ardent prayer and sincere faith.

ātmāvalokana: direct vision of the self; self-realization.

āveśa: to take possession of; infusion of divine power into a body.

āyudha: weapons.

baddha: bound; the soul in bondage.

bala: strength.

bhagavadapacāra: offences committed in respect of God.

bhagavān: the Supreme Being endowed with six principal attributes, Viṣṇu.

bhāgavata: worshipper of Bhagavān or Viṣṇu, devotees of Viṣṇu.

bhāgavadapacāra: offences committed to devotees of Viṣṇu.

bhakta: a devotee of God.

bhakti: devotion to God; loving meditation on God.

bhakti-yoga: observance of unceasing meditation on God as a means to *mokṣa*.

bheda: difference.

bhedābheda: difference cum non-difference.

bhīti: fear.

bhogya: the object of experience; what is enjoyable.

bhoktā: one who experiences pleasure and pain; the individual self.

bhrama: error; delusion.

bhūmā: limitless; the infinite blissful reality.

bhūta-hita: compassion towards all living beings.

brahmā: the Vedic deity entrusted with the task of creation of the universe.

Brahman: the Absolute of philosophy; the ultimate Reality; the personal God according to Viśiṣṭādvaita.

Brahma-loka: the abode of Brahman; eternal transcendental realm of Viṣṇu.

Brahmānubhava: experience of Brahman.

Brahmasākṣātkāra: direct realization of Brahman.

Brahmavidyā: meditation on Brahman.

Brahma-vit: the knower of Brahman.
buddhi: mind; internal organ.
buddhi-yoga: higher stage of *bhakti-yoga* (*para-bhakti*).

caitanya: consciousness.
cakra: discus; wheel.
cakṣus: visual organ; eye.
cāturya: cleverness.
cetana: sentient; that which possesses consciousness.
caturmukha-brahmā: four-faced Brahmā.
chāga: goat.
cintana: contemplation.
cit: sentient being; the individual self.

dama: self-restraint.
dampatī: couple.
daṇḍadhara: dispenser of punishment for sins committed by an individual.
darśana: vision; a system of philosophy.
dāna: giving away as charity.
dānava: a demon.
dāsa: subordinate; one who is subservient to the Lord.
dāsa kūṭa: a band of devotees of Viṣṇu singing His glory.
dāsatva: subordination.
deśa: place; space.
devatā: vedic deity; celestial being.
dharma: a quality of a substance; an attribute; righteousness; religious duty.
dharmabhūtajñāna: knowledge as an essential attribute of self.
dharmī: that in which a quality inheres; a substrate.
dhyāna: contemplation; meditation.
dhāraṇa: concentration.
dhruvāsmṛti: steadfast meditation.
divi: heaven, sky.
divya: divine.
doṣa: defect.
dravya: that which is associated with modification; a substance.
duḥkha: suffering; sorrow.
duṣkṛta: evil deed.

dvaya: an esoteric Vaiṣṇava *mantra* comprising two sentences referring to self-surrender (*śaraṇāgati*).
dvaita: pluralism; a system of Vedānta founded by Madhva.
dveṣa: hatred.
dyuloka: higher region; heaven.

eka: one; one Reality.

gadya: a prose lyric; devotional prose hymn.
gandha: odour; sandal paste.
Garuḍa: divine bird; Viṣṇu's mount.
gāḍhopagūḍha: intimately united as inseparable.
gāmbhīrya: incomprehensible character.
gauṇa: secondary.
goptṛtva-varaṇa: prayer seeking protection.
guṇa: quality; three cosmic attributes.
guru: preceptor imparting spiritual knowledge.

heya-guṇa: defiling qualities or attributes.
heya-pratyanīka: opposed to everything that is defiling or evil.
hiraṇya: gold.
Hiraṇyagarbha: the vedic deity entrusted with the function of cosmic creation; Brahmā; name of Viṣṇu.
Hiraṇmaya: golden; description of God.
hita: means to achieve the supreme goal of life.
homa: offering oblations in the consecrated fire.
Hrī: name of Goddess Bhū-devī; also Lakṣmī.

icchā: will.
īḍu: the commentary on the hymns of Nammāḷvār known as *muppattiyārāyirappaḍi* (36000).
indriyas: sense organs.
indriya-saṁyama: control of sense organs.
ijyā: formal worship of God; third Part of the five-fold religious duty of a Vaiṣṇava.
Iśvara: God; the Supreme Being as the controller of all beings.
Iśvarī: the sovereign of the universe; Goddess.
Iśāna: the ruler of the universe; god; also applicable to Śiva.
Iśānā: goddess Lakṣmī; The sovereign of the universe.

iṣṭaprāpti: attainment of what is desired.
itihāsa: the two epics—Rāmāyaṇa and Mahābhārata.

jaḍa: non-sentient; inert object.
jagat: physical universe.
jagat-kāraṇa: the primary cause of the universe.
janma: origin; birth.
jijñāsā: enquiry into the nature of Brahman; desire to know Brahman.
jīva: individual self.
jīva-koṭi: category of jīvas.
jīvātman: individual self as distinct from Paramātman.
Jīyar: respectful name for an ascetic of the religious centre (*maṭham*).
jñāna: knowledge; consciousness.
jñātā: subject of knowledge; knower.
jyotis: light.

kalyāṇa-guṇa: auspicious attributes.
kaivalya: the state of existence of self in its true form as free from bondage; a state of *mokṣa*.
karma: action; rituals; past deeds and their results in the form of merit and sin.
karma-kāṇda: the earlier part of the Vedas dealing primarily with the rituals.
karma-yoga: observance of religious act as a means for self-realization.
kartā: agent of action; individual self as doer.
kartṛtva: responsibility for action.
kāla: time.
kāma: passion; attachment; desire.
kāmya-karma: religious observances prompted by desire for specific results.
kāraṇa: cause.
kārayitā: one who prompts an individual to act.
kāruṇya: compassion.
kārya: effect.
kāyika: physical act.
kīrtana: singing the glory of God.

kīrti: renown; synonymous with *Lakṣmī*.
kṛpā: compassion.
kṛtajñatā: gratitude; feeling of satisfaction even with the smallest good deed.
kṛtakṛtya: one who has accomplished *prapatti* for *mokṣa*.
kṛti: effort.
kṛtitva: feeling of having fulfilled the obligations.
kriyā: activity; the performance of rites.
krodha: anger.
kṣamā: forgiveness.
kṣetrajña: the knower of body; the individual self.
kumbha: pot; a vessel to keep water.
kuṭumba: family.

Lakṣmī: name of Goddess who is the consort of Viṣṇu.
līlā: sport.
līlā-vibhūti: divine glory serving as play ground for God; physical universe.
liṅga: identity mark.
loha: metal.

mahad-bhūtaṁ: the Supreme Being.
mahat: the great; the evolute of the primordial matter (*prakṛti*).
mahimā: greatness.
mamatā: the feeling of mineness; the sense of ownership.
manana: logical reflection.
maṇḍala: a division of the Ṛgveda (the whole collection being divided into ten *maṇḍalas*).
maṅgala: auspiciousness.
maṇipravāla: Sanskritised Tamil prose.
mantra: esoteric syllables or words signifying spiritual ideas, a Vedic hymn.
mata: a religious cult; a religious system.
maṭham: a religious centre headed by an ascetic; a monastery.
mārdava: soft-heartedness; an attribute of God.
māyā: cosmic principle which gives rise to world illusion; the phenomenal character of the universe; the primordial matter (*prakṛti*); that which is an instrument of wonderful creation.

māyā-vāda: the doctrine of Advaita Vedānta which advocates that everything other than Brahman is illusory.
medhā: knowledge; synonymous with Lakṣmī.
mithyā: illusory.
mokṣa: liberation of soul from bondage; a complete and comprehensive experience of Brahman; attainment of Brahman.
mukta: the soul which is liberated from bondage.
mumukṣu: an aspirant for *mokṣa*; one who is desirous of release from bondage.

namaḥ: salutation; the mental notion that the soul is not mine but of the Lord.
namaskāra: offering salutation; self-surrender.
nāma: name; one of the five Vaiṣṇava sacraments.
nidāna: cause.
nididhyāsana: steadfast meditation.
Nara: the Supreme Being.
Nārāyaṇa: the Supreme Being who is the ground of all sentient and non-sentient entities in the universe and also immanent in them.
naimittika-karma: rituals prescribed for specific occasions and purposes.
nigraha: unfavourable disposition of God.
nimitta-kāraṇa: instrumental cause.
niratiaśya: greatness beyond comprehension.
nirguṇa: devoid of all characteristics; undifferentiated; devoid of defiling attributes.
nirhetuka-kṛpā: unconditioned flow of compassion.
nirukta: a treatise containing glossarial explanation of vedic terms.
nirvikāra: immutable.
nirviśeṣa: undifferentiated; devoid of all attributes.
niṣkāma: free from any desire for results.
nitya: eternal.
nitya-karma: mandatory religious duties.
nitya-sūris: eternally existing souls.
nitya-vibhūti: eternal transcendental realm.
nivṛtti: removal.
niyantā: controller of all beings; God.

niyantṛī: Goddess who controls all.
niyāmaka: one who controls.
nyāsa: self-surrender to God.
nyāsa-vidyā: the observance of self-surrender as means to *mokṣa.*

padmanābha: name of one of the twelve sub-vyūhas.
pañcabhūta: five physical elements.
pañcakāla-prakriyā: five-fold religious duty of a Vaiṣṇava.
pañca-saṁskāra: five-fold Vaiṣṇava sacrament.
pañcīkaraṇa: quintuplication of five elements.
pāñcarātra: religious system followed by the Bhāgavatas; the religious treatises dealing with modes of worship of God and matters relating to temples.
para: the highest; the Supreme.
para-bhakti: the perfected stage of meditation serving as direct means to *mokṣa.*
para-brahma: the ultimate metaphysical Reality; the supreme personal God.
para-devatā: the supreme deity.
parajñāna: vision of God; a stage of meditation giving rise to temporary vision of God.
parama-bhakti: highest stage of meditation culminating in the liberation of soul from bondage.
paramapada: the supreme abode of Viṣṇu.
paraṁ-jyotis: the transcendental light; Brahman.
parama-vyoma: the highest heaven; the eternal abode of God.
paramāṇu: the atom; the infinitesimal, suprasensible reals.
paramātman: the supreme Self; Brahman; God.
parāk: that which manifests for the self as, for example, *jñāna.*
parākrama: supreme power.
parāpti: attainment of supreme Deity.
parārtha: what is intended for the use of others.
paratantra: dependent.
pariṇāma: modification; evolution.
paripūrṇa: perfect; comprehensive.
paśu: animal; individual soul (according to Śaivism).
paśupati: Lord of the *jīvas*; Rudra; Śiva.
pati: Lord; husband.
pādukā: holy sandals of the idol of God.

pādya: water offered to wash the feet.
pāśupata: the cult advocating the worship of Paśupati (Śiva).
prabhā: light; luminosity.
pradhāna: cosmic matter; *prakṛti*.
pradyumna: one of the four *vyūhas*.
prakāra: mode; attribute; jīva as *prakāra* of Brahman.
prakārin: a substance which has modes; Brahman.
prakāśa: illumination.
prakṛti: primordial cosmic matter.
pralaya: dissolution of the universe.
pramāṇas: means of valid knowledge; evidence.
prapanna: one who has performed *prapatti*.
prapatti: total self-surrender to God as the sole refuge.
prasādana: grace.
pratijñā: the statement of the proposition to be proved.
pratikūla: disagreeable.
pratimā: image of worship; an idol.
pratyak: that which reveals for itself such as *jīva* and *Īśvara*.
pratyakṣa: perception.
prayatna: effort; endeavour.
prādurbhāva: manifestation of God; incarnation.
prākṛta: material; made of material substance.
prāmāṇya: validity.
prāṇa: vital breath; also applicable to Brahman.
prāptā: one who seeks to attain God; the individual self.
prāptyupāya: the means of attaining God.
prāpya: the goal to be achieved; God.
prārabdha-karma: *karma* which has already begun to give result.
prātikūlya-varjanam: to refrain from acts which cause displeasure to God.
preritāra: the controller of the universe of *cit* and *acit*; God.
prīti: love; devotion.
pṛthivī: earth.
puṇya: merit; good deed.
purāṇa: Hindu mythological works.
puruṣa: the self (according to Sāṅkhya); the Supreme Being (according to Vaiṣṇavism); the creator of the universe.
puruṣakāra: an interceder; mediatrix of grace.
puruṣa-sūkta: the vedic passage dealing with the *puruṣa*.

puruṣārtha: the goal of human endeavour.
puruṣottama: the supreme Self; the personal God.
purovāda: the statement made earlier.
pūjā: worship.

rahasya: secret.
rahasya-grantha: a treatise dealing with the esoteric doctrines.
rajas: one of the three cosmic attributes; the quality which causes suffering, passion etc.
rakṣaka: saviour, god.
retas: semen.
Rudra: a vedic deity; Śiva as conceived in post-vedic period; also synonymous with Viṣṇu according to Rāmānuja.
rūpa: colour; divine personality.

sadācāra: right conduct.
sad-vidyā; meditation on Brahman as the *sat*, as described in Chāndogya Upaniṣad.
saguṇa-brahmaṇ: Brahman endowed with attributes.
sahakāri-kāraṇa: accessory cause.
sahasranāma: thousand names.
sahetuka-kṛpā: showering of grace in response to human effort.
saiddha: idols consecreted by sages.
samānādhikaraṇa-vākya: a sentence or judgment where terms are found in apposition.
samarpaṇa: to offer; to surrender.
samasta: all.
samaṣṭi-sṛṣṭi: aggregate evolution of the universe.
samavāya: internal relation.
samādhi: trance; final stage of eightfold yoga discipline.
saṃbandha: relation.
saṁhitā: composition of Vedic hymns; a religious treatise.
saṁjñāpada: specific proper name applicable exclusively to one individual or entity.
saṁkarṣaṇa: one of the four vyūhas.
saṁpradāya: tradition.
saṁskāra: sacrament; latent impression of past experience.
saṁyoga: conjunction; external relation.
sandhyā: prayer offered at the time of sun-rise and sun-set.

saṅkalpa: will of God, will of an individual soul; a vow to observe a religious act.
saṅkoca: contraction.
sarvajña: omniscient.
sarvamedha-yāga: a sacrifice in which everything including oneself is offered as oblation.
sarvarakṣaka: saviour of all; God.
sarvaśakta: omnipotent; all-powerful God.
sarvātiśaya: greatest of all.
sarvavyāpi: all-pervasive.
sarva-vit: knower of all; omniscient.
sarveśvara: Lord of all; the Supreme Being.
satkāryavāda: the theory of causality upholding that effect exists in the causal substance.
sattā: existence.
sattva: one of the three attributes of *prakṛti*; the quality which represents whatever is fine or light.
satyakāma: ever desired God and His auspicious attributes.
satya-saṅkalpa: firm resolve of God.
satyaṁ: truth; reality; an essential attribute of Brahman.
saurya: the cult worshipping the Sun.
sauśīlya: gracious condescension.
saviśeṣa: differentiated.
sādhana: method or means adopted to achieve a goal.
sādhana-bhakti: *bhakti-yoga* adopted as means to *mokṣa*.
sādharmya: equality; attainment of equal status.
sādhu: pious devotee of God.
sādhya: what is to be achieved; spiritual goal.
sādhya-bhakti: *bhakti* manifested in the form of service to God (*phala-bhakti*).
sākāra: having a physical form.
sālagrāma: a special kind of black stone in the shape of a pebble obtained from the Gandak river in Nepal which is used as a symbol of God for worship.
sālokya: residing in *Viṣṇu-loka*.
sāmya: equality.
sāmīpya: staying close to Viṣṇu.
sātvata: cult of the Bhāgavatas who are devoted to the worship of Bhagavān Viṣṇu; pāñcarātra system.

sāyujya: the state of *mokṣa* in which the individual self enjoys equal status with Brahman.

setu: causeway.

sevā: service.

siddhānta: final view; an established school of thought or system.

siddhopāya: one who is ever existent serving as principal cause of *mokṣa*; God.

skanda: the cult worshipping the deity known as skanda or murugan.

smaraṇa: remembering the glory of Lord.

smṛti: texts based on Revealed Scripture such as Epics, Purāṇas, Dharma-śāstras, Āgamas.

sthairya: steadfastness.

sthitaprajña: one who has acquired perfect mental tranquillity through *karma-yoga*.

sthūla: gross.

suhṛt: friend.

sukha: happiness.

sukṛta: merit.

sūkṣma: subtle.

sūris: eternal souls.

sūrya: Sun.

sūrya-loka: the realm of Sun.

sūtra: an aphorism; a short, concise technical sentence used as a memorial rule as, for example, *Vedānta-sūtra*.

svabhāva: essential attribute; natural form.

svabhāva-vāda: the theory upholding the spontaneous emergence of the universe.

svarga: heaven.

svarūpa: essential nature of a substance.

svarūpanirūpaka-dharma: the attribute which defines the essential nature of a substance.

svarūpanirūpita-viśeṣaṇa: the secondary qualities of a substance which become known after the *svarūpa* is comprehended.

svataḥ-siddha: self-established.

svatantra: one who is independent; God.

svayaṁ-prakāśa: self-revelation; that which does not require to be manifested by anything else.

svayaṁvyakta: self-manifested; incarnation of God as an idol out of His own will.

svecchā: one's free will.

svābhāvika: natural; unconditioned.

svādhyāya: recitation of Vedas; study of sacred texts.

swāmin: Lord of the universe.

śabda: sound; verbal testimony.

śakti: power; potency; the supreme female deity; import of a word.

śama: tranquillity; mental calmness.

śaṅkha: conch; a weapon of Viṣṇu.

śaraṇa: refuge; protection.

śaraṇāgati: surrendering to God as the sole refuge.

śaraṇya: one who grants refuge; God.

śarīra: body; that which is necessarily supported by the self, controlled by it and subserves its purpose.

śarīrin: the owner of *śarīra*; the Supreme Being.

śarīra-śarīri-saṁbandha: the organic relation of the body to the soul and of the cosmic universe of *cit* and *acit* to Brahman, according to Rāmānuja.

śaivism: the religious cult upholding the worship of Śiva as Supreme Deity.

śambhu: Śiva; giver of auspiciousness (Viṣṇu).

śāktaism: the religious cult worshipping *śakti* or female Deity as Supreme Being.

śānti: mental tranquillity.

śāstra: sacred texts.

śeṣa: one who exists for the purpose of the Lord; individual self as *śeṣa* of God; the dependent.

śeṣin: one who utilizes the *śeṣa* for his purpose; the Lord.

śiva: name of the supreme Deity of śaivism; auspiciousness, Viṣṇu.

śiśya: disciple.

śila: development of ethical virtues.

śraddhā: faith; synonymous with Lakṣmī.

śravaṇa: hearing; comprehending what is taught by a teacher.

Śrī: the name of Goddess Lakṣmī; the consort of Viṣṇu; a prefix indicating veneration.

Śriyaḥ-pati: the consort of Śrī; Viṣṇu as inseparably related to *Śrī*.

śrotriya: one who is well versed in Vedas and other sacred works.

śrotra: ear.

śruti: Revealed Scripture; Vedas including the Upaniṣads.

śubhāśraya: the divine image serving as object of meditation and also auspicious.

śuddha-sattva: pure unalloyed *sattva* quality; transcendental spiritual matter.

ṣaḍaṅga-yoga: six components of *prapatti*-yoga.

ṣaḍ-darśana: six orthodox systems of Indian Philosophy.

ṣaḍguṇa: six principal attributes of God.

ṣāḍguṇya: God endowed with six principal attributes viz., *jñāna*, *bāla*, *aiśvarya*, *vīrya*, *tejas* and *śakti*.

tamas: one of the three attributes of *prakṛti*; the quality causing lethargy; darkness; primordial cosmic matter.

tanian: a verse paying obeiscence to a preceptor.

tanmātra: subtle elements.

tantra: a religious treatise; religious practice.

tapas: austerity.

tarka: logic.

tattva: ultimate Reality; metaphysical category.

tattva-jñāna: knowledge of Reality.

tattva-sākṣātkāra: realization of Reality; direct intuition of Brahman.

tattva-traya: three ontological categories or entities such as *Iśvara*, *cit* and *acit*.

tādātmya: identity.

tejas: splendour; the element of fire.

tenkalai: literally southern school; a sect of Vaiṣṇavas owing allegience to Maṇavālamāmuni; the school of thought giving greater importance to the Tamil hymns of Āḻvārs.

Tiruvāymoḻi: Tamil hymns of Nammāḻvār.

trāta: protector; saviour.

tredhā: three-fold.

triguṇa: three qualities.

trimūrti: trinity of deities—Brahmā, Viṣṇu and Rudra.

tripād-vibhūti: transcendental infinite glory of God.
tyāga: renouncement.

ubhayaliṅgatva: the twofold characteristic of Brahman or God as endowed with auspicious attributes and free from all defects.
ubhaya-vedānta: Vedānta developed on the basis of the Upaniṣads and Tamil hymns of Āḻvārs.
upabrahmaṇa: that which elucidates the meaning of Śruti texts; the Smṛtis, Itihāsas and Purāṇas.
upādāna: collection of material for worship of God; one of the five religious duties of Vaiṣṇavas according to Pāñcarātra.
upādāna-kāraṇa: material cause.
upādhi: adjunct; a limiting condition.
upāsanā: meditation on Brahman.
upāsaka: one who is engaged in *upāsanā.*
upāya: means, spiritual discipline adopted for *mokṣa.*
upeya: goal.
utpatti: origin; production.
utsava-mūrti: idol used for procession.
uttarakāṇḍa: the later part of the Vedas dealing with Brahman-knowledge; the Upaniṣads.
uttara-Mīmāṁsā: the Vedānta system dealing with Brahman.
uttarānuvāka: the later part of a Vedic passage (*puruṣa-sūkta*).
ūrdhva-puṇdra: caste mark worn on forehead.

vaḍakalai: literally northern school; a sect of Vaiṣṇavas owing allegience to Vedānta Deśika; a school of thought ascribing greater importance to Vedānta works in Sanskrit.
vandana: prostrating before God.
vaikhānasa: the Āgamas taught by Sage Vikhanas; the followers of Vaikhānasa system.
vaikuṇṭha: the eternal abode of Viṣṇu.
vaināyaka: a cult devoted to the worship of Vināyaka or Gaṇapati.
vairāgya: absence of worldly desires.
vaiṣamya: partiality; arbitrariness.
vaiṣṇava: a devotee of Viṣṇu; one who has realized that he is a *dāsa* of Viṣṇu.

vaiṣṇava-mata: Religion of Vaiṣṇavas; Vaiṣṇavism.

varṇāśrama-dharma: religious duties prescribed by the Sacred texts according to one's caste and stages of life.

vācika: oral.

vāda: discussion of a philosophic topic or issue; dialectical argument.

vāk: speech; synonymous with Lakṣmī as *Vāg-devī*.

vākya: sentence; scriptural statement.

vākyārtha-jñāna: knowledge derived from the study of Upaniṣads.

vāsanā: latent impression of past experience.

Vāsudeva: the Supreme Being as described in the pāñcarātra system; Viṣṇu.

vātsalya: tender affection; an attribute of God.

vedana: knowledge of Brahman; meditation on Brahman according to Rāmānuja.

vibhava: incarnation of God as human and other living being.

vibhu: all-pervasive.

vibhūti: property or glory of God.

vidyā: *upāsanā* or meditation on Brahman; knowledge of Brahman.

vidyut: lightning.

vigraha: idol of God; icon.

vijñāna: knowledge: philosophic wisdom.

viraja: name of the river in the divine realm.

virakti: sense of non-attachment towards worldly pleasures.

virodha: obstacles; opposition.

viśeṣaṇa: a quality of a substance; an attribute.

viśeṣya: that in which the *viśeṣaṇa* inheres; substrate.

viśiṣṭa: that which is qualified; a characterised entity.

viśiṣṭādvaita: non-dualism in the sense of organic unity; a system of Vedānta expounded by Rāmānuja.

Viṣṇu: the supreme deity of Vaiṣṇavism; the all-pervasive God; the Sun (according to some Vedic commentators).

Viṣṇu-dāsa: subordinate to Viṣṇu; individual self.

Viṣṇu-loka: the eternal abode of Viṣṇu.

Viṣṇumaya: immanence of Viṣṇu in all sentient and non-sentient entities in the universe.

Viṣṇu-patnī: consort of Viṣṇu; Lakṣmī.

viśvaksena: the divine angel.

viśvarūpa: universal form.

viśvāsa: unshakable faith.

viśvātmā: universal Soul; God as immanent in the universe.

viveka: discriminatory knowledge.

vṛtta: good conduct.

vyaṣṭi-sṛṣṭi: creation of the universe of space and matter with all its diversity.

vyākhyāna: commentary; a treatise devoted to the elaboration of what is contained in the original texts/teachings.

vyāpāra: activity; function of an individual.

vyāsajya-vṛtti: the principle of a single quality or property belonging to two.

vyoma: heaven; eternal abode of God.

vyūha: one of the five incarnations of the Supreme Being; the four divine manifestations as Vāsudeva, Saṁkarṣaṇa, Pradyumna and Aniruddha.

yajña: offering of sacrifice in the consecrated fire; a ritual prescribed by Sacred texts.

yāga: religious sacrifice; formal worship of God.

yoga: ethico-religious discipline as means to attain self-realization or God-realization; one of the five daily religious duties of a Vaiṣṇava.

yuga: epoch.

BIBLIOGRAPHY

The basic source books are of two kinds—general and specific. The general books cover the Vedas, Upaniṣads, Itihāsas, Purāṇas and the Āgamas. The specific ones are the independent philosophical and religious treatises including commentaries thereon contributed by Vaiṣṇava Ācāryas between 10th and 15th century. There have been mentioned in the first chapter (pp. 35-38). The present list is confined to such select books in Sanskrit, Maṇipravāḷa language and English as have direct bearing on Vaiṣṇavism.

SANSKRIT WORKS

Ālavandār (Yāmuna): *Āgamaprāmāṇyam*, Ramanuja Research Society, Madras, 1971.

———: *Catuḥ-ślokī* with *Catuḥ-ślokī-bhāṣyam* of Vedānta Deśika, ed. P.B. Annangaracharya, Conjeevaram, 1940.

———: *Gītārtha-saṁgraha* with *Gītārtha-saṁgraha-rakṣā* of Vedānta Deśika, ed. P.B. Annangaracharya, Conjeevaram, 1941.

———: *Siddhitraya* with English Translation by R. Ramanuja Chari, Annamalai University Philosophy Series, 1972.

———: *Stotraratna* with *Stotraratna-bhāṣyam* of Vedānta Deśika, ed., P.B. Annangaracharya; Conjeevaram, 1941.

Nañjīyar: *Śrī-sūkta Bhāṣyam*, ed. A. Srinivasa Raghavan, Pudukota, 1937.

Parāśara Bhattar: *Bhagavadguṇa-darpaṇa*—commentary on *Viṣṇu-sahasranāma* with English Translation by A. Srinivasa Raghavan, Viśiṣṭādvaita Prachāriṇī Sabhā, Madras, 1983.

———: *Aṣṭaślokī*
Śrī-guṇaratnakośa
Śrī-raṅgarājastava
(All three included in Stotramāla)
ed. P.B. Annangaracharya, Conjeevaram.

Rāmānuja: *Brahmasūtra Śrī-bhāṣya* with *Śrutaprakāśikā* (commentary of Sudarśana Sūri), (2 volumes), Viśiṣṭādvaita Prachāriṇī Sabhā, Madras, 1967.

———: *Gadyatrayam* with the commentaries of Vedānta Deśika and Sudarśana Sūri (in Sanskrit) and Periyavācchān Piḷḷai (in Tamil), Vaiṣṇava Grantha Mudrāpaka Sabha, Conjeevaram, 1916.

———: *Gītā-bhāṣya* with *Tātparya-candrikā*, ed. P.B. Annangaracharya, Conjeevaram, 1941.

———: *Nityagrantha*, Granthamala Office, Conjeevaram, 1956.

———: *Vedānta-dīpa* with Tamil and English Translation (2 volumes), Ubhayavedānta Granthamala, Madras, 1957-58.

———: *Vedānta-sara* with English Translation by M.B. Narasimha Iyengar, Adyar Library, Madras, 1953.

———: *Vedārtha-saṁgraha* with *Tātparya-dīpikā* (commentary of Sudarśana Sūri), T.T. Devasthanam, Tirupati, 1953.

Raṅgarāmānuja: *Bṛhadāraṇyakopaniṣad-bhāṣya*, ed. Uttamur T. Viraraghavacharya, T.T.D. Press, Tirupati, 1954.

———: *Chāndogyopaniṣad-bhāṣya*, Ubhayavedānta Granthamala, Madras, 1952.

———: *Kenādyopaniṣad-puruṣasūkta-śrīsūkta Bhāṣya*, Ubhaya Vedānta Granthamala, Madras, 1972.

———: *Onnbadināyirappaḍi* (commentary in Sanskrit on *Tiruvāymoli*), Parakālayatīndra Granthamala, Conjeevarām, 1941.

Śrīnivāsadāsa: *Yatīndramatadīpikā* with English Translation by Swami Adidevananda (2nd edn.), Ramakrishna Math, Madras, 1967.

Śrīnivāsācārya, Lakshmipuram: *Darśanodaya*, Mysore, 1933.

Śrivatsāṅka Miśra (Kuresa): *Pañcastava* in two volumes with Tamil commentary, ed. Srivatsankacharya, Viśiṣṭādvaita Pracariṇī Sabha, Madras, 1986.

Sundarajāmatṛmuni (Aḻahiyamaṇavāla Jīyar): *Tattvadīpa* with *Tattva-prakaśikā*, Vaiṣṇava Grantha Mudrāpaka Sabha, Conjeevaram.

Vangivaṁśeśvara: *Ahnika-kārikā*, ed. V. Ananthachar, Madras, 1941.

Vardācārya Vātsya: *Tattvasāra*, Madras Government Oriental Series, Madras, 1951.

Varavara Guru: *Aṣṭādaśabheda-vicāra*, Conjeevaram, 1909.

Vedānta Deśika: *Adhikaraṇa-sārāvalī*, ed. P.B. Annangaracharya

Dramiḍopaniṣad-tātparya Ratnāvali, ed. P.B. Annangaracharya.

Nyāya-siddāñjana, -do-

Nikṣepa-rakṣā, -do-

Pāñcarātra-rakṣā -do-

Saccaritra-rakṣā -do-

Śatadūṣaṇī, -do-

Tattva-muktā-kalāpa with *Sarvārthasiddhi*, -do-

Vedāntarāmānuja (Sākṣāt Swāmi): *Śri-tattva Siddhāñjana*, *Nyāsavidyā-darpaṇa*, ed. Uttamur T. Veeraraghavacharya, New Delhi, 1981.

Venkatacharya, Jaggu: *Divyasūri-caritāni*, ed. Jaggu Sudarśanācharya, Mysore, 1969.

Villivalam Krishnamacharya: *Śrī-vaiṣṇavasadācāranirṇaya* (A treatise on *Ahnika*), Madras, 1990.

Viṣṇucitta: *Śrīviṣṇucittīya* commentary on *Viṣṇu-purāṇa* in Telugu Script, ed. Iyyani Jagannathacharya, Madras, 1882.

MAṆIPRAVĀḶA WORKS

Aḻahiamaṇvāla Jīyar: *Pannirāyirappaḍi* (commentary on *Tiruvāymoli*), Bhagavadviṣaya Committee, Madras, 1901-3.

Brahmatantra Parakāla Swāmi: *Mūvāyirappaḍi Guruparamparā Prabhāvam*, LIFCO, Madras, 1970.

Nañjīyar: *Onbadināräyirappaḍi* (9000), (commentary on *Tiruvāymoli*), ed. S. Krishnamacharya (in Tamil Script), Noble Press, Madras, 1925-30.

Nāyanāräccān Pillai: *Catuḥślokī Vyākhyānam*, ed. S. Krishnaswamy Ayyangar, Tiruchy, 1977.

———: *Tattvasaṅgraham*, Sri Vaiṣṇavagrantha Mudrapaka Sabha, Conjeevaram, 1908.

Periya Parakāla Swāmi: *Padinennāyirappaḍi* (commentary on Tiruvāymoḻi), ed. P.B. Annangaracharya, Conjeevaram, 1941-42.

Periyavāccān Piḷḷiai: *Irupattunālāyirappaḍi* (commentary on *Tiruvāymoli*), ed. S. Krishnamacharya, Noble Press, Madras, 1925-30.

———: *Vyākhyānam* on other Divyaprabandhas, Sri Vaiṣnavagrantha Mudrapaka Sabha, Madras, 1901-2.

———: *Catuḥślokī Vyākhyānam* ed. S. Krishnaswamy Iyengar, Tiruchy, 1977.

Gadyatraya Vyākhyānam -do-

Parandarahasyam -do-

Stotraratna Vyākhyānam -do-

Piḷḷailokācārya: *Aṣṭādaśa Rahasyangal*, ed. S. Krishnaswamy Iyengar, Tiruchy, 1987.

Pinpalahiya Perumāl Jīyar: *Ārāyirappaḍi Guruparamparā Prabhāvam*, ed. S. Krishnaswamy Iyengar, Tiruchy, 1975.

Tirukkuruhaippirān Piḷḷān: *Ārāyairappaḍi* (commentary on *Tiruvāymoli*), ed. P.B. Annangaracharya, Conjeevaram, 1942.

Vadakkuttiruvīdi Piḷḷai: *Īḍu Muppattiyārāyirappaḍi* (commentary on *Tiruvāymoli*) in 10 volumes, Bhagavadviṣya Committee, Madras, 1901-3.

Varavara Muni: *Mumukṣuppaḍi Vyākhyānam*
Tattvatraya Vyākhyānam
Śrivacanabhūṣaṇa Vyākhāynam
Ācāryahṛdaya Vyākhyānam
Varavaramunidra Granthamala, Conjeevaram, 1966.
Upadeśa-rattinamālai
Ārtiprabandham
Tiruvāymoli Nūttrandādi
ed. with commentary in Tamil, P.B. Annangaracharya, Conjeevaram, 1947.

Vedāntarāmānuja (Sākṣāt Swami): *Irupattinālāyirappadi* (commentary on Pillarn's *Ārāyirappadi*) with *Śabdārtham* (word by word meaning of the *Tiruvāymoli*) in 2 volumes. ed. A.R. Venkatacharya, Śundapalyam, 1913.

Vedānta Deśika: *Rahasyatraya-sāra*,
Rahasya ratnāvali Hṛdaya,
Tattva-traya Culuka,
Rahasyatraya Culuka,
Sārasāra,
Abhayapradānasāra,

Pradhāna-śataka,
Virodhaparihāra,
Paramapada-sopāna,
Paramata-bhaṅga,
Twenty two other *Rahasya Granthas*
Vedānta Deśika Granthamala Series (Sampradāya Vibhāga), Conjeevaram, 1941.

ENGLISH WORKS

Aiyangar, S.K.: A History of Early Vaiṣṇavism in South India, Madras University, Madras, 1920.

Anantharangachar, N.S.: The Philosophy of Sādhana in Viśiṣṭādvaita, Mysore University, Mysore, 1967.

Bhandarkar, R.G.: Vaiṣṇavism, Śaivism and Minor Religion (Reprint), Asian Educational Services, N. Delhi, 1983.

Bharadwaj, K.D.: The Philosophy of Rāmānuja, New Delhi, 1958.

Bhatt, S.R.: Studies in Rāmānuja Vedānta, Delhi, 1975.

Buitenen, J.A.B. Van: Rāmānuja on the Bhagavadgīta (Reprint), Motilal Banarsidass, New Delhi, 1968.

Carman, John Braisted: The Theology of Rāmānuja (Indian Reprint), Bombay, 1981.

Dasgupta, S.N.: History of Indian Philosophy, Vol. III.

Gonda, J.: Aspects of Early Viṣṇuism, Motilal Banarsidass, Delhi, 1969.

———: Vaiṣṇavism and Śaivism, London, 1970.

Gopinath Rao, T.A.: History of Śrīvaiṣṇavas, Madras University, Madras, 1923.

Goswami, K.G.: A Study of Vaiṣṇavism, Calcutta Oriental Book Agency, Calcutta, 1956.

Govindacharya, Alkondavilli: The Divine Wisdom of the Drāviḍa Saints, Madras, 1902.

Hiriyanna, M.: Outlines of Indian Philosophy, George Allen and Unwin, London, 1932.

Hooper, J.S.M.: Hymns of the Āḻvārs, Association Press, Calcutta, 1929.

John C. Plott: Philosophy of Devotion, Motilal Banarsidass, Delhi, 1974.

Kaylor, R.D. and K.K.A. Venkatachari: God Far, God Near, Ananthacharya Indological Research Institute, Bombay, 1981.

Kumarappa Bharatan: Hindu Conception of the Deity as Culminating in Rāmānuja, London, 1934.

Lott, Eric. J.: God and the Universe in the Vedantic Theology of Rāmānuja, Ramanuja Research Society, Madras, 1976.

Narasimhachary, M.: Contribution of Yamuna to Viśiṣṭādvaita, Madras, 1971.

Otto Schrader: Introduction to the Pāñcarātra and Ahirbudhnya Saṁhitā, The Theosophical Society, Madras (Second Edition), 1973.

Radhakrishnan, S.: Indian Philosophy (2 vols.), George Allen and Unwin, London, 1948.

Raghavachar, S.S.: Rāmānuja on the Gītā, Ramakrishna Asrama, Mangalore, 1959.

———: Introduction to the Vedārtha-saṁgraha (2nd Ed.) Ramakrishna Asrama, Mangalore, 1973.

———: Śrī Rāmānuja on the Upaniṣads, Madras, 1972.

———: *Śrī Bhāṣya* on the Philosophy of the *Brahma-sūtra*, Bangalore, 1986.

Raghavan, V.K.S.N.: History of Viśiṣṭādvaita Literature, Ajanta Publications, Delhi, 1979.

Rajagopala Ayyangar, M.R.: Śrīmad-Rahasyatrayasāra—English Translation with Introduction, Kumbakonam, 1956.

Rajagopalachariar, T.: Vaiṣṇava Reformers of India, G.A. Natesan and Co., Madras, 1909.

Ramachandra Rao, S.K.: *Pāñcharātrāgama*, Kalpataru Research Academy, Bangalore, 1991.

———: *Vaikhānasa Āgama*, Kalpataru Research Academy, Bangalore, 1990.

Ramanujachari, V.K.: The Three Tattvas, Kumbakonam, 1932.

Roychoudhary, H.: Early History of the Vaiṣṇava Sect, University of Calcutta, 1930.

Satyamurthi Ayyangar, S.: *Tiruvāymoli*—English Glossary in four volumes Ananthachārya Indological Research Institute, Bombay, 1981.

Satyavrta Singh: Vedānta Deśika, His Life, Works and Philosophy—A Study, Banaras, 1958.

Seshadri, R.K.: Abiding Grace, T.T. Devasthanam, Tirupati, 1988.

Sreenivasa Murthy, H.V.: Vaiṣṇavism of Śaṁkardeva and Rāmānuja, Motilal Banarsidass, Delhi, 1973.

Srinivasachari, P.N.: Philosophy of Viśiṣṭādvaita, Adyar Library and Research Centre, Madras (Reprint) 1978.

———: Rāmānuja's Idea of the Finite Self, Longmans, Madras, 1928.

Srinivasachari, S.M.: Advaita and Viśiṣṭādvaita (A Study based on Śatadūṣaṇī), Asia Publishing House, New York, 1961.

———: Fundamentals of Viśiṣṭādvaita Vedānta—A study based on Tattva-muktā-kalāpa, Motilal Banarsidass, Delhi, 1988.

Subbu Reddiar, N.: Religion and Philosophy of Nālāyiram with special Reference to Nammālvār, Sri Venkatesvara University, Tirupati, 1977.

Thibaut, G.: Vedānta-Sūtras with the commentary by Rāmānuja Translation, Sacred Books of the East, Vol. 48, (Reprint) 1962.

Varadachari, K.C.: Theory of Knowledge, T.T.D. Press, Tirupati, 1956.

———: The Idea of God, T.T.D. Press, Tirupati, 1950.

———: Alvars of South India, Bharatiya Vidya Bhavan, Bombay, 1966.

Varadachari, V.: Āgamas and South Indian Vaiṣṇavism, M. Rangacharya Memorial Trust, Madras, 1982.

Venkatachari, K.K.A.: Śrīvaiṣṇava Maṇipravāḻa, Anantacharya Indological Research Institute, Bombay.

Vidyarthi, B.P.: Rāmānuja's Philosophy and Religion, M. Rangacharya Memorial Trust, Madras, 1977.

———: Knowledge, Self and God in Rāmānuja, Worlds Wisdom Series, New Delhi, 1978.

INDEX

Abbreviations: R = Rāmānuja; S = Śaṁkara; VD = Vedānta Deśika; VS = Vedānta-sūtra; V = Vaiṣṇavism; VV = Viśiṣṭādvaita Vedānta; accg. to = according to; re. = regarding